lonely planet

Kuala Lumpur, Melaka & Penang

"All you've got to do is decide to go and the hardest part is over.

So go!"

TONY WHEELER, COFOUNDER – LONELY PLANET

Contents

Plan Your Trip 4

Welcome to Kuala Lumpur 4
Kuala Lumpur's Top 10 ...6
What's New 13
Need to Know 14
Top Itineraries 16
If You Like 18
Month By Month 20
With Kids 22
Like a Local 24
Eating 25
Drinking & Nightlife 31
Entertainment 34
Shopping 36

Explore Kuala Lumpur 40

Neighbourhoods at a Glance 42
Bukit Bintang & KLCC 44
Chinatown, Merdeka Square & Bukit Nanas ...67
Masjid India, Kampung Baru & Northern KL 83
Lake Gardens, Brickfields & Bangsar .. 92
Day Trips from Kuala Lumpur 112
Sleeping 124
Melaka City 133
Penang 155

Understand Kuala Lumpur 185

Kuala Lumpur Today 186
History 188
Life in Kuala Lumpur ...197
Multiculturalism, Religion & Culture 200
Arts & Architecture 207
Environment 212

Survival Guide 217

Transport 218
Directory A–Z 222
Language 229

Kuala Lumpur Maps 245

(left) Hindu statue, Batu Caves (p113)

(above) Merdeka Square (p70)

(right) Royal Museum (p99)

Masjid India, Kampung Baru & Northern KL p83

Bukit Bintang & KLCC p44

Chinatown, Merdeka Square & Bukit Nanas p67

Lake Gardens, Brickfields & Bangsar p92

Welcome to Kuala Lumpur

Imagine a city, its skyline punctuated by minarets, Mogul-style domes and skyscrapers, its colourful, food-stall-lined streets shaded by a leafy canopy of banyan trees

Multicultural Modernity

Kuala Lumpur (KL), Malaysia's sultry capital is packed with historic monuments, steel-clad skyscrapers, lush parks, mega malls, bustling street markets and lively nightspots. An essential part of the vibrant mix are the incense-wreathed, colourfully adorned mosques and temples of the Malay, Chinese and Indian communities. Reverence for these ancient cultures is balanced with a drive toward the contemporary world, evident from the exciting contemporary-art and design scene, an ambitious riverbank-regeneration project and cutting-edge architecture.

Historical Canvas

Today's KLites are separated by only a few generations from the Chinese and Malay tin prospectors who founded the city. By the time the British made it the capital of Peninsular Malaysia in the late 19th century, erecting grand colonial buildings, KL had only been in existence for a few decades. The city has since been the scene of history-defining moments for Malaysia. Stadium Merdeka was where, in 1957, the country's first prime minister, Tunku Abdul Rahman, punched his fist seven times in the air and declared independence.

Shoppers' Paradise

Join locals in two of their favourite pastimes: shopping and eating. Malaysian consumer culture achieves its zenith in KL, where you could spend all day browsing glitzy air-conditioned malls such as Pavilion Kuala Lumpur, Suria KLCC and Mid Valley Megamall in search of designer fashion and bargains. Bangsar and Publika are the places to go for lesser-known labels and the work of offbeat independent designers. Alternatively, explore Central Market for locally made handicrafts and hunt out the few remaining artisans and antiques dealers still keeping shop in and around Chinatown.

Street Feast

Despite the heat, this is a city best explored on foot. Walk and you can catch all the action and save yourself the frustration of becoming entangled in one of KL's all-too-frequent traffic jams. You'll be sure to come across some of the city's best dining spots: the hawker stalls and traditional neighborhood *kopitiam* (coffee shops) that beckon you over with the aroma of freshly cooked food.

MARTIN PUDDY/GETTY IMAGES ©

Why I Love Kuala Lumpur

By Isabel Albiston, Writer

For such a frenetic city, KL has an uncanny way of charming its visitors. Of course, the food helps: the sheer variety of delicious dining options that reflect the very best of Malaysian cuisine. But it's more than that. It's the way the city has embraced modernity with its towering skyscrapers and technological connectivity, all the while retaining a deeply entrenched adherence to the traditional customs and religions of its residents. Beyond the traffic and malls lies a complex cultural patchwork formed of distinct, coexisting communities, united by the warm welcome they extend to guests.

For more about our writers, see p264.

Above: Petronas Towers and the KLCC

Kuala Lumpur's Top 10

Street Food *(p55)*

1 In KL some of your best dining experiences will happen on the street. Delicious, freshly cooked meals served from mobile carts, stalls and humble shophouse *kopitiam* (coffee shops) are the way to go. Jalan Alor is the city's most famous eats street, jammed with al-fresco tables. Prices will be higher here than at more locally patronised hawker gourmet destinations such as Lucky Gardens, Glutton Street or the stalls scattered around Brickfields.

BELOW: JALAN ALOR (P55)

Petronas Towers *(p46)*

2 The 452m-high Petronas Towers are beautiful to look at, as well as being the embodiment of Malaysia's transformation into a fully developed nation. Designed by architect Cesar Pelli, this is the focal point of the Kuala Lumpur City Centre (KLCC), a 40-hectare development that also includes an imaginatively designed tropical park, a fun aquarium, an excellent kids' museum, a world-class concert hall and one of KL's best shopping malls.

Bukit Bintang & KLCC

1

2
SURIA KLCC

4

Islamic Arts Museum *(p94)*

3 The dazzling collection of objects housed in this fine museum prove that religious devotion can be married with exquisite craftsmanship. The building itself – with its Iranian-tiled facade and decorated domes – is a stunner, its galleries filled with natural light and amazing works gathered from around the Islamic world. Don't miss the architecture gallery, with models of some of the great Islamic buildings. The museum's gift shop is also one of the best places in KL to buy beautifully designed and expertly made items from across the Islamic world.

TOP LEFT: THE CEILING OF THE ISLAMIC ARTS MUSEUM (P94)

Lake Gardens, Brickfields & Bangsar

Chinatown *(p43)*

4 Plumes of smoke curl upwards from smouldering coils of incense, flower garlands hang like pearls from the necks of Hindu statues and the call to prayer punctuates the honk of traffic. The temples and mosques of the city's Hindus, Muslims and Chinese Buddhists are crammed shoulder to shoulder in this atmospheric neighbourhood along the Klang river – where KL was born. Don't miss eating at the daytime Madras Lane hawker stalls or savouring the bustle and fun of the night market along Jln Petaling.

BOTTOM LEFT: INCENSE COILS IN CHINATOWN (P72)

Chinatown, Merdeka Square & Bukit Nanas

Batu Caves *(p122)*

5 It's always a very busy and colourful scene at this sacred Hindu shrine but, if you can, time your visit for a holy day, the biggest of which is Thaipusam. Guarding the 272 steps that lead up to the main Temple Cave is a 43m gilded statue of Lord Murugan, assisted by a platoon of lively macaques who show little fear in launching raids on tourists' belongings. A new cable car at the foot of the giant limestone outcrop takes the sweat out of reaching Temple Cave.

ABOVE: STATUE OF LORD MURUGAN (P113)

Day Trips from Kuala Lumpur

Tun Abdul Razak Heritage Park *(p95)*

6 KL's major recreation area, this park is named after the country's second prime minister. The botanical garden laid out during the British days remains at the park's heart and is flanked by one of the city's top attractions, the KL Bird Park. Visit the National Planetarium, Kuala Lumpur Butterfly Park and the striking National Monument, commemorating those who lost their lives fighting communists during the Emergency. BELOW: FLAMINGOS, KL BIRD PARK (P95)

Lake Gardens, Brickfields & Bangsar

Shopping Malls *(p63)*

7 Come for the air conditioning, stay for the designer bargains! The roll call of brands in malls Pavilion KL, Suria KLCC and Publika will impress even the most sophisticated of shoppers. Refreshments are never far away, with masses of restaurants and excellent food courts always part of the retail mix, along with everything from luxury spas to vast multiplex cinemas and karaoke rooms. It's the unexpected finds – the feng shui stores, art galleries and Hindu temples – that really set these malls apart. TOP RIGHT: SURIA KLCC (P65)

Bukit Bintang & KLCC

Merdeka Square *(p70)*

8 Stand beside the Victorian fountain next to the empty expanse of lawn and take in the impressive scene. When it was called the Padang, members of the Royal Selangor Club would politely clap as another wicket fell in a colonial cricket match. At midnight on 31 August 1957, the flag of the independent nation of Malaya was hoisted on the 95m flagpole. The eastern flank is dominated by the handsome Sultan Abdul Samad Building, decorated with copper-clad domes and barley-sugar-twist columns.

Chinatown, Merdeka Square & Bukit Nanas

FRIM *(p115)*

9 The Forest Research Institute Malaysia (FRIM) offers a leafy escape from KL's urban grind. Feel your soul start to calm as soon as you enter this 600-hectare reserve, where hard concrete and traffic pollution give way to soft foliage, fresh air and forest trails. Get the blood pumping on the steep hike up to the thrilling 200m-long Canopy Walkway that hangs a vertigo-inducing 30m above the forest floor and provides panoramic views back to the city.

Thean Hou Temple *(p97)*

10 KL has plenty of Buddhist temples but none other as visually striking as this. Rising out of the leafy surrounds of Robson Heights in four terraced levels, this architecture is the stuff of pure Chinese fantasy, with dazzling mosaic dragons and phoenixes flying off the eaves and snaking around columns. It was built to house effigies of the heavenly mother Thean Hou as well as Kuan Yin, the goddess of mercy, and Shuiwei Shengniang, goddess of the waterfront. Visit on festival days and weekends to see the temple at its liveliest.

What's New

Street Art

New murals in KL including boy in a canoe and goldsmith, red metal sculptures by Kuen Stephanie and the caricatures of cartoonist Lat brighten the streets in and around Chinatown. (p76)

Dewakan

It's worth making the trip out to Shah Alam to sample the innovative cooking of the exciting young chefs at this restaurant making a bid for Michelin stars. (p120)

TREC

This new KL entertainment complex is home to superclub Zouk as well as a whole street of bars, restaurants and music and comedy venues, such as COMO and Live House. (p58)

Jln Petaling Hangouts

The southern end of KL's Chinatown has become a magnet for the hip, with the new speakeasy-style cocktail bar PS150 (p79) and supercool cafes Merchant's Lane (p77) and Chocha Foodstore (p79).

Visit KL

The new home of KL's official tourist information office is in a fully restored 1903 mansion once owned by tin-mining magnate Loke Chow Kit. (p228)

Menara KL Open Deck

Now you can step outside onto the 300m-high open deck at Menara KL and take a photo in the new sky box, which puts nothing but glass between you and the ground below. (p69)

Old Malaya

A row of 100-year-old crumbling buildings in central KL has been beautifully renovated and transformed into this cluster of bars and restaurants that includes Antara. (p78)

The Habitat

At this excellent new nature reserve atop Penang Hill treetop walkways and bridges, giant swings and zip lines put you at eye level with the rainforest canopy. (p182)

Entopia by Penang Butterfly Farm

Be mesmerised by around 120 species of tropical butterfly, plus multiple other insects and reptiles, at this upgraded tourist attraction on Penang Island. (p179)

Art & Garden by Fuan Wong

Mother nature and human creativity combine at this beautiful concept garden on Penang Island, packed with bromeliads, glass sculptures and so much more. (p179)

Cheah Kongsi

A major restoration has left Penang's oldest Straits Chinese clan association looking fabulous. Also learn about Chinese immigrant life and secret societies in the early days of the colony. (p168)

The Top at KOMTAR

A major revamp of part of George Town's iconic KOMTAR tower has resulted in the addition of the Rainbow Skywalk on the 68th floor rooftop and theme park attractions on lower levels. (p163)

For more recommendations and reviews, see **lonelyplanet.com/kuala-lumpur**

Need to Know

For more information, see Survival Guide (p217)

Currency
Malaysian ringgit (RM)

Language
Bahasa Malaysia, English

Visas
Generally not required for stays of up to 60 days.

Money
ATMs widely available; credit cards accepted in most hotels and restaurants.

Mobile Phones
Local SIM cards can be used in most phones; if not, set your phone to roaming.

Time
Malaysia Time (GMT/UTC plus eight hours)

Tourist Information
Visit KL (Kuala Lumpur Tourism Bureau; Map p252; ☎03-2698 0332; www.visitkl.gov.my; 11 Jln Tangsi; ⏲8.30am-5.30pm Mon-Fri; 📶; Ⓜ Masjid Jamek)

Malaysia Tourism Centre (MaTiC; Map p250; ☎03-9235 4900; www.matic.gov.my/en; 109 Jln Ampang; ⏲8am-10pm; Bukit Nanas)

Daily Costs

Budget: Less than RM100
- Dorm bed: RM17–50
- Hawker stalls and food courts for meals
- Use public transport; plan sightseeing around walking tours, free museums and galleries

Midrange: RM100–500
- Double room in a comfortable hotel: RM100–400
- Two-course meal in a neighbourhood restaurant: RM40–60
- Take taxis and guided tours

Top end: More than RM500
- Luxury double room: RM450–1000
- Meal in top restaurant plus bottle of wine: RM200

Advance Planning

Two months before Book tickets for a concert at the Dewan Filharmonik Petronas.

One month before Plan your itinerary, checking to see if there are any events or festivals you may be able to attend.

One week before Book online for a tour of Petronas Towers and for a foodie walking tour. Make reservations at any top-end restaurants.

Useful Websites

Visit KL (www.visitkl.gov.my) Official city tourism site.

Time Out KL (www.timeoutkl.com) Monthly listings magazine with an excellent website.

Zafigo (http://zafigo.com) Founded by Marina Mahathir (daughter of the former prime minister), this online travel guide specialises in advice for women travellers in the region.

Lonely Planet (www.lonelyplanet.com/malaysia/kuala-lumpur) Destination information, hotel bookings, traveller forum and more.

WHEN TO GO

KL is busy during Chinese New Year (January/February) and Ramadan. In July and August haze can be caused by smoke from field-clearing fires in Indonesia.

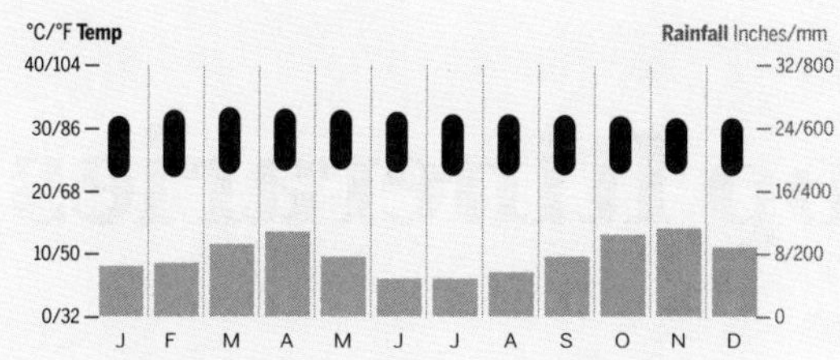

Arriving in Kuala Lumpur

Most likely you'll arrive at Kuala Lumpur International Airport (KLIA), although a handful of flights land at SkyPark Subang Terminal. Coming overland, arrival points include KL Sentral for trains and Terminal Bersepadu Selatan (TBS) for buses. Ferries from Sumatra (Indonesia) dock at Pelabuhan Klang, which is connected by rail with KL Sentral.

Kuala Lumpur International Airport (KLIA) Trains RM55; every 15 minutes from 5am to 1am; 30 minutes to KL Sentral. Buses RM10; every hour from 5am to 1am; one hour to KL Sentral. Taxis from RM75; one hour to central KL.

KL Sentral Transport hub with train, light rail (LRT), monorail, bus and taxi links to rest of city.

Terminal Bersepadu Selatan (TBS) Long-distance buses from most destinations now arrive here. It's connected to KL by LRT.

For much more on **arrival** see p218

Getting Around

KL Sentral is the hub of a rail-based urban network consisting of the KTM Komuter, KLIA Ekspres, KLIA Transit, light rail (LRT) and monorail systems. Though the systems are poorly integrated, you can happily get around much of central KL on a combination of rail and monorail services. Buy the MyRapid card (www.myrapid.com.my; RM10) at monorail and LRT stations; it can also be used on Rapid KL buses.

- **Monorail** Stops in mostly convenient locations; gets very crowded during evening rush hour.
- **Light Rail Transit (LRT)** Handy for Chinatown, Kampung Baru and KLCC, but network is poorly integrated.
- **Bus** The GOKL City Bus has four free loop services connecting many city-centre destinations.
- **Taxi** Can be flagged down with metered fares. Some designated taxi ranks operate a prepaid coupon system for journeys.

For much more on **getting around** see p219

Sleeping

There are plenty of budget hostels, hotels and five-star properties, but reserve in advance, especially if visiting during busy Asian travel seasons such as Chinese New Year and the end of Ramadan. You can often snag great online deals for top-end accommodation, which compensates for the dearth of characterful midrange options. Serviced apartments are also well worth considering, especially for longer stays. Rates at the cheaper places usually include all taxes and service charges, but many midrange and all top-end options quote prices without these added, so count on an extra 16% on the bill.

Useful Websites

iBilik (www.ibilik.my) Room rentals in Malaysia.

Asia Homestay (http://asiahomestay.com) Malaysian homestay booking site.

Lonely Planet (www.**lonelyplanet.com/malaysia/kuala-lumpur/hotels) Recommendations and bookings.**

For much more on **sleeping** see p124

Top Itineraries

Day One

Bukit Bintang & KLCC (p44)

Head to the Kuala Lumpur City Centre (KLCC), where you've prebooked tickets up the **Petronas Towers**. Afterwards, browse the shops in **Suria KLCC** and see a free art exhibition at the excellent **Galeri Petronas**.

Lunch Try one of the restaurants at Suria KLCC (p65 or Avenue K (p65).

Bukit Bintang & KLCC (p44)

Take a postlunch stroll around **KLCC Park**, admiring the view of the towers, then take a look at contemporary Malaysian art at the **ILHAM** in the Foster + Partners-designed tower. Join the 3pm tour of the Malay-style wooden house **Rumah Penghulu Abu Seman** next to **Badan Warisan Malaysia**, or learn about sea life at **Aquaria KLCC**.

Dinner Enjoy chicken wings and grilled fish at Wong Ah Wah (p55) on Jln Alor.

Bukit Bintang & KLCC (p44)

Go mall hopping to **Pavilion KL**, **Starhill Gallery**, **Lot 10** and **Sungei Wang Plaza** along Jln Bukit Bintang until 10pm, then head to Changkat Bukit Bintang and Jln Mesui for the bars; **Pisco Bar** is a good choice. Also check out **No Black Tie** for jazz and classical concerts.

Day Two

Chinatown, Merdeka Square & Bukit Nanas (p67)

Admire the historic buildings of **Merdeka Square** (if you can, sign up for one of Visit KL's free tours), then either cycle on a hired bike or take a taxi to the **Tun Abdul Razak Heritage Park**. Start at the **National Monument**, then walk through the **Perdana Botanical Garden** to the **National Museum**; if you're there by 10am you can take the free guided tour.

Lunch Feast on a buffet of traditional Malay dishes at Rebung (p102)

Lake Gardens, Brickfields & Bangsar (p92)

Continue to enjoy the leafy surrounds of the park at the **KL Bird Park** or **KL Butterfly Park**. Save a couple of hours for the splendid **Islamic Arts Museum**, then admire the architecture of **Masjid Negara** and **KL Railway Station**.

Dinner Sample Malaysian and Western food at Merchant's Lane (p77).

Chinatown, Merdeka Square & Bukit Nanas (p67)

Go souvenir shopping at the **Central Market**, then push your way through the crowds at Chinatown's **Petaling Street Market**. Finish up with a cocktail at speakeasy-style bars **PS150** or **Omakase + Appreciate**.

Kampung Baru (p85)

Day Three

Masjid India, Kampung Baru & Northern KL (p83)

Have breakfast at **Bazaar Baru Chow Kit**, one of KL's most atmospheric wet markets, then amble through the Malay area of **Kampung Baru** admiring the traditional wooden houses and flower gardens.

Lunch Go old school at the Hainanese *kopitiam* Yut Kee (p88).

Chinatown, Merdeka Square & Bukit Nanas (p67)

Walk from Masjid India to **Bukit Nanas**, where you can traverse the canopy walkway of **KL Forest Eco Park** and then go much higher up the **Menara Kuala Lumpur**, to get your bearings in the city from the observation deck, and, weather permitting, the new outdoor deck.

Dinner Chinese at Robson Heights (p104) or Indian food in Brickfields.

Lake Gardens, Brickfields & Bangsar (p92)

For another panoramic perspective of KL, stand on the upper terraces of the gloriously decorative **Thean Hou Temple**. Walk around the many religious sites of Brickfields in the cool of the evening and enjoy a cocktail at the rooftop **Mai Bar** overlooking KL Sentral.

Day Four

Batu Caves (p122)

Climb the 272 steps at **Batu Caves** to pay your respects at the Hindu **Temple Cave** and learn about bats and other cave dwellers in the **Dark Cave**, then take a taxi up to the **Muzium Orang Asli** in Gombak.

Lunch Tuck into Thai at Samira (p88) in Sentul Park.

Masjid India, Kampung Baru & Northern KL (p83)

View the city skyline from **Titiwangsa Lake Gardens**, where you can hire a bike, take a boat out on the lake or even take a spin in a helicopter. Nearby is the **National Visual Arts Gallery**.

Dinner Splash out on dinner at Antara Restaurant (p78) at Old Malaya.

Bukit Bintang & KLCC (p44)

Sink a sunset cocktail at **Heli Lounge Bar**. If your budget doesn't stretch to fine dining, a meal at **Jalan Imbi Hawker Stalls** or **Glutton Street** will be equally memorable and delicious. End the night at the new entertainment complex TREC: see some stand-up comedy or live music at **Live House** or club until the early hours at **Zouk**.

If You Like...

Historic Buildings

Sultan Abdul Samad Building Glorious brick structure with Moorish architectural influences and 43m clock tower. (p70)

Old KL Train Station A Mogul fantasy, once the rail hub of the peninsula. (p99)

Stadium Merdeka Sporting venue where independence of the Federation of Malaya was declared in 1957. (p72)

Loke Mansion Restored home of tin tycoon Loke Yew, now a law firm's office. (p85)

Sultan Sulaiman Club City's oldest Malay club, in the heart of Kampung Baru. (p85)

Rumah Penghulu Abu Seman Traditional wooden stilt house from Kedah in the grounds of Badan Warisan Malaysia. (p48)

Loke Chow Kit Mansion Visit KL's new office is in the beautifully restored building once owned by the tin-mining magnate. (p228)

Malayan Railway Administration Building Mirrors the Mogul style of the Old KL Train Station. (p99)

Modern Architecture

Petronas Towers Iconic twin towers that lord it over the city. (p46)

Putrajaya Showcase of modern urban planning and vaulting architectural ambition. (p122)

Old KL Train Station (p99)

Bank Negara Malaysia Museum & Art Gallery Hijjas Kasturi–designed complex. (p85)

Istana Budaya Traditional Malay design is applied to this performing-arts hall. (p90)

Animal Encounters

KL Bird Park Giant aviary that's home to some 200 mostly Asian species. (p95)

Aquaria KLCC Pools swimming with everything from starfish to sand tiger sharks. (p48)

KL Butterfly Park Hundreds of species of fluttering insect and other critters. (p96)

Zoo Negara Feed elephants, camels and deer; watch orangutans and tigers. (p114)

Forest Research Institute Malaysia (FRIM) Macaques and langurs (leaf monkeys) hang out in this jungle-like reserve. (p115)

Art Galleries

National Visual Arts Gallery KL's top public gallery, with permanent and temporary collections. (p87)

ILHAM Hosts changing exhibitions that showcase modern and contemporary Malaysian art. (p48)

Sekeping Tenggiri Outstanding private collection worth making an appointment to view. (p131)

Ruang Pemula Appointment-only private gallery with excellent contemporary collection. (p53)

Publika Mall stacked with commercial art galleries and the MAP exhibition space. (p110)

Religious Sites

Masjid Negara The National Mosque is a classic piece of modern architecture. (p99)

Temple Cave A 42m statue of Lord Murugan guards the entrance to the Hindu shrine at Batu Caves. (p113)

Sri Mahamariamman Temple Venerable Hindu shrine in Chinatown. (p205)

Masjid Jamek Recently restored mosque sporting elegant Mogul-influenced design. (p76)

Sin Sze Si Ya Temple Atmospheric Chinese temple dedicated to one of KL's founding fathers. (p72)

Thean Hou Temple Fabulous Buddhist temple on a leafy hill overlooking the city. (p97)

Buddhist Maha Vihara Historic Sinhalese Buddhist temple in Brickfields. (p101)

Museums

Islamic Arts Museum Marvel at gorgeous works of art inspired by the Muslim faith. (p94)

National Museum Covering the region's history from prehistoric times to the present day. (p98)

National Textiles Museum Admire skilful weaving, embroidery, knitting and batik printing. (p71)

Petrosains Science-focused discovery centre at Suria KLCC. (p48)

Royal Museum A look inside the former Istana Negara (National Palace). (p99)

Royal Malaysian Police Museum Excellent small museum that explores the history of Malaysia through the story of policing. (p96)

For more top Kuala Lumpur spots, see the following:

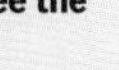

- Eating (p25)
- Drinking & Nightlife (p31)
- Entertainment (p34)
- Shopping (p36)

Parks & Gardens

KLCC Park Jogging track, great kids' playground, top views of Petronas Towers. (p48)

Titiwangsa Lake Gardens Serene park surrounding a large lake in northern KL. (p87)

KL Forest Eco Park Traverse the canopy walkway in this lowland dipterocarp forest in the heart of the city. (p74)

Taman Botani Landscaped gardens beside the lake in Putrajaya. (p123)

Perdana Botanical Garden KL's oldest park showcases a variety of native and introduced plants and trees. (p111)

Viewpoints

Menara KL Dine in the revolving restaurant atop this telecom tower. (p69)

Petronas Towers Watch fearless window cleaners from the 86th-floor observation deck. (p46)

Thean Hou Temple City panoramas and decorative dragons and phoenixes. (p97)

Heli Lounge Bar Bottoms up at the cocktail bar on the helipad. (p57)

Chin Woo Stadium Peaceful Chinatown spot to view sunset across the city. (p81)

Month By Month

TOP EVENTS

Thaipusam, January/ February

Chinese New Year, January/February

Urbanscapes, April/ May

Wesak Day, May

Petronas Malaysian Grand Prix, September

January

New Year is a busy travel period, so plan ahead. Both Chinese New Year and Thaipusam can fall in February in some years.

Thaipusam

Enormous crowds converge at Batu Caves north of KL and at Nattukottai Chettiar Temple in Penang for this dramatic Hindu festival involving body piercing.

February

Chinese New Year

Dragon dances and pedestrian parades mark the start of the New Year. Families hold open house and everybody wishes you *kong hee fatt choy* (a happy and prosperous new year). Celebrated on 16 February 2018, 5 February 2019 and 25 January 2020.

March

One of KL's wettest months, so bring an umbrella and watch out for flash flooding.

Birthday of the Goddess of Mercy

Offerings are made to the popular Chinese goddess Kuan Yin at temples across the region; a good one to visit is Thean Hou Temple in KL. The goddess is also honoured three times more during the year, in April/May, July/August and October/November.

Putrajaya International Hot Air Balloon Fiesta

Held over four days in Putrajaya, this festival (http://myballoonfiesta-putrajaya.com) has hosted hot-air-balloon pilots from as far afield as New Zealand and Switzerland, as well as attracting over 100,000 spectators.

April

The end of the light monsoon season on Malaysia's west coast, but not the end of rain, for which you should always be prepared.

☆ Urbanscapes

Held in various venues across the city over three weekends in April and May, this long-running creative arts festival (www.urbanscapes.com.my) brings together art, music, film and design with a series of performances and events.

May

In 2018, 2019 and 2020 Ramadan will fall mostly in May, so look out for night food markets and buffets around the city. There are also a couple of big parades this month.

Wesak Day (Vesak Day)

In celebration of Buddha's birth, enlightenment and death there's a major procession with illuminated floats and thousands of people carrying candles through KL, starting from the Buddhist Maha Vihara. Celebrated on 29 May 2018, 18 May 2019 and 6 May 2020.

June

The first Saturday of the month is the official birthday of Malaysia's king, marked by a parade at the national palace, an address to the nation and an award ceremony.

Hari Raya Aidlifitri

The end of Ramadan is followed by a month of breaking-the-fast parties, many of them public occasions where you can enjoy a free array of Malay culinary delicacies. The Malaysian prime minister opens his official home in Putrajaya to the public.

Putrajaya Floria

This flower and garden festival (www.floriaputrajaya.com.my) lasts nine days and is a big affair. Expect colourful displays of exotic blooms including orchids and bougainvillea.

August

Haze from forest and field-clearance fires in Indonesia can create smog in KL, so avoid visiting during this month and the next if you are prone to respiratory complaints and asthma.

Festival of the Hungry Ghosts

Chinese Malaysians perform operas, host open-air concerts and lay out food for their ancestors. The ghosts eat the spirit of the food but thoughtfully leave the substance for mortal celebrants. Celebrated towards the end of the month and in early September.

National Day

Join the crowds at midnight on 31 August to celebrate the anniversary of Malaysia's independence in 1957. Events are held in Merdeka Sq and across KL.

September

A month packed with festivals, making it a great time to visit the city, though haze from forest fires may still be a problem.

DiverseCity

KL's international arts festival (http://diversecity.my) runs throughout September and offers a packed program of contemporary and traditional dance, music shows, literature readings, comedy and visual-arts events.

KL International Jazz & Arts Festival

A cracking line-up of artists perform at this festival (www.klinternationaljazz.com), held on the University of Malaya campus in September.

Petronas Malaysian Grand Prix

Formula 1's big outing in Southeast Asia is held at the Sepang International Circuit (www.sepangcircuit.com) over three days. Associated events and parties are held in KL.

Cooler Lumpur Festival

Multidisciplinary arts festival (www.coolerlumpur.com) with a different annual theme and events staged at Publika.

Malaysian International Gastronomy Festival

Prestigious restaurants and master chefs all pitch in with their best efforts during this month-long celebration of edible creativity in KL that includes food fairs and cooking classes. Full details at www.migf.com.

November

In the run-up to Deepavali, KL's Little Indias are packed with stalls selling textiles and celebratory sweets.

Deepavali

Tiny oil lamps are lit outside Hindu homes to attract the auspicious gods Rama and Lakshmi. Indian businesses start the new financial year. Little India is ablaze with lights.

December

School holidays can see hotels booked up towards the end of the month, when many people arrive in the region to vacation over the Christmas and New Year breaks.

Winter Solstice Festival

Called Dong Zhi in Mandarin and Tang Chek in Hokkien, this Chinese festival offers thanks for a good harvest and usually occurs between 21 and 23 December. It's celebrated by eating glutinous rice balls served in a clear sugar syrup.

With Kids

KL has a lot going for it as a family-holiday destination. Its textbook Southeast Asian cultural mix offers chances to watch temple ceremonies and sample an amazing range of food. Nature is also close at hand, along with clean accommodation, modern malls and fun amusement parks.

STEFAN CRISTIAN CIOATA/GETTY IMAGES ©

Public playground in KL

Animal & Jungle Attractions

It's not so long ago that tigers and other beasts of the jungle prowled the outskirts of KL. Abundant swaths of greenery within the city and in its surrounds mean that wildlife is still very much present.

At Batu Caves and the Forest Research Institute Malaysia (FRIM), encountering wild monkeys, such as macaques and langurs, is pretty much guaranteed. Zoo Negara (p114) is one of the region's better-managed facilities and offers visitors a chance to become a volunteer for a day.

In the heart of KL there's the Aquaria KLCC with its many sea creatures and touch pools, as well as the excellent KL Bird Park, KL Butterfly Park and Deer Park, all at the Tun Abdul Razak Heritage Park (p102).

Parks & Theme Parks

For small kids, the following parks have top-grade playgrounds with slides, splash pools and the like: Perdana Botanical Garden (p111), KLCC Park (p48) and Titiwangsa Lake Gardens (p87).

Brave kids and teens will be thrilled by the chance to make like a monkey in the treetops by traversing the canopy walkways at KL Forest Eco Park (p74) and FRIM (p115).

When the weather turns too hot or rainy, the Berjaya Times Square Theme Park (p66) provides an indoor energy-burning and fun-injecting experience. Scheduled to open in 2017, the theme park **20th Century Fox World** at Genting Highlands is set to be a major attraction, with rides based on movies such as *Ice Age, Life of Pi, Planet of the Apes* and *Night at the Museum.*

Pack your swimsuits and sunscreen and head to Sunway Lagoon (p121) for a brilliant watery theme park, featuring water slides and a surfing beach along with other attractions including a mall and an ice rink. There's also a water park at the City of Digital Lights at i-City (p119) outside Shah Alam.

Museums, Temples & Heritage Buildings

Heading up the Petronas Towers (p46) is not just an opportunity to gawk at the city from on high but also to learn about the tower's construction and, afterwards, visit the hands-on science museum Petrosains (p48), within the Suria KLCC mall.

Batu Caves (p113), with its Hindu temples, colourful tableaux of Hindu tales and legends, monkeys, and natural Dark Cave, holds much to capture a child's imagination. The dazzlingly decorated Thean Hou Temple (p97) is similarly appealing, with photo ops of Chinese zodiac statues, flying dragons and a pool teeming with tortoises.

Dining Out

KL's myriad dining outlets offer meals that will appeal to the fussiest of kids. Although you may not think it, a busy food stall is usually the safest place to eat – you can see the food being prepared, the ingredients are often fresh and if the wok stays hot there's little chance of bacteria. Grown-ups can also try adventurous dishes while the kids get something more familiar.

If outdoor eating is something you're not comfortable with, then there are plenty of indoor food courts – all the major malls have them, and choice and standards are universally fantastic. Many restaurants attached to hotels and guesthouses will serve familiar Western food, while international fast food is ubiquitous. Midrange and upscale restaurants often have high chairs, but most budget places don't.

NEED TO KNOW

Time Out KL (www.timeout.com/kuala-lumpur/kids) publishes a *Malaysia for Kids* guide and its website has up-to-date listings and features on what to do with your kids.

Malaysian drinks are very sweet and even fresh juices usually have sugar added. To cut down on sugar, ask for drinks without sugar or order bottled water.

Markets & Malls

KL's crowded wet markets and street markets are no place to be pushing a pram around. The butchering stalls can also be the stuff of childhood nightmares. But if you have curious older kids then markets can be a great opportunity for learning about and tasting unfamiliar tropical fruits and veggies.

Some shopping malls go overboard to embrace the family. At Avenue K, don't miss the interactive dinosaur exhibition Discoveria (p48). Publika (p110) has a particularly good selection of shops for kids and parents, including ones offering clothing, toys, crafts and books. Play spaces and crèches are available at Megakidz in Mid Valley Megamall (p108) and Kizsport & Gym in Bangsar Village II.

Older kids and teens will love exploring the warren of youth-oriented outlets at Sungei Wang Plaza (p64). The Tokyo Street section of Pavilion KL (p63) is also a dream for those into Japanese fashion and comic cultures.

Like a Local

In Kuala Lumpur, the traditional greeting is not 'How are you?' but 'Sudah makan?' (Have you eaten yet?), underlining the national obsession with food. Hawker stalls, kopitiam (coffee shops) and mamaks (Muslim Indian-Malay hawker stalls) are where locals catch up on news and gossip with friends and family.

LIM_JESSICA/GETTY IMAGES ©

Devotee carrying a *kavadi* (p205)

Eating & Shopping

Tap into what truly makes this city tick: the search for the next great meal. There are many online blogs and sites – such as www.eatdrinkkl.blogspot.com and http://theyumlist.net/en/ – devoted to the local dining scene and some great food tours that get you walking the streets, grazing along the way.

Next to eating, KLites' favourite pastime has to be shopping. These two obsessions dovetail in the city's multiplicity of malls. More local shopping experiences can be had at classic Southeast Asian fresh-produce day markets, such as Pudu Market and Bazaar Baru Chow Kit, and at several atmospheric night markets, the most famous of which is the one along Jln Petaling. Craft markets are becoming popular, with monthly ones to attend at Bangsar Shopping Centre and Publika.

Festivals

Being a multicultural, multifaith city, KL sees few weeks unadorned by some sort of religious or cultural celebration. As well as ceremonies at mosques, shrines and temples, this often means special things to eat and drink.

Securing a reservation at popular restaurants in the weeks leading to Chinese New Year can be tricky, as friends, colleagues and family gather over endless banquets. Ramadan bazaars (special afternoon food markets) and buffets are reason enough to visit KL during the Muslim holy month. For weeks before Deepavali, KL's Little Indias are awash in stalls selling clothing, textiles, household goods and special sweets and savoury snacks.

Drinking & Nightlife

KL's traditional *kopitiam* now sit side by side with hip new venues where coffee-making is a scientific process involving beakers and tubes, performed by baristas who compete in latte-art contests.

Come nightfall, join KLites in their quest to find the city's best cocktail, sampling the wares of mixologists at rooftop bars and a growing number of speakeasy-style joints as you go.

KEVIN MILLER/GETTY IMAGES ©

Beef and chicken satay skewers

Eating

KL is a nonstop feast. You can dine in incredible elegance or mingle with locals at street stalls, taking your pick from a global array of cuisines. Ingredients are fresh, cooking is high quality and hygiene standards are excellent. Most vendors speak English, and the final bill is seldom heavy on the pocket.

Hawker Stalls, Markets & Food Courts

The tastiest and best-value food is found at hawker stalls, and locals are fiercely loyal to their favourite vendors. Many hawkers have been in business for decades or operate a business inherited from parents or even grandparents; the best enjoy reputations that exceed geographical reach. To sample Malaysian hawker food, simply head to a stand-alone streetside kitchen-on-wheels, a *kopitiam* (coffee shop) or food court. Place your order with one or multiple vendors, find a seat (shared tables are common) and pay for each dish as it's delivered to your table. You'll be approached by someone taking drink orders after you've sat down – pay for these separately as well.

Intrepid eaters shouldn't overlook *pasar* (markets). Morning markets include stalls selling coffee and other beverages, as well as vendors preparing foods such as freshly griddled roti and curry and *chee cheong fun* (rice-noodle roll). *Ta pao* (takeaway) or eat in – most can offer at least a stool. *Pasar malam* (night markets) are also excellent places to graze.

NEED TO KNOW

Price Ranges

The following price ranges refer to the cost of an average main course.

$ less than RM15

$$ RM15–60

$$$ more than RM60

Opening Hours

Cafes and food stalls 7.30am–midnight

Restaurants noon–2.30pm and 6–10.30pm

Blogs & Online Resources

Eat Drink KL (http://eatdrinkkl.blogspot.com)

FriedChillies (www.friedchillies.com)

The Yum List (http://theyumlist.net)

CC Food Travel (www.cumidanciki.com)

KYspeaks.com (http://kyspeaks.com)

Reservations

Only recommended for top-end places or large groups.

Smoking

Banned in air-conditioned cafes and restaurants.

Tipping & Service Charges

At some midrange and all top-end places prices will be '++', meaning 6% government tax and a 10% service charge will be added to the bill. Tipping is not expected, but leaving small change will be appreciated.

Cooking Courses

➡ **LaZat Malaysian Home Cooking Class** (p101)

➡ **Sarang Cookery** (p81)

➡ **Starhill Culinary Studio** (p65)

➡ **Nathalie's Gourmet Studio** (p110)

Food Tours

➡ **Food Tour Malaysia** (p82)

➡ **Simply Enak** (p82)

There's little to fear about eating from outdoor hawker stalls or food markets, but if you want some air-conditioning and a little more comfort, there's no shortage of indoor food courts in KL's malls.

Coffee Shops & Restaurants

While some *kopitiam* operate like food courts, with different vendors under one roof, others are single-owner establishments. Expect to be served noodle and rice dishes, strong coffee and other drinks, and all-day breakfast fare such as half-hard-boiled eggs and toast spread with *kaya* (coconut cream jam).

Restoran (restaurants) range from casual, decades-old Chinese or Malay restaurants to upscale establishments boasting international fare, slick decor and a full bar.

Vegetarians & Vegans

Given the inclusion of prawn paste and fish in many dishes, vegetarians and vegans will find it difficult to negotiate their way around most menus. Chinese vegetarian restaurants and hawker stalls (signage will include the words *'sayur-sayuran'*) are safe bets – they are especially busy on the 1st and 15th of the lunar month, when many Buddhists adopt a vegetarian diet for 24 hours.

Indian vegetarian restaurants are another haven for snacks such as steamed *idli* (rice cakes) served with dhal and *dosa*, as well as thali (full set meals consisting of rice or bread with numerous side dishes). Look also for Chinese eateries displaying rows of stainless-steel pans and advertising 'economy rice'; this type of restaurant will have several purely vegetarian dishes.

Chinese cuisine

Thanks to generations of immigrants from all parts of China, KL boasts a notable range of regional Chinese cuisines, including Cantonese, Sichuanese, Teochew, Hokkien and Hakka.

Homegrown Chinese dishes that the city is famous for include *pan mee*. Literally 'board noodles', these are substantial hand-cut or hand-torn wheat noodles tossed with dark soy sauce and garlic oil, garnished with chopped pork and crispy *ikan bilis* (dried sardines or anchovies), and served with soup on the side. Some versions include a poached egg.

More expensive than your average noodle dish but well worth it are *sang har mee* (literally 'fresh sea noodles'): huge freshwater prawns in gravy flavoured with Chinese rice wine and the fat from the shellfish

Eating by Neighbourhood

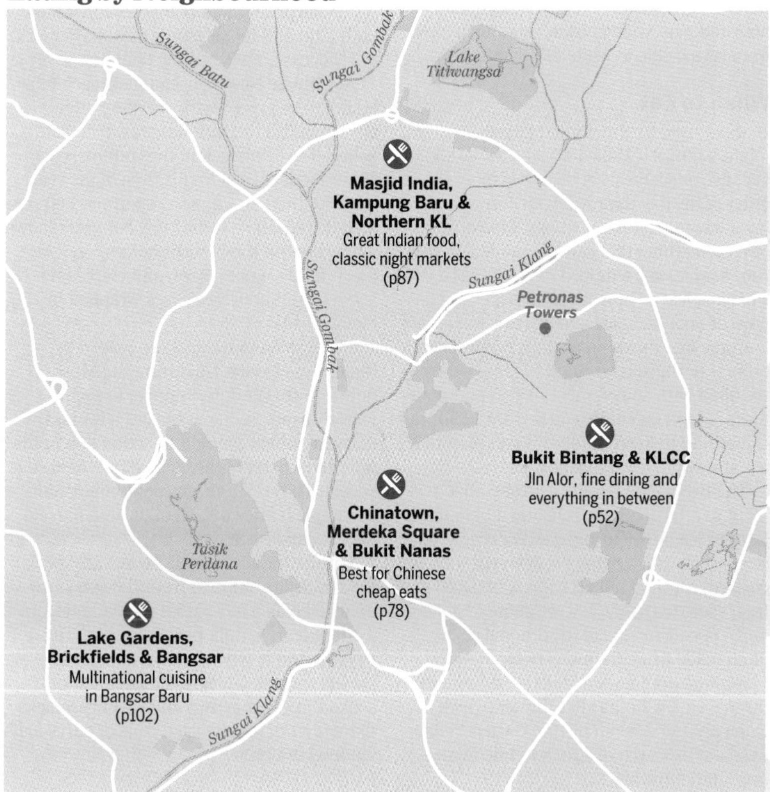

heads, served over *yee mee* (crispy fried noodles).

Hainanese immigrants were the private cooks of the British during colonial rule, which has led to a hybrid style of Western cuisine still served in old-school places such as Yut Kee, the Coliseum Cafe and, in a much more fancy version, the Colonial Cafe at the Majestic Hotel.

Malay & Peranakan cuisine

Head to Kampung Baru to sample the specialities of Malaysia's eastern states, such as Kelantanese *nasi kerabu* and *ayam percik* (barbecued chicken smothered in chilli-coconut sauce) and, from Terengganu, *nasi dagang* (nutty, coconut milk–cooked red rice).

Also look out across the city for restaurants serving Peranakan (or Nonya/Nyonya) cuisine, a fusion of Chinese and Malay ingredients and cooking techniques.

Indian cuisine

KL's two Little Indias – the official one in Brickfields and the other around Masjid India – are the places to sample Indian cooking, although you'll find the cuisine of the subcontinent served right across the city. Further afield, Klang's Little India also has an excellent array of Indian eateries.

A very KL experience is taking supper late at night at a Muslim Indian-Malay eatery known as a *mamak;* these typically run 24 hours, serve comfort-food dishes such as *roti canai* (flaky, flat bread), mee goreng (fried noodles) and *murtabak* (roti stuffed with meat).

Other Cuisines

KL's dining scene is fully international and – thanks to Malaysia's huge immigrant workforce – you needn't look far to find inexpensive Thai, Burmese, Nepalese, Indonesian, Bangladeshi and Pakistani fare. Among the more upmarket dining options are restaurants serving Italian, French, fusion, Japanese and pan-Asian cuisine, ranging in style from casual chic to white tablecloth.

When to Eat

To those used to 'three square meals', it might seem as if Malays are always eating. In fact, five or six meals or snacks is more the order of the day than strict adherence to the breakfast-lunch-dinner trilogy. Breakfast is often something that can be grabbed on the run: *nasi lemak* wrapped to go *(bungkus)* in a banana leaf or brown waxed paper, a quick bowl of noodles, toast and eggs, or *roti canai.*

Come late morning a snack might be in order – perhaps a *karipap* (deep-fried pastry filled with spiced meat or fish and potatoes). Lunch generally starts from 12.30pm, something to keep in mind if you plan to eat at a popular establishment.

The British left behind a strong attachment to afternoon tea, consumed here in the form of tea or coffee and a sweet or savoury snack such as *tong sui* (sweet warm soup or custard), various Indian fritters, battered and fried slices of cassava, sweet potato, banana and – of course – *kueh* (traditional cakes often made from glutinous rice).

Mamak and hawker stalls see a jump in business a few hours after dinner (which is eaten around 6.30pm or 7pm), when Malays head out in search of a treat to tide them over until morning.

Festivals & Celebrations

It's no surprise that a people as consumed with food and its pleasures as Malays mark every occasion with edible delights.

At Chinese New Year banquets each table is sure to be graced with *yee sang* (literally 'fresh fish'; a Cantonese raw-fish dish believed to bring luck in the coming year). Other foods special to this time of the year (look for them in Chinese supermarkets) include pineapple tarts, *kueh bangkit* (snow-white, melt-in-the-mouth cookies), *nga ku* (deep-fried Chinese arrowroot chips) and *ti kueh* (glutinous rice cakes wrapped in banana leaf).

The Ramadan bazaars are reason in themselves to visit KL during the Muslim holy month. Vendors compete to secure a lucrative spot at one of the city's Ramadan markets, which swing into action late in the afternoon to serve those breaking the fast at sunset. They offer an excellent opportunity to sample home-cooked, otherwise hard-to-find Malay dishes.

For the Indian festival Deepavali, special foodstuffs are shipped from the subcontinent, such as hand-patted pappadams and *kulfi* (a frozen, milk-based dessert). Head to Little India, where you'll find special sweets such as *jalebi* (deep-fried fritters soaked in sugar syrup) and savoury snacks like *muruku* (crispy fried coils of curry-leaf-studded dough).

EATING HABITS

- You'll rarely find a knife on the Malaysian table – fork and spoon are the cutlery of choice. Forks aren't used to carry food to the mouth but to nudge food onto the spoon.
- Chinese food is usually eaten with chopsticks (Westerners may be offered a fork and a spoon as a courtesy).
- Malays and Indians eat rice-based meals with their right hand (the left is reserved for unclean tasks), using their thumb to manoeuvre rice onto the balls of their fingers and then transferring the lot to their mouth. Moistening your rice with curries and side dishes helps things along and, as with any new skill, practice makes perfect.
- Before and after eating, wash your hands with water from the teapot-like container on your table (Malaysian eateries) or at a communal sink to the rear or side of the room.
- Napkins on the table (and a towel to wipe your wet hands) aren't a given, so it's always a good idea to carry a pack of tissues when heading out to graze.
- In some Chinese eateries, after you've placed your order a server will bring a basin of hot water containing saucers, chopsticks, bowls and cutlery to the table. This is meant to allay hygiene concerns – remove the items from the water and dry them off with a napkin (or shake them dry).
- Restaurants adhering to Muslim dietary rules are classed as halal and will not serve alcohol. Restaurants advertising themselves as pork free don't use pig products in any of their dishes.

TOP TASTES

Don't even think about leaving KL without sampling these much-loved specialities:

- *Nasi lemak* – rice steamed in coconut milk and served with *ikan bilis*, fried peanuts, half a hard-boiled egg, *sambal* (chilli sauce) and a selection of curries; often eaten for breakfast.
- *Char kway teow* – wide rice noodles stir-fried with prawns, cockles, bean sprouts and egg; it vies with *nasi lemak* for the title of 'national dish'.
- *Roti canai* – flaky unleavened bread griddled with ghee until crisp and eaten with curry or dhal; it's another breakfast favourite.
- *Asam laksa* – hailing from Penang, this is a sour and chilli-hot bowlful of round rice noodles in a fish-based soup, garnished with slivered torch ginger flower, chopped pineapple and mint.
- *Cendol* – a wonderfully refreshing sweet of shaved ice mounded over toothsome mung-bean noodles, all doused in fresh coconut milk and luscious palm-sugar syrup.

Eating by Neighbourhood

- **Bukit Bintang & KLCC** Jln Alor, fine dining and everything in-between.
- **Chinatown, Merdeka Square & Bukit Nanas** Best for Chinese cheap eats.
- **Masjid India, Kampung Baru & Northern KL** Great Indian food, classic night markets.
- **Lake Gardens, Brickfields & Bangsar** Multinational cuisine in Bangsar Baru.

Lonely Planet's Top Choices

Rebung (p102) Seemingly endless buffet of typically Malay dishes.

Dewakan (p120) Innovative fine dining in Shah Alam.

Jalan Alor (p55) KL's premier eats street is an unmissable culinary experience.

Sambal Hijau (p101) Authentic Malay cooking with more than 50 dishes to try.

Restoran Yarl (p103) An array of tasty Tamil food from northern Sri Lanka.

Best by Budget

$

Madras Lane Hawkers (p75) Sample the best *asam laksa* and *yong tau fu* in Chinatown.

Glutton Street (p49) Head to Pudu in the evening for this street of hawker stalls.

Kin Kin (p87) This bare-bones joint serves KL's best chilli *pan mee*.

$$

Rebung (p102) Feast on a buffet of expertly made Malay dishes.

Limapulo (p88) Homestyle authentic Peranakan food.

Merchant's Lane (p77) Lofty cafe serving a mash-up of Eastern and Western dishes.

$$$

Bijan (p55) Malay cuisine with fine-dining flair in a relaxed atmosphere.

Antara Restaurant (p78) Modern Malaysian dishes with a French twist in a restored colonial building.

Sushi Hinata (p55) Exquisite sushi prepared by expert Japanese chefs.

Best Malaysian & Peranakan

Sambal Hijau (p101) Traditional buffet-style Malay cooking.

Wondermama (p56) Contemporary twists on Malaysian classics.

Limapulo (p88) Homely, Nonya-style cooking.

Best Chinese

Sek Yuen (p49) Pudu landmark with dishes made in a wood-fired kitchen.

Yut Kee (p87) Classic Hainanese *kopitiam* known also for its Western-style dishes.

Kin Kin (p87) Dry *pan mee* specialist; it also offers a vegetarian version.

Kedai Makanan Dan Minuman TKS (p55) Feel the heat at this Sichaunese joint on Jln Alor.

Best Indian

Lawanya Food Corner (p103) Homestyle cooking at a family-run curry joint in Brickfields.

Sri Nirwana Maju (p104) Banana-leaf heaven in Bangsar.

Saravana Bhavan (p88 There are several outlets of this famous vegetarian operation.

Best International & Fusion

Antara Restaurant (p78) French inflections on modern Malaysian dishes.

Cilantro (p57) Serves an eclectic range of Japanese-French-inspired dishes

Merchant's Lane (p77) Tasty mash-up of Eastern and Western dishes.

Best French

Yeast Bistronomy (p105) Brilliant bistro-bakery in the heart of Bangsar Baru.

French Feast (p55) Comforting cassoulet and other French bistro-style dishes in Bukit Bintang.

Nathalie's Gourmet Studio (p110) Expertly prepared meals at Publika.

Italian

Strato (p57) Tasty pasta and pizza high up the Norman Foster-designed Troika building.

Nerovivo (p55) Classy Italian eatery in a bungalow close to Changkat Bukit Bintang.

Prego (p56) Family-friendly pizza joint.

Hawker

Madras Lane Hawkers (p75) A treasure hidden behind Chinatown's wet market.

Glutton Street (p49) Pudu alleyway crammed with delicious hawker food.

Jalan Imbi Hawker Stalls (p52) A great alternative to touristy Jln Alor – and much cheaper.

Best Japanese

Sushi Hinata (p55) Sublime sushi, sashimi and other haute-Japanese creations.

Santouka (p54) Rich pork-broth ramen noodles in Pavilion KL.

Fukuya (p56) Full range of Japanese dishes, served in an elegant bamboo-surrounded bungalow.

Vegetarian

Dharma Realm Guan Yin Sagely Monastery Canteen (p48) Join office workers for a healthy breakfast or lunch.

Ganga Cafe (p106) Wholesome South Indian food on Bangsar's Lg Kurau.

Blue Boy Vegetarian Food Centre (p52) Remarkable hawker-style cafe at the base of a backstreet apartment block.

Bakery & Patisserie

Bunn Choon (p76) Purveyers of KL's best egg tarts.

Jaslyn Cakes (p104) Tiny shop in Bangsar selling a delectable range of sweet treats.

Tommy Le Baker (p90) Top-grade sourdough bread, pastries, sandwiches and quiches.

Best Market Food

Bazaar Baru Chow Kit (p85) Sample noodles in a rich cow's-liver soup and an array of Malay desserts.

Masjid India Pasar Malam (p88) A wide range of excellent food stalls at this Saturday-night market.

Bangsar Sunday Market (104) Noodles, satay and fresh juices at this lively and mainly daytime market.

Best Local Breakfast

Imbi Market at ICC Pudu (p49) Try the *popiah*, congee and egg tarts.

Chee Cheong Fun Stall (p49) Best rice noodles in Chinatown.

LOKL Coffee Co (p77) Choose between delicious dessert toasties or a full English.

Best Afternoon Tea

Colonial Cafe at the Majestic Hotel (p103) High tea with all the trimmings served in a gorgeous orchid-filled conservatory.

Atmosphere 360 (p78) Gorge on the buffet in Menara KL's revolving restaurant.

Rococo (p52) Choose from a table piled high with bread, pastries, cakes and scones.

Best of the Chain Gang

Ben's (p54) Tempting range of Western and Malay foods.

Little Penang Kafé (p56) Offering excellent versions of Peranakan specialities.

Delicious (p106) Reliable, elegant restaurant with something for everyone.

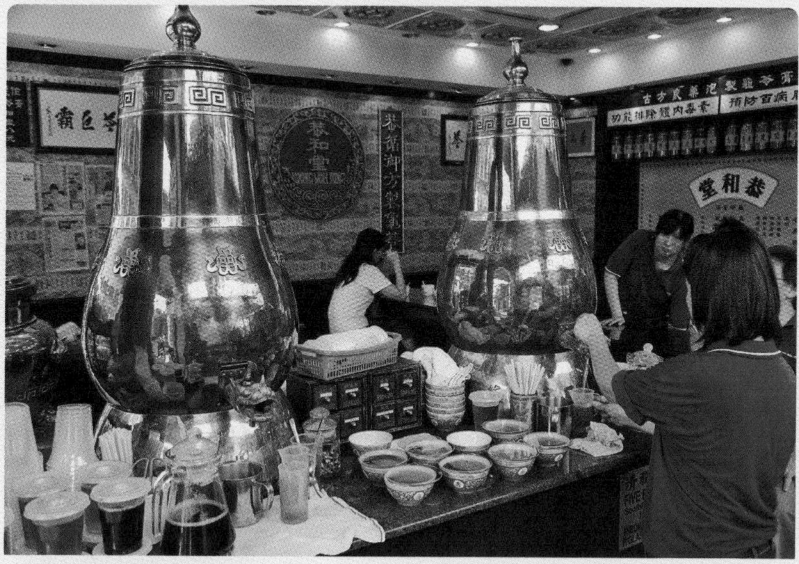

Tea served from brass urns

Drinking & Nightlife

Bubble tea, iced kopi-o, a frosty beer or a flaming Lamborghini – KL's cafes, teahouses and bars offer a multitude of ways to wet your whistle. Muslim mores push coffee and tea culture to the fore, but there's no shortage of sophisticated cocktail bars and other alcohol-fuelled venues where you can party the night away with abandon.

Time for Tea

British colonial rule left Malaysians with a taste for tea. The leaf is grown on the peninsula in the Cameron Highlands, with BOH the largest producer of black tea; there's also plenty of tea imported from China, India and Sri Lanka.

One of the best shows at hawker stalls and *kopitiam* (coffee shops) is watching the tea wallah toss-pour an order of *teh tarik*. The result is one very frothy cuppa. A true *teh tarik* is made using condensed milk, but this ingredient has largely been replaced by condensed creamer made from palm oil.

Other tea drinks of note are *teh halia* (tea flavoured with ginger), *teh ais* (milky iced tea), *teh-o-ais* (iced tea without milk) and *teh limau* (tea with lime juice). For an especially rich cuppa, ask for *teh susu kerabau* (hot tea with boiled fresh milk).

Coffee Culture

Traditional Malaysian *kopi* is also popular. This dark, bitter brew is served in Chinese coffee shops and is an excellent antidote to a case of jet lag. Another unique-to-Malaysia caffeinated drink is *cham* or Hainan tea, a blend of milky coffee and tea.

NEED TO KNOW

Opening Hours

Bars 5pm to 1am Sunday to Thursday, to 3am Friday and Saturday. Happy hours offering two-for-one drinks and other deals typically run from opening until around 8pm.

Clubs 9pm to 3am Tuesday to Saturday; Zouk and Zion Club are open until 5am.

How Much?

- Local beer: RM15
- Imported beer: RM25
- Cocktail: RM40
- Coffee: RM10
- Tea: RM5

Drinking Water

- Filtered tap water is usually fine, but check first.
- Avoid ice if a place looks dodgy.

Cover Charges

Club admission ranges from RM30 to RM60 depending on the venue and event.

Bar Crawl

The Kuala Lumpur Pub Crawl (p55) meets at 8.45pm every Thursday and Saturday at Nagaba on the corner of Jln Nagasari and Jln Mesui in the Changkat Bukit Bintang area. Includes five drinks and discounts on others.

Information

Time Out KL (www.timeoutkl.com) Latest info on cafes and bars.

Utopia Asia (www.utopia-asia.com) For local GLBT info.

Eat Drink KL (http://eatdrinkkl.blogspot.com) Reviews of KL's latest drinking spots.

There's no need to go without your daily dose of latte or espresso, though. The *kopitiam* and their contemporary counterparts – chains such as Coffee Bean & Tea Leaf, PappaRich and Old Town White Coffee – are rivalled by a host of excellent independent cafes that deal in single-origin beans and employ baristas trained to use classic coffee-making machines.

Juices & Other Nonalcoholic Drinks

Caffeine-free beverages include freshly blended fruit and vegetable juices; sticky-sweet, green, sugar-cane juice; and coconut water, consumed straight from the nut with a straw. More unusual drinks include *barley peng* or *ee bee chui* (barley boiled with water, pandan leaf and rock sugar served over ice); *air mata kucing* (a sweet dried longan beverage); and *cincau* (a herbal grass-jelly drink).

Sweetened kalamansi juice and Chinese salted plums may sound a strange combination but make for a thoroughly refreshing potion called *asam boi*. There's also a whole range of bubble teas, drinks that come with various sago pearls, jellies and other edible additives floating in them.

Wine, Beer & Spirits

Sky-high duties on alcohol can make a boozy night out awfully expensive. The cheapest beers are those brewed locally, such as Tiger and Carlsberg; they're best enjoyed alfresco while watching the streetside theatre of Jln Alor or Chinatown's Jln Hang Lekir. KLites are also partial to an expertly mixed cocktail, which can be sampled at one of the city's many rooftop bars or one of the growing number of speakeasy-style 'secret' bars.

Clubbing

Wednesday to Saturday are the main clubbing nights, with plenty of different events happening to suit all musical tastes. What's in and out is fairly fluid, so it's best to check local media listings before heading out. Be prepared for cover charges, which typically include your first drink.

LGBT Scene

There's a fairly open LGBT scene in KL, with several established gay dance nights, the main ones being DivineBliss at G Tower and Lovemachine at Marketplace. Don't miss the monthly party Rainbow Rojak (www.facebook.com/RainbowRojak); this laid-back and inclusive event for all sexual persuasions is currently held at Marketplace.

Drinking & Nightlife by Neighbourhood

➡ **Bukit Bintang & KLCC** Home to Changkat Bukit Bintang, new entertainment complex TREC and several classy sky-high bars.

➡ **Chinatown, Merdeka Square & Bukit Nanas** Backpacker bars and some speakeasy-style cocktail bars worth hunting for.

➡ **Masjid India, Kampung Baru & Northern KL** Heritage drinking spots at the Coliseum and the Row.

➡ **Lake Gardens, Brickfields & Bangsar** Bangsar is the place for classy cocktail bars and cool cafes.

Lonely Planet's Top Choices

Heli Lounge Bar (p57) Amazing city views from this helicopter-pad-turned-cocktail-lounge.

Marini's on 57 (p62) Toast the close-up views of the Petronas Towers.

Omakase + Appreciate (p79) Speakeasy joint on the edge of Chinatown.

PS150 (p79) Shanghai-style drinking den concealed behind a fake toyshop.

Coliseum Cafe (p90) Colonial charmer where Somerset Maugham enjoyed a drink or two.

Best Clubs

Zouk (p58) Multizoned dance space that keeps on pumping till 5am.

Zion Club (p57) Stumble home in the early hours from this club on Changkat Bukit Bintang.

Nagaba (p58) Come for the Rooftop Mojito Bar and the 2nd-floor club.

Best for Coffee

VCR (p79) Latte-art-contest-winning baristas serve up quality brews.

Feeka Coffee Roasters (p58) Choose from microlot beans or espresso-based drinks.

Coffea Coffee (p107) Slick Bangsar operation by a Korean barista champ.

Best for Tea

TWG Tea (p58) Classy tea emporium in Pavilion KL.

Chocha Foodstore (p79) Sample the hot and cold blends selected by the in-house 'tea sommelier'.

Newens (p59) Nibble macarons with your lapsang souchong.

Best Cocktail Bars

Omakase + Appreciate (p79) Top-secret retro cocktail bar.

PS150 (p79) Concealed behind a fake toyshop in a hip hood.

Coley (p106) Tiny cocktail bar serving expertly mixed drinks.

Ril's Bar (p106) Sophisticated assignation spot with inventive mixologists.

Best for Views

Heli Lounge Bar (p57) Thrilling rooftop drinks in the heart of Bukit Bintang.

Marini's on 57 (p62) Book a seat for a bird's-eye view of the KLCC.

Mantra Bar KL (p106) Look across the suburbs to the KL skyline from the rooftop of Bangsar Village II mall.

Mai Bar (p106) Fun poolside bar overlooking KL Sentral.

Best LGBT Friendly

DivineBliss (p62) Saturday-night rooftop party with renowned guest DJs.

Marketplace (p62) Sweat it out on the dance floor, cool off on the roof.

Moontree House (p79) Come here to tap into KL's discreet lesbian scene.

Entertainment

KL has plenty of entertainment options, but you have to keep your ear to the ground to discover the best of what's going on. Conservative tastes and censorship mean that quite a lot of what is on offer can be bland and inoffensive, but occasionally controversial and boundary-pushing performances and events are staged.

Theatre & Traditional Performing Arts

If you want to see and hear traditional Malaysian dance and music, there are regular shows at Malaysia Tourism Centre (p225) during the day, as well as every night at the nearby restaurant Saloma (p63). Central Market's Kasturi Walk is the stage for free music and dance events at the weekends. The beautifully renovated Panggung Bandaraya theatre is the venue for Mud (p80), a light-hearted musical telling the story of Kuala Lumpur.

The NGO Pusaka (www.senipusaka.com) works to keep traditional Malaysian arts alive by introducing them to the general public with free shows and exhibitions, and by training a new generation in such forms as *wayang kulit* (shadow puppetry), *mak yong* (dance-theatre) and various Chinese performing arts. Shows are by donation and often feature some outstanding older performers and the occasional young phenom.

Live Music

Major international popular-music artists often add KL to their Asia tours, but they sometimes have to adapt their shows to accommodate devout Muslim sensibilities.

Various restaurants and bars, including Pisco Bar (p57), have live music, and Live House (p58) at the new entertainment complex TREC hosts regular live comedy and music. Jazz is also popular (check out the line-up at No Black Tie (p62), and the accomplished Malaysian Philharmonic Orchestra is well worth catching in concert at the Dewan Filharmonik Petronas (p62).

At the Movies

KL's many multiplexes screen major international and local movies. The venues are generally top class. Tickets, which range from RM15 to RM30, can be booked online and are cheaper for screenings earlier in the day.

Cultural centres including **Alliance Française** (Map p258; ☎03-2694 7880; http://alliancefrancaise.org.my/en; 15 Lg Gurney; ⊙9am-7pm Tue-Thu, to 6pm Fri, to 5pm Sat; Ⓜ Ampang Park) and **Goethe Institut** (Map p251; ☎03-2164 2011; www.goethe.de; 6th fl Menara See Hoy Chan, 374 Jln Tun Razak; ⊙9am-6pm Mon-Fri; Ⓛ Ampang Park) screen foreign movies with subtitles; check the websites for details.

Spectator Sports

KLites are fans of football (soccer) – for details of upcoming games, check the website of the Football Association of Malaysia (www.fam.org.my). Basketball games take place at the MABA Stadium (p80). The city also gets caught up in the Formula 1 Malaysian Grand Prix, held at the Sepang International Circuit (www.sepangcircuit.com).

Entertainment by Neighbourhood

➡ **Bukit Bintang & KLCC** Orchestral classical music, intimate jazz and pop performances all get a showing at venues in these central areas.

➡ **Chinatown, Merdeka Square & Bukit Nanas** Free dance and martial-arts performances at Central Market on the weekend.

➡ **Masjid India, Kampung Baru & Northern KL** Istana Budaya and Kuala Lumpur Performing Arts Centre are two of the city's major performing-arts venues.

➡ **Lake Gardens, Brickfields & Bangsar** Performing-arts events at Publika or classical Indian dance shows in Brickfields.

Lonely Planet's Top Choices

No Black Tie (p62) Intimate space hosting jazz and classical-music concerts.

Dewan Filharmonik Petronas (p62) Gorgeous classical concert hall at the foot of the Petronas Towers.

Kuala Lumpur Performing Arts Centre (p90) Progressive theatre and dance venue set in a beautiful park.

Publika (p110) Events at the MAP performance spaces; free movies in the central courtyard.

Live House (p58) Comedy and live music at the new entertainment complex TREC.

Panggung Bandaraya (p80) The old City Hall has transformed into an elegant theatrical venue for the musical *Mud*.

Best for Movies

GSC Pavilion KL (p63) Treat yourself to the Gold Class section.

TGV Cineplex (p63) Get your Hollywood fix at this multiplex.

Coliseum Theatre (p90) Go Bollywood at this historic Masjid India theatre.

Best Dance Venues

Temple of Fine Arts (p107) Brickfields home of classical Indian dance.

Sutra Dance Theatre (p90) Shows choreographed by a Malaysian dance legend.

Istana Budaya (p90) Major venue for dance and theatre performances.

Best for Jazz

No Black Tie (p62) Discover some of the best talents on the local scene.

Sino The Bar Upstairs (p107) First Monday of the month is a jazz jamming event.

Forbidden City (p63) Hear jazz and blues at this new live-music venue on Changkat Bukit Bintang.

NEED TO KNOW

Tickets

Ticketpro (www.ticketpro.com.my)

TicketCharge (www.ticketcharge.com.my)

Information

KL Dance Watch (http://kldancewatch.wordpress.com) Blog with info and reviews on local contemporary-dance scene.

Kakiseni (http://kakiseni.com) Event listings and more.

Courses

Kuala Lumpur Performing Arts Centre (p90) Acting, dance and courses in traditional instruments such as the gamelan (traditional Malay orchestra).

Sutra Dance Theatre (p90) Courses in Odissi and other forms of classical Indian dance.

Temple of Fine Arts (p107) Courses in classical Indian dance, song and music.

Arts & Music Festivals

Urbanscapes (www.urbanscapes.com.my) User-generated arts festival that brings together art, music and design.

KL International Jazz & Arts Festival (www.klinternationaljazz.com) Held in September at the University of Malaya.

Cooler Lumpur Festival (www.coolerlumpur.com) Publika is the venue for this cultural fest that focuses on a different artistic genre each year.

JOHAN DESIGN ASSOCIATES/GETTY IMAGES ©

Textiles stall

Shopping

Kuala Lumpur is a prizefighter on the Asian shopping parade, a serious rival to retail heavyweights Singapore, Bangkok and Hong Kong. On offer are appealing handicrafts, major international brands (both legit and fake versions), masses of malls and decent sale prices. The city's traditional markets are hugely enjoyable and atmospheric experiences, regardless of whether you have a purchase in mind.

Malls & Department Stores

KL and the Klang Valley are liberally peppered with air-conditioned malls, some so big it would take several days to do them justice – Mid Valley Megamall and Sunway Pyramid, for example, are communities unto themselves, with hotels, entertainment facilities and, in the former, a 100-year-old Hindu temple!

Anchoring the malls are department stores:

AEON At Mid Valley Megamall (p108).

Metrojaya At Mid Valley Megamal (p108).

Parkson At Pavilion KL (p63).

Isetan At Suria KLCC (p65) and the Gardens Mall (p108).

Markets

Day markets focused on fresh produce include Pudu, Chow Kit and Chinatown. Vendors at *pasar malam* (night markets) sell prepared food, clothing, accessories, DVDs and CDs and the like. Some occur daily, such as the one along Jln Petaling in KL's Chinatown; others are once or twice a week.

Look out for flea, fashion and craft markets, such as the monthly events at Publika and Bangsar Shopping Centre.

What to Buy

Skilled artisans may be a dying breed, but you can still find great handmade craft items for sale in KL. Fashion, contemporary-art galleries, antique stores and interior-design shops are also worth a look.

There are bargain buys, but Malaysia is too affluent to offer dirt-cheap prices. Counterfeit goods are a problem – not just Prada handbags and Rolex watches but also software and electronics. Buyer beware!

FASHION

The area around KWC Fashion Mall (p49) is home to KL's rag trade, importing the latest looks from factories and designers across Asia. Major labels:

British India (http://britishindia.com.my) For high-quality linen and cotton pieces at Pavilion KL, Mid Valley Megamall, Bangsar Shopping Centre and Publika; its cheaper brand JustB has outlets in Publika and Gardens Mall.

Padini (www.padini.com) Offering many brands, several of which – such as Seed, Padini Authentics and Vincci (for shoes and accessories) – can be spotted at all the major malls.

Bonia (www.bonia.com) Quality Italian-style leather fashions and accessories for men and women.

If you're wanting to snap up some designer-brand bargains, visit **Melium Outlet** (http://meliumoutlet.com; 63 Jln Tasik Utama 3, Lake Fields, Sungai Besi; ⏲10am-7.30pm; Ⓜ Sungai Besi), the end-of-line and bargain sale outlet for luxury brand retailer Melium; its 50-plus labels include D&G and Hugo Boss, as well as Malaysian and Asian designer ready-to-wear garments.

TEXTILES

Batik is produced by drawing or printing a pattern on fabric with wax, then dyeing the material. The wax resists the various colours and, when washed away, leaves the pattern. Batik can be made into clothes or homewares or simply displayed as works of art.

Another textile to look out for is *kain songket*, a luxurious fabric with gold and silver threads woven throughout the material.

NEED TO KNOW

Opening Hours

Hours vary, but most places are open from around 9.30am to 7pm Monday to Saturday. Department stores and malls are open 10am to 10pm daily.

Sales Times

Malaysia Grand Prix Sale Coincides with the dates of the sporting event

Malaysia Mega Sale Carnival June to August

Malaysia Year-End Sale End November to early January

Refunds

Policies vary from shop to shop; as a rule, you'll find more flexible, consumer-friendly service at international-brand stores.

Shopping Festivals

Hari Kraf Kebangsaan (www.kraftangan.gov.my) February-March

Malaysian International Shoe Festival (www.misfshoe.com) April

Malaysian Fashion Week (www.malaysia-fashionweek.my) November

Handicrafts Courses

Aziz Ma'as (p82) Learn traditional and innovative batik from master artist Aziz Ma'as at his studio at the foot of Bukit Nanas.

Kompleks Kraf (p65) Kuala Lumpur Try your hand at traditional Malay crafts such as batik at the craft village in the grounds of this one-stop crafts complex.

Royal Selangor Pewtersmithing Workshops (p91) Entertaining classes where you make your own pewter bowl or jewellery; bookings required.

My Batik Visitor Centre (p53) Batik-painting classes for adults and children in an attractive compound with frangipani trees.

BASKETRY & MENGKUANG

All sorts of useful household items are made using rattan, bamboo, swamp nipah grass and pandanus leaves. Mengkuang (a local form of weaving) uses pandanus leaves and strips of bamboo to make baskets, bags

Shopping by Neighbourhood

Sungai Batu
Sungai Gombak
Lake Titiwangsa
Masjid India, Kampung Baru & Northern KL
Jln TAR's fabric shops, Chow Kit's wet market, and night markets in Masjid India and Kampung Baru (p91)
Sungai Klang
Petronas Towers
Sungai Gombak
Bukit Bintang & KLCC
Best for malls and the traditional wet market at Pudu (p63)
Chinatown, Merdeka Square & Bukit Nanas
Jln Petaling's night market and interesting local stores, from florists to funerary goods (p80)
Tasik Perdana
Lake Gardens, Brickfields & Bangsar
Bangsar Baru is packed with boutiques; go-to malls include Bangsar Village and Publika (p107)
Sungai Klang

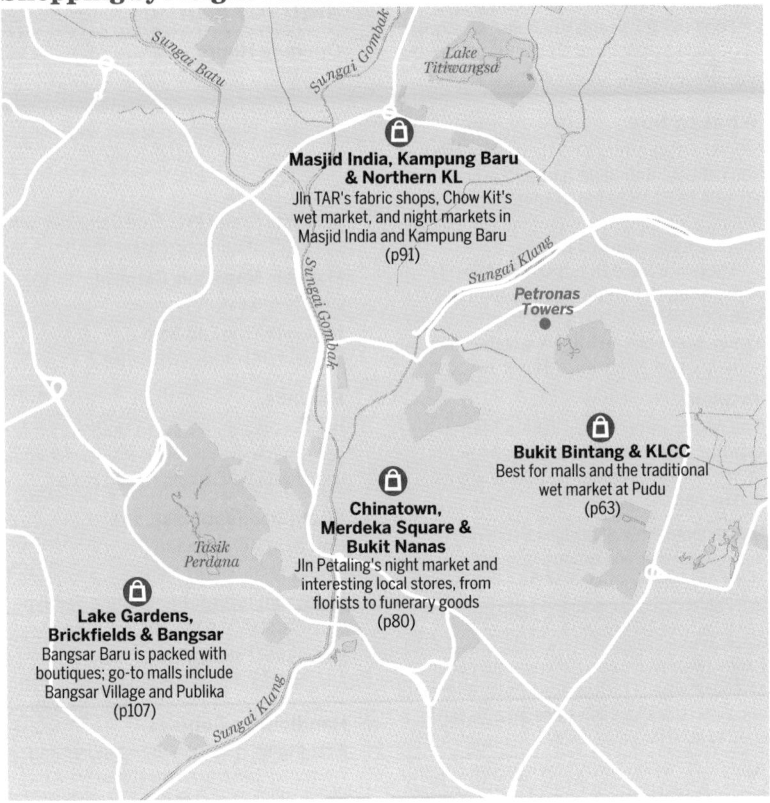

and mats. Look in the Central Market and around Chinatown for these items.

KITES & PUPPETS

Eye-catching *wayang kulit* (shadow puppets) are made from buffalo hide to portray characters from epic Hindu legends, while kites are made from paper and bamboo strips in a variety of traditional designs. The crescent-shaped *wau bulan* (moon kite) can reach 3m in length and breadth, while the *wau kucing* (cat kite) is the logo of Malaysia Airlines. You can find kites and puppets in Central Market.

METALWORK

Malaysia's skilled silversmiths specialise in filigree and repoussé work, where designs are hammered through the silver from the underside. Objects crafted out of pewter are synonymous with Selangor. Royal Selangor (p63) has several outlets in major malls, including Suria KLCC and Pavilion KL.

WOODCARVING

The Mah Meri tribe from Pulau Carey off the coast of Selangor are particularly renowned for their sinuous carvings of animist spirits. You can find these Orang Asli crafts at a stall in Central Market.

Shopping by Neighbourhood

- **Bukit Bintang & KLCC** Best for malls and the traditional wet market at Pudu.
- **Chinatown, Merdeka Square & Bukit Nanas** Jln Petaling's night market and interesting local stores from florists to funerary goods.
- **Masjid India, Kampung Baru & Northern KL** Jln TAR's fabric shops, Chow Kit's wet market and the night market in Masjid India.
- **Lake Gardens, Brickfields & Bangsar** Bangsar Baru is packed with boutiques; go-to malls are Publika and Bangsar Village.

Lonely Planet's Top Choices

Publika (p110) Innovative complex combining culture, art and great food with retail.

Thisappear (p109) Independent, designer-owned boutique selling a range of local labels.

Central Market (p74) Best selection of local arts and crafts.

Wei-Ling Gallery (p107) Invest in a piece of contemporary art.

Museum of Ethnic Arts (p74) Antique tribal pieces from Borneo and elsewhere.

Best For Local Handicrafts

Asli Craft (p80) Beautiful items handmade by indigneous groups from across Malaysia.

Wau Tradisi (p80) Traditional paper and bamboo kites.

Rhino (p80) Hand-painted clogs and other handicrafts.

Best Bookshops

Kinokuniya (p65) KL's best printed-matter pit stop.

Silverfish Books (p111) Local publisher with its own small bookstore.

Junk Bookstore (p81) Shelves piled high with secondhand books.

Best Fashion Designers

Khoon Hooi (p64) Luxury fashion with an edge from an award-winning designer.

Comoddity (p109) Original pieces by local menswear designer Vincent Siow.

d.d.collective (p109) Contemporary high-end fashion by Paris-based Malaysian designer Jonathan Liang.

Mimpikita (p109) Local fashion made wih gorgeous printed fabrics.

Aseana (p65) Plenty of blingtastic frocks, including pieces by top designer Nurita Harith.

Best Boutiques

Thisappear (p109) Designer-owned boutique selling pieces by Joe Chia, Kozo and Alia Bastaman among others.

Lonely Dream (p109) Offering own-label clothing and other designers' wares.

Shoes Shoes Shoes (p109) A shoe- and accessory-lover's dream store, with branches in Bangsar and Publika.

Fabspy (p108) Urban unisex fashion by a range of Malaysian designers.

League of Captains (p91) Sells T-shirts and caps by local label Pestle & Mortar Clothing.

Best Malls

Publika (p110) Schedule a day to browse the shops, galleries and the many great places to eat.

Pavilion KL (p63) Setting the gold standard for Bukit Bintang's gaggle of malls.

Sungei Wang Plaza (p64) Who knows what you'll discover in this multilevel warren of youth cool and fashion.

Suria KLCC (p65) A retail nirvana at the base of the Petronas Towers.

Best Museum Shops

Islamic Arts Museum (p94) Top-notch range of arts and crafts, plus design and art books.

Gahara Galleria (p80) The National Textiles Museum shop sells quality batik and local designer goods.

Museum of Ethnic Arts (p74) Nearly everything is for sale at this extraordinary private collection of local tribal arts.

Kompleks Kraf Kuala Lumpur (p65) The Karakenya section is stacked with all kinds of batik prints.

Best Markets

Pudu Market (p49) There's always plenty of activity at KL's biggest wet market.

Bazaar Baru Chow Kit (p85) A heady sensory experience awaits at this long-established wet market.

Bangsar Sunday Market (p104) Weekly fresh-produce market with plenty of hawker stalls for grazing.

Petaling Street Market (p81) Piles of pirated goods alongside the real deal.

Explore Kuala Lumpur

Bukit Bintang & KLCC....44
Top Sights....46
Sights....48
Eating....52
Drinking & Nightlife....57
Entertainment....62
Shopping....63
Sports & Activities....65

Chinatown, Merdeka Square & Bukit Nanas..67
Top Sights....69
Sights....72
Eating....75
Drinking & Nightlife....78
Entertainment....80
Shopping....80
Sports & Activities....81

Masjid India, Kampung Baru & Northern KL....83
Top Sights....85
Eating....87
Drinking & Nightlife....90
Entertainment....90
Shopping....91
Sports & Activities....91

Lake Gardens, Brickfields & Bangsar..92
Top Sights....94
Sights....99
Eating....102
Drinking & Nightlife....106
Entertainment....107
Shopping....107
Sports & Activities....111

Day Trips from Kuala Lumpur....112
Top Sights....113
Bukit Fraser (Fraser's Hill)....116
Klang Valley....118
Putrajaya....122

Sleeping....124

Melaka City....133
Sights....135
Eating....144
Drinking & Nightlife....147
Shopping....148
Activities....150
Sleeping....151

Penang....155
George Town....159
Sights....159
Eating....164
Drinking & Nightlife....170
Shopping....173
Activities & Tours....174
Sleeping....174
Batu Ferringhi & Teluk Bahang....178
Sights....179
Eating & Drinking....180
Activities....180
Sleeping....181
The Rest of Penang...182
Air Itam & Penang Hill....182
Southeast Penang Island.183
Balik Pulau & Kampung Pulau Betong....184

KUALA LUMPUR'S TOP SIGHTS

Petronas Towers & KLCC ... 46

Menara KL ... 69

Merdeka Square ... 70

Sri Mahamariamman Temple ... 72

Masjid Jamek ... 75

Islamic Arts Museum ... 94

Tun Abdul Razak Heritage Park ... 95

Thean Hou Temple ... 97

National Museum ... 98

Batu Caves ... 113

Forest Research Institute Malaysia ... 115

Neighbourhoods at a Glance

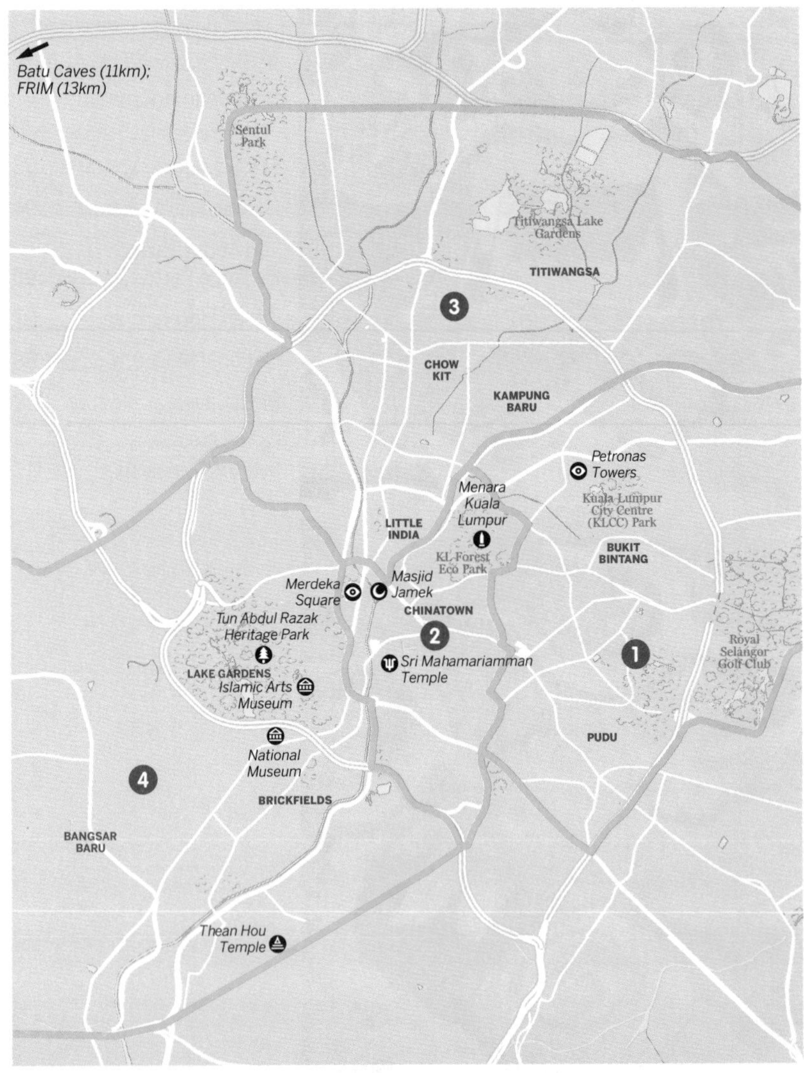

❶ Bukit Bintang & KLCC (p44)

Bukit Bintang (Star Hill) – also known as the Golden Triangle – is home to a cluster of major shopping malls and many excellent places to eat and drink, not least of which is Jln Alor, KL's most famous food street. KLCC, which stands for Kuala Lumpur City Centre, is the vast development anchored by the Petronas Towers. East of here are places of interest along Jln Tun Razak and Jln Ampang. South of Bukit Bintang is the distinctly Chinese district of Pudu, home to an atmospheric wet market.

❷ Chinatown, Merdeka Square & Bukit Nanas (p67)

You don't have to look too hard to find traces of old KL in Chinatown's shophouse-lined streets, which border the confluence of the Klang and Gombak rivers. This is where the city was born, reached its teenage years with the development of Chinatown and celebrated its late 20s with the establishment of the British colonial ensemble around Merdeka Square. The Malay fort that once topped the jungle-clad hill Bukit Nanas has long gone, replaced by one of the city's most recognisable landmarks, the Menara KL telecommunications tower.

❸ Masjid India, Kampung Baru & Northern KL (p83)

Surrounding the mosque of the same name, Masjid India is not to be missed for its Saturday night market. To the east are the traditional wooden houses of Kampung Baru, a Malay village within the heart of the modern city. Chow Kit, north along Jln TAR, has a reputation for drugs and vice, but by day it also hosts a wonderful wet market. Further north are the leafy surrounds of Lake Titiwangsa and Sentul, both providing respite from the city with parks and the chance to watch performing arts.

❹ Lake Gardens, Brickfields & Bangsar (p92)

Born of the British desire to conquer the teeming jungle and fashion it into a pleasant park, the Lake Gardens remains a lush breathing space in the heart of KL. It's mainly covered by the Tun Abdul Razak Heritage Park and includes major institutions such as the Islamic Arts Museum, National Museum and Masjid Negara. KL Sentral and neighbouring Brickfields are immediately south of here, while the upscale residential area of Bangsar – one of the top locations in the city in which to shop and eat – is to the southwest.

Bukit Bintang & KLCC

Neighborhood Top Five

❶ **Petronas Towers** (p46) Admiring the architectural wonder from within at the 86th-floor observation deck and strolling across the Skybridge that connects the twin skyscrapers.

❷ **KLCC Park** (p48) Exploring the imaginatively designed park and joining the evening crowds gathered to watch the Petronas Towers light up and the Lake Symphony fountains' show.

❸ **Jalan Alor** (p55) Enjoying a variety of tasty dishes washed down with a cold beer at the bustling food street.

❹ **Pavilion KL** (p63) Shopping for international and local brand bargains at Bukit Bintang's stellar malls.

❺ **ILHAM** (p48) Viewing the latest exhibition at the cutting-edge gallery housed in the stunning 60-storey ILHAM tower designed by Foster & Partners.

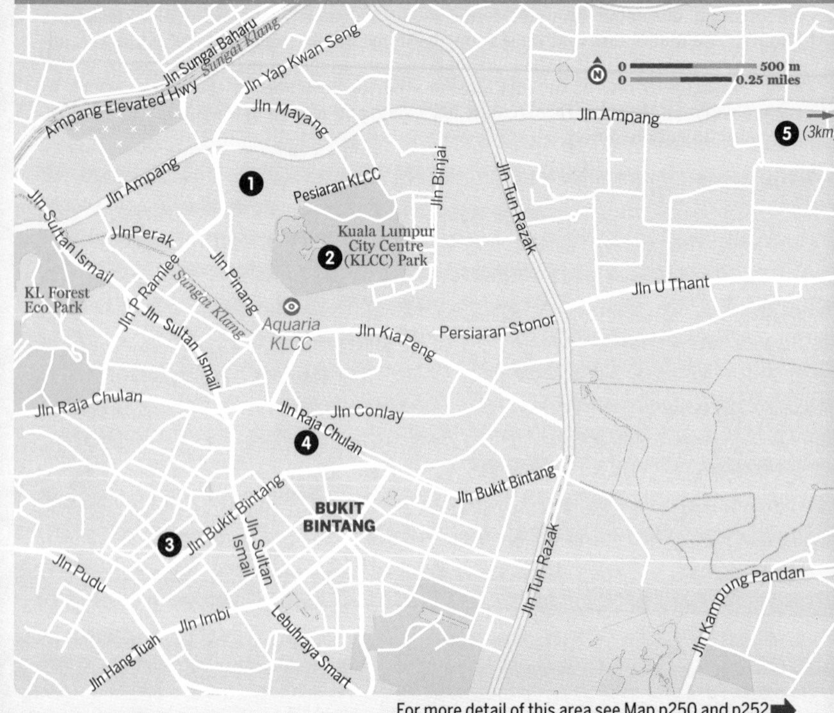

For more detail of this area see Map p250 and p252

Explore Bukit Bintang & KLCC

The intersection of Jln Sultan Ismail and Jln Bukit Bintang marks the heart of Bukit Bintang, KL's premier shopping, dining and nightlife district, an area studded with office towers, condominiums and glitzy shopping malls. The construction of a new MRT underground station here, due to open by July 2017, has meant several years of building works and hoardings.

Changkat Bukit Bintang is the city's most raucous nightlife area and has some good restaurants, while nearby Jln Mesui is more laid-back. The new entertainment complex TREC, a taxi ride east of Bukit Bintang on Jln Tun Razak, is where you'll find KL's biggest club, Zouk (p58), and a number of bars and live music venues which come to life on Friday and Saturday nights.

An elevated, covered walkway links Bukit Bintang with Kuala Lumpur City Centre (KLCC), anchored by the iconic Petronas Towers (p46). Also here is a spacious landscaped park, huge convention centre, aquarium, excellent children's museum, world-class concert hall and Suria KLCC (p65), another of KL's great shopping malls.

Out towards Jln Tun Razak you'll find a few interesting things to see and do, as well as in the Imbi and Pudu areas and the city's financial district, Tun Razak Exchange.

Local Life

- **Hawker heaven** Join the locals for breakfast at the Imbi Market stalls at ICC Pudu (p49) and stick around for great eats at the evening hawker stalls on Jln Sayur, aka Glutton Street (p49).
- **Markets** Rise early to stroll Pudu Market (p49), where price-conscious KL residents shop for groceries.
- **Meditation and lunch** The vegetarian canteen at the serene Dharma Realm Guan Yin Sagely Monastery (p56) is popular with office workers.
- **Food courts** Food courts are the best place to refuel during a hard day's shopping at the malls. Feel spoilt for choice at Food Republic (p52) and sample food from the city's top hawker stalls at Lot 10 Hutong (p52).

Getting There & Away

- **Monorail** The best way to access the area with stops along Jln Imbi and Jln Sultan Ismail. Avoid the evening weekday rush hour, 6pm to 8pm.
- **Bus** There are four free GOKL City Bus loop services, but they can get snarled in traffic.
- **Walking** The fastest way to get around during rush hour. Take advantage of the partly air-con covered walkway between KLCC and Pavilion KL.
- **MRT** New stations Bukit Bintang and Tun Razak Exchange due to open in 2017.

Lonely Planet's Top Tip

Go to concierge desks in each of the major malls to sign up for free discount shopping cards that may entitle you to free gifts and often save you 10% or more on prices at many outlets.

Best Places to Eat

- Kedai Makanan Dan Minuman TKS (p55)
- Bijan (p55)
- Sushi Hinata (p55)
- Glutton Street (p49)
- Imbi Market at ICC Pudu (p49)

For reviews, see p52

Best Places to Drink

- Heli Lounge Bar (p57)
- Marini's on 57 (p62)
- Fuego (p57)
- Pisco Bar (p57)
- Zouk (p58)

For reviews, see p57

Best Places to Shop

- Pavilion KL (p63)
- Sungei Wang Plaza (p64)
- Suria KLCC (p65)
- Starhill Gallery (p64)
- Kompleks Kraf Kuala Lumpur (p65)

For reviews, see p63

TOP SIGHT

PETRONAS TOWERS & KLCC

Resembling two silver rockets preparing for take-off, the twin towers of Kuala Lumpur's iconic landmark are the perfect allegory for the meteoric rise of the city from tin-miners' hovel to 21st-century metropolis. The magnificent stainless steel skyscrapers are the crowning glory of the KLCC.

Petronas Towers

Opened in 1998, the Petronas Towers reach up nearly 452m; for six years they were the tallest structure in the world and they remain the world's tallest twin towers. The design for the 88-storey-high tower blocks, by Argentinian architect César Pelli, is based on an eight-sided star that echoes arabesque patterns. Islamic influences are also evident in each tower's five tiers – representing the five pillars of Islam – and in the 63m masts that crown them, calling to mind the minarets of a mosque and the Star of Islam.

The starting point for guided 45-minute tours of the towers is the ticket office in the towers' basement. First stop is the **Skybridge** connection on the 41st floors of the towers at 170m. Having walked across this you'll then take the lift up to the 86th-floor **observation deck** at 370m.

DON'T MISS...

- Observation deck
- Skybridge
- KLCC Park
- Dewan Filharmonik Petronas

PRACTICALITIES

- Map p250
- ☎03-2331 8080
- www.petronastwin-towers.com.my
- Jln Ampang
- adult/child RM85/35
- 9am-9pm Tue-Sun, closed 1-2.30pm Fri
- (child-friendly icon)
- (train icon) KLCC

Dewan Filharmonik Petronas

Tucked away at the base of the Petronas Towers is KLCC's premier concert hall, Dewan Filharmonik Petronas (p62), a handsomely decorated space with excellent acoustics. The polished Malaysian Philharmonic Orchestra (www.mpo.com.my) plays here (usually Friday and Saturday evening and Sunday matinee, but also other times) as well as other local and international ensembles.

KLCC Park

The Petronas Towers are the star attraction of the KLCC (Kuala Lumpur City Centre), a development covering 40 hectares of land that was once the Selangor Turf Club. The site includes the imaginatively landscaped KLCC Park (p48), designed by Brazilian Roberto Burle Marx, who never lived to see its completion. Naturally, the park is the best vantage point for photos of the Petronas Towers. In the early evening, it can seem like everyone in town has come down here to watch the glowing towers punching up into the night sky.

Galeri Petronas

Swap consumerism for culture at the excellent Galeri Petronas (p48) showcasing contemporary photography and paintings. It's a bright, modern space with interesting, professionally curated shows that change every few months.

Petrosains

Fill an educational few hours at this interactive science discovery centre (p48) with all sorts of buttons to press and levers to pull. Many of the activities and displays focus on the wonderful things that fuel has brought to Malaysia – no prizes for guessing who sponsors the museum. As a side note, 'sains' is not pronounced 'sayns' but 'science'.

TOP TIPS

Buy your ticket online. Up to half of the 1500 tickets issued daily can be bought via the website until 24 hours before the visit time.

If you don't have an advance booking, get in line around 8.30am to be sure of securing one of the remaining tickets.

Go early for the best views. Mornings in KL tend to be clearer than afternoons, when it is more likely to rain or be hazy.

For a lip-smackingly good bowl of noodles head to Little Penang Kafe (p56), one of tens of dining options at Suria KLCC, the mall adjacent to the towers.

Across the road at Avenue K is the family-friendly restaurant Wondermama (p56) selling tasty modern Malaysian food.

SIGHTS

PETRONAS TOWERS TOWER

See p46.

★ILHAM GALLERY

Map p250 (www.ilhamgallery.com; 3rd & 5th fl, Ilham Tower, 8 Jln Binjai; 11am-7pm Tue-Sat, to 5pm Sun; Ampang Park) FREE KL's latest public art gallery provides an excellent reason to admire close-up the slick 60-storey ILHAM Tower designed by Foster + Partners. With a mission to showcase modern and contemporary Malaysian art, ILHAM kicked off with a blockbuster show of works by Hoessein Enas (1924–95). There's no permanent collection, with exhibitions changing every three to four months.

Talks, performances, film screenings and children's workshops are also held here, often tying in with the theme of the current exhibition. Outside the tower the giant copper-clad sculptures are the first permanent public work by Chinese artist Ai Weiwei to be installed in Southeast Asia.

★KLCC PARK PARK

Map p250 (Jln Ampang, KLCC; 7am-10pm; KLCC) The park is the best vantage point for eyeballing the Petronas Towers (p46). In the early evening, it can seem like everyone in town has come down here to watch the glowing towers punching up into the night sky. Every night at 8pm, 9pm and 10pm the Lake Symphony fountains play in front of the Suria KLCC.

A 1.3km soft-surface jogging track winds its way around the park past the excellent children's playground, paddling pool and Masjid Asy-Syakirin.

AQUARIA KLCC AQUARIUM

Map p250 (03-2333 1888; www.aquariaklcc.com; Concourse, KL Convention Centre, Jln Pinang; adult/child RM64/53; 10am-8pm, last admission 7pm; ; KLCC) The highlight of this impressive aquarium in the basement of the KL Convention Centre is its 90m underwater tunnel: view sand tiger sharks, giant gropers and more up close. Daily feeding sessions for a variety of fish and otters are complemented by ones for arapaimas, electric eels and sharks on Monday, Wednesday and Saturday (see website for schedule). Free dives (RM424), cage dives (RM211), and a Sleep with Sharks (RM211) program for kids aged six to 13 are also available.

DISCOVERIA MUSEUM

Map p250 (03-2181 7218; www.discoveria.com.my; level 4, Avenue K, Jln Ampang; adult/child RM40/50; 11am-6pm Mon-Fri, 10am-8pm Sat & Sun; ; KLCC) Kids will love this interactive exhibition with animatronic dinosaurs, climbing walls, treasure hunts and games.

DHARMA REALM GUAN YIN SAGELY MONASTERY BUDDHIST TEMPLE

Map p250 (www.drba.org; 161 Jln Ampang; 7am-4pm; Ampang Park) FREE The calm spaces, potted plants, mandala ceilings and giant gilded statues create an appropriately contemplative mood for quiet meditation at this colourful modern temple. The complex is dedicated to Guan Yin, the Buddhist goddess of compassion, represented by the central statue in the main building. There's an excellent vegan canteen (p56) behind the complex staffed by volunteers and monks.

RUMAH PENGHULU ABU SEMAN HISTORIC BUILDING

Map p251 (2 Jln Stonor; suggested donation RM10; tours 11am & 3pm Mon-Sat; Raja Chulan) This glorious wooden stilt house, which was once the family home of a village headman in Kedah, was built in stages between 1910 and the 1930s and later moved to the grounds of Badan Warisan Malaysia (p48). Worthwhile tours of the property provide an explanation of the house's architecture and history and of Malay customs and traditional village life. You can wander around outside tour times (and since it's built with ventilation in mind, you can easily look in).

Check out the stunning hand-carved canoe under the house. The boat was used in religious ceremonies in Kelantan and has the head of a fantastic-looking bird carved into the prow.

MUZIUM KRAF MUSEUM

Map p251 (03-2162 7459; www.muzium-kraf.blogspot.co.uk; Jln Conlay; adult/child RM3/1; 9am-5pm; Raja Chulan) At the back of the Kompleks Kraf shop (p65) is this surprisingly good museum dedicated to Malaysia's traditional crafts. There are special exhibits and regular displays of batik, wood carving, pewter, kites and drums. Exhibits are nicely accompanied by informative posters.

BADAN WARISAN MALAYSIA HISTORIC BUILDING

Map p251 (Heritage of Malaysia Trust; 03-2144 9273; www.badanwarisan.org.my; 2 Jln Stonor;

WORTH A DETOUR

PUDU

Once a Chinese village on the edge of the city, Pudu is now firmly part of KL, hosting a lively fresh produce market, a street of wonderful hawker stalls and one of the city's best Chinese restaurants. Its most famous landmark, **Pudu Jail**, was demolished in 2010 and is now the site of the **Bukit Bintang City Centre** (BBCC) development, an ambitious complex featuring a shopping mall, a concert hall, a 1.2-hectare rooftop public park and an 80-floor signature tower, due to be completed by 2025. Only the original entrance gate to the jail remains.

Sights

Pudu Market (Pasar Besar Pudu; Jln Pasar Baharu; ⏲4am-2pm; Pudu), KL's biggest wet and dry market, is a frenetic place, full of squawking chickens, frantic shoppers and porters. Stalls here sell everything from goldfish to pigs' heads, cows' tongues and durians in baskets. Arrive early in the morning to experience the market at full throttle. From Pudu LRT station; go south along Jln Pudu, left on to Jln Pasar, then right down Jln Pasar Baharu, passing the colourful **Choon Wan Kong**, a Chinese temple dating from 1879.

Eating & Drinking

ICC Pudu (Map p253; Jln 1/77C; dishes RM5-10; ⏲6am-2pm; Pudu) The famous Imbi Market vendors now dish up tasty breakfasts at their new home, the ground floor of the Integrated Commercial Complex in Pudu. Several stalls – including Sisters Crispy Popiah – are located in the *kopitiam* **Ah Weng Koh Hainan Tea** (www.facebook.com/AhWengKohHainanTea/; Lot G85, dishes RM3-10; ⏲5.30am-2pm). Look for **Ah Fook Chee Cheong Fun** (lot G-31); there will probably be a queue for his delicious rice flour noodles.

Glutton Street (Pudu Wai Sek Kai; Jln Sayur; noodles RM5-10; ⏲most stalls 5pm-midnight; Pudu) This atmospheric alley of hawker stalls is best visited at night. Grazing could include addictive fried chicken, *chai tow kway* (radish cake stir-fried with soy sauce, bean sprouts and egg), prawn fritters and barbecued dried squid, all for bargain prices.

Sek Yuen (☎03-9222 0903; 315 Jln Pudu; mains RM30-45; ⏲noon-2.30pm & 5.30-9pm Tue-Sun; Pudu) Occupying the same beautiful, time-worn, art deco building for the past 60 years, Sek Yuen serves up meals that offer an experience of KL food history. There's no written menu but you can trust the aged chefs toiling in the wood-fired kitchen to make something delicious. Their *kau yoke* (pork belly), char siu (barbecued pork), village chicken and crispy-skin roast duck are all classics.

Fei Por (Map p252; ☎03-2143 4798; 211 Jln Pudu; mains RM7-14; ⏲6.30pm-4am Fri-Wed; Pudu) Famous for its chicken rice served into the early hours, this long-running operation in an art deco shophouse also serves congee (rice porridge) and char siu.

Wong Kee (Map p252; ☎03-2145 2512; 30 Lg Baba, Jln Nyonya; pork plates RM17; ⏲12.30-2.30pm Mon-Sat; Imbi) Get here early as there's only a two-hour window of opportunity to sample chef Wong Peng Hui's famous roasted pork. Chicken rice is also on the menu.

Shopping

Eu Yan Sang (Map p252; www.euyansang.com.my; Shaw Parade, Jln Changkat Thambi Dollah; ⏲9.30am-6.30pm; Imbi) Eu Kong opened his first Yang Sang (meaning 'caring for mankind') Chinese medicine shop in 1879 in Malaysia. There are now scores of outlets carrying the company's herbal remedies across the globe, including this impressive one.

Purple Cane Tea Square (Map p252; ☎03-2145 1200; www.purplecane.my; 1st fl, Shaw Parade, Jln Changkat Thambi Dollah; ⏲11am-9pm; Imbi) All things to do with tea are catered for at the main branch of this tea retailer.

KWC Fashion Mall (Map p252; www.kenangacity.com.my; 28 Jln Gelugor, off Jln Kenanga; ⏲10am-7pm Sun-Thu, to 8pm Fri & Sat; Hang Tuah) This complex in a strikingly modern high-rise block offers head-to-toe fashion items from some 800 wholesale dealers. The Kenanga Food Court on level 7 has some good outlets and an outdoor seating area with awesome views across the train tracks back to Bukit Bintang.

Architecture

From the Moorish Mogul–inspired civic buildings of the late 19th century to the millennial splendour of the Petronas Towers, KL's architecture is nothing if not eye-catching. Explore the city to also find traditional wooden Malay homes, various styles of shophouses in Chinatown and the bold modernist style of buildings such as Masjid Negara and the National Parliament.

1

2

ANDREW TB TAN/GETTY IMAGES ©

4

ALAN COPSON/GETTY IMAGES ©

1. Masjid Asy-Syakirin backed by the Petronas Towers (p46)
The 452m-high twin towers are the crowning glory of the KLCC area.

2. Malayan Railway Administration Building and Old KL Train Station (p99)
These public buildings are prime examples of Mogul (or Indo-Saracenic) architecture.

3. Sultan Abdul Samad Building (p70)
The Moorish domes and 43m clocktower of this building grace the east side of Merdeka Square.

4. Guandi Temple (p72)
This colourful Taoist temple dates back to 1886.

3

SIMONLONG/GETTY IMAGES ©

⌚10am-4pm Tue-Sat; Raja Chulan) FREE This heritage preservation society has its head office in a 1920s colonial bungalow. The building, once part of a neighbourhood of British officers' quarters, is one of the few remaining, though it's worth strolling Jln Conlay to see what's left. The trust holds exhibitions and has a small shop stocking wooden antique furniture, local handcrafted items and books.

TABUNG HAJI ARCHITECTURE
Map p250 (201 Jln Tun Razak; Ampang Park) Designed by celebrated Malay architect Hijjas Kasturi, this distinctive tower houses the *hajj* funding body. The five main exterior columns represent the five pillars of Islam, while the overall structure recalls the drum used to summon pilgrims to the *hajj* and the shape of a traditional Arabic perfume vessel.

EATING

Bukit Bintang

★TONG SHIN HOKKIEN MEE HAWKER $
Map p252 (Tengkat Tong Shin, near cnr Jln Tong Shin; mains RM7; ⌚7.30pm-midnight Wed-Mon; AirAsia-Bukit Bintang) This unassuming stall has been serving up its satisfyingly thick, slippery noodles for more than 20 years. The Hokkien mee here is prepared in the traditional style with pork lard, soy sauce, lardons and prawns, cooked over a charcoal flame to add a smoky flavour. It's a popular place, but once you tuck in you'll be glad you waited.

BLUE BOY VEGETARIAN FOOD CENTRE CHINESE $
Map p252 (☎011-6695 0498; Jln Tong Shin; mains RM5-10; ⌚8am-6pm; ; Imbi) Run by Chung Ching Thye and his son for the last 40 years, this remarkable hawker-style cafe at the base of a backstreet apartment block serves only vegetarian dishes. If you bypass a couple of stalls that use egg, it's also vegan. Try the *char kway teow* (noodles fried in chilli and black-bean sauce).

JALAN IMBI HAWKER STALLS HAWKER $
Map p252 (cnr Jln Imbi & Jln Barat; dishes RM6; ⌚5pm-midnight; AirAsia-Bukit Bintang) A car park by day turns into a great open-air hawker stall area by night. All the usual hawker favourites are here, as well as stalls selling fresh *amra* (a local, sweet, plum-like fruit) and star-fruit juice and coconut water. Try the dried chilli *lajoia pan mee* topped with mushrooms and anchovies.

RESTORAN WIN HENG SENG HAWKER $
Map p252 (183 Jln Imbi; dishes RM5-10; ⌚6.30am-midnight; AirAsia-Bukit Bintang) This street-side *kopitiam* is a popular spot for a local breakfast. Try the famous **Jln Imbi Pork Noodle** stall (open 6.30am to 3pm). Come evening time, the **Fatt Kee Hokkien Mee** stall (open from 5pm to midnight) is considered one of KL's top purveyors of the filling, fried noodle dish.

LOT 10 HUTONG HAWKER $
Map p252 (basement, lot 10, 50 Jln Sultan Ismail; dishes RM9-18; ⌚10am-10pm; AirAsia-Bukit Bintang) Lot 10 Hutong was the first mall to encourage top hawkers to open branches in a basement food court. In its well-designed space it has pulled in names such as Soong Kee, which has served beef noodles since 1945. Look also for Kong Tai's oyster omelettes, Hon Kee's Cantonese porridge, Kim Lian Kee's Hokkien *mee* and Penang Famous Fried Koay Teow.

FOOD REPUBLIC FOOD HALL $
Map p252 (☎03-2142 8006; www.foodrepublic.com.my; level 1, Pavilion KL, 168 Jln Bukit Bintang; mains RM5-17; ⌚10am-10pm; AirAsia-Bukit Bintang) An excellent choice of meals and snacks and slick design make this one of the best shopping mall food courts in KL. It's also surrounded by scores of proper restaurants.

ROCOCO CAFE $$
Map p252 (☎012-974 0192; www.facebook.com/RococoCafeMY; 7th fl, Melange Boutique Hotel, 14 Jln Rembia; mains RM14-30; ⌚11am-10.30pm Wed-Mon; AirAsia-Bukit Bintang) This atmospheric cafe with views across the rooftops of Jln Alor and Tengkat Tong Shin has a tempting central display of freshly baked bread and homemade pastries, cookies and cakes. Also serves brunch from 11am to 3pm and an all-day menu of salads, sandwiches, pasta and rice dishes. Opens for dinner from 6pm to 10.30pm by reservation only.

LIMA BLAS PERANAKAN $$
Map p252 (☎03-2110 1681; www.facebook.com/limablas25; 25 Jln Mesui; mains RM19-33; ⌚kitchen

WORTH A DETOUR

AMPANG

Ampang means 'dam' a reference to the dams created during KL's heyday as a boom town for tin mining. Jln Ampang is one on KL's most historic streets, once leading from the mansions of the tin tycoons to the mines themselves - this is why the area to the northwest of the city is called Ampang. Only a handful of the old mansions remain including the one used for the Malaysia Tourism Centre.

Further west of the KLCC along and around Jln Ampang are a few places worth searching out and best accessed by taxi.

Sights & Activities

Ruang Pemula (RuPé; 03-4279 7720; www.rupe.com.my; Block 1, Pusat Perdagangan Taman Dagang, Jln Dagang Besar, Ampang; by appointment) Pakhruddin Sulaiman and his wife, Fatimah, have been amassing one of Malaysia's top private art collections since around 1996, when they bought two major works, *Brothers* and *Does History Change?*, in the first solo exhibition of Bayu Utmo Radjikin. These works by the now-prominent contemporary Malaysian artist are among hundreds displayed and stored in the must-see private gallery nicknamed RuPé and meaning 'beginner's space'. Call to arrange a time to visit and get directions from Ampang LRT station.

Other established and up-and-coming artists with works here include many from the art collective Matahati, Fuad Osman, Shukri Mohammed, Amron Omar and Fadilah Karim. Figurative forged-metal sculptures by Raja Shahrima, a cross between ancient Malay warriors and manga robots, are dotted among the gallery spaces, which are arranged to resemble living rooms, with designer chairs and Pakhruddin's extensive art and design library.

My Batik Visitor Centre (03-4251 5154, 016-220 3190; www.mybatik.org.my; 333 Persiaran Ritchie, off Jln Ritchie; 8am-5pm; Ampang Park) Founded by artist Emilia Tan and set in a pretty compound with frangipani trees, My Batik sells colourful batik-print fashions and offers demonstration sessions and DIY batik-painting classes for adults and children (weekends are popular with families). The outdoor **Green Tomato Cafe** (www.facebook.com/greentomatocafe.com.my; mains RM15-20; 8am-5pm;) serves all-day Western breakfasts. Call to arrange workshop bookings.

Eating

Zaini Satay (013-369 3934; www.zainisatay.com; Naan Corner, Jln Kerja Ayer Lama; satay sticks RM1-1.50; 6-11.30pm; Ampang LRT) Mohamed Zaini comes from a long line of satay-stall owners – his grandfather was known as the 'King of Satay' in the 1960s – and these days KLites regularly make the trip to Ampang to satisfy their craving for the best satay in town. The stall (find it opposite a 7-Eleven) closes once the meat sells out.

Tamarind Springs (03-4256 9300; www.tamarindrestaurants.com; Jln 1, Taman TAR, Selangor; mains RM42-110; noon-3pm & 6pm-midnight) With an open-sided, Balinese-style wooden dining room, backed by jungle and overlooking a golf course, Tamarind Springs makes for a romantic setting. The extensive cocktail list and Indochinese dishes served here more than live up to the lush surroundings. Make reservations.

Mei Keng Fatt Seafood Restaurant (03-4256 6491; www.meikengfatt.com; 1 Lg Awan 6, Kuala Ampang; fresh seafood per person approx RM60-100; 11.30am-2.30pm & 4pm-midnight) This long-running seafood restaurant, famous for its chilli crab, is great for group dining, but check the prices before ordering.

Shopping

Great Eastern Mall (www.greateasternmall.com.my; 303 Jln Ampang; 10am-10pm; Ampang Park) This upscale mall houses the flagship branch of British India (www.britishindia.com.my), Malaysian fashion and accessories store **Pedlars** and local shoemaker **Thomas Chan**, as well as **Alexis Ampang** (03-4260 2288; www.alexis.com.my; ground fl), a bistro by day and at weekends one of the city's top venues for live jazz music.

11am-3pm & 6-10.30pm Mon-Sat, bar to midnight Mon-Thu, to 1am Fri & Sat; ; Raja Chulan) With a hip, bric-a-brac design that channels old Malaysia to a T, this restaurant and open-air bar is a top spot for a casual night out of exotic food and postdinner drinks. Try the Nonya fried chicken, aubergine in sambal sauce and the *sago gula melaka* (sago pearls in a brown-sugar sauce).

BEN'S — INTERNATIONAL $$

Map p252 (03-2141 5290; www.thebiggroup.co/bens; level 6, Pavilion KL, 168 Jln Bukit Bintang; mains RM25-78; 11am-11pm; ; AirAsia-Bukit Bintang) The flagship brand of the BIG group of dining outlets delivers on both style and substance. There's a tempting range of Eastern and Western comfort foods, appealing living-room design and nice touches such as a box of cards with recipes and talk topics on each table. Other branches are in Suria KLCC (p65), Publika (p110) and Bangsar Shopping Centre (p111).

PINCHOS TAPAS BAR — TAPAS $$

Map p252 (03-2145 8482; www.pinchos.com.my; 18 Changat Bukit Bintang; tapas RM18-66; food 5-11pm, bar to 3am, Tue-Sun; Raja Chulan) This is the real deal for tapas, run by a Spaniard and packed with KL's approving Spanish-speaking community. A great place for a solo meal and drink or fun with a group while you munch your way through the wide-ranging menu.

LEVAIN — CAFE $$

Map p252 (03-2142 6611; www.levain.com.my; 7 Jln Delima; pastries from RM5, mains RM17-24; 7.30am-10.30pm; AirAsia-Bukit Bintang) You can see the fresh bread being taken out of the oven at this appealing bakery, cake shop and cafe in a quiet part of the city centre. The outdoor patio is a pleasant spot for a lunch of homemade pizza or a pastry with a local inflection, like a curry chicken doughnut or seaweed, ham and chicken-floss roll.

SANTOUKA — JAPANESE $$

Map p252 (03-2143 8878; www.santouka.co.jp/en; level 6, Pavilion KL, 168 Jln Bukit Bintang; ramen sets RM30-40; 11am-10pm; AirAsia-Bukit Bintang) Slurp tasty ramen noodles in a rich pork broth at this joint in Pavilion's Tokyo Street, an outlet of a famous stall originating from the Japanese island of Hokkaido.

SAO NAM — VIETNAMESE $$

Map p252 (03-2144 1225; www.saonam.com.my; 25 Tengkat Tong Shin; mains RM30-70; noon-2.30pm & 7.30-10.30pm Tue-Sun; AirAsia-Bukit Bintang) This reliable place is decorated with colourful communist propaganda posters and has a courtyard for dining outside. The kitchen turns out huge plates of delicious Vietnamese food, garnished with basil, mint, lettuce and sweet dips. The starter *banh xeo* (a huge Vietnamese pancake with meat, seafood or vegetables) is a meal in itself.

AL-AMAR LEBANESE CUISINE — LEBANESE $$

Map p252 (03-2166 1011; www.al-amar.com; level 6, Pavilion KL, 168 Jln Bukit Bintang; mains RM25-63; noon-12.30am; AirAsia-Bukit Bintang) There's no shortage of restaurants in Bukit Bintang serving Middle Eastern food but few are as consistently good as Al-Amar. Choose from a tasty range of meze and grilled meats or go simple with a shawarma sandwich. If you've got a big appetite, feast on the Sunday lunch buffet (RM80).

RESTAURANT MUAR — MALAYSIAN $$

Map p252 (03-2144 2072; 6g Tengkat Tong Shin; mains RM10-20; 11am-3pm & 6-10pm Tue-Sun; AirAsia-Bukit Bintang) Ever-reliable home cooking at an unpretentious place with some outdoor tables. Try the *petai* squid and prawns, crispy fried eggs and *cendol* (shaved ice, coconut milk and jelly noodle dessert).

NEROTECA — ITALIAN $$

Map p252 (03-2070 0530; www.neroteca.com; ground fl, Seri Bukit Ceylon, 8 Lg Ceylon; mains RM22-119; 11.30am-11.30pm; Raja Chulan) This stylish Italian joint will satisfy your cravings for authentic pizza and pasta.

TWENTY ONE KITCHEN & BAR — INTERNATIONAL $$

Map p252 (03-2142 0021; www.drbar.asia; 20-1 Changkat Bukit Bintang; mains RM18-46; noon-3am; ; Raja Chulan) Plenty of choice on the menu here, including snacks like pandan chicken skewers and reasonably priced mains (think burgers, risotto and pasta as well as a number of local dishes). The bar upstairs, with a deck overlooking the street, gets cranking at weekends when a DJ spins chill and dance tunes.

LOCAL KNOWLEDGE

JALAN ALOR

The collection of roadside restaurants and stalls lining **Jln Alor** (Map p252; 24hrs; AirAsia-Bukit Bintang) is the great common denominator of KL's food scene, hauling in everyone from sequinned society babes to penny-strapped backpackers. From around 5pm till late every evening, the street transforms into a continuous open-air dining space with hundreds of plastic tables and chairs and rival caterers shouting out to passers-by to drum up business (avoid the pushiest ones!). Most places serve alcohol and you can sample pretty much every Malay Chinese dish imaginable, from grilled fish and satay to *kai-lan* (Chinese greens) in oyster sauce and fried noodles with frogs' legs. Thai food is also popular.

Recommended options:

Kedai Makanan Dan Minuman TKS (Map p252; 32 Jln Alor; small mains RM15-35; 6pm-4am; AirAsia-Bukit Bintang) for mouth-tingling Sichuan dishes.

Restoran Beh Brothers (Map p252; 21a Jln Alor; dishes RM5-10; 24hr; AirAsia-Bukit Bintang), one of the few places open from 7am for breakfast, where **Sisters Noodle** (Map p252; 21a Jln Alor; noodles RM6; 7am-4pm; AirAsia-Bukit Bintang) serve delicious 'drunken' chicken *mee* (noodles) with rice wine, and there's also a good Hong Kong–style dim sum stall.

Wong Ah Wah (WAW; Map p252; 1-9 Jln Alor; chicken wings per piece RM3.20; 5pm-4am; AirAsia-Bukit Bintang) is unbeatable for addictive spicy chicken wings, as well as grilled seafood, tofu and satay.

SAHARA TENT — MIDDLE EASTERN $$

Map p252 (03-2144 8310; 41 Jln Sultan Ismail; mains RM27-52; 11am-3pm; AirAsia-Bukit Bintang) A long-established Middle Eastern restaurant serving meaty kebabs, couscous and Turkish coffee.

★SUSHI HINATA — JAPANESE $$$

Map p251 (03-2022 1349; www.shin-hinata.com; St Mary Residence, 1 Jln Tengah; lunch/dinner set meals from RM77/154; noon-3pm & 6-11pm Mon-Sat; Raja Chulan) It's quite acceptable to use your fingers to savour the sublime sushi served at the counter, one piece at a time, by expert Japanese chefs from Nagoya. There are also private booths for more intimate dinners. The kaiseki-style full course meals are edible works of art.

★BIJAN — MALAYSIAN $$$

Map p252 (03-2031 3575; www.bijanrestaurant.com; 3 Jln Ceylon; mains RM30-90; 4.30-11pm; Raja Chulan) One of KL's best Malaysian restaurants, Bijan offers skilfully cooked traditional dishes in a sophisticated dining room that spills out into a tropical garden. Must-try dishes include *rendang daging* (dry beef curry with lemongrass), *masak lemak ikan* (Penang-style fish curry with turmeric) and *ikan panggang* (grilled skate with tamarind).

FRENCH FEAST — FRENCH $$$

Map p252 (03-2110 6283; www.frenchfeast.com.my; 20 Tengkat Tong Shin; mains RM52-159; 6.30-10.30pm Tue-Fri, 10am-10.30pm Sat, 10am-2pm Sun; AirAsia-Bukit Bintang) Occupying a beautifully restored old family home, French Feast is the new venture from the team behind former KL eatery La Vie En Rose. Classic French-bistro style dishes here include cassoulet, house-smoked sausages with puy lentils and imported cheeses and wines, as well as an indulgent weekend brunch menu accompanied by freshly baked pastries and breads.

NEROVIVO — ITALIAN $$$

Map p252 (03-2070 3120; www.nerovivo.com; 3a Jln Ceylon; mains RM74-165, pizzas RM28-68; noon-3pm Sun-Fri, 6-11.30pm daily; Raja Chulan) This long-standing Italian joint serves a range of solid appetisers, pastas, risottos and of course pizzas in a chic, partly open-air dining room

ENAK — MALAYSIAN $$$

Map p253 (03-2141 8973; www.enakkl.com; feast fl, Starhill Gallery, 181 Jln Bukit Bintang; mains RM26-95; noon-11pm; AirAsia-Bukit Bintang) Hidden at the back of Starhill's Feast floor, Enak is worth searching out for its finely presented Malay cuisine with a sophisticated twist.

FUKUYA JAPANESE $$$

Map p253 (03-2144 1022; www.fukuya.com.my; 9 Jln Delima; set lunches/dinners from RM40/92; noon-2.30pm & 6.30-10.30pm Mon-Sat, 6-10pm Sun; AirAsia-Bukit Bintang) The quality of Chef Takao Ando's beautifully presented sushi, sashimi and tempura dishes more than lives up to this restaurant's elegant setting in a Zen-style bungalow surrounded by bamboo.

PREGO ITALIAN $$$

Map p253 (03-2773 8338; www.westindining.com.my; Westin Kuala Lumpur, 199 Jln Bukit Bintang; mains RM50-90, 4-course set menus RM190; noon-2.30pm & 6.30-10.30pm; AirAsia-Bukit Bintang) Quality Italian pasta and pizzas in family-friendly surroundings.

MARCO POLO CHINESE $$$

Map p251 (03-2141 2233; http://marcopolo.com.my; 1st fl, Wisma Lim Foo Yong, 86 Jln Raja Chulan; mains RM30-118; 11am-2.30pm & 6-10.30pm Mon-Sat, 9.30am-10.30pm Sun; Raja Chulan) At lunch, pick from the steamed baskets of dim sum being wheeled in carts at this classy, old-fashioned Chinese joint. It also offers a dim sum buffet on Sunday. The extensive menu includes traditional Chinese dishes as well as more inventive items such as venison with dragon fruit.

EL CERDO EUROPEAN $$$

Map p253 (03-2145 0511; http://elcerdokl.com/; 43-45 Changkat Bukit Bintang; mains RM38-108; noon-2.30pm & 6-10.30pm Sun-Thu, to 11pm Fri & Sat; AirAsia-Bukit Bintang) If you're craving pork, this 'nose-to-tail eating' joint specialising in ham, sausages and all things piggy is the place to go. The Sunday beer brunch special includes all-you-can-eat pork dishes and free-flowing cava, wine or beer for RM168.

KLCC & Around

DHARMA REALM GUAN YIN SAGELY MONASTERY CANTEEN CHINESE $

Map p250 (161 Jln Ampang; mains RM6-10; 11am-2.30pm Mon-Fri; Ampang Park) Join office workers for a tasty vegetarian lunch of various fried rice and noodle dishes, dumplings and delicious *yong tao-fu* (vegetables stuffed with a tofu paste) in this airy canteen behind the monastery. The food contains no onions or garlic and there are drinks and fruit, too. For the best selection of dishes try to get here before noon.

WONDERMAMA MALAYSIAN $$

Map p250 (www.wondermama.my; ground flr, Ave K, 156 Jln Ampang; mains RM13-27; 10am-9.30pm; KLCC) A good choice for a modern take on classic Malaysian dishes such as *nasi lemak* and Nonya laksa in a fun, contemporary setting.

MELUR & THYME FUSION $$

Map p250 (03-2181 8001; www.melurandthyme.com; ground fl, Suria KLCC, Jln Ampang; mains RM14-59; 8am-9.30pm; KLCC) This appealingly designed restaurant's name, conjoining Malay and Western ingredients, hints at its game plan: offering Malay and Western tapas-sized portions to be mixed and shared. For breakfast (8am to 11am) the coconut pancakes with caramelised honeydew melon is a very tasty precursor to a day's shopping in Suria KLCC. There is also a branch at Nu Sentral (p107).

LITTLE PENANG KAFÉ MALAYSIAN $$

Map p250 (03-2163 0215; level 4, Suria KLCC, Jln Ampang; mains RM14-22; 11.30am-9.30pm; KLCC) At peak meal times expect a long line outside this mall joint serving authentic food from Penang, including specialities such as curry mee (spicy soup noodles with prawns).

NASI KANDAR PELITA FOOD HALL $$

Map p250 (03-2162 5532; www.pelita.com.my; 149 Jln Ampang; mains RM10-25; 24hr; KLCC) There's round-the-clock eating at the Jln Ampang branch of this chain of excellent *mamak* (Muslim Indian-Malay) food courts. Among the scores of dishes available from the various stalls are magnificent *roti canai* (flat, flaky bread) and spiced chicken cooked in the tandoor.

MAMA SAN INDONESIAN $$

Map p250 (019-787 5810; www.mamasankualalumpur.com; lot 46, ground fl, Suria KLCC, Jln Ampang; mains RM42-75; 8.30am-10.30pm; KLCC) A KL offshoot of the original Bali Mama San, this stylish joint at Suria KLCC (p65) occupies a prime position overlooking the park's fountains. The menu is peppered with appealing Asian ingredients such as ginger flowers, lime leaves, tamarind and chilli. The dishes are a bit hit and miss, though, so choose carefully and don't over-order as portions are large.

ACME BAR & COFFEE INTERNATIONAL **$$$**

Map p250 (☎03-2162 2288; www.acmebarcoffee.com; unit G1, The Troika, 19 Persiaran KLCC; mains RM44-99; ⏲11am-midnight Mon-Thu, to 1am Fri, 9.30am-1am Sat, to midnight Sun; Ⓜ Ampang Park) Blink and you might be in a chic bistro in New York, Paris or Melbourne. The menu changes seasonally so there's always something new to try, from tasty nibbles such as battered salted egg yolk–battered chicken strips to bigger dishes like chargrilled cod steak with ABC *kicap* (a type of soy sauce), chickpea ratatouille and papaya-pineapple salsa.

CILANTRO FRENCH, JAPANESE **$$$**

Map p250 (☎03-2179 8082; www.cilantrokl.com; MiCasa All Suite Hotel, 68b Jln Tun Razak; mains RM188-218, set lunches/dinners from RM150/298; ⏲noon-2pm Fri, 6-10.30pm Mon-Sat; 📶; Ⓜ Ampang Park) Takashi Kimura is often lauded as one of KL's most accomplished chefs. The eclectic range of Japanese-French-cuisine inspired dishes might include the likes of *unagi* (eel) paired with foie gras and mesclun, Japanese sole with noisette butter, with a vintage rum baba for dessert.

DRINKING & NIGHTLIFE

Bukit Bintang

★HELI LOUNGE BAR COCKTAIL BAR

Map p251 (☎03-2110 5034; www.facebook.com/Heliloungebar; level 34, Menara KH, Jln Sultan Ishmail; ⏲5pm-midnight Mon-Wed, to 2am Thu, to 3am Fri & Sat, to 11am Sun; 📶; Raja Chulan) If the weather's behaving, this is easily the best place for sundowners in KL. Nothing besides your lychee martini and the cocktail waiter stands between you, the edge of the helipad and amazing 360-degree views. Steady your hands as you have to buy your first drink at the somewhat cheesy bar below and carry it up yourself.

Go early to catch the sunset shortly after 7pm and for the 6pm to 9pm happy hour prices. After 9pm a dress code applies and your group will need to stump up for a bottle in order to enter.

> **LOCAL KNOWLEDGE**
>
> **TROIKA SKY DINING**
>
> Sophisticated dining with outstanding views of KLCC's glittering high rises are the highlights of the Troika complex of restaurants and bars. Try **Cantaloupe** (Level 23a, tower B; set lunches RM120, 4-/6-/8-course dinners RM250/360/450; ⏲noon-2pm Mon-Fri, 6.30-10.30pm daily) for modern French, and **Strato** (Level 23a, tower B; mains RM45-120; ⏲noon-3pm & 6-11pm) for Italian that aims for homely authenticity. Troika's bars include Latin-themed **Fuego** (Level 23a, Tower B; ⏲6pm-midnight), wine bar **Claret** and cocktail bar **Coppersmith**. (☎03-2162 0886, www.troikaskydining.com; The Troika, Persiaran KLCC; Ⓜ Ampang Park)

★PISCO BAR BAR

Map p253 (☎03-2142 2900; www.piscobarkl.com; 29 Jln Mesui; ⏲5pm-1am Tue, Thu & Sun, to 2am Wed, to 3am Fri & Sat; Raja Chulan) Take your pisco sour in the cosy, exposed-brick interior or the plant-filled courtyard of this slick tapas joint. The chef is half Peruvian, so naturally the ceviche here is good. DJs regularly spin the decks at the upstairs dance space on Friday and Saturday nights.

ZION CLUB CLUB

Map p253 (www.facebook.com/theZionKL; 31 Changkat Bukit Bintang; cover charge RM50; ⏲5pm-3am Sun-Tue, to 5am Wed-Sat; AirAsia-Bukit Bintang) This slick new club smack in the middle of the Changkat Bukit Bintang strip has three separate spaces where DJs pump out dance and house, hip-hop and reggae until 5am. There's a happy hour in the reggae bar from 5pm until the club opens at 10pm, after which drink prices skyrocket and a RM50 cover charge applies.

RABBIT HOLE BAR

Map p253 (☎010-899 3535; www.rabbithole.com.my; lot 14 & 16, Changkat Bukit Bintang; ⏲4pm-2am Sun-Thu, to 3am Fri & Sat; Raja Chulan) Not much evidence of Alice or a Wonderland here but it is one of the more convivial bars at the head of KL's rowdiest nightlife strip. There's plenty of seating and

LOCAL KNOWLEDGE

TREC

The city's newest entertainment complex, **TREC** (www.trec.com.my), is located a short taxi ride east of Bukit Bintang on Jln Tun Razak.

TREC's prime attraction is **Zouk** (Map p253; www.zoukclub.com.my; TREC, 436 Jln Tun Razak; RM60; ⏲10pm-3am Sun-Tue, to 4am Thu, to 5am Fri & Sat; AirAsia-Bukit Bintang): if you're going to visit one club in KL, make it this one. The seven interlinked DJ spaces include the Main Room, which reverberates to trance, electro, techno and trance, Velvet Underground for commercial house music and Ace, a hip-hop and R & B club.

Next to Zouk is Electic Blvd, a strip of food and beverage outlets. Along here you'll find the excellent new live music and comedy venue **Live House** (Map p253; ☎012-372 2374; www.facebook.com/livehousekl; TREC, 436 Jln Tun Razak; RM30; ⏲noon-3pm & 6pm-3am Mon-Wed, to 5am Thu & Fri, 6pm-5am Sat, to 3am Sun; AirAsia-Bukit Bintang) hosting regular stand-up gigs by international comedians as well as bands and DJs. It also serves tasty Southern-style soul food (fried chicken, burgers and wraps) by the popular burger makers KGB.

Supperclub (Map p253; ☎03-2110 0866; www.supperclubkl.com; TREC, Jln Tun Razak; ⏲5pm-3am; AirAsia-Bukit Bintang) is so-called for its nightly transformation from gastro-bar to club. It's a polished place, pumping out house music from the early evening and set-up for DJs and dancing later at night. Also check out **COMO** (Map p253; ☎014-711 2185; www.facebook.com/comokl/; TREC, 436 Jln Tun Razak; ⏲5pm-2am Sun-Thu, to 3am Fri & Sat; AirAsia-Bukit Bintang) a tunnel-like bar with curved, exposed brick walls and bright graffiti-style murals is a great spot for some Spanish tapas, expertly mixed cocktails and live music.

a variety of differently themed areas as well as a long bar and pool tables.

FEEKA COFFEE ROASTERS — CAFE

Map p253 (www.facebook.com/feeka.coffeeroasters; 19 Jln Mesui; ⏲9am-10.30pm Mon-Thu, to 11.30pm Fri-Sun; 📶; Raja Chulan) Set in a minimally remodelled shophouse on hip Jln Mesui, Feeka delivers both on its premium coffee (choose from microlot beans or espresso-based drinks) and its food (breakfast items served from 10am to 6pm and a menu including omelettes and pulled-pork sandwiches served from noon to 10pm, as well as delicious cakes).

There's a lovely tree-shaded patio area and a gallery space upstairs, making this a place to linger.

TWG TEA — TEAHOUSE

Map p253 (www.twgtea.com; level 2, Pavilion KL, 168 Jln Bukit Bintang; ⏲10am-10pm; AirAsia-Bukit Bintang) Offering a mind-boggling range of more than 400 teas and infusions, this KL offshoot of the original Singaporean TWG is a luxurious place to refresh during your rounds of the mall. The teas are beautifully packaged for gifts, too. As well as afternoon tea (2pm to 6pm), it also serves brunch from 10am to 3pm and meals from noon to 10pm.

Don't miss TWG's delectable tea-infused macarons, with flavours such as Moroccan mint tea and matcha, black tea and blackcurrant and Earl Grey and chocolate.

NAGABA — BAR

Map p253 (☎03-2141 0858; www.facebook.com/nagaba.kualalumpur; 31 Jln Mesui; ⏲4pm-1am Mon & Tue, to 2am Wed & Thu, to 3am Fri & Sat; Raja Chulan) This three-level bar and club has a ground-floor industrial-style bar with comfy chairs, and a club on the next floor up. The Rooftop Mojito Bar, with fairy lights, big shared tables and benches, and a DJ deck, has a relaxed, urban vibe. Come from 8pm to 10pm for the all-you-can-drink mojito buffet, with free-flowing cocktails for RM60 per person.

TAPS BEER BAR — MICROBREWERY

Map p252 (www.tapsbeerbar.my; One Residency, 1 Jln Nagasari; ⏲5pm-1am Mon-Sat, noon-1am Sun; 📶; Raja Chulan) Taps specialises in ale from around the world with some 80 different microbrews on rotation, 14 of them on tap. There's live music Thursday to Saturday at 9.30pm and regular beer festivals and events. Taps also serves pub grub (mains RM15 to RM50) and a Sunday roast (RM35 to RM38).

NEWENS TEAHOUSE

Map p252 (☎03-2719 8550; www.newenstea-house.com; Indulge fl, Starhill Gallery, 181 Jln Bukit Bintang; ⏰10am-11pm Sun-Thu, to midnight Fri & Sat; AirAsia-Bukit Bintang) Serving the Maids of Honour egg tarts made famous by the UK-based tea shop of the same name, Newens offers a genteel place to indulge in afternoon tea (RM60, 2.30pm to 5.30pm) that's a world away from the bustle of Bukit Bintang's malls.

NEO TAMARIND BAR

Map p250 (☎03-2148 3700; www.tamarindres-taurants.com; 19 Jln Sultan Ismail; ⏰6-11pm; Raja Chulan) This sophisticated restaurant-bar feels like a slice of Bali smuggled into the heart of KL. Sip cocktails by flickering lights and a waterfall running the length of the long bar. The Thai and Indochinese food is also lovely, should you want to start with dinner.

LUK YU TEA HOUSE TEAHOUSE

Map p253 (☎03-2782 3850; www.starhillgal-lery.com; Feast fl, Starhill Gallery, 181 Jln Bukit Bintang; ⏰11am-10pm; AirAsia-Bukit Bintang) On the Feast Floor of Starhill Gallery (p64) but away from the heady Feast Village area, the secluded Luk Yu offers fine Chinese and Taiwanese teas along with dim sum and other dainty snacks.

VILLAGE BAR BAR

Map p253 (☎03-2782 3852; Feast fl, Starhill Gallery, 181 Jln Bukit Bintang; ⏰11am-11pm; AirAsia-Bukit Bintang) The village in question is the Feast Village (a collection of bars and restaurants) in the basement of the Starhill Gallery mall (p64). Columns of glasses and bottles and cascades of dangling lanterns lend an *Alice in Wonderland* quality to this establishment, which is best visited for a pre- or postmeal evening drink. There's a happy hour from 5pm to 8pm.

WHISKY BAR KUALA LUMPUR BAR

Map p253 (☎03-2143 2268; www.thewhiskybarkl.com; 46 Changkat Bukit Bintang; ⏰3pm-1am Sun-Thu, 4pm-3am Fri & Sat; Raja Chulan) This specialist bar stocks more than 500 different whiskies, including single malts, blends and bourbons. Also offers a good selection of cigars.

SNOWFLAKE CAFE

Map p253 (http://snowflake.com.my; 4th fl, Pavilion KL; ⏰10am-10pm; AirAsia-Bukit Bintang) We're prepared to believe the cute marketing blurb saying that Jimmy learned how to make these refreshing jelly-based drinks and desserts from his Taiwanese gran – they make you realise how much more there is to soft drinks in Asia than canned soda.

WINGS BAR

Map p253 (www.wingsmusicafe.com; 16 Lg 1/77a; ⏰6pm-1.30am; 📶; Imbi) This youthful hang-out has regular live music, though most drinkers prefer to chill out on the front terrace.

J CO DONUTS & COFFEE CAFE

Map p253 (www.jcodonuts.com; basement, Pavilion KL, 168 Jln Bukit Bintang; ⏰10am-10pm; AirAsia-Bukit Bintang) The wacky creations may have cheesy names (Tira Miss U or Copa Banana anyone?) but they look so damn tasty that it's difficult to pass by this fried dough and coffee operation.

BLUEBOY DISCOTHEQUE GAY & LESBIAN

Map p252 (☎03-2142 1067; https://www.facebook.com/blueboydiscotheque/home; 50 Jln Sultan Ismail; ⏰9pm-2am; AirAsia-Bukit Bintang) This two-decades-old bar is the dinosaur of the KL gay scene, with cabaret shows from Wednesday to Sunday. Friday and Saturday nights are most popular – expect a crowd of older expats, locals and drag divas.

CEYLON BAR BAR

Map p253 (http://ceylonbar.com; 20-2 Changkat Bukit Bintang; ⏰4pm-2am Sun-Thu, to 3am Fri, 2pm-3am Sat; Raja Chulan) Big, comfy

KUALA LUMPUR PUB CRAWL

Kuala Lumpur Pub Crawl (☎017-394 1191; www.facebook.com/KualaLumpurpubcrawl; RM70; ⏰8.45pm-1am Thu & Sat; Raja Chulan) KL's only pub crawl includes five drinks and discounts on others. Meet at **Nagaba** on the corner of Jln Nagasari and Jln Mesui in the Changkat Bukit Bintang area.

Markets

Although Western-style supermarkets have become the norm, Kuala Lumpur still sustains several traditional wet and dry food markets as found across Southeast Asia. Arrive around dawn to experience them at full throttle. *Pasar malam* (night markets) are also very popular and fun to explore for their street-food offerings.

1

TOM BONAVENTURE/GETTY IMAGES ©

GWOEII/SHUTTERSTOCK ©

1. Masjid India Pasar Malam (p88)
Sample Malay, Indian and Chinese snacks at this Saturday-night market.

2. Petaling Street Market (p81)
Bargain hunt or browse through this popular market.

3. Hawker stalls (p25)
Don't miss trying some of KL's tasiest and best-value food.

4. Durian stall, Bazaar Baru Chow Kit (p85)
Browse stalls loaded with fresh produce.

5. Clothing stall, Jln Masjid India (p86)
Shop among locals on this busy street, packed with sari stalls and gold jewellers.

JEMBANTOLA/GETTY IMAGES ©

lounges and board games set the tone at one of the friendliest drinking holes in KL. It's noticeably more relaxed than others along this frantic strip. Come early to bag one of the terrace tables or one of the sofas inside. Tuesday is quiz night and there's live music on Thursday and Friday.

KLCC & Around

★MARINI'S ON 57 BAR

Map p250 (03-2386 6030; www.marinis57.com; level 57, Menara 3, Petronas KLCC; 5pm-1.30am Sun-Thu, to 3am Fri & Sat; KLCC) This is about as close as you can get to eyeballing the upper levels of the Petronas Towers from a bar. The stellar views are complemented by sleek interior design and attentive service. When booking (advised) be aware that it's the lively bar not the laid-back whisky lounge that has the view of the towers. There's also a dress code.

DIVINEBLISS GAY & LESBIAN

Map p250 (G Tower Rooftop; www.facebook.com/Divine.KL; rooftop, G Tower, 199 Jln Tun Razak; RM45; 10pm-3am Sat; Ampang Park) On Saturday nights the swanky rooftop bar at the G Tower hotel hosts the popular gay night DivineBliss. International DJs and quality sound and light systems attract a young crowd, who pack the dance floor until the early hours. Bring photo ID for entry.

RGB AT THE BEAN HIVE CAFE

(03-2181 1329; www.rathergoodbeans.com; 35 Jln Damai; 9am-4pm Mon, 8.30am-4pm Tue-Fri, 9am-6.30pm Sat & Sun; ; Ampang Park) This is what you get when a boutique coffee roaster teams with health-conscious cooks in a quiet green oasis. RBG serves excellent hand-drip coffees and espresso-based drinks as well as vegan and vegetarian breakfasts, sandwiches and pastas, all in a cute bungalow with an inner courtyard and big grassy yard.

TATE COCKTAIL BAR

Map p250 (03-2161 2368; www.thebiggroup.co/tate; ground fl, Intermark, 182 Jln Tun Razak; 5pm-2am Mon-Sat; ; Ampang Park) It's bordering on self-mockery to have a 'secret' speakeasy cocktail bar in a shopping mall, but once you get past that, Tate's sophisticated atmosphere, complete with cushy leather armchairs and a great cocktail menu, is perfect for a relaxing late-night drink.

MARKETPLACE GAY & LESBIAN

Map p250 (03-2166 0750; www.facebook.com/love.mpkl; 4a Lg Yap Kwan Seng; RM40; 10pm-3am Fri & Sat; KLCC) As Saturday night turns into Sunday morning DJs take to the decks for Lovemachine at Marketplace and KL's gay community dances and drinks like there's no tomorrow. Friday nights are also gay friendly. The rooftop has a superb view of the Petronas Towers.

SKY BAR BAR

Map p250 (03-2332 9888; www.skybar.com.my; level 33, Traders Hotel, KLCC, off Jln Kia Peng; 10.30am-1am Sun-Thu, to 3am Fri & Sat; KLCC) Head to the rooftop pool area of this hotel for a grand circle view across to the Petronas Towers – it's a great spot for sundowner cocktails or late-night flutes of bubbly. There's a happy hour from 6pm to 9pm.

APARTMENT DOWNTOWN BAR

Map p250 (www.atheapartment.com; ground fl, Suria KLCC, Jln Ampang; 11.45am-11.45pm; ; KLCC) With outdoor seating facing the fountains of KLCC Park, the Apartment, styled to resemble an upmarket condo, is a pleasant spot to revive after a hard day's shopping.

☆ ENTERTAINMENT

★NO BLACK TIE LIVE MUSIC

Map p253 (03-2142 3737; www.noblacktie.com.my; 17 Jln Mesui; live music RM30-70; 5pm-1am Mon-Sat; Raja Chulan) Blink and you'd miss this small live-music venue, bar and bistro as it's hidden behind a grove of bamboo. NBT, as it's known to its faithful patrons, is owned by Malaysian concert pianist Evelyn Hii, who has a knack for finding the talented singer-songwriters, jazz bands and classical-music ensembles who play here from around 9pm.

DEWAN FILHARMONIK PETRONAS CONCERT VENUE

Map p250 (03-2051 7007; www.dfp.com.my; box office, Tower 2, Petronas Towers, KLCC; box office 10.30am-6.30pm Tue-Sat; KLCC) Don't miss the chance to attend a show at this gorgeous concert hall at the base of the Petronas Towers (p46). The polished Malaysian Philharmonic Orchestra plays here (usually Friday and Saturday evenings and Sunday matinees, but also other times), as do other local and international ensembles. There is a smart-casual dress code.

FORBIDDEN CITY LIVE MUSIC
Map p253 (03-2110 2088; www.forbiddencitykl.com; 50a Changkat Bukit Bintang; 9pm-1am Tue-Thu, to 2am Fri & Sat; AirAsia-Bukit Bintang) This new live-music venue on Changkat Bukit Bintang hosts mostly jazz and blues musicians in a classy, intimate setting.

KL LIVE LIVE MUSIC
Map p250 (03-2162 2570; www.kl-live.com.my; 1st fl, Life Centre, 20 Jln Sultan Ismail; Raja Chulan) A boon to KL's live-music scene, this spacious venue packs in rock and pop fans with an impressive lineup of overseas and local big-name artists and DJs.

KUALA LUMPUR CONVENTION CENTRE CONCERT VENUE
Map p250 (03-2333 2888; www.klccconventioncentre.com; Jln Pinang; KLCC) The largest of the convention centre's conference rooms and events spaces is Plenary Hall, which is sometimes used for concerts and seats up to 3000.

TGV CINEPLEX CINEMA
Map p250 (www.tgv.com.my; 3rd fl, Suria KLCC, Jln Ampang; adult/child RM14/9; KLCC) Take your pick from the mainstream offerings at this 12-screen multiplex. Book in advance or be prepared to queue, particularly at weekends.

GSC PAVILION KL CINEMA
Map p252 (www.gsc.com.my; level 6, Pavilion KL, 168 Jln Bukit Bintang; tickets RM11-20; AirAsia-Bukit Bintang) Expect queues for hit movies at this multiplex in the popular Pavilion mall. This is one of the few multiplexes in the GSC chain that has an International Screens program showing art-house and foreign movies.

GSC BERJAYA TIMES SQUARE CINEMA
Map p252 (03-8312 3456; www.gsc.com.my; 3rd fl, Berjaya Times Square, 1 Jln Imbi; tickets RM9-22; Imbi) Among the screens at the Berjaya Times Square branch of the GSC chain is the 3D Maxx, the largest of its kind in Malaysia.

LOCAL KNOWLEDGE

DANCE & CULTURAL SHOWS

If you'd like to see and hear traditional Malaysian dances and music, there are good shows at the **Malaysian Tourism Centre** (p225) at 3pm Monday to Thursday and Saturday, and 3.30pm Friday. There's also an evening dance show at 8.30pm daily in the attached restaurant **Saloma** (Map p250; 03-2161 0122; www.saloma.com.my; 139 Jln Ampang, Malaysia Tourism Centre; show only RM60, buffet & show RM100; show 8.30-9.30pm, buffet 7-10pm; Bukit Nanas).

HARD ROCK CAFÉ LIVE MUSIC
Map p250 (03-2715 5555; www.hardrock.com/cafes/kuala-lumpur; ground fl, Wisma Concorde, 2 Jln Sultan Ismail; 11.30am-2am Sun-Thu, to 3am Fri & Sat; Bukit Nanas) The KL branch of the cheesy international chain has nightly live performances by local rock bands, with musicians hitting the stage from 10pm. There is cover charge of RM40 (includes a drink) on Friday and Saturday.

SHOPPING

Bukit Bintang

★**PAVILION KL** MALL
Map p253 (www.pavilion-kl.com; 168 Jln Bukit Bintang; 10am-10pm; AirAsia-Bukit Bintang) Pavilion sets the gold standard in KL's shopping scene. Amid the many familiar international brands, there are some good local options, including British India (p64) for fashion, offering well-made linen, silk and cotton clothing for men and women; and the more affordable Padini Concept Store. For a quick trip to Japan, head to the Tokyo Street of stalls on the 6th floor.

There's also an excellent food court in the basement. Note that when you enter the mall from Jln Bukit Bintang, you are already on level 3.

ROYAL SELANGOR ARTS & CRAFTS
Map p252 (www.royalselangor.com; level 3, Pavilion KL, 168 Jln Bukit Bintang; 10am-10pm; AirAsia-Bukit Bintang) This well-regarded chain of handcrafted pewter claims ori-

WORTH A DETOUR

Taman Connaught Night Market

In the southeast of the city, stretching along Jln Cerdas, is the longest *pasar malam* (night market, ⏲7pm-1am Wed) in Malaysia. It stretches for around 2km, with over 500 stalls selling mainly clothing, household goods and food. At the western end near Jln Pantas, fuel up on *kway teow mee goreng* (noodles), fresh juices and baked birds' eggs on a stick.

To reach the market, take the LRT or Komuter Train to Bandar Tasik Selatan, then hop in a taxi (around RM10).

gins in 1885 when a Chinese pewtersmith arrived during KL's tin-mining boom. You can still find old pieces in Central Market antique shops but the newer works on sale here are outstanding. If you have time, visit the factory and visitor centre, located 8km northeast of the city centre.

KHOON HOOI FASHION & ACCESSORIES

Map p253 (www.khoonhooi.com; Explore Fl, Starhill Gallery, 181 Jln Bukit Bintang; ⏲10am-10pm; AirAsia-Bukit Bintang) Interesting fabric textures are a signature of this Malaysian designer's work. What sets his clothes apart is attention to detail, such as pleated belts made from zips or shifts sewn from lace.

SUNGEI WANG PLAZA MALL

Map p252 (www.sungeiwang.com; Jln Sultan Ismail; ⏲10am-10pm; AirAsia-Bukit Bintang) A little confusing to navigate but jam-packed with youth-oriented fashion and accessories, this is one of KL's more interesting malls with a focus on street fashion and bargains rather than glitzy international brands. You'll find vintage pieces at Gallery 80s and unique, customised items at MODO. There's also a hawker centre on the 4th floor.

FAHRENHEIT88 MALL

Map p252 (www.fahrenheit88.com; 179 Jln Bukit Bintang; ⏲10am-10pm; AirAsia-Bukit Bintang) This youth-orientated mall houses a large branch of Japanese clothes store Uniqlo. Shoe lovers should check out Shoes Gallery by Parkson and South Korean footwear emporium Shoopen. Local fashion legend Bernard Chandran also has a boutique here on the 1st floor.

STARHILL GALLERY MALL

Map p253 (www.starhillgallery.com; 181 Jln Bukit Bintang; ⏲10am-10pm; AirAsia-Bukit Bintang) With its design crossing Louis Vuitton with Louis XIV, and a basement restaurant 'village' that's a maze of cobbled alleys, grey slate walls and bamboo partitioning, this upscale mall is worth popping into just for a look. Fashion outlets such as Alexander McQueen are also here, as well as an excellent culinary school, and a 'Pamper' floor for spas.

PLAZA LOW YAT ELECTRONICS

Map p252 (http://plazalowyat.com; 7 Jln Bintang, off Jln Bukit Bintang; ⏲10am-10pm; Imbi) This is Malaysia's largest IT mall, with six floors of electronic goods and services. Head to the top-floor shops for repairs. There have been reports of credit-card details being recorded after transactions, so it's best to use cash here.

HOUSE OF SUZIE WONG ANTIQUES

Map p252 (www.houseofsuziewong.com; unit 9, 4th fl, Lot 10 Shopping Centre, 50 Jln Sultan Ismail; ⏲10am-10pm; Bukit Bintang) Antiques from across Asia, from Chinese furniture to textiles, paintings and rugs, are gathered together for sale at this eclectic shop.

BRITISH INDIA CLOTHING

Map p252 (www.britishindia.com.my; level 2, Pavilion KL, Jln Bukit Bintang; ⏲10am-10pm; AirAsia-Bukit Bintang) Branch of the local clothing and home furnishing chain selling high-quality pieces made with gorgeous, Indian-style fabrics.

COCOA BOUTIQUE CHOCOLATE

Map p250 (www.cocoaboutique.com.my; 139 Jln Ampang; ⏲10am-8pm; Bukit Nanas) Brave the tour groups being pushed through this chocolate emporium and small-scale production line to sample unusual local variations such as durian-filled chocolates.

JADI BATEK CENTRE ARTS & CRAFTS

Map p253 (☎03-2145 1133; www.jadibatek.com; 30 Jln Inai; ⏲9am-5.30pm; AirAsia-Bukit Bintang) On the tour-bus circuit, this batik goods and Malaysian handicrafts showroom and workshop offers plenty of handmade pieces – colourful and pretty things, but no extraordinary designs.

BERJAYA TIMES SQUARE MALL

Map p252 (www.berjayatimessquarekl.com; 1 Jln Imbi; ⏲10am-10pm; Imbi) Lacking the glitz of rival malls, Berjaya's mammoth effort is best visited for its entertainment options – which include a bowling alley (p66), karaoke, multiplex cinema (p63) and giant indoor theme park (p66) – rather than for any original shopping.

LOT 10 MALL

Map p252 (www.lot10.com.my; 50 Jln Bukit Bintang; ⏲10am-10pm; AirAsia-Bukit Bintang) Fronted by branches of fashion retailers H&M and Zara, Lot 10 is yet another of the Bukit Bintang malls that's worth a browse. Lot 10 Hutong (p52), the mall's fine basement food court, has stalls run by some of the city's most famous hawkers.

KLCC & Around

SURIA KLCC MALL

Map p250 (☎03-2382 2828; www.suriaklcc.com.my; KLCC, Jln Ampang; ⏲10am-10pm; KLCC) Even if shopping bores you to tears, you're sure to find something to interest you at this fine shopping complex at the foot of the Petronas Towers. It's mainly international brands but you'll find some local retailers here too including Royal Selangor for pewter, Vincci for shoes and accessories and Aseana for designer fashion.

ASEANA FASHION & ACCESSORIES

Map p250 (www.melium.com; ground level, Suria KLCC, Jln Ampang; ⏲10am-10pm; KLCC) Billed as Malaysia's 'largest luxury multibrand boutique', Aseana is noted for accessories, bags and jewellery. It also boasts an extensive selection from international and local fashion luminaries, such as Malaysian Farah Khan (www.farahkhan.com), who specialises in beaded and sequinned glamour wear.

KINOKUNIYA BOOKS

Map p250 (www.kinokuniya.com; level 4, Suria KLCC, Jln Ampang; ⏲10am-10pm; KLCC) Kinokuniya is the kind of bookshop where you can lose hours browsing the covetable stationery supplies and excellent selection of English-language titles, as well as books in all the other major languages of Malaysia. The upper-floor cafe has great views.

PROTOTYPE GALLERY ART

Map p250 (www.facebook.com/prototypegallery; level 2, Wisma Central, Jln Ampang; ⏲10am-6pm Tue & Thu-Sat; KLCC) Search out this small gallery of local arts products, ranging from 3D-printed items to prints and magazines, for the chance to see the awesome murals painted on the ceilings of this old-school mall. On the same floor is the KL outpost of Ipoh-based indie publishers and arts collective Projek Rabak.

KOMPLEKS KRAF KUALA LUMPUR ARTS & CRAFTS

Map p250 (☎03-2162 7533; www.kraftangan.gov.my/en/craft-complex-2; Jln Conlay; ⏲9am-8pm; Raja Chulan) A government enterprise, this huge complex caters mainly to coach tours, but it's worth a visit to browse the shops and stalls selling batik prints and fashion, wood carvings, pewter, basket ware, glassware and ceramics. You can also watch artists and craftspeople at work in the surrounding Craft Village or take a look around the attached Muzium Kraf (p48).

AVENUE K MALL

Map p250 (www.avenuek.com.my; 156 Jln Ampang; ⏲10am-10pm; KLCC) Anchored by a huge branch of fast-fashion retailer H&M, Avenue K has undergone a serious revamp in recent years and is now packed with shops and appealing places to eat, as well entertainment such as a branch of the escape game Breakout and the interactive prehistoric exhibition Discoveria (p48).

ISETAN DEPARTMENT STORE

Map p250 (www.isetankl.com.my; Suria KLCC; ⏲10am-10pm; KLCC) At this vast department store spread over five floors you'll find cosmetics and beauty products, children's wear, menswear and womenswear, including labels such as Anya Hindmarch, Dior, Celine and Ralph Lauren.

SPORTS & ACTIVITIES

STARHILL CULINARY STUDIO COOKING

Map p253 (☎03-2782 3810; www.starhillculinarystudio.com; Starhill Gallery, Muse Fl, 181 Jln Bukit Bintang; public classes RM188; ⏲10am-9.30pm Tue-Sun; AirAsia-Bukit Bintang) Sign up for a two- to three-hour class (usually focusing

LOCAL KNOWLEDGE

SPAS & REFLEXOLOGY

Bukit Bintang is stacked with spas and massage parlours offering all manner of pampering, from luxurious treatments with exotic potions to simple salons for foot reflexology.

Practically all KL's five-star hotels offer a luxurious spa experience. One of the best is the Ritz Carlton's **Spa Village** (Map p252; 03-2782 9090; www.spavillage.com; Ritz-Carlton, 168 Jln Imbi; treatments RM410-995; 10am-10pm; AirAsia-Bukit Bintang), with its resortlike atmosphere and wide-ranging menu of Chinese, Indian and Southeast Asian healing and toning therapies.

The 'Pamper' floor of swish shopping mall **Starhill Gallery** (p64) is dedicated to exclusive spa and beauty treatments. Among the less pricey options (ie treatments from around RM260) here are **Asianel Reflexology Spa** (Map p253; 03-2142 1397; www.asianel.com; Pamper fl, 1½-hr treatments from RM250; 10am-10pm) and the Balinese-style **Donna Spa** (Map p252; 03-2141 8999; www.donnaspa.net; Pamper Fl, 10am-midnight). Another sybaritic possibility over at **Berjaya Times Square** (p65) is **JoJoBa Spa** (Map p252; 03-2141 7766; www.jojoba.com.my; 15th fl, East Wing, 1hr massages from RM98; 11am-midnight), which claims to be Malaysia's largest tourist spa – come for seaweed wraps, coconut and green tea body scrubs and ginger tea.

If the top-end spas are beyond your budget, there are numerous Chinese massage and reflexology centres strung along Jln Bukit Bintang. Pricing is fairly consistent – around RM100 per hour for a full body massage and RM55 for 30 minutes of foot reflexology, though you can bargain down – but standards vary and some places are slightly seedy. Be prepared: a good foot massage can be rather painful, but the results will be remarkable.

on a single dish) and you'll not only get top instruction in this gleaming, well-designed culinary art studio, but you'll also be well fed. Classes vary daily and include Malay and Nonya (Peranakan) dishes, Japanese cuisine, baking and Asian and Western desserts. Private classes can also be arranged.

BERJAYA TIMES SQUARE THEME PARK — AMUSEMENT PARK

Map p252 (03-2117 3118; www.berjayatimessquarethemeparkkl.com; Berjaya Times Sq, 1 Jln Imbi; adult/child RM51/41; noon-10pm Mon-Fri, 11am-10pm Sat & Sun; Imbi) Despite the mall location, there's a full-sized looping coaster here, plus a good selection of thrill rides for teenagers and gentler rides for families. (Avoid the DNA Mixer unless you want to see your *nasi lemak* a second time.)

AMPANG SUPERBOWL — BOWLING

Map p252 (03-2144 8323; www.ampangsuperbowl.com; 5th fl, Berjaya Times Square, 1 Jln Imbi; RM6-9; 10am-midnight; Imbi) Forty-eight lane ten-pin bowling alley. Shoe rental costs RM3.30.

ROYAL SELANGOR GOLF COURSE — GOLF

(03-9206 3333; www.rsgc.com; Jln Kelab Golf, off Jln Tun Razak; 18 holes RM450; AirAsia-Bukit Bintang) KL offers more than 40 courses in and around the city, including the Royal Selangor Golf Course. You'll need to be invited by a member to play or be staying at the associated hotel. Take a taxi from AirAsia-Bukit Bintang.

CELEBRITY FITNESS — GYM

Map p252 (03-2145 1000; www.celebrityfitness.com.my; rooftop, Lot 10, 50 Jln Sultan Ismail; day passes RM75; 6.30am-midnight Mon-Fri, 8am-8pm Sat & Sun; AirAsia-Bukit Bintang) Fully equipped gym with classes on the rooftop of Lot 10.

Chinatown, Merdeka Square & Bukit Nanas

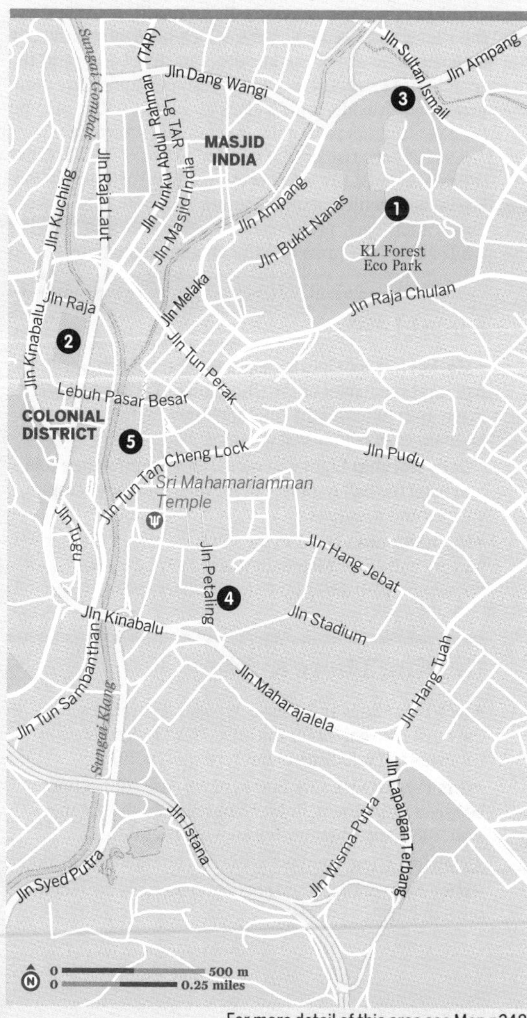

For more detail of this area see Map p248

Neighborhood Top Five

❶ **Menara KL** (p69) Getting treetop views from the canopy walkway in KL Forest Eco Park and ascending the tower for a thrilling panoramic lookout from the open-air deck.

❷ **Merdeka Square** (p70) Standing at the city's colonial heart, surrounded by a handsome ensemble of heritage buildings.

❸ **Kuala Lumpur Heritage Trail** (p81) Exploring the newly signposted walks around Chinatown and Merdeka Sq.

❹ **PS150** (p79) Sipping the creations of some of the city's top mixologists in retro surroundings.

❺ **Central Market** (p74) Shopping for souvenirs and viewing cultural performances.

Lonely Planet's Top Tip

Gain access to the exclusive members-only **Royal Selangor Club** (p71) by joining a free two-and-a-half hour **walking tour** (p81) around Merdeka Sq, laid on by Visit KL every Monday, Wednesday and Saturday at 9am.

Best Places to Eat

- Madras Lane Hawkers (p75)
- Merchant's Lane (p77)
- Bunn Choon (p76)
- Antara Restaurant (p78)
- LOKL Coffee Co (p77)

For reviews, see p75

Best Places to Drink

- Omakase + Appreciate (p79)
- PS150 (p79)
- Aku Cafe & Gallery (p79)
- Barlai (p79)

For reviews, see p78

Best Places to Shop

- Central Market (p74)
- Petaling Street Market (p81)
- Museum of Ethnic Arts (p74)
- Gahara Galleria (p80)

For reviews, see p80

Explore Chinatown, Merdeka Square & Bukit Nanas

If there's one part of Kuala Lumpur that's a microcosm of Malaysia's ethnic and historic mix, it's Chinatown. Jln Petaling is its central spine, hosting a bustling night market and bracketed by Chinese arch gates. Alongside the traditional, the neighbourhood's hipper side can be seen in new street art, cafes and cocktail bars clustered around the southern end of Jln Petaling.

Ringed by impressive colonial-era buildings, Dataran Merdeka Square (p70) is a hugely symbolic location, where the British handed over control of Malaya to its citizens in 1957. Nearby, the graceful Masjid Jamek (p75), the city's oldest surviving mosque, sits at the muddy confluence of the Klang and Gombak rivers, which bequeathed the city its name. The site of the mosque, the river banks and the surrounding streets have been revamped and made more pedestrian friendly with wider pavements, public art and heritage trails as part of the River of Life project (p187).

East of here rise up the wooded slopes of Bukit Nanas (Pineapple Hill), the oldest protected piece of jungle in Malaysia, atop which stands Menara KL (p69). The tower's observation deck provides 360-degree views of the city; while at the base are a handful of other attractions.

Local Life

- **Market life** Join locals shopping for fresh fish, meat, fruit and vegetables at the Chinatown Wet Market (p74). From 4pm to midnight Petaling Street Market (p81) sells all manner of counterfeit goods.
- **Daily worship** Light joss sticks, have your fortune told and heed the call to prayer at the area's historic temples, shrines and mosques.
- **Hip hang-outs** Head to the southern end of Chinatown for cafe culture at Merchant's Lane (p77), Chocha Foodstore (p79) and Aku Cafe & Gallery (p79).

Getting There & Away

- **LRT** Pasar Seni and Masjid Jamek LRT stations are the most convenient for the area. Plaza Rakyat station connects to Pudu Sentral bus terminal (p219).
- **Bus** Free GO-KL City Buses (p220) ease connection between Chinatown, Bukit Nanas and Bukit Bintang. Kota Raya and Muzium Telekom are useful stops.
- **Walking** These compact areas can be explored on foot.
- **MRT** New stations Pasar Seni and Merdeka are set to open in 2017.

TOP SIGHT
MENARA KL

Located within the KL Forest Eco Park, this 421m telecommunications tower, the tallest in Southeast Asia and seventh tallest in the world, offers the city's best views. Come to appreciate the phenomenal growth of the city while enjoying a Malay banquet or afternoon tea at its sky-high revolving restaurant, or to explore the park's treetops on the canopy walkway.

Observation Deck

Although the Petronas Towers are taller structures, the Menara KL (KL Tower) provides a higher viewpoint as its base is already nearly 100m above sea level atop Bukit Nanas. A lift whisks you up 276m to the indoor observation deck in the bulb at the top of the tower, its shape inspired by a Malaysian spinning toy. More thrilling yet is the **open air deck** at 300m, access to which is weather dependent. Here you can take photos unencumbered by windows and step (if you dare) into the new **sky box** jutting out from the deck which puts nothing but glass between you and the ground below.

A free shuttle bus runs from the gate on Jln Punchak, or you can walk up through the KL Forest Eco Park and its canopy walkway.

Other Attractions

There's plenty of touristy hoopla at the tower base including a zoo, an F1 simulator and a small aquarium. Look out too for the 150-year-old **Jelutong tree** that was saved during the tower's construction – find it to the left of the tower lobby.

DON'T MISS...

- Observation deck
- Open deck and sky box
- Canopy walkway in KL Forest Eco Park

PRACTICALITIES

- KL Tower
- Map p248
- ☎03-2020 5444
- www.menarakl.com.my
- 2 Jln Punchak
- observation deck adult/child RM52/31, open deck adults only RM105
- ⏲observation deck 9am-10pm, last tickets 9.30pm
- 🚉KL Tower

TOP SIGHT MERDEKA SQUARE

The large, grassy square where Malaysian independence was declared in 1957 is ringed by heritage buildings and dominated by an enormous flagpole and fluttering Malaysian flag. Come here to learn about the city's history and to admire the grand colonial architecture.

History of the Square

During KL's founding in the mid-19th century, this patch of land was used by the tin prospectors and other settlers to grow fruit and vegetables. In 1884, after the founding of the Selangor Club, the land was transformed into a games pitch and was called the Padang (meaning field).

For the next 70-odd years the Padang remained the green nucleus of colonial power on the Malay peninsula, a place for cricket, parades and civic celebrations. It became cemented in the national consciousness at midnight on 31 August 1957, when the Union flag was lowered and the Malayan States' flag hoisted on the Padang's 95m flagpole.

In 1989, a year after the city took over the Padang from the Royal Selangor Club, the square was renamed Dataran Merdeka (Independence Square), although it's commonly called Merdeka Square.

Heritage Buildings

Many of the colonial buildings that ring the square were designed by AC Norman, who arrived in Kuala Lumpur from England in 1883 and was appointed the government's official architect in 1890.

The architect's masterpiece is the **Sultan Abdul Samad Building** gracing the east side of the square. This glorious brick building, with Moorish domes and a 41m clock tower, is dramatically illuminated at night. Constructed as the secretariat for the colonial administration

DON'T MISS...

- KL City Gallery
- National Textiles Museum
- Sultan Abdul Samad Building
- St Mary's Anglican Cathedral

PRACTICALITIES

- Dataran Merdeka
- Map p248
- Masjid Jamek

in 1897, it is named after the Sultan of Selangor at the time. It now houses the national Ministry of Information, Communications and Culture.

Norman's obsession with Indian architecture can be seen in the elegant Mogul-Islamic building on the square's southeast corner, originally constructed for the railway works department. It now houses the excellent **National Textiles Museum** (Muzium Tekstil Negara; ☎03-2694 3457; www.muziumtekstilnegara.gov.my; Jln Sultan Hishamuddin; ⌚9am-6pm) FREE. The lower floors cover the history of textiles, in particular Malaysian fabrics such as *songket* (silk or cotton with gold threading), and the traditional processes and machinery used in manufacturing. Gorgeous examples of clothing and fabric abound. The upper floors cover Malaysian fabrics and design motifs in greater detail, as well as items for personal adornment such as jewellery and headgear.

At the north end of Merdeka Sq is the striking former Standard Charter Bank building, built in 1891 and another Norman design. Now the **Music Museum** (Music Museum; www.jmm.gov.my; Jln Raja, Merdeka Sq; ⌚9am-6pm) FREE, it has one floor of exhibits on the history and variety of traditional music from the region. Among the things you'll learn from the displays is that Orang Asli believe music can ward off evil spirits, and there's also a large display on the life of iconic Malaysian musician and film star P Ramlee.

When it came to **St Mary's Anglican Cathedral** (☎03-2692 8672; www.stmaryscathedral.org.my; Jln Raja), Norman ditched the Moorish and Mogul influences and stuck with the traditional blueprint of an English country church. Built in 1894, the Anglican cathedral has beautiful stained-glass windows and a fine pipe organ dedicated to Sir Henry Gurney, the British high commissioner to Malaya, assassinated in 1951 during the Emergency.

Built in mock Tudor style and founded in 1884, the exclusive **Royal Selangor Club** (www.rscweb.my; Jln Raja) remains a refuge for the KL elite. This is where the running-and-drinking club, the Hash House Harriers, kicked off in 1938. For many years women have been barred from its long bar, which has a view of the former playing fields

Raising the Flag

Apart from New Year's Eve, National Day and occasional special events, such as the Colours of Malaysia parade, crowds rarely gather at Merdeka Square.

Don't miss the **ceremonial flag-raising ceremony** held 9.45am to 10am every Monday on the square. Around the base of the flagpole (at 102m, it's the tallest in the world) are mosaics depicting the famous scenes of independence from 1957.

TOP TIPS

Start at the KL City Gallery (☎03-2691 1382; www.klcitygallery.com; 27 Jln Raja; RM5; ⌚9am-6.30pm) to get a quick overview of the city's history and see the huge scale model of the city created by Arch Kuala Lumpur.

Join the free walking tour (p81) offered by Visit KL and you'll also gain access to the Royal Selangor Club, one of KL's most exclusive private member clubs.

Refuel with a plate of nasi lemak or some cake at ARCH Cafe (www.klcitygallery.com; KL City Gallery, 27 Jln Raja, mains RM10-18; ⌚9am-6.30pm; 📶) at the KL City Gallery.

Mosaic portraits of all of Malaysia's prime ministers line a wall next to the 1904 Victorian Fountain, said to be have been built in memory of an inspector of the Selangor Military.

Stop for healthy salads, Malaysian dishes and tempting desserts at the Canteen by Chef Adu (p78) on the ground floor of the National Textiles Museum.

SIGHTS

Chinatown

SRI MAHAMARIAMMAN TEMPLE HINDU TEMPLE
See p72.

★SIN SZE SI YA TEMPLE TEMPLE
Map p249 (Jln Tun HS Lee; ⏲7am-5pm; 🚇Pasar Seni) FREE Kuala Lumpur's oldest Chinese temple was built on the instructions of Kapitan Yap Ah Loy and is dedicated to Sin Sze Ya and Si Sze Ya, two Chinese immigrants instrumental in Yap's ascension to Kapitan status. Beautiful objects decorate the temple, including two hanging carved panels, but the best feature is the almost frontier-like atmosphere. This is still an important temple for the community, much as it was in 1883 when 10,000 people turned out for opening day.

Fortune-telling sticks are provided for devotees; just rattle the pot until a stick falls out, then find the paper slip corresponding to the number on the stick. Staff will translate the fortune on the slip for RM1. On your way out, note the two old wooden sedan chairs used to carry the deity statues during religious processions.

GUANDI TEMPLE TEMPLE
Map p249 (Jln Tun HS Lee; ⏲7am-5pm; 🚇Pasar Seni) FREE Founded in 1886, this atmospheric temple is dedicated to Guandi, a historical Chinese general known as the Taoist god of war, but more commonly worshipped as the patron of righteous brotherhoods: he is in fact patron of both police forces and triad gangs. The temple's high ceilings, red walls, tiled eaves and pointy gable ends give it a distinctive look that's great for photos.

STADIUM MERDEKA HISTORIC BUILDING
Map p249 (Jln Stadium; Maharajalela) Built for the declaration of independence in 1957, this open-air stadium is where Malaysia's first prime minister, Tunku Abdul Rahman, famously punched his fist in the air seven times shouting *'Merdeka!'* (Independence!). Other big events during its history include a boxing match between Muhammad Ali and Joe Bugner, and a concert by Michael Jackson. There are panoramic views of the city from the grandstands and evocative photographic murals in the entrance hall.

TOP SIGHT
SRI MAHAMARIAMMAN TEMPLE

This venerable Hindu shrine – the oldest in Malaysia and rumoured to be the richest – was founded by the Pillai family from the Indian state of Tamil Nadu in 1873. For 50 years it was their private shrine until opening to the public in the 1920s.

Flower-garland vendors crowd the entrance and the temple is crowned by a five-tiered **gopuram** (temple tower), built in 1972 and covered in riotously colourful statues of Hindu deities. Passing through the gate symbolises the move from the material to the spiritual world.

The **main prayer hall** has several shrines to different Hindu deities. The main shrine, found at the rear of the complex, is for Mariamman, the South Indian mother goddess, an incarnation of Durga, also known as Parvati. On the left side of the complex is a shrine to Ganesh, the elephant-headed god, and on the right is the shrine where Lord Murugan is worshipped.

The temple also houses the **silver chariot** in which statuettes of Lord Murugan and his consorts are transported to Batu Caves during the Thaipusam festival in January or February each year. Non-Hindus are welcome to visit; leave your shoes at the entrance.

DON'T MISS...

- Gopuram
- Main prayer hall

PRACTICALITIES

- Map p249, B6
- 163 Jln Tun HS Lee
- admission free
- ⏲6am-8.30pm
- 🚇Pasar Seni

Neighbourhood Walk Chinatown Architecture

START MASJID JAMEK LRT STATION
END PETALING STREET MARKET
LENGTH 1.6KM; 1½ HOURS

From the station head south down the new river embankment path parallel to Jln Benteng for a great view of **1 Masjid Jamek** (p75) with its newly uncovered steps down to the river. At the junction with Lr Ampang is **2 Medan Pasar**, site of KL's original market square. In the southwestern corner of the square, stop to look at **3 Cafe Old Market Square** (p75) built by tin magnate Loke Yew in 1906.

Where Medan Pasar meets Lr Pasar Besar you'll see the **4 OCBC Building**, a graceful art deco structure built in 1938 for the Overseas Chinese Banking Company. Around the corner with Jln Tun HS Lee is **5 MS Ally Company**, a pharmacy in business since 1909.

Cross Lr Pudu, turn right and, after 25m, duck left into an alley leading to **6 Sin Sze Si Ya Temple** (p72). Exit the way you came in, cross the street and walk two blocks up to **7 Central Market** (p74).

Exit the market, turn left on to Jln Tun Tan Cheng Lock, then right on to Jln Tun HS Lee. The shophouses along here are among Chinatown's oldest; note the unique feature of a five-foot way (pavement) lower than the road level. On the south corner is the pale-yellow art deco **8 Lee Rubber Building**.

Opposite, next to the bright-red, incense-wreathed **9 Guandi Temple** (p72), is Jln Sang Guna, a covered arcade housing Chinatown's atmospheric **10 wet market** (p74). Back on Jln Tun HS Lee pause to admire the **11 Sri Mahamariamman Temple** (p72) and to breathe in the sweet jasmine of the flower sellers outside.

At the junction with Jln Sultan turn left, then right on to Jln Petaling. Further south, around the busy traffic roundabout of Bulatan Merdeka, you find the ornate ancestral **12 Chan She Shu Yuen Clan Association Temple** (p74) and, across Jln Stadium, the **13 Guan Yin Temple** (p74), dedicated to the goddess of mercy.

Finish at **14 Maharajalela MRT station** or return to Jln Petaling to browse the **15 Petaling Street Market** (p81).

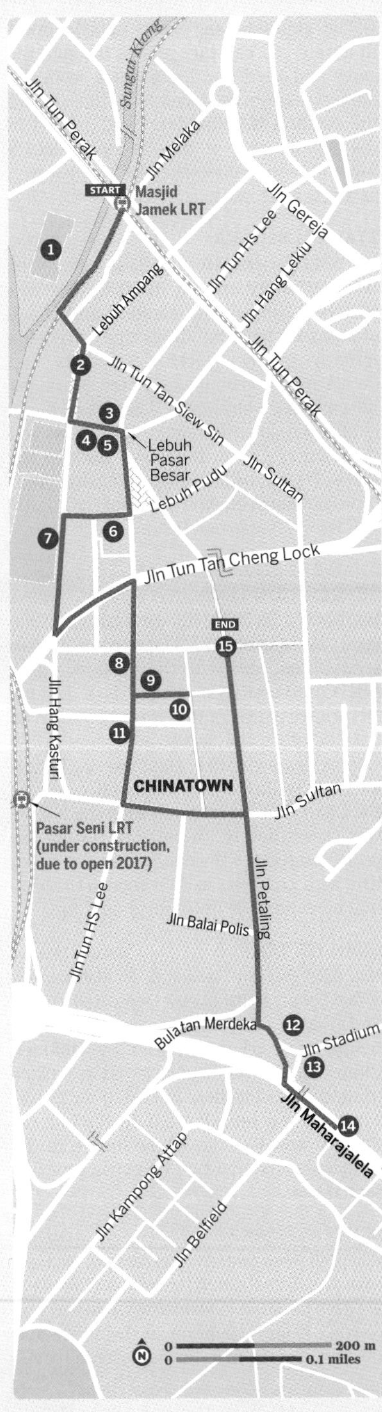

The stadium isn't open outside event times but you can take a peek through the gates and there's a decent view from the monorail train as it passes. Land around the stadium is being developed as part of the construction of the 118-storey KL118 tower (due to be completed by 2020) as well as a new MRT station.

STADIUM NEGARA HISTORIC BUILDING

Map p249 (Jln Hang Jebat; Hang Tuah, Hang Tuah) Officially opened in 1962, this was Malaysia's first indoor stadium and is one of many heritage buildings that have been recently given a facelift. Concerts and events are occasionally held here. Murals in the entrance lobby depict the cultural dances of Malaysia's different ethnic groups and the country's main industries back in the 1960s. It's not officially open outside event times but between 9am and 5pm the guards will likely let you look inside.

CHAN SHE SHU YUEN CLAN ASSOCIATION TEMPLE TEMPLE

Map p249 (03-2078 1461; Jln Petaling; 9am-6pm; Maharajalela) FREE Opened in 1906 to serve immigrants with the surname Chan, this Cantonese-style temple is a beauty. Decorative panels of 100-year-old Shek Wan pottery adorn the facade and eaves, while side gables swirl like giant waves. Inside, an altar enshrines the three ancestors of the Chan clan. At research time the temple was closed due to an ongoing restoration project to replace the distinctive green roof tiles with grey ones in deference to the original model temple in Guangzhou, China.

GUAN YIN TEMPLE BUDDHIST TEMPLE

Map p249 (cnr Jln Stadium & Jln Maharajalela; 7am-5pm; Maharajalela) Dedicated to the Bodhisattva of compassion, this cement temple was originally built by Hokkien Chinese in the 1890s and served as a place to say prayers for those buried in the graveyard that was once located on the hill. On the first and 15th day of the month in the Chinese calendar, a free vegetarian meal is served here.

CENTRAL MARKET MARKET

Map p249 (www.centralmarket.com.my; Jln Hang Kasturi; 10am-10pm; Pasar Seni) This 1930s art deco building (a former wet market) was rescued from demolition in the 1980s and transformed into a tourist-oriented arts-and-crafts centre. Nonetheless, there are some excellent shops, good restaurants, and the fascinating private **Museum of Ethnic Arts** (Map p249; 03-2301 1468; 2nd fl, the Annexe, 10 Jln Hang Kasturi; 11am-7pm; Pasar Seni) in the Annexe. The adjacent Kasturi Walk – the arch is a series of *wau bulan* (moon kites) – is bordered by handsome restored shophouses. Check the website for details of events that happen around the market.

CHINATOWN WET MARKET MARKET

Map p249 (off Jln Tun HS Lee; 7am-1pm; Pasir Seni) If you want your chicken freshly plucked, this is where to get it. The market is squished in darkened alleys between Jln Petaling and Jln Tun HS Lee and it's where locals shop for their groceries.

MEDAN PASAR SQUARE

Map p248 (Masjid Jamek) Pedestrianised Medan Pasar (which translates as Market Square) was once the heart of Chinatown. Kapitan Yap Ah Loy lived here, and in addition to holding the city's wet market, it was a place of brothels and illegal gambling dens (now long gone). In the centre stands an art deco clock tower built in 1937 to commemorate the coronation of King George VI.

Merdeka Square & Bukit Nanas

MENARA KUALA LUMPUR TOWER

See p69.

MERDEKA SQUARE SQUARE

See p70.

★KL FOREST ECO PARK NATURE RESERVE

Map p248 (Taman Eko Rimba KL; 03-2026 4741; www.forestry.gov.my; 7am-6pm; KL Tower) FREE Don't miss traversing the lofty **canopy walkway** set in this thick lowland dipterocarp forest covering 9.37 hectares in the heart of the city. The oldest protected jungle in Malaysia (gazetted in 1906), the park is commonly known as Bukit Nanas (Pineapple Hill), and is threaded through with short trails up from either Jln Ampang or Jln Raja Chulan. Pick up a basic map to the trails from the Forest Information Centre on Jln Raja Chulan.

TELEKOM MUSEUM LANDMARK

Map p248 (www.muziumtelekom.com.my; Jln Raja Chulan; adult/child RM11/5; ⏲9am-5pm Mon-Fri; 🚉Masjid Jamek) Housed in the beautifully renovated former telephone exchange building, this interesting museum has creatively designed displays on the history of communications in Malaysia, from the earliest stone carvings through the use of messenger elephants and carrier pigeons to the latest digital technology. Highlights include a section of the original switchboard from the 1920s with wires that had to be manually connected and photographs of the glamorous telephone operators of the 1950s who competed in the Miss Golden Voice contest.

EATING

Chinatown & Around

★MADRAS LANE HAWKERS HAWKER $

Map p248 (Madras Lane; noodles RM5-6; ⏲8am-4pm Tue-Sun; 🚉Pasar Seni) Enter beside the Guandi Temple to find this alley of hawker stalls. It's best visited for breakfast or lunch, with standout operators including the one offering 10 types of *yong tau fu* (vegetables stuffed with tofu and a fish and pork paste). The *bak kut teh* (pork and medicinal herbs stew) and curry laksa stalls are also good.

CAFE OLD MARKET SQUARE CAFE $

Map p248 (☎03-2022 2338; www.cafeoldmarketsquare.com; 2 Medan Pasar; mains RM2-14; ⏲7am-4.30pm Mon-Fri, to 3pm Sat; 🚉Masjid Jamek) Come for a local breakfast of Hainanese coffee, soft-boiled eggs and *kaya* toast at this newly restored *kopitiam* serving the same dishes as it did over 80 years ago. The original wall tiles and mosaic floors have been scrubbed clean, historical photographs hung on the walls and the 2nd floor turned into a gallery space.

Note the fine Dutch gables, yellow shutters and glassless windows of the building, one of three shophouses built by tin magnate Loke Yew in 1906.

RESTORAN SANTA INDIAN $

Map p248 (☎019-269 9771; 11 Jln Tun HS Lee; chapatis RM1.50; ⏲6.30am-6.30pm Mon-Sat; 🚉Masjid Jamek) You won't find Christmas presents at this no-frills cafe but freshly made chapatis, loved by the surrounding Indian community. Paired with a side dish of curried chickpeas

TOP SIGHT
MASJID JAMEK

Chinatown's Muslim population prays at this beautiful onion-domed mosque designed by British architect AB Hubback, who sought inspiration from the Moghul mosques of northern India. Constructed in 1907 at the confluence of the Klang and Gombak rivers, it was the first brick mosque in Malaysia and the city's centre of Islamic worship until the opening of the National Mosque in 1965.

An extensive relandscaping of the mosque's surroundings is under way as part of the River of Life project. The original steps at the back of the mosque, once used to access the building by boat, have been uncovered and reinstated. They form an elegant addition to the view of the mosque from the adjoining riverbank, which has also been done-up as part of the project. A pedestrian bridge will link Masjid Jamek with **Merdeka Square** (p70), while the entrance to the mosque will be fronted by a landscaped plaza with shaded areas and fountains.

Visitors are welcome outside prayer times, but shoes should be removed and women should cover their heads, legs and shoulders; robes are available to borrow.

DON'T MISS...

- Prayer hall
- Steps down to the river

PRACTICALITIES

- Friday Mosque
- off Jln Tun Perak
- ⏲9am-12.30pm & 2.30-4pm Sat-Thu
- 🚉Masjid Jamek
- FREE

LOCAL KNOWLEDGE

KL'S STREET ART

Following in the wake of Penang's street-art revolution, a number of KL's buildings have been brightened with large-scale paintings, including one by Lithuanian artist Ernest Zacharevic. The eponymously named **Ernest Zacharevic Mural** of a boy in a canoe (Map p248; Wisma Allianz, 33 Jln Gereja; Masjid Jamek) can be seen on the wall of Wisma Allianz, next to a car park on Jln Gereja. On the end of a terrace of shophouses on Jln Panggong in Chinatown, Russian artist Julia Volchkova painted her evocative **Goldsmith Mural** (Map p249; Jln Panggong; Pasar Seni).

Other murals to look out for are the**#tanahairku mural**, a huge painting of a boy in a tiger hat (Map p248; Jln Raja Chulan; Muzium Telekom) opposite the Muzium Telekom, artist Kenji Chai's giant **Cockerel** (Map p248; Jln Tun Tan Cheng Lock; P-laza Rakyat) on the side of the Nando's building on Jln Tun Tan Cheng Lock, and the **#distinctivecreative #artforlife** (Jln Imbi; Imbi) explosion of colour overlooking a car park on Jln Imbi opposite the Park Royal Hotel.

As part of the River of Life project, a number of sculptures have been commissioned, including the red-painted metal **Kuen Stephanie Sculptures** (Map p249; www.kuenstephanie.com; Bangkok Bank Sq, Lebuh Pudu; Masjid Jamek) depicting scenes from Malaysian life in the style of paper cuttings. These can be seen on Bangkok Bank Sq and Lebuh Pudu. **Lat Cartoon Sculptures** are fun, life-size sculptures based on the cartoonist (Map p248; Jln Melaka; Masjid Jamek); humorous characters are dotted along the trail from Jln Melaka to the KL Forest Eco Park on Jln Raja Chulan.

If the city's public art leaves you feeling inspired, you can join the **Kuala Lumpur Urban Sketchers** (www.facebook.com/KLUrbanSketchers) FREE at one of their monthly sketching sessions. Run by artist KC Lee and his daughter, the group meets every third Sunday of the month to draw on location. Before sketching, KC Lee usually gives a short talk on the history of the spot, which is often a heritage building. Check the group's Facebook page to find out what's planned.

or dhal, they are the perfect fast, cheap snack if you need a break any time of day.

BUNN CHOON BAKERY $

Map p249 (www.facebook.com/bunnchoonmy; 153 Jln Petaling; pastries RM1.40-2.50; 10.30am-5pm Mon-Fri, 9am-6pm Sat; Maharajalela) It's worth coming early to Bunn Choon to sample their egg tarts warm from the oven. Fourth generation owner-baker Wong Kok Tong and his wife use the family's original egg-tart recipe, and have branched out to create charcoal-black-sesame and green-tea versions. If the egg tarts are sold out the pineapple sticks are pretty good, too.

LAI FOONG HAWKER $

Map p249 (Kedai Kopi Lai Foong, 138 Jln Tun Tan Cheng Lock; noodles RM8; 7am-3.30pm; P-laza Rakyat) The stall that lends its name to this old-school hawker cafe has been dishing up beef ball noodles since 1956; on Mondays you can ask for its special 'steak and balls' soup made with beef penis and testicles. Other stalls in the complex keep longer hours.

CHEE CHEONG FUN STALL CHINESE $

Map p249 (cnr Jln Petaling & Jln Hang Lekir; noodles RM3-6; 7am-4pm Thu-Tue; ; Pasar Seni) Just off Jln Petaling on Jln Hang Lekir, in the heart of the pedestrian area, this stall has been soothing early morning appetites for decades with melt-in-the-mouth *chee cheong fun* (rice noodles) doused with sweet and spicy sauces and a sprinkle of sesame seeds.

HON KEE CHINESE $

Map p249 (93 Jln Hang Lekir; congee RM6.50; 4am-3pm; Pasar Seni) A great Cantonese porridge place – frogs' leg porridge is their speciality.

SANGEETHA INDIAN $

Map p248 (03-2032 3333; 65 Lg Ampang; mains RM13.50-18; 8am-11pm; ; Masjid Jamek) This vegetarian restaurant serves lots of North Indian delights such as *idli* (savoury, soft, fermented-rice-and-lentil cakes) and *masala dosa* (rice-and-lentil crepes stuffed with spiced potatoes). From 4pm try the Punjabi *chaat* (snacks) including vegetable samosas and *pani puri* (stuffed dough balls) – perfect for afternoon munchies.

TANG CITY FOOD HALL $

Map p249 (21-27 Jln Hang Lekir; mains RM5-12; 6am-11pm; Pasar Seni) Set back from the open-air tables on the main drag of Jln Hang Lekir, this food court serves a good variety of inexpensive Chinese, Indian and Malay dishes and cold beers.

KHUKRI NEPALESE $

Map p249 (03-2072 0663; 1st fl, 26 Jln Tun Tan Siew Sin; mains RM9-13; 9am-9pm; Masjid Jamek) A gathering point for Nepalis in KL, this simple restaurant serves authentic Nepalese cuisine including great momos (dumplings), steamed or fried, and spicy chicken and mutton dishes.

RESTORAN YUSOOF DAN ZAKHIR INDIAN $

Map p249 (03-2026 8685; Jln Hang Kasturi; mains RM3.50-8; 6am-11pm; Pasar Seni) This huge banana-yellow and palm-tree-green canteen opposite Central Market on the pedestrian street serves delicious *mamak* (Muslim Indian-Malay) food, and is perfect for a roti or *dosa* and curry sauce snack. The fresh fruit drinks are also good here.

★MERCHANT'S LANE FUSION $$

Map p249 (03-2022 1736; www.facebook.com/merchantslane/home; level 1, 150 Jln Petaling; mains RM20-30; 11.30am-10pm Mon, Tue, Thu & Fri, 9.30am-10pm Sat & Sun; ; Maharajalela) Look for the narrow doorway at the end of the block for the stairs leading up to this high-ceilinged charmer of a cafe with a gorgeous, plant-filled outdoor terrace. The vibe is relaxed, the staff young, hip and friendly and the food a very tasty mash-up of Eastern and Western dishes, such as Italian chow mein.

KIM LIAN KEE CHINESE $$

Map p249 (03-2032 4984; www.facebook.com/KimLianKee; 49 Jln Petaling; mains RM15-35; 11am-11pm; Pasar Seni) Kim Lian Kee has been serving some of the city's best Hokkien mee since 1927, when Ong Kim Lian arrived in KL from Fujian, China, and opened his first noodle stall in the city. Choose a table upstairs for aircon and a view of Petaling Street Market, or sit downstairs, alley-side. There is also a stall at Lot 10 Hutong (p52).

LOKL COFFEE CO INTERNATIONAL $$

Map p249 (http://loklcoffee.com; 30 Jln Tun HS Lee; mains RM16-30; 8am-6pm Tue-Sun; ; Masjid Jamek) From its clever name and slick design to its tasty twists on comfort foods such as deep-fried Hainanese meatloaf sandwiches and dessert toasties, LOKL ticks all the right boxes. Also does great breakfasts (8am to 11am).

There's an internal courtyard with outdoor seating at the back – part of the hostel BackHome (p129), to which the cafe is attached.

IKAN PANGGANG HAWKER $$

Map p249 (019-315 9448; Jln Hang Lekir; mains RM15; 5-11pm Tue-Sun; Pasar Seni) Tuck into spicy fish and seafood dishes and luscious chicken wings from this stall labelled only Ikan Panggang (which means grilled fish) outside Hong Leong Bank. Order ahead: it generally takes 20 minutes for your foil-wrapped pouch of seafood to cook, allowing time to explore the market.

OLD CHINA CAFÉ MALAYSIAN $$

Map p249 (03-2072 5915; www.oldchina.com.my; 11 Jln Balai Polis; mains RM10-43; 11.30am-10.30pm; Pasar Seni) Housed in an old guild hall of a laundry association, this long-running restaurant continues to not only conjure retro charm but also serve good-value Peranakan food. Try the beef rendang, the succulent Nonya fried chicken, and tasty appetisers such as the top hats (small pastries shaped like a hat and stuffed with veggies).

PRECIOUS OLD CHINA MALAYSIAN $$

Map p249 (03-2273 7372; www.oldchina.com.my; mezzanine fl, Central Market, Jln Hang Kasturi; mains RM13-46; 11am-10pm; Pasar Seni) Run by the owners of Old China Café, this restaurant inside Central Market has an upscale, Shanghai-1930s look, with lacquered chairs and pricey porcelain on display, and serves similar, excellent Southeast Asian and Nonya dishes. Try the bitter gourd soup for something different. The restaurant also functions as a bar, if you just want a drink.

WINS BOULANGERIE BAKERY $$

Map p248 (03-2022 2288; www.facebook.com/winsboulangerie; 9 Jln Tun HS Lee; breakfasts & sandwiches RM18; 8am-8pm Mon-Fri, to 3pm Sat & Sun; Masjid Jamek) The smell of freshly baked bread wafts into the street. The vast array of loaves, baguettes, cakes and pastries, artfully arranged on shelves and in crates, are a feast for the eyes as well as the stomach. A good place for a baked-goods based breakfast or a satisfyingly 'giant' lunchtime sandwich.

CHA BOU KITCHEN CHINESE $$

Map p249 (03-2272 3090; www.purplecane.com.my; 1 Jln Maharajalela; mains RM23-69; 11am-10pm; Maharajalela) Tucked behind the Chinese Assembly Hall, Cha Bou uses tea as an ingredient in most of its dishes – it's part of the Purple Cane family of tea shops and restaurants. Intriguing specials include green tea curry chicken, vegetables with oolong tea and beef simmered in lychee tea.

MALAYA HAINAN MALAYSIAN $$

Map p249 (019-329 7899; lot 16, section 24, Jln Panggong; mains RM9-13; 10am-10pm; Pasar Seni) It's good to see this long-shuttered mock-Tudor-meets-the-tropics post office revamped as an appealing restaurant with a choice of breezy open-air and retro-themed indoor dining areas. Pick from a good range of colonial Hainanese and Nonya dishes such as roast chicken, sambal prawns and sweet-sour fish.

Merdeka Square & Bukit Nanas

CANTEEN BY CHEF ADU MALAYSIAN $$

Map p248 (www.chefaduamran.com; National Textiles Museum, Jln Sultan Hishamuddin; mains RM13-25; 9am-6pm; Masjid Jamek) You'll be happy to linger over coffee in this serene space, styled with mismatched antique furniture, wood-cut screens and fabulous textiles. *MasterChef Malaysia* judge Chef Adu's new cafe specialises in dishes from his native state of Johor, such as laksa Johor and *soto ayam Johor* (a yellow spicy chicken soup), and also does a mean rendang cottage pie. It's also a great place for dessert – try the banana brownies or the *ondeh-ondeh* (pandan-flavoured cake).

MOGHUL MAHAL INDIAN $$

Map p248 (03-2070 8288; www.moghulmahal.com.my; ground fl, Menara Kuala Lumpur; mains RM20-48; 10am-11pm; KL Tower) At the foot of Menara KL is this Punjabi restaurant dishing up tasty tandoori platters, curries and naans as well as teh tarik, masala tea and traditional north Indian sweets.

ANTARA RESTAURANT FUSION $$$

Map p248 (03-2078 8881; www.antararestaurant.com; lot 2 Old Malaya, 66-68 Jln Raja Chula; mains RM25-115; noon-2.30pm & 6-11.30pm; KL Tower) Chef Isadora Chai's new venture is Antara at Old Malaya, a row of 100-year-old colonial buildings that have been immaculately renovated to accommodate a cluster of upscale restaurants and bars. The menu is modern Malaysian with French inflections and features creative dishes such as scallop *popiah* rolled at the table using pancake wraps and tiffin tins of tasty fillings.

ATMOSPHERE 360 MALAYSIAN, INTERNATIONAL $$$

Map p248 (03-2020 2121; www.atmosphere360.com.my; Menara Kuala Lumpur, 2 Jln Punchak; buffet lunch/afternoon tea/dinner RM92/60/208; 11.30am-1pm, 3.30-5.30pm & 6.30-11pm; KL Tower) There are 360-degree views from this tower-top revolving restaurant. The lunch and dinner buffets offer an ample choice of Malay dishes, though they can be hit and miss. Book ahead (you can do this online) for meals, especially sunset dining, but you can usually just drop in for high tea.

Note there's a smart-casual dress code in the evening and it costs extra to sit by the window (per table RM25 at lunch and RM50 at dinner).

DRINKING & NIGHTLIFE

Chinatown is home to a couple of pricey, speakeasy-style cocktail bars as well as a cluster of stylish coffee joints. Sinking cold beers at the open-air restaurants around Jln Petaling night market is what many visitors quite rightly prefer to do. Many of the backpacker lodges also have bars, some, such as Reggae Mansion (p129), on their roofs.

★PS150 COCKTAIL BAR

Map p248 (03-2022 2888; www.ps150.my; ground fl, 150 Jln Petaling; 6pm-2am Tue-Sat, 3-10pm Sun; Maharajalela) The southern end of Petaling St's evolution into a hip hood is helped along by PS150, a cocktail bar concealed behind a fake toyshop in a building that was once a brothel. Inside, the dim red lights and vintage-style booths bring to mind the films of Wong Kar-Wai; the open-air courtyard and back bar are more-modern spaces.

★OMAKASE + APPRECIATE COCKTAIL BAR

Map p248 (www.facebook.com/OmakaseAppreciate; basement, Bangunan Ming Annexe, 9 Jln Ampang; 5pm-1am Tue-Fri, 9pm-1am Sat; ; Masjid Jamek) This cosy, retro cocktail bar is one of KL's top-secret drinking spots. The expert mixologists here each have their own menu of speciality cocktails or, if nothing appeals, ask them to create a drink tailored to your tastes. Part of the fun is finding the entrance: look for the sign saying 'no admittance'.

★VCR CAFE

Map p249 (03-2110 2330; www.vcr.my; 2 Jln Galloway; 8.30am-11pm; ; Hang Tuah) Set in an airy prewar shophouse, VCR serves first-rate coffee, excellent all-day breakfasts (RM19 to RM35) and desserts. The crowd is young and diverse, but anyone will feel welcome here. Behind the shop, check out Jln Sin Chew Kee, a photogenic row of colourful shophouses.

★AKU CAFE & GALLERY CAFE

Map p249 (03-2857 6887; www.oldchina.com.my; 1st fl, 8 Jln Panggong; 11am-8pm Tue-Sun; ; Pasar Seni) This relaxed coffee haunt serves good hand-drip brews starting at RM10. There are also flavoured cold drinks such as orange, ginger and mint, plus iced coffee, cakes, desserts (try the pandan panna cotta), and light *kopitiam*-style meals. Exhibitions change on a monthly basis and there are some nice local craft souvenirs for sale.

Keep climbing the stairs to find the contemporary-arts space **Lostgens'** (Map p249; www.facebook.com/lostgens; 3rd fl, 8c Jln Panggong; 1-7pm Tue-Sun; Pasar Seni) FREE and, a floor above, the edgy performance space Findars (p80).

CHOCHA FOODSTORE CAFE

Map p249 (03-2022 1100; www.facebook.com/chocha.foodstore; 156 Jln Petaling; 11am-6pm Tue-Sun; Maharajalela) The abandoned Mah Lian Hotel has been transformed into a multifunctional hipster's paradise. Behind the building's raw concrete and timber facade is a ground-floor cafe and events space with a sunny plant-filled courtyard and the original hotel tiles, where Chocha's 'tea sommelier' Youn serves an extensive selection of speciality brews. Coffee is handled by in-house coffee bar @addicted.

There's also a menu of Malaysian-inspired dishes made with ingredients bought directly from farmers. Upstairs there's a wine bar and architect's office and there are plans to open a bike workshop and design bookshop in the coming months.

BARLAI COCKTAIL BAR

Map p249 (03-2141 7850; http://thebiggroup.co; 3 Jln Sin Chew Kee; 5pm-3am Mon-Fri, 3pm-3am Sat & Sun; ; Hang Tuah) Occupying the ground floor of a beautifully restored heritage building – the fab rental apartment Sekeping Sin Chew Kee (p130) is upstairs – this chilled bar is a sophisticated place to sip a lemongrass G&T or a bacon bourbon Bloody Mary. There are cosy nooks inside and a leafy courtyard garden outside.

MOONTREE HOUSE CAFE

Map p249 (www.moontree-house.blogspot.com; 1st fl, 6 Jln Panggong; 10am-8pm Wed-Mon; ; Pasar Seni) Apart from being a quiet space for a well-prepared hand-drip or siphon coffee in an old Chinatown shophouse, Moontree also sells cute handicrafts and feminist literature and is probably the best central place to make enquiries about KL's discreet lesbian scene.

Coffee beans are mostly directly sourced and include the local Johor-grown Liberica and Peabody Liberica. The latter makes for a sweet and slightly pungent ice-dripped coffee.

KOONG WOH TONG TEAHOUSE

Map p249 (www.kwt.my; 111 Jln Petaling; 8.45am-11pm; Pasar Seni) This little herbal drink shop is part of a Chinese chain that has spread into Southeast Asia. There are branches at either end of Petaling Street Market, with resplendent gold interiors and a range of jellies and refreshing traditional herbal drinks – try the Five Flower tea.

REGGAE BAR BAR

Map p249 (www.facebook.com/reggaechinatown; 158 Jln Tun HS Lee; ⊙11am-3am; Pasar Seni) Travellers gather in droves at this pumping bar in the thick of Chinatown, which has outdoor seats for those who'd like to catch the passing parade. There are beer promos, pool tables and pub grub served until late.

ENTERTAINMENT

MUD THEATRE

Map p248 (www.mudKL.com; Panggung Bandaraya, Jln Raja; tickets RM80; ⊙performances 3pm & 8.30pm; Masjid Jamek) This lively musical show mixes a modern multicultural Malaysia theme with historical vignettes from KL's early days. The young, talented cast give it their all and there's some fun to be had with audience participation. It's staged in a beautiful historic **theatre** (DBKL City Theatre; Jln Raja; Masjid Jamek), the intimate auditorium based on the shape of a Malaysian kite.

FINDARS LIVE MUSIC

Map p249 (www.facebook.com/FINDARS; 4th fl, 8c Jln Panggong; Pasar Seni) Check the Facebook page of this edgy, graphic arts space for details of gigs by local and visiting musicians and performance artists – they often happen on the weekends. The quirky street-art-style cafe-bar is an installation in itself, complete with Darth Vader mask.

MABA STADIUM STADIUM

Map p249 (03-2078 0055; www.maba.com.my; 6 Jln Hang Jebat; ⊙9am-6pm Mon-Fri, to 1pm Sat; Pasar Seni) Check the MABA website to find out about matches held at the headquarters of the Malaysian Basketball Association. There's also a training court on the roof.

SHOPPING

★**GAHARA GALLERIA** CLOTHING

Map p248 (www.ruzzgahara.com; National Textiles Museum, 26 Jln Sultan Hishamuddin; ⊙10am-6pm Mon-Fri, 11am-5pm Sat & Sun; Masjid Jamek) This boutique at the National Textiles Museum (p71) sells pieces by the Malaysian label Ruzz Gahara. Batik artisans – many of them based in the villages of rural Kelantan – use traditional printing methods to create the textiles from which Ruzz Gahara's beautiful contemporary designs are made. And since the textiles are hand-printed, no two garments are exactly alike.

LOCAL KNOWLEDGE

CENTRAL MARKET

Based in a beautiful 1920s art deco building, **Central Market** (p74) offers KL's best selection of souvenirs, gifts and traditional crafts such as batik clothing and hangings, *songket* (fine cloth woven with silver and gold thread), *wau bulan* (moon kites) and baskets, as well as vintage items from daily life.

Don't miss the fascinating private **Museum of Ethnic Arts** (p74) in the Annexe where most items are for sale; even if you're not interested in buying, it's fascinating to browse this extraordinary private collection of tribal arts from Borneo and ethnographic arts from as far afield as Tibet. Other top shops include the following:

Asli Craft (Map p249; G23 ground fl, main building⊙10am-9.30pm) Handmade indigenous items.

Rhino (KB17 ground fl, main bldg,⊙9am-10.30pm) Hand-painted clogs and handicrafts.

Songket Sutera Asli (M53 mezzanine fl, main bldg,⊙10am-9.30pm) Weavings and embroidery.

Tanamera (www.tanamera.com.my; G25 ground fl, main bldg, ⊙10am-9.30pm) Natural spa products.

Wau Tradisi (M51 mezzanine fl, main bldg, ⊙10am-9.30pm) Striking traditional kites.

PETALING STREET MARKET MARKET

Map p249 (Jln Petaling; ⏲10am-10.30pm; 🚉Pasar Seni) Malaysia's relaxed attitude towards counterfeit goods is well illustrated at this heavily hyped night market bracketed by fake Chinese gateways. Traders start to fill Jln Petaling from midmorning until it is jam-packed with market stalls selling everything from fake Mulberry handbags to jackfruit. Visit in the afternoon if you want to take pictures or see the market without the crowds.

HOUSE OF RINPO ANTIQUES

Map p248 (C30, Dataran Underground, Merdeka Sq; ⏲10am-6pm; 🚉Masjid Jamek) In the underground mall at the southern end of Merdeka Sq is this small antique shop run as a hobby by affable Uncle Khoo. The quality of items varies but there are usually some good finds to be had among the ceramics, paintings, and daily-life items from the past.

JUNK BOOKSTORE BOOKS

Map p248 (☎03-2078 3822; 78 Jln Tun HS Lee; ⏲8.30am-5pm Mon-Fri, to 2pm Sat; 🚉Masjid Jamek) One of KL's best secondhand bookshops, with thousands of titles piled high on a couple of jam-packed floors. Ask staff to show you their selection of antique local titles, but don't expect to get them for bargain prices!

CHOP SANG KEE ARTS & CRAFTS

Map p248 (64 Jln Tun Perak; ⏲9am-3pm Mon-Fri; 🚉Masjid Jamek) A photogenic rattan-cane and bamboo basket and furniture shop that has been in business since 1920. These days most items come from China.

KWONG YIK SENG ARTS & CRAFTS

Map p249 (☎03-2078 3620; 144 Jln Tun HS Lee; ⏲9am-5pm Mon-Sat; 🚉Pasar Seni) Looking for traditional Chinese teapots, bowls or a kitsch ornament for your mantelpiece? Your search is over at this shop specialising in new and antique-style china and porcelain.

PURPLE CANE TEA ARTS TEA

Map p249 (www.purplecane.com.my; 11 Jln Sultan; ⏲10am-9pm; 🚉Pasar Seni) One of several specialist tea shops in Chinatown where you can sample and buy Chinese teas (mostly Pu-erh) and all manner of tea-making paraphernalia.

LOCAL KNOWLEDGE

VISIT KL GUIDED WALKS

Visit KL (p228) offers two free guided walks in the Chinatown and Merdeka Sq areas.

Kuala Lumpur Night Walk (Map p249; ☎03-2698 0332; ⏲6.30-9pm Sat) FREE Starting in Chinatown at the Arch Cafe on Jln Hang Kasturi, this tour loops past Masjid Jamek and Masjid India and through the packed streets of the bustling night market, tasting and sampling along the way, popping into old-school tailor shops and retro barbers.

Kuala Lumpur Heritage Trail (Dataran Merdeka Heritage Walk; Map p248; ☎03-2698 0332; ⏲9-11.30am Mon, Wed & Sat) FREE A guided walk around Merdeka Sq, starting at the KL City Gallery in the square.

BASKET SHOP ARTS & CRAFTS

Map p249 (www.thebasketshop.com.my; 10 Jln Panggong; ⏲9.30am-5.30pm Mon-Sat; 🚉Pasar Seni) All kinds of bamboo and woven straw baskets and decorative boxes are to be found here, many of them handmade.

SPORTS & ACTIVITIES

SARANG COOKERY COOKING

Map p249 (☎012-210 0218; http://sarangcookery.com; 8 Jln Galloway; 4hr classes RM250; ⏲9am-1pm & 2-6pm Mon-Fri; Hang Tuah) Learn to cook four different Peranakan (Nonya), Malay or Indian dishes at these fun, hands-on cooking classes run by B&B owners Christina and Michael at one of their properties. Ingredients from the herb garden such as lemongrass, turmeric and basil are incorporated into the dishes, which are consumed at the end of the class in a sit-down meal.

CHIN WOO STADIUM SWIMMING

Map p249 (☎03-2072 4602; www.chinwoo.org.my; Jln Hang Jebat; swimming adult/child RM5/2; ⏲2-8pm Mon-Fri, 9am-8pm Sat & Sun; 🚉Pasar Seni) This historic sports stadium sits atop a hill overlooking Chinatown.

The highlight here is its 50m outdoor pool. Note that all swimsuits must be tight-fitting, ie no baggy shorts even with an inner mesh lining, and you need a cap as well.

AZIZ MA'AS ART

(☎012-314 0443; a2zstone@yahoo.com; Wariseni, lot 231 Bukit Nanas, Jln Ampang; 3 session courses RM480; Bukit Nanas) This innovative artist has his studio in the Wariseni complex where he teaches courses (three sessions of around three hours each) in traditional and innovative batik, applying the designs to wood and glass as well as fabric. Call or email Aziz to arrange a course.

SIMPLY ENAK FOOD & DRINK

(☎017-287 8929; www.simplyenak.com; tours RM200-250) Daily tours to places such as Chow Kit and Petaling St to experience authentic Malaysian food with resident experts.

FOOD TOUR MALAYSIA FOOD & DRINK

(www.foodtourmalaysia.com; walking/driving tours RM110/160) Expert guides lead these walking tours around some of KL's best street-food and dining destinations. They also offer a full day tour out to the foodie destination of Ipoh, plus food tours in Penang.

Masjid India, Kampung Baru & Northern Kuala Lumpur

Neighbourhood Top Five

❶ **Kampung Baru** (p85) Meandering around the low-rise Malay village in the heart of the high-rise city, where many residents live in traditional wooden houses fronted by flower gardens.

❷ **Titiwangsa Lake Gardens** (p87) Jogging, cycling or strolling around Lake Titiwangsa while admiring the view of the city skyline, or viewing the buildings at eye level on a helicopter tour.

❸ **Masjid India Pasar Malam** (p88) Immersing yourself in the Saturday night market around Masjid India, KL's other Little India.

❹ **Bazaar Baru Chow Kit** (p85) Stimulating your senses at the market and pausing to sample local delicacies.

❺ **National Visual Arts Gallery** (p87) Viewing works by Malaysia's top modern and contemporary artists.

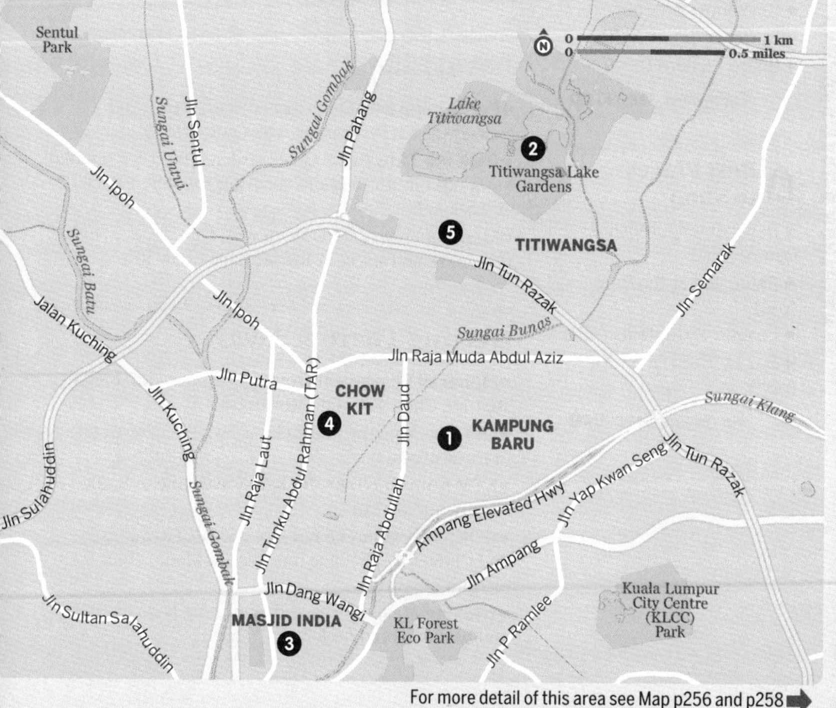

For more detail of this area see Map p256 and p258

Lonely Planet's Top Tip

If you're in town during the Muslim fasting month don't miss the Ramadan street markets in Kampung Baru, where you can buy all manner of tasty delicacies to break the fast. Just remember not to start eating until after sundown.

Best Places to Eat

- Kin Kin (p87)
- Limapulo (p88)
- Ikan Bakar Berempah (p88)
- Yut Kee (p88)
- Capital Café (p88)

For reviews, see p87

Best Places to Drink

- Coliseum Cafe (p90)
- Butter & Beans (p90)
- Bistro Richard (p90)

For reviews, see p90

Best Places to Shop

- Royal Selangor Visitor Centre (p91)
- Peter Hoe at the Row (p91)
- League of Captains (p91)
- Bazaar Baru Chow Kit (p85)

For reviews, see p90

Explore Masjid India, Kampung Baru & Northern Kuala Lumpur

For decades the area around **Masjid India** was known as 'Little India', until, in 2010, Brickfields was dubbed KL's 'official' Little India. But being stripped of its title has done nothing to alter the character of Masjid India, sandwiched between Jln TAR and Jln Munshi Abdullah. Visit during the bustling pasar malam (p88) on Saturday for maximum India-meets-Malaysia atmosphere.

Mostly northeast of Jln Sultan Ismail is **Kampung Baru** (p85), meaning 'new village'. The leafy residential streets are lined with charming wooden houses. It's a lovely area to stroll around, marvelling at the contrast with the skyscrapers of the KLCC and Bukit Bintang in the background.

Spread around the northern end of Jln TAR, **Chow Kit** is named after tin miner and city councillor Loke Chow Kit. The zone's rep for sex and drugs means it can be slightly shady at night, but don't miss it by day for its magnificent wet and dry market and tasty places to eat.

North of here are a couple of green spaces that also merit exploration: **Lake Titiwangsa** for the park (p87) and National Visual Arts Gallery (p87); and **Sentul West** (p87), a redevelopment of railway yards into a gorgeous private park, home to the excellent Kuala Lumpur Performing Arts Centre (p90) and a couple of pleasant places to eat and drink.

Local Life

- **Performing arts** Catch local drama, dance and concerts at KL Performing Arts Centre (p90).
- **Park life** Titiwangsa Lake Gardens (p87) is a popular hang-out for families and courting couples, especially at weekends.
- **Markets** Browse stalls laden with fruit, veggies, meat, fish, herbs and spices at Bazaar Baru Chow Kit.

Getting There & Away

- **Monorail** Convenient stops for this area are Medan Tuanku, Chow Kit and Titiwangsa.
- **LRT** The Ampang and Kelana Jaya lines have stations in these areas.
- **KTM Komuter** Take the Batu Caves line to Bank Negara and Sentul.
- **GOKL City Bus** The red line goes to Titiwangsa and Chow Kit. The blue line goes to Medan Tuanku monorail station.
- **Walking** Masjid India and Kampung Baru are easily and best explored on foot.

SIGHTS

Masjid India & Around

LOKE MANSION HISTORIC BUILDING

Map p256 (03-2691 0803; 273a Jln Medan Tuanku; 9am-5pm Mon-Fri; Medan Tuanku) Rescued from the brink of dereliction by the law firm Cheang & Ariff, Loke Mansion was once the home of self-made tin tycoon Loke Yew. The Japanese high command set up base here in 1942. After years of neglect, the mansion has been beautifully restored; access to the interior is by appointment only, but you're welcome to pause in the driveway and admire the whitewashed exterior any time.

BANK NEGARA MALAYSIA MUSEUM & ART GALLERY MUSEUM

Map p256 (03-9179 2784; www.museum.bnm.gov.my; Sasana Kijang, 2 Jln Dato Onn; 10am-6pm; Bank Negara) FREE This well-designed complex of small museums focuses on banking, finance and money and is not dull in the least. Highlights include a collection of ancient coins and money (and a slick interactive screen to examine their history), a gallery of the bank's private art collection, a surreal 3m-long tunnel lined with RM1 million (in the Children's Gallery), and a history of the Islamic banking system (which must comply with sharia law, including prohibitions against usury). Get a taxi from Bank Negara.

MASJID INDIA MOSQUE

Map p256 (Jln Masjid India; Masjid Jamek) The original wooden mosque that gave the area its name was built in 1883, and replaced by a bulky red-granite tiled modern structure in 1963. It's not much to look at, and you can't go inside, but it's fronted by a busy market and surrounded by stalls selling religious items and traditional Malay costumes. The area's famous Saturday night market (p88) runs along Lg TAR, behind the mosque.

Chow Kit & Kampung Baru

BAZAAR BARU CHOW KIT MARKET

Map p256 (Chow Kit Market; 469-473 Jln TAR; 8am-5pm; Chow Kit) This daily wet-and-sundry market serving the Chinese and Malay working class of Chow Kit may occupy a slick new building and the surrounding alleyways, but it hasn't lost its heady, chaotic atmosphere. Though the stalls are now easier to navigate, you'll find the same hangars loaded with fruit, veggies and freshly butchered meat, with vendors shouting their prices to drum up business.

TATT KHALSA DIWAN GURDWARA SIKH TEMPLE

Map p256 (24 Jln Raja Alang; Chow Kit) FREE This is the largest Sikh temple in Southeast Asia and the spiritual home of KL's 75,000 Sikhs. There's been a temple and school here since 1924, though the present building dates from the 1990s. Visitors are welcome to enter and see the main shrine with a guide but they must wear a headscarf (headwrap for men, which will be provided at the entrance) and pants or a long dress. There's a free vegetarian lunch on Sundays, open to all visitors.

SULTAN SULAIMAN CLUB HISTORIC BUILDING

Map p259 (Bangunan Warisan Kelab Sultan Suleiman; Jln Datuk Abdul Razak; Kampung Baru, Medan Tuanku) Dating back to 1901, this is the oldest Malay club in KL and is said to be where the meetings took place that led to the foundation of the United Malays National Organisation (UMNO; the lead party in the ruling coalition). The original club building was demolished in the late '60s. In 2007 a local architectural firm constructed an exact replica, which is located across from the new club at the back of a field.

HISTORY OF KAMPUNG BARU

Worried about the declining number of Malay residents in the capital, the British set aside 224 hectares of land in the late 1890s – on what was then the outskirts of Kuala Lumpur – as protected Malay agricultural land. Settlers were encouraged to plant crops in this new village: Kampung Baru. In what seems like a miracle in 21st-century KL, Kampung Baru continues to look very much like a Malay village – albeit minus the vegetable patches and rice paddies. This means that alongside well-maintained traditional wooden homes you also have unsightly shanty shacks. Apart from Malays, immigrant Indonesians and Thai Muslims also live here.

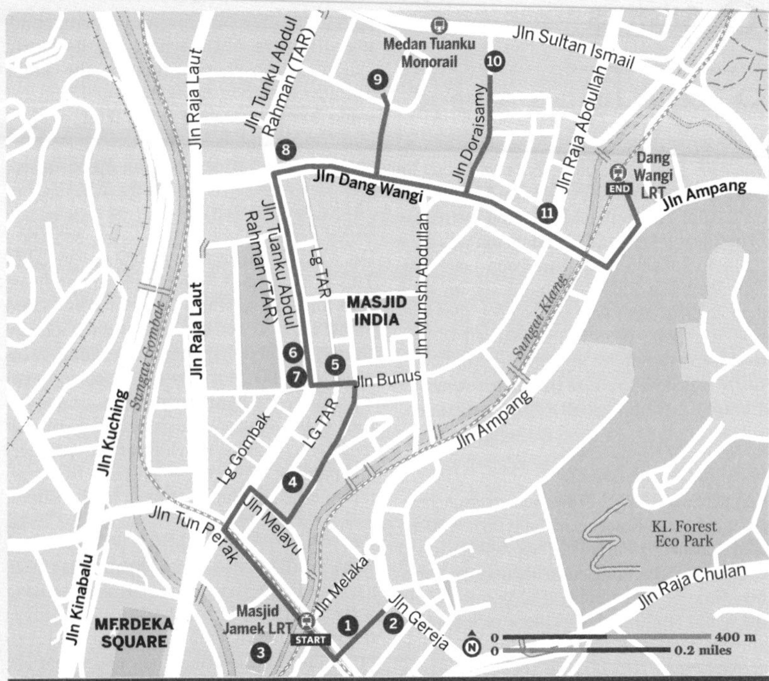

Neighbourhood Walk
Masjid India Ramble

START MASJID JAMEK LRT STATION
END DANG WANGI LRT STATION
LENGTH 1.5KM; 1½ HOURS

From the LRT station walk one block southeast to Lr Ampang. Lined with money changers, Indian cafes and street vendors selling sweets and flower garlands, this street has long been the preserve of the Chettiars from south India. Note the ❶**old shophouses** at Nos 16 to 18 and 24 to 30, and the ceramic peacock tiles on ❷**Chettiar House**.

Return to the station, next to which is the venerable ❸**Masjid Jamek Kampung Baru**. Opposite, Jln Melayu curves around to the covered arcade of market stalls at the pedestrianised end of Jln Masjid India. Pick your way through the tightly packed stalls to find the Indian mosque ❹**Masjid India** (p85). The area is a riot of sari stalls, gold jewellers and DVD and CD shops playing Bollywood soundtracks at full blast. The atmosphere is enhanced on Saturday afternoon when a ❺**night market** (p88) sets up along Lg TAR, the lane sandwiched between Jln TAR and Jln Masjid India.

Next door to the ❻**Coliseum Theatre** (p90), at the south end of Jln TAR, is another colonial relic – the ❼**Coliseum Cafe** (p90), where Somerset Maugham once drank. Stop here for a reviving beer or meal, then continue north along Jln TAR past scores of colourful fabric shops.

An art deco movie house barely recognisable beneath huge banner ads, the ❽**Odeon** is on the corner at the crossroads of Jln Dang Wangi and Jln TAR. Head east along Jln Dang Wangi, taking the first road on the left: on the next corner, opposite the car park, is grand colonial era ❾**Loke Mansion** (p85).

The parallel street to the east is Jln Doraisamy, a strip of restored shophouses turned into bars and restaurants and rebranded ❿**the Row**. Continue down Jln Dang Wangi and turn left on to Jln Kamunting to reach the much-loved *kopitiam* (coffee shop) ⓫**Yut Kee** (p88). Dang Wangi LRT is nearby.

MASJID JAMEK KAMPUNG BARU MOSQUE

Map p259 (http://masjidmjkb.org.my; Jln Raja Alang; 9am-noon, 3-4pm & 5.30-6.30pm; Kampung Baru) FREE Founded in the late 1880s, this is Kampung Baru's principal mosque; it has recently been expanded and sports a handsome gateway decorated with eye-catching tiles in traditional Islamic patterns. Entry is permitted outside of prayer times, as long as you are respectfully attired.

Stalls around the mosque sell religious paraphernalia, including white *kopia* and black songkok, the traditional head coverings for Malay Muslim men. Outside the mosque, look for the map that shows the seven smaller villages that make up Kampung Baru.

Titiwangsa & Sentul

★NATIONAL VISUAL ARTS GALLERY GALLERY

Map p258 (NVAG, Balai Seni Lukis Negara; 03-4026 7000; www.artgallery.gov.my; 2 Jln Temerloh; 10am-6pm; Titiwangsa) FREE Occupying a pyramid-shaped block, the NVAG showcases modern and contemporary Malaysian art, including a variety of temporary shows of local and regional artists, as well as a permanent collection of 4000 pieces in which you'll find paintings by Zulkifli Moh'd Dahalan, Wong Hoy Cheong, Ahmad Fuad Osman and renowned batik artist Chuah Thean Teng. On the ground floor, the National Portrait Gallery hosts regularly changing exhibitions.

The interior is dominated by a swirly Guggenheim Museum–style staircase that provides access to the main galleries. The side staircases are also used to showcase artworks.

★TITIWANGSA LAKE GARDENS PARK

Map p258 (Taman Tasik Titiwangsa; Jln Tembeling; Titiwangsa) For a postcard-perfect view of the city skyline, head to Lake Titiwangsa and the relaxing tree-filled park that surrounds it. If you're feeling energetic, hire a motor boat (p91), go for a jog, hire a bike, play some tennis or even go for a spin in a helicopter (p91). The park is a favourite spot for courting Malaysian couples. It's a 10-minute walk east of the monorail station.

SENTUL WEST PARK

(Jln Strachan; Sentul) On the western edge of the city the industrial and natural heritage of an old railway depot and workshop was transformed into a park called Sentul West. The back half is exclusively for residents, but anyone can wander the leafy grounds and photograph the ageing brick shops and warehouses. The KL Performing Arts Centre (p90) is also here, and around a pretty lake you'll find several restaurants and cafes with decks for taking in the bucolic scene.

EATING

Masjid India

★KIN KIN CHINESE $

Map p256 (40 Jln Dewan Sultan Sulaiman; noodles RM7.50; 8am-6.30pm Tue-Sun; Medan Tuanku) This bare-bones shop is famous throughout the city for its chilli *pan mee* (board noodles). These 'dry' noodles, topped with a soft-boiled egg, minced pork, *ikan bilis* (small, deep-fried anchovies),

LOCAL KNOWLEDGE

P RAMLEE MEMORIAL

The brief life of P Ramlee, the charismatic singer, actor and movie director who was Malaysia's biggest star in the 1950s, is chronicled at the **P Ramlee Memorial** (Pustaka Peringatan P Ramlee; www.arkib.gov.my; 2 Jln Dedap, Taman P Ramlee, Setapak; 10am-5pm Tue-Sun, closed noon-3pm Fri; Titiwangsa) FREE, a short taxi ride north of Titiwangsa. The modest bungalow Ramlee shared with his wife, Saloma, has been remodelled to incorporate displays about his 250-plus songs and the 66 movies he starred in, along with personal items such as handwritten lyrics and his piano.

Ramlee may be a legend today, with a road named after him in Kuala Lumpur, but when he died in 1973 from a heart attack aged only 44 he was reportedly penniless, his style of music and movies having gone out of vogue. His final song, and the title of an unmade movie, was *Air Mata di Kuala Lumpur (Tears of Kuala Lumpur)*, its melancholic lyrics reflecting Ramlee's feelings of failure and loss. His grave lies beside that of Saloma in the **Muslim Cemetery** (Map p259; off Jln Ampang; 7am-7pm; Bukit Nanas).

fried onion and a special spicy chilli sauce, are a taste sensation. If you don't eat pork, staff do a version topped with mushrooms.

MASJID INDIA PASAR MALAM HAWKER $
Map p256 (Night Market; Lg Tuanku Abdul Rahman; street food RM5-10; ⏲3pm-midnight Sat; Masjid Jamek) Stalls pack out the length of Lg Tuanku Abdul Rahman, the alley between Jln TAR and Masjid India. Amid the headscarf and T-shirt sellers are plenty of stalls serving excellent Malay, Indian and Chinese snacks and colourful soya- and fruit-based drinks.

CAPITAL CAFÉ MALAYSIAN $
Map p256 (213 Jln TAR; dishes RM4-6; ⏲7.30am-7.30pm Mon-Sat; Bandaraya) Since it opened in 1956, this truly Malaysian cafe has had Chinese, Malays and Indians all working together, cooking up excellent renditions of Malay classics such as mee goreng, *rojak* (salad doused in a peanut-sauce dressing) and satay (only available in the evenings).

YUT KEE CHINESE $
Map p256 (03-2698 8108; 1 Jln Kamunting; meals RM6.50-16; ⏲7.30am-4.30pm Tue-Sun; Medan Tuanku) This beloved *kopitiam* (in business since 1928), run by a father-and-son team and a crew of friendly, efficient staff, serves classic Hainanese and colonial-era food: try the chicken chop, *roti babi* (French toast stuffed with pork) or toast with homemade *kaya* (coconut-cream jam).

★**LIMAPULO** MALAYSIAN $$
Map p256 (03-2698 3268; 50 Jln Doraisamy; mains RM17-45, set lunches RM9.90; ⏲noon-3pm & 6-10pm Mon-Sat; Medan Tuanku) Its tag line is 'baba can cook', baba being genial Uncle John who is often found greeting guests at this atmospheric and justly popular restaurant. The Nonya-style cooking is very homely, with dishes such as *ayam pong teh* (a chicken stew) and shrimp and petai beans cooked in sambal. The set lunches are good value.

SARAVANA BHAVAN INDIAN $$
Map p256 (03-2698 3293; www.saravanabhavan.com; Selangor Mansion, Jln Masjid India; meals RM10-20; ⏲8am-10.30pm; ; Masjid Jamek) This global chain offers some of the best-quality Indian food you'll find in KL. Their banana-leaf and mini-tiffin feasts are supremely tasty and you can also sample southern Indian classics such as *masala dosa* (rice-and-lentil crepe stuffed with spiced potatoes).

Chow Kit & Kampung Baru

★**IKAN BAKAR BEREMPAH** HAWKER $
Map p259 (Jln Raja Muda Musa; mains RM5-10; ⏲7am-10pm; Kampung Baru) This excellent barbecued-fish stall sits within a hawker-stall market covered by a zinc roof and is one of the best places to eat in Kampung Baru. Pick your fish off the grill and add *kampung*-style side dishes to it off the long buffet.

KAK SOM MALAYSIAN $
Map p259 (Jln Raja Muda Musa; meals RM10-15; ⏲8am-3am; Kampung Baru) Specialising in east coast Peninsular Malaysian dishes such as *nasi kerabu* (blue rice), this is a good place to dine inexpensively on the main Kampung Baru restaurant strip. Take your rice and pick of items from the buffet along with rice and the waitstaff will come to take a drink order and tally up your bill.

MUNGO JERRY CHINESE $
Map p256 (292 Jln Raja Laut; dishes RM8-12; ⏲6pm-2.30am; Sultan Ismail) This late-night supper hotspot on the edge of Chow Kit is a bare-bones joint famous for its thicker take on *bak kut teh* (chilli-infused pork curry stew), as well as for the original version.

Titiwangsa & Sentul

D'ISTANA JALAMAS CAFÉ MALAYSIAN $
Map p258 (Jln Tun Razak; mains RM5-10; ⏲7am-8pm Mon-Fri; Titiwangsa, Titiwangsa) A good eating option in the Titiwangsa area, this cafe at Istana Budaya (p90), the national theatre, offers an appealing serve-yourself buffet of Malay and *mamak* (Indian Muslim) favourites such as fish-head curry, as well as salads, snacks and fresh fruit. Try the local coffee: it's filtered here and not simply a powdered mix. Balcony seats are shaded by trees.

SAMIRA THAI $$
(03-4042 3880; www.samiraasianterrace.com; Sentul Park, Jln Strachan; mains RM20-90; ⏲noon-3.30pm & 6-10.30pm Mon-Fri, noon-10.30pm Sat & Sun; Sentul) Overlooking the koi pond and lake at Sentul Park, and very romantic at night when lit by flickering candles, Samira serves good Thai and Vietnamese food. Can get booked up in advance when there is a show on at the nearby KL Performing Arts Centre.

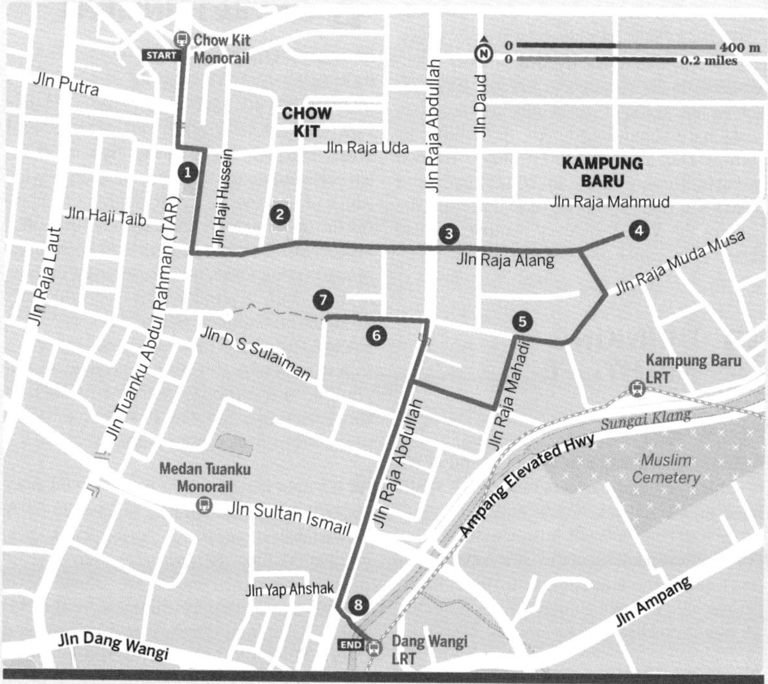

Neighbourhood Walk
Architecture of Chow Kit & Kampung Baru

START CHOW KIT MONORAIL STATION
END DANG WANGI LRT STATION
LENGTH 3.5KM; TWO HOURS

From Chow Kit station, walk south along Jln TAR and cross over to the entrance to **1 Bazaar Baru Chow Kit** (p85). Explore the market's shaded alleys and hangars, pausing for a snack or a drink along the way. Emerge, blinking into the bright light, on Jln Raja Alang, heading east to the Sikh temple **2 Tatt Khalsa Diwan Gurdwara** (p85). Visitors are welcome to go inside to see the prayer hall or stop for a free cup of tea or simple meal in the canteen. Further along is **3 Masjid Jamek Kampung Baru** (p87), the area's principal mosque.

Where Jln Raja Alang turns south, continue on the smaller road ahead to the end where you'll turn right at a two-level apartment block: **4 two palms** in a small field perfectly frame the Petronas Towers. Continue south past the site of the former Saturday night market where a flash new residential skyscraper is under construction.

At the junction of Jln Raja Muda Musa and Jln Raja Mahadi stands a photogenic **5 turquoise and white painted house** dating from 1931; explore Jln Raja Mahadi and the cross streets to see more such traditional wooden houses. Cross Jln Raja Abdullah to Jln Datuk Abdul Razak. At the end of a playing field is the handsome black-and-white painted reconstruction of the original **6 Sultan Sulaiman Club** (p85). Continue west along Jln Datuk Abdul Razak, stopping at the corner to look at **7 Master Mat's house,** a handsome blue home built in 1921 by a former school headmaster. Look for the coconut trees in the garden; the family planted one for each child. Turn left and continue past the new Sultan Sulaiman Club building.

South along Jln Raja Abdullah, off to the left, you'll pass more wooden homes as the concrete city starts to resume. Just before the end of this walk, at the footbridge across to Dang Wangi LRT station, look carefully for one more **8 wooden yellow house**.

TOMMY LE BAKER — BAKERY $$

(☎03-4043 2546; www.tommylebaker.wordpress.com; A-1-3A Viva Residency, 378 Jln Ipoh; sandwiches RM16-26; ⏲8am-6pm Tue-Sun; Sentul) You're not going to meet anyone in KL as passionate about sourdough and baking as Tommy Lee, aka Tommy Le Baker. Trained in Paris, Tommy bakes amazing breads and pastries at this tiny outlet tucked around the back of the Viva Residency complex. It also serves good coffee and hearty sandwiches.

DRINKING & NIGHTLIFE

COLISEUM CAFE — BAR

Map p256 (www.coliseum1921.com; 100 Jln TAR; ⏲10am-10pm; Masjid Jamek) The kind of bar in which colonial planters and clerks would have knocked back stouts and G&Ts, this retro watering hole (in business since 1921) oozes nostalgia. It's worth visiting even if you don't eat at the adjoining grill room, where little seems to have changed since Somerset Maugham tucked into its sizzling steaks.

BUTTER & BEANS — CAFE

Map p256 (☎03-2060 2177; www.facebook.com/butterbeans.my; 42 Jln Doraisamy; ⏲7.30am-11pm Mon-Fri, 9.30am-11pm Sat & Sun; Medan Tuanku) Jln Doraisamy's reinvention as the Row has thrown up a few cool cafes and restaurants to hang out in, including this one, handy for cold-brew coffee and other drinks. Next door is Slate, a space where events and music performances are held.

BISTRO RICHARD — BAR

(☎03-4041 3277; www.bistrorichard.com; Lot 268 Jln Strachan; ⏲5-11pm Tue-Fri, noon-11pm Sat & Sun; ; Sentul) A French-style cafe-bar, complete with checked red tablecloths, in the surrounds of a Japanese Zen rock garden is slightly culturally confusing. Nonetheless, it's a very pleasant place for a drink, whether or not you happen to be attending a show at adjacent KL Performing Arts Centre .

ENTERTAINMENT

★KUALA LUMPUR PERFORMING ARTS CENTRE — PERFORMING ARTS

(KLPAC; ☎03-4047 9000; www.klpac.org; Sentul Park, Jln Strachan; Sentul) Part of the Sentul West regeneration project, this modernist performing-arts complex puts on a wide range of progressive theatrical events including dramas, musicals and dance. Also on offer are performing-arts courses and screenings of art-house movies (noncensored). Combine a show with a stroll in the peaceful leafy grounds and dinner. Sentul Park is 2.5km west of Titiwangsa Lake Gardens.

A variety of performing-arts courses – including in traditional instruments such as those used in a gamelan (traditional Malay orchestra) – are on offer here.

★ISTANA BUDAYA — PERFORMING ARTS

Map p258 (National Theatre; ☎03-4026 5555; www.istanabudaya.gov.my; Jln Tun Razak; tickets RM100-300; Titiwangsa) Large-scale drama and dance shows are staged here, as well as music performances by the National Symphony Orchestra and National Choir. The building's soaring roof is based on a traditional Malay floral decoration of betel leaves, while the columned interior invokes a provincial colonialism. There's a dress code of no shorts and no short-sleeved shirts.

SUTRA DANCE THEATRE — DANCE

Map p258 (☎03-4021 1092; www.sutrafoundation.org.my; 12 Persiaran Titiwangsa 3; Titiwangsa) The home of Malaysian dance legend Ramli Ibrahim has been turned into a showcase for Indian classical dance as well as a dance studio, painting and photography gallery and cultural centre near Lake Titiwangsa. See the website for upcoming events. Also offers courses in Odissi and other forms of classical Indian dance.

COLISEUM THEATRE — CINEMA

Map p256 (94 Jln TAR; Masjid Jamek) One of KL's oldest still-functioning cinemas, this art deco–style building dates back to 1920 and screens Tamil and other Indian-language movies.

WORTH A DETOUR

ROYAL SELANGOR VISITOR CENTRE

Located 8km northeast of the city centre, the **Royal Selangor Visitor Centre** (☎03-4145 6122; www.royalselangor.com/visitor-centre; 4 Jln Usahawan 6, Setapak Jaya; ⊙9am-5pm; Wangsa Maju) is the main factory of the world's largest pewter manufacturer. For sale in the centre's galleries are some very appealing souvenirs made from this malleable alloy of lead and silver, as well as the company's silver pieces under the Comyns brand and its Selberam jewellery.

You can tour the factory and sign up for a **pewtersmithing workshop** (30min class RM63.60, 60min class RM159). Try your hand at creating a pewter dish at the **School of Hard Knocks** or designing and making your own jewellery at **the Foundry**. The centre is fronted by a nearly 2m-tall pewter tankard and has an appealing cafe. If you don't make it out here, Selangor's products are sold at its retail outlets in Kuala Lumpur's malls, including Suria KLCC (p65) and Pavilion KL (p63).

SHOPPING

PETER HOE AT THE ROW — HOMEWARES

(☎012-334 7123; Lot 56-1, 1st fl, the Row, Jln Doraisamy; ⊙10am-7pm; Medan Tuanku) Peter Hoe's explosively colourful and creative emporium is a KL institution and is looking better than ever in its new digs at the Row. It stocks all manner of original fabric products, such as tablecloths, cushions and robes (many handprinted in India directly for Peter Hoe), as well as woven baskets, lanterns, silverware, candles and knickknacks galore. There's also an excellent cafe.

★LEAGUE OF CAPTAINS — FASHION & ACCESSORIES

Map p256 (www.facebook.com/leagueofcaptains; Lot 42-50 the Row, Jln Doraisamy; ⊙boutique noon-9pm; Medan Tuanku) T-shirts and caps by local label Pestle & Mortar Clothing and accessories by other hip young designers are artfully displayed at this boutique. It doubles as a cafe selling excellent coffee, homemade cakes and beef rendang pie.

RATTAN ART ENTERPRISES — ARTS & CRAFTS

Map p256 (☎017-622 2530; www.gekguan.com; 343 Jln Tuanku Abdul Rahman; ⊙10am-6pm Mon-Sat, to 4pm Sun; Medan Tuanku) Handmade rattan rocking chairs, baskets, bags and mats.

SEMUA HOUSE — DEPARTMENT STORE

Map p256 (cnr Jln Masjid India & Jln Bunus 6; ⊙10am-10pm; Masjid Jamek) Two floors of Indian wedding shops can be found at this department store, right in the heart of Masjid India and the Saturday night *pasar malam*.

SPORTS & ACTIVITIES

KAMPUNG BARU WALKING TOUR — WALKING

Map p258 (Jalan-Jalan at Kampung Baru; ☎03-2698 0332; www.visitkl.gov.my/visitklv2; ⊙4.15-7.15pm Tue, Thu & Sun; Medan Tuanku) FREE This free walking tour from Visit KL (p228) takes you into the heart of the traditional Malay village at the centre of a modern metropolis. The route takes in not only the neighbourhood sights – the Masjid Jamek (p87), Sultan Sulaiman Club (p85) and beautiful old wooden houses – but also traditional shops, popular dishes and food venues, and Malay customs. Tours start at the Sultan Sulaiman Club. Dress conservatively and bring an umbrella.

KL SKY TOUR — SCENIC FLIGHTS

Map p258 (☎019-258 6818; www.cempaka.com.my; Titiwangsa Helipad, Titiwangsa Lake Gardens; 6/15/30/45min tours for up to 3 people RM600/1500/3000/4500; ⊙10am-6pm; Titiwangsa) Departing from a helipad on the edge of Titiwangsa Lake, KL's new helicopter tours allow you to swing between the city's skyscrapers in style. A six-minute whizz around the lake gardens will cost you RM600 for up to three people; for the 15-minute tour (RM1500) you'll get as far as Batu Caves. Flights are weather dependent.

TUBESTER — BOATING

Map p258 (☎03-7733 4181; www.tubesterinc.com; Titiwangsa Lake Gardens; 20-min rides adult/child RM35/25; ⊙10am-7pm Tue-Fri, 9am-7.30pm Sat & Sun; Titiwangsa) Get taken for a 20-minute spin on the lake with a Tubester boater, or hire one of the six- or 10-seater motorboats and sail it yourself (from RM60 for 30 minutes). Life jackets are provided.

Lake Gardens, Brickfields & Bangsar

Neighborhood Top Five

❶ **Islamic Arts Museum** (p94) Admiring the beautiful objects and artworks gathered from around the world in this top-class museum, which occupies an impressive building embellished with decorative domes and mosaic tiles.

❷ **Tun Abdul Razak Heritage Park** (p95) Strolling the leafy gardens and visiting the the KL Bird Park.

❸ **Buddhist Maha Vihara** (p101) Exploring this peaceful complex of Buddhist temples and the neighbouring places of worship in Brickfields.

❹ **Thean Hou Temple** (p97) Marvelling at the architectural detail and the views from its elevated terraces.

❺ **Bangsar** (p99) Sampling some of KL's top food and fashion picks, and relaxing over a coffee or cocktail in Bangsar Baru.

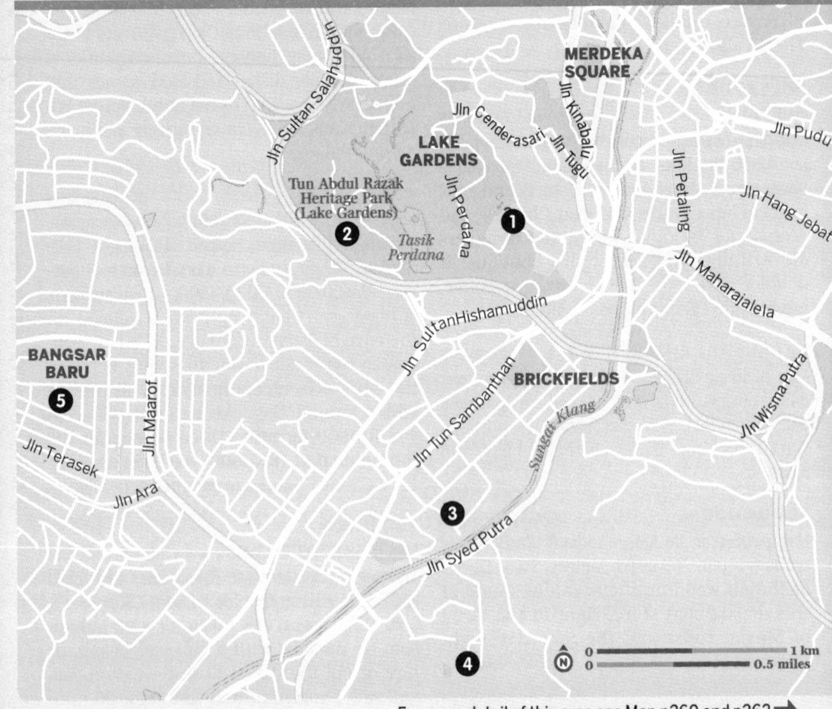

For more detail of this area see Map p260 and p262

Explore Lake Gardens, Brickfields & Bangsar

The Lake Gardens were created in the late 19th century as an urban retreat for the colonial Brits to escape the hurly-burly of downtown. Now named the Tun Abdul Razak Heritage Park after Malaysia's second prime minister, this lush, landscaped area continues to act as KL's green relaxation zone and includes three museums, six themed parks and other monuments and sights.

Following devastating fires in the late 19th century, KL's colonial administration decreed that bricks would henceforth be used to construct the city's buildings. The area where they were manufactured became known as Brickfields. Many Indian labourers, mainly Tamils from southern India and Sri Lanka, settled here, giving the area its still-predominant Indian atmosphere – that's why it's KL's official Little India. However, in this ethnically diverse suburb you'll also find a Chinese temple and various Christian churches alongside the Hindu and Buddhist shrines. All are overshadowed by the skyscrapers of KL Sentral, the city's transportation hub, around which several new shopping complexes and offices towers have sprouted.

To the south ripple the green hills that are home to KL's main Chinese Cemetery as well as the spectacular Thean Hou Temple and the old Istana Negara, now the Royal Museum. North of here is Bangsar, a century ago a rubber plantation, now an upscale residential area of luxury bungalows and condominiums. Its commercial hub, Bangsar Baru, is one of KL's most pleasant places to eat and shop.

Local Life

- **Malls** Browse the shops at Mid Valley Megamall (p108), Bangsar Village (p109) or Bangsar Shopping Centre (p111).
- **Markets** Go grocery shopping and enjoy great hawker food at the Bangsar Sunday Market (p104).
- **Drumming** Join the Tugu Drum Circle (p111) as they bang out some beats near the National Monument.

Getting There & Away

- **Train, monorail and LRT** KL Sentral is close to both Brickfields and the Tun Abdul Razak Heritage Park; Bank Rakyat-Bangsar is one stop southwest on the LRT.
- **Walking** Tun Abdul Razak Heritage Park can easily be accessed by foot from Chinatown.
- **Bus** The KL Hop-On-Hop-Off bus stops at Masjid Negara, KL Bird Park, the National Monument and the National Museum. The GOKL free city bus red line stops at KL Sentral, Masjid Negara and the National Museum.
- **Bicycle** Pedal around the Lake Gardens area with a rental bike from KL By Cycle (p220).

Lonely Planet's Top Tip

The Tun Abdul Razak Heritage Park is huge, and in KL's heat and humidity getting to and from the sights can be a slog. The free GOKL city bus red line links KL Sentral with Masjid Negara, the National Museum and Merdeka Sq.

Best Places to Eat

- Rebung (p102)
- Restoran Yarl (p103)
- Lawanya Food Corner (p103)
- Ganga Cafe (p106)
- Jaslyn Cakes (p104)

For reviews, see p102

Best Places to Drink

- Coley (p106)
- Mantra Bar KL (p106)
- Mai Bar (p106)
- Pulp by Papa Palheta (p106)
- Ril's Bangsar (p106)
- Sino The Bar Upstairs (p107)

For reviews, see p106

Best Places to Shop

- Thisappear (p109)
- Shoes Shoes Shoes (p109)
- d.d.collective (p109)
- DR.Inc (p109)
- Lonely Dream (p109)
- Fabspy (p108)

For reviews, see p107

ALIZADA STUDIOS/SHUTTERSTOCK ©

TOP SIGHT
ISLAMIC ARTS MUSEUM

On the southern edge of the Tun Abdul Razak Heritage Park, this outstanding museum houses one of best collections of OLD decorative arts in the world. Aside from the quality of the exhibits, which include fabulous textiles, jewellery, calligraphy-inscribed pottery and scale architectural models, the building itself is a stunner, with beautifully decorated domes and glazed tile work on its facade.

The Galleries

Spread over four levels, the museum has 12 permanent galleries and two galleries for special exhibitions. Start on the 3rd floor in the **Architecture Gallery**, which has scale models of important Islamic buildings, including Islam's holiest mosque, the Masjid al-Haram in Mecca. There's also a re-creation of a mosque interior. On the same floor, in the **Quran and Manuscripts Gallery**, look for the 19th-century Qurans from Malaysia's east coast decorated in red, gold and black, as well as a full *kiswah* (an embroidered door panel from the holy Kaaba in Mecca). Other highlights include the **Ottoman Room**, a magnificent reconstruction of an 1820s decorative room from Syria; **Chinese calligraphy scrolls**; the weft silk ikat **limar**, a fabric patterned with Islamic calligraphy and no longer made as the tradition has died out; and **Uzbek pectoral plates**.

DON'T MISS...

- Ottoman Room
- Architecture Gallery
- Quran & Manuscripts Gallery
- China Gallery
- Textiles Gallery
- Gift Shop

PRACTICALITIES

- Muzium Kesenian Islam Malaysia
- Map p260
- 03-2092 7070
- www.iamm.org.my
- Jln Lembah Perdana
- adult/child RM14/7
- 10am-6pm
- Kuala Lumpur

The Museum Building

Flooded with natural light, the Islamic Arts Museum is a contemporary building with airy, open spaces and wall-to-ceiling glass. The vaulted, *iwan*-style entrance resembles a ceramic tapestry and is inscribed with verses from the Quran. Iranian artisans were contracted to tile the turquoise domes on the museum roof, while the building's striking internal inverted domes were constructed by craftspeople from Uzbekistan.

TOP SIGHT
TUN ABDUL RAZAK HERITAGE PARK

Covering 173 hectares, KL's major recreational park is better known by its colonial moniker of the Lake Gardens. Ranging over undulating, landscaped hills, it's a park with something for everyone, the main attractions being the KL Bird Park and Perdana Botanical Garden. The Islamic Arts Museum, National Museum (p98), Masjid Negara (p99) and National Monument also fall within the park's boundaries.

Park History

In 1888 Alfred Venning, Selangor State Treasurer, secured permission from British Resident Frank Swettenham to create a botanical garden around the small stream Sungai Bras Bras. It took more than a decade to clear and landscape the area, which today stretches from Parliament House to the National Museum. The stream was dammed to give the park Sydney Lake (Tasik Perdana) – hence the name Lake Gardens. In 2011 the park was renamed after Abdul Razak, Malaysia's second prime minister (1970–76). Abdul Razak lived in a house in the park between 1962, when he was deputy PM, and 1976, when he died; the home is now the Memorial Tun Abdul Razak (p99) museum.

KL Bird Park

This fabulous 21-hectare **aviary** (Map p260; ☎03-2272 1010; www.klbirdpark.com; Jln Cenderawasih; adult/child RM50/41; ⏲9am-6pm; 👪; 🚆Kuala Lumpur) houses some 3000 birds comprising 200 species of (mostly) Asian birds. The park is divided into four sections: in the first two, birds fly freely beneath an enormous canopy. Section three features the native hornbills (so-called because of their enormous beaks), while section four offers the less-edifying spectacle of caged species. Feeding times are scattered throughout the day (see the website for times) and there are bird shows at 12.30pm and 3.30pm.

DON'T MISS...

- KL Bird Park
- Perdana Botanical Garden
- KL Butterfly Park
- Royal Malaysia Police Museum

PRACTICALITIES

- Lake Gardens
- Map p260
- www.visitkl.gov.my
- ⏲7am-8pm
- 🚆Kuala Lumpur

EATING IN THE PARK

Bird Park's Hornbill Restaurant (p102)offers Western and Malay staples, best enjoyed (with the free-flying fowl) on the wood deck overlooking the park.

For local food, try the hawker stalls at Kompleks Makan Tanglin (p102).

The KL Hop-On-Hop-Off bus stops at Masjid Negara, KL Bird Park, the National Monument and the National Museum, and the GOKL free city bus red line stops at KL Sentral, Masjid Negara and the National Museum.

TOP TIPS

Rent bicycles (as well as a helmet and lock) and pick up a route map from KL By Cycle (p220). Take care crossing busy roads at the start of the route.

A hop-on, hop-off electric tram (RM4) shuttles around the park's major attractions from 9.30am to 5pm daily.

Pick up a map of the Perdana Botanical Garden at the information booth.

Perdana Botanical Garden & Around

The vast Perdana Botanical Garden showcases a wide variety of native and introduced plants with sections dedicated to ferns, rare trees, trees that have lent their names to places in Malaysia, medicinal herbs, aquatic plants and so on. The gardens are well laid out with gazebos and boardwalks (be careful of rotten wood that might break underfoot), but there is only limited signage to identify the plants.

The **Hibiscus** (Taman Bunga Raya; Map p260; Jln Cenderawasih; 9am-6.30pm; Kuala Lumpur) FREE and **Orchid** (Taman Orkid; Map p260; Jln Cenderawasih; Sat & Sun RM1, Mon-Fri free; 9am-6pm; Kuala Lumpur) gardens are adjacent to the Botanical Garden. Among the 800-odd species of orchid are Vandas and exotic hybrids.

Other Attractions

A short walk north of the KL Bird Park is the **KL Butterfly Park** (Taman Rama Rama; Map p260; 03-2693 4799; www.klbutterflypark.com; Jln Cenderasari; adult/child RM22/11; 9am-6pm; Kuala Lumpur). Among the 101 different species of colourful butterflies fluttering around the covered grounds are some real monsters, and there's a bug gallery where you can shudder at the size of Malaysia's giant centipedes and spiders.

Between the Islamic Arts Museum and the planetarium is the surprisingly interesting **Royal Malaysia Police Museum** (Map p260; 5 Jln Perdana; 10am-6pm Tue-Sun, closed 12.30-2.30pm Fri; Kuala Lumpur) FREE, where the standout display is a gallery of weapons, from handmade guns and knives to automatic weapons, and from hand grenades to swords, all seized from members of criminal 'secret societies' and communists during the Emergency.

National Monument

At the northern end of the park, across Jln Parlimen, an impressive **monument** (Tugu Negara; Map p260; Plaza Tugu Negara, Jln Parlimen; 7am-6pm; Masjid Jamek) FREE commemorates the defeat of the communists in 1950 and provides fine views across the park and city. The giant militaristic bronze sculpture was created in 1966 by Felix de Weldon, the artist behind the Iwo Jima monument in Washington, DC, and is framed beautifully by an azure reflecting pool and graceful curved pavilion. Nearby is a cenotaph to the Malay fighters who died in WWI and WWII.

IHOR PASTERNAK/SHUTTERSTOCK ©

TOP SIGHT
THEAN HOU TEMPLE

Sitting atop Robson Heights, this imposing, multilayered Chinese temple is one of the most visually impressive in Malaysia. Dedicated to the heavenly mother, Thean Hou, it provides wonderful views of KL and is a great place to visit on a Buddhist festival such as Wesak Day or during Chinese New Year.

History & Design

The temple was officially opened in 1989 and cost the Selangor and Federal Territory Hainan Association RM7 million to build. You can see pretty much every ringgit in its rich architectural detail, which includes decorative balustrades, beams, eaves, murals, and flying dragons and phoenixes. Arranged on four levels, the temple is fronted by a **statue of Thean Hou** beside a wishing well and a garden studded with large statues of the **signs of the Chinese zodiac**. On the ground floor there are souvenir stalls, a canteen and a marriage registration office – this is a very popular spot for weddings. The 1st floor has a large hall where religious and cultural events are held while the 2nd has the temple's administrative offices.

Main Prayer Hall

Thean Hou's statue takes centre stage in the main hall on the 3rd floor with Kuan Yin (the Buddhist goddess of mercy) on her right and Shuiwei Shengniang (goddess of the waterfront) to her left. Smaller statues of Milefo (the laughing Buddha), Weituo and Guandi contribute to this Taoist–Buddhist hotchpotch. Climb to the terrace above for wonderful views and then go back down behind the temple past a medicinal herb garden and a pond packed with tortoises.

DON'T MISS...

- Main prayer hall
- Chinese zodiac statues
- Rooftop terrace

PRACTICALITIES

- Map p260
- 03-2274 7088
- www.hainannet.com.my/en
- off Jln Syed Putra
- admission free
- 8am-10pm
- Tun Sambanthan

TOP SIGHT
NATIONAL MUSEUM

This museum offers a rich look at Malaysian history, with four main galleries covering everything from the formation of the rainforest through to Malaysia today. The best exhibits are Early History, with artefacts from Neolithic and Bronze Age cultures; and the Malay Kingdoms, which highlights the rise of Islamic kingdoms in the Malay Archipelago. Note that the museum may close for renovations in 2017.

The Main Building

The four main galleries are housed in a building with a distinctive Minangkabau-style roof. Flanking the main entrance are a pair of giant friezes, designed by Cheong Lai Tong and made of Italian mosaic glass, depicting scenes from Malaysian life and history.

Apart from the Early History and Malay Kingdoms galleries, the **Colonial Era** gallery has exhibits from the Portuguese through to the Japanese occupation; and **Malaysia Today** charts the country's post-WWII development. Free museum tours are offered at 11am Monday to Saturday and again at 2pm on Thursday.

Other Galleries

Outside the main building, there's a section with a regularly changing exhibition; two excellent small permanent galleries – the **Museum of Malay World Ethnology** (Map p260; ☎03-2267 1000; www.jmm.gov.my; Jln Damansara; adult/child RM5/2; ⏲9am-6pm; 🚉KL Sentral) with displays on Malay musical instruments, games, textiles and metalwork; and the **Orang Asli Craft Museum** (Map p260; ☎03-2282 6255; www.jmm.gov.my; Jln Damansara; adult/child RM5/2; ⏲9am-6pm; 🚉KL Sentral) with wood carvings and masks produced by the Mah Meri and Jah Hut peoples – both covered by a joint entry ticket; a gorgeous traditional raised house; and ancient burial poles from Sarawak.

DON'T MISS...

- Guided tours
- Exterior friezes
- Orang Asli Craft Museum
- Museum of Malay World Ethnology

PRACTICALITIES

- Muzium Negara
- Map p260, C4
- ☎03-2282 6255
- www.muziumnegara.gov.my
- Jln Damansara
- adult/child RM5/2
- ⏲9am-6pm
- 🚉KL Sentral

SIGHTS

Lake Gardens

ISLAMIC ARTS MUSEUM MUSEUM

See p94.

TUN ABDUL RAZAK HERITAGE PARK PARK

See p95.

NATIONAL MUSEUM MUSEUM

See p98.

MASJID NEGARA MOSQUE

Map p260 (National Mosque; www.masjidnegara.gov.my; Jln Lembah Perdana; 9am-noon, 3-4pm & 5.30-6.30pm, closed Fri morning; Kuala Lumpur) FREE The main place of worship for KL's Malay Muslim population is this gigantic 1960s mosque, inspired by Mecca's Masjid al-Haram. Able to accommodate 15,000 worshippers, it has an umbrella-like blue-tile roof with 18 points symbolising the 13 states of Malaysia and the five pillars of Islam. Rising above the mosque, a 74m-high minaret issues the call to prayer, which can be heard across Chinatown. Non-Muslims are welcome to visit outside prayer times; robes are available for those who are not dressed appropriately.

NATIONAL PLANETARIUM PLANETARIUM

Map p260 (03-2273 4301; http://planetarium.angkasa.gov.my; 53 Jln Perdana; gallery free, planetarium adult/child RM12/8; 9am-4.30pm Tue-Sun; Kuala Lumpur) Part of the National Space Agency, the planetarium offers shows in the Space Theatre throughout the day. It has an observation deck (for looking at KL) and a space observatory, and in the grounds are small-scale models of famous historic observatories such as Stonehenge. Parts of the rocket that launched Malaysia's first satellite are displayed in the main gallery.

MEMORIAL TUN ABDUL RAZAK MUSEUM

Map p260 (www.arkib.gov.my/memorial-tun-abdul-razak; Jln Perdana; 10am-5.30pm Tue-Sun, closed noon-3pm Fri; Kuala Lumpur) FREE The house where Tun Abdul Razak lived while serving as Malaysia's second prime minister has been turned into a memorial museum displaying his personal effects, speedboat and golf cart. Upstairs you can see the bedroom where Tun Abdul Razak's son Najib, the current prime minister of Malaysia, sometimes stayed.

Behind the museum is Rumah Felda, a small wooden house in the style of those built to provide rural housing during Tun Abdul Razak's premiership.

OLD KL TRAIN STATION HISTORIC BUILDING

Map p260 (Jln Sultan Hishamuddin; Kuala Lumpur) One of KL's most distinctive colonial buildings, this 1910 train station (replaced as a transit hub by KL Sentral in 2001) is a grand if ageing structure designed by British architect AB Hubback in the Mogul (or Indo-Saracenic) style. The building's walls are white plaster, rows of keyhole and horseshoe arches provide ventilation on each level, and large *chatri* (elevated pavilions) and onion domes adorn the roof.

Note that only KTM Komuter trains still stop here. Across from the station is the **Malayan Railway Administration Building** (Jln Sultan Hishamuddin; Kuala Lumpur), opened in 1917 and another beautiful Indo-Saracenic piece of architecture.

Brickfields, Bangsar & Around

THEAN HOU TEMPLE TEMPLE

See p97.

ROYAL MUSEUM MUSEUM

Map p260 (Muzium Diraja; www.jmm.gov.my; Jln Istana; adult/child RM10/5; 9am-5pm; Tun Sambanthan) With the 2011 opening of the new RM800 million Istana Negara (National Palace; official residence of Malaysia's head of state) in the city's north, the former palace became the Royal Museum. You can tour the first two floors of the mansion, originally built as a family home in 1928 by Chinese tin tycoon Chan Wing. The palace exterior, with its eclectic European style, looks much the same as it did in Chan Wing's day.

Used as the Japanese military's officers' mess during KL's WWII occupation, in 1957 it became the National Palace, the residence of the king and queen of Malaysia. The interior was obviously altered to suit both royal tastes and royal needs. There are major and minor waiting rooms, a small throne room (for royal events), an office for the king, a family room (including KTV), and a dozen or so bedrooms for guests and family alike. Floral wallpaper, upholstered furniture, thick carpets, crystal chandeliers and some gaudy posters reveal the Down-

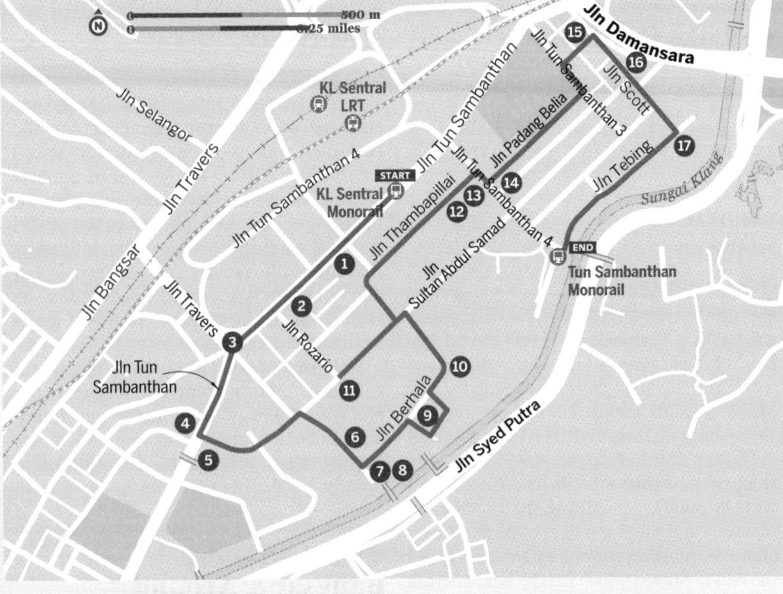

Neighbourhood Walk
Brickfields' Temples & Street Food

START KL SENTRAL MONORAIL STATION
END TUN SAMBANTHAN MONORAIL
LENGTH 3.3KM; TWO HOURS

From the station walk one block west along Jln Tun Sambanthan to the 1 **Ammars**, where you can pick up a lentil *vadai* (fritter, RM1), prepared in a giant wok. Continue on to the 2 **Vivekananda Ashram** (p102), built in 1904 and recently granted heritage status to protect it from developers.

At the next corner, cross the road to see the 3 **Little India Fountain** (p102). Continue along Jln Tun Sambanthan and on the right, follow the scent of jasmine to find an alley of 4 **garland stalls**; where stall holders skilfully weave the brightly coloured flowers into garlands used in religious ceremonies.

Cross Jln Tun Sambanthan. At the corner with Jln Sultan Abdul Samad, look for a series of 5 **murals** depicting the history of Brickfields. Walk down Jln Sultan Abdul Samad, taking the second turning on the right on to Jln Berhala to the 6 **Buddhist Maha Vihara** (p101).

Continue on, passing a traditional Malay wooden house at number 120, to the 7 **Temple of Fine Arts** (p107) on the right. Here you can stop for lunch at 8 **Annalakshmi** (p103). Take the next turn on the right and loop up; on your left, beneath a tree, is the 9 **Sri Maha Kaaliamman shrine**, while opposite it on your right is the 10 **Sri Sakthi Vinayagar Temple** (p102).

Turn right on to Jln Sultan Abdul Samad and at the pedestrian bridge cross over to the 11 **Tamil Lutheran Church**. Backing up, turn right and then right again onto Jln Thambapillai. Stop to look inside the 12 **Sam Kow Tong Chinese Temple** (p101). Pass 13 **Brickfields Pisang Goreng** and the 14 **ABC stall**, sampling the goods on the way, and walk down Jln Padang Belia. Turn left on to Jln Tun Sambanthan 3, and right on to Jln Scott. Follow the road down past the 15 **Wei-Ling Gallery** (p107), 16 **Sree Veera Hanuman Temple** (p102) and Indian sweet stalls to the impressive 17 **Sri Kandaswamy Temple** (p101). From here turn right down Jln Tebing until you reach Tun Sambanthan station.

ton Abbey-meets-'70s-suburbia tastes of the royals, though Malay colours and motifs remind you of where you are. To get here, take a taxi from Tun Sambanthan.

SEKEPING TENGGIRI GALLERY

Map p262 (017-207 5977; www.sekeping.com/tenggiri; 48 Jln Tenggiri, Taman Weng Lock; by appointment; Bank Rakyat-Bangsar) FREE If you're not a guest at the adjoining guesthouse (p131) you'll need to make an appointment to view landscape architect Ng Seksan's superb collection of Malaysian contemporary art, so large that he's turned over a whole house to store and display it. View pieces by top talents including Phuan Thai Meng, Samsudin Wahab, Justin Lim and Rajinder Singh.

SRI KANDASWAMY TEMPLE HINDU TEMPLE

Map p260 (www.srikandaswamykovil.org; 3 Lg Scott; 5.30am-9pm; Tun Sambanthan) FREE This temple, fronted by an elaborate modern *gopura* (gateway), was founded by the Sri Lankan community in 1909 as a place to practise Shaiva Siddhanta, a major Hindu sect popular with the diaspora community. One of the temple's major events (it has many festivals) is the 10-day **Mahotchava Festival** held around May or June, with celebrations including processions of the painted wooden deities. Check the temple's Facebook page (www.facebook.com/SriKandaswamyTemple) for detailed information and schedules.

SAM KOW TONG TEMPLE TEMPLE

Map p260 (16 Jln Thambapillai; 7am-5pm; KL Sentral) FREE Established in 1916 by the Heng Hua clan, the 'three teachings' temple has a beautiful Hokkien-style temple roof, with graceful curving ridgelines that taper at the ends like swallowtails. The colourful rooftop dragons, and other figures, are actually three-dimensional mosaics, another traditional decorative feature of southern Chinese temples (though these are new works). Inside, look for photos of the original temple, a simple timber-frame structure with a thatched roof.

BUDDHIST MAHA VIHARA BUDDHIST TEMPLE

Map p260 (03-2274 1141; www.buddhistmahavihara.org; 123 Jln Berhala; KL Sentral, KL Sentral) Founded in 1894 by Sinhalese settlers, this is one of KL's major Theravada Buddhist temples. It's a particular hive of activity around Wesak Day, the Buddha's birthday, when a massive parade with multiple floats starts from here before winding round the city. Meditation classes take place on Monday and Thursday at 8pm on a by-donation basis.

WORTH A DETOUR

SUNGAI PENCHALA

In the city's far northwest, this sleepy Malay village, nestling in a hilly, jungly landscape, seems a million miles from urban KL, even though it's less than a 30-minute taxi drive from Chinatown. The main reasons to visit, apart from the relaxing atmosphere, are to eat and learn to cook.

A visit to a local market, followed by learning to cook several Malaysian dishes, is the format at **LaZat** (019-238 1198; www.malaysia-klcookingclass.com; Malay House at Penchala Hills, Lot 3196, Jl Seri Penchala, Kampong Sg; RM290; 8.30am-2pm Mon-Sat). Teaching takes place in a traditional Malay house with an open kitchen looking out into the jungle, where you might see silver leaf monkeys scampering by. A different menu is taught on each day of the week, so book your class for a date when the list of dishes appeals.

If cooking isn't your idea of fun, let the chefs do the work and enjoy the exquisite Malay buffet at **Sambal Hijau** (03-7731 2045; www.sambalhijau.my; Lot 2990, Jln Sungai Penchala, Kampung Sungai Penchala; buffet dishes RM1-35; 8am-1am). Here you'll find more than 50 traditional Malay dishes to sample, including *ikan bakar* (barbecued fish) with *sambal hijau* green chilli sauce. The restaurant is also known for its *gulai daging* (beef curry).

On the main road before the turnoff to LaZat, **Subak** (03-7729 9030; www.subak.com.my; Lot 3213, Jln Penchala Indah, Bukit Lanjan; mains RM26-40; 11am-11pm) serves Indonesian, Malaysian and international dishes in a leafy, relaxed setting.

A taxi to Sungai Penchala from KL Sentral takes around 30 minutes and costs RM25.

VIVEKANANDA ASHRAM HISTORIC BUILDING

Map p260 (220 Jln Tun Sambanthan; KL Sentral) This historic ashram, built in 1904 and part of the global Ramakrishna movement, is a well-loved subject for photographers. It offers courses in yoga, as well as various social programs for the underprivileged. After the board of trustees sold the surrounding land, a campaign to save the ashram led to the government granting the building national heritage status in 2016, protecting it from developers.

SRI SAKTHI VINAYAGAR TEMPLE TEMPLE

Map p260 (Jln Berhala; 6am-noon & 5.30-9.30pm; Tun Sambanthan) The original shrine for Lord Vinayagar (the remover of obstacles) in Brickfields was a squatter shack on Jln Sultan Abdul Samad. Such was the humble start of many temples in this immigrant community. It's still rather simple but there is a tender devotional atmosphere to the place, and one statue of Lord Vinayagar inside is made of bananas and brown sugar.

The current temple (in essence an open colonnaded, or hypostyle, gallery) on Jln Berhala is reached via a short staircase from the street.

KWONG TONG CEMETERY CEMETERY

Map p261 (www.ktc.org.my; 8.30am-4.30pm; KL Sentral, KL Sentral) This fascinating cemetery lies directly south of the Royal Museum and is notable not just for its immense size (333 hectares of rolling grassy hills and fragrant frangipani trees) but also for the many notables buried within. These include Kapitan Yap Ah Loy, founder of KL. There are also memorials to WWII dead. Pick up a map at the cemetery office. Take a taxi from KL Sentral.

SREE VEERA HANUMAN TEMPLE HINDU TEMPLE

Map p260 (www.veerahanuman.com; Jln Scott; 7am-9pm; Tun Sambanthan) Honouring Hanuman, this temple has been under reconstruction for years, and should be a striking sight when its *gopura* (gateway) is revealed: the tower rises with the coiled tail of the monkey god. Various puja (special prayer) services happen here – check the website for details.

Don't confuse this temple with the Sri Maha Muneswar to the left or the shrine to Krishna to the right (though both are worth a look, too).

LITTLE INDIA FOUNTAIN FOUNTAIN

Map p260 (cnr Jln Tun Sambanthan & Jln Travers; KL Sentral) This eye-catching fountain is the focal point of KL's official 'Little India'. Symbolic elements in the fountain's design include elephants, swans, lotuses and seven different colours. Flanking the fountain are two abstract metal sculptures of Bharatanatyam dancers created by **Sculpture at Work** (http://sculptureatwork.com).

EATING

Lake Gardens

KOMPLEKS MAKAN TANGLIN HAWKER $

Map p260 (Jln Cenderasari; meals RM5-10; 7am-4pm Mon-Sat; Kuala Lumpur) This small hawker complex up the hill behind Masjid Negara is a popular lunch spot for nearby workers and local families visiting the Tun Abdul Razak Heritage Park. Try the *nasi lemak* (rice boiled in coconut milk, served with fried anchovies and peanuts), Hokkien mee, or *ikan bakar* (grilled fish).

★**REBUNG** MALAYSIAN $$

Map p260 (03-2276 3535; www.restoranrebungdatochefismail.com; 5th fl, 1 Jln Tanglin, Perdana Botanical Garden; buffet lunch/dinner RM42/53; 8am-10pm; Masjid Jamek) Occupying the top level of a multistorey car park overlooking the Botanical Garden, flamboyant celebrity chef Ismail's restaurant Rebung is one of KL's best. The seemingly endless buffet spread is splendid, with all kinds of dishes that you'd typically only be served in a Malay home. Herbs grown on the terrace are used in the recipes. Book ahead at weekends.

Ask staff for help identifying the food: start by loading your plate with rice and then work your way round the spread of vegetable, meat and fish dishes and fiery sambals. Don't miss the additional food stations outside for noodles, barbecued fish and banana fritters. Go hungry! Get a taxi from Masjid Jamek.

HORNBILL RESTAURANT INTERNATIONAL $$

Map p260 (03-2693 8086; www.klbirdpark.com; KL Bird Park, 920 Jln Cenderawasih; mains RM17-30; 9am-7.30pm; Kuala Lumpur) Providing a ringside view of the feathered inhabitants of KL Bird Park, this rustic place offers good food without fleecing the tourists too much. Go local with its *nasi lemak* and fried noodles, or please the kids with fish and chips or the homemade chicken or beef burgers.

COLONIAL CAFE MALAYSIAN $$$

Map p260 (03-2785 8000; www.majestickl.com; Majestic Hotel, 5 Jln Sultan Hishamuddin; mains RM60-170; noon-2.30pm, 3-6pm & 6.30-11pm; Kuala Lumpur) British-Malay cuisine, as interpreted by Hainanese chefs of yore, is on the menu at this elegant restaurant in the heritage wing of the Majestic, probably the best spot in KL to feel the privilege and grace of the colonial era. Highlights of the menu include the chicken rice served Melaka style, and the Hainanese chicken chop.

In the attached tea lounge you can enjoy a very fancy afternoon tea (RM60), which can also be served in the luscious orchidarium (RM110). Book ahead.

Brickfields & Around

★LAWANYA FOOD CORNER INDIAN $

Map p260 (016-220 2117; 1077/8 Lg Scott; meals RM8; 6am-4pm; KL Sentral) Don't be put off by the low-key appearance of this simple joint with a few ramshackle tables lined up against a lime green wall under a sheet of corrugated iron. The same family has been preparing delicious curries here for more than 30 years, with a spread of meat and vegetarian dishes served from clay pots. Rice and three types of vegetables costs RM6, add meat for RM8.

VISHAL INDIAN $

Map p260 (03-2274 1995; 22 Jln Scott; meals from RM6; 7.30am-10.45pm; ; Tun Sambanthan) Sit at one of the tables and allow the army of servers to dollop out the great-tasting food on to a banana leaf for you. If you're hungry, supplement the standard meal with a good range of side dishes or a huge mound of chicken biryani. Good for tiffin snacks and a refreshing lassi, too.

ANNALAKSHMI VEGETARIAN RESTAURANT INDIAN $

Map p260 (03-2274 0799; www.facebook.com/AnnalakshmiVegetarianRestaurantKualaLumpur; Temple of Fine Arts, 116 Jln Berhala; dinner mains RM10-18; 11.30am-3pm & 6.30-10pm Tue-Sun; ; KL Sentral, KL Sentral) Inside the fancy main hall at the Temple of Fine Arts (p107), this well-regarded vegetarian restaurant has set prices at night and a daily lunch buffet for RM18 (RM20 Friday to Sunday); or you can eat at the humbler **Annalakshmi Riverside** next to the car park behind the main building, where it's 'eat as you wish, give as you feel'.

IKAN BAKAR JALAN BELLAMY HAWKER $

Map p261 (Jln Bellamy; meals RM10; 11am-11pm Mon-Sat; Tun Sambanthan) When the king lived nearby it was said he occasionally sent his minions to get an order of grilled stingray from one of the justifiably popular barbecued-fish hawker stalls on the hill behind the former royal palace. There's little to choose between the three of them; wander around and see what takes your fancy.

★RESTORAN YARL SRI LANKAN $$

Map p260 (www.yarl.com.my; 50 Jln Padang Belia; meals RM10-15; 7am-10pm Tue-Sun; KL Sentral, KL Sentral) This simple restaurant in Brickfields serves tasty Tamil dishes from northern Sri Lanka. Help yourself from clay pots of spicy mutton, chicken and fish *peratal* (dry curry), squid curry, aubergine *sothi* (mild curry with coconut milk) and vegetable dishes. Don't miss the house speciality, crab curry – try a ladle of the sauce if you don't fancy grappling with claws.

JASSAL TANDOORI RESTAURANT INDIAN $$

Map p260 (03-2274 6801; 84 Jln Tun Sambanthan; dishes RM17-37; 11am-11pm Mon-Thu, to 11.30pm Fri-Sun; KL Sentral, KL Sentral) Jassal serves great-tasting tandoori specialities, what must be the city's best dhal *makhani* (thick dark spicy lentils), and a load of other dishes including a variety of naans, rotis and *parathas*. Cheap Indian beer is also on offer. At the entrance to the restaurant is Jesal Sweet House, a counter selling delicious North Indian sweets.

GEM RESTAURANT INDIAN $$

Map p260 (03-2260 1373; 124 Jln Tun Sambanthan; mains RM10-24; 11.30am-5pm & 6.15-11pm; ; KL Sentral) A Brickfields stalwart, this calm, air-conditioned restaurant serves good South Indian food, including specialities from Chettinad, Andhra Pradesh and the Malabar coast. The thali is great value.

SIU SIU CHINESE $$

(☎016-370 8555; 15-11 Lg Syed Putra Kiri; mains RM40-60; ⏰11am-11pm Tue-Sun; Tun Sambathan) On the way to Kwong Tong Cemetery from Thean Hou Temple, this is a very good no-frills, partly al fresco place. Order the milk curry prawns with buns to soak up the tasty gravy, or any type of fish.

ROBSON HEIGHTS SEAFOOD RESTAURANT CHINESE $$

(☎03-2274 6216; 10b Jln Permai, off Jln Syed Putra; mains RM30-60; ⏰11am-3pm & 5.30-11pm; Tun Sambanthan) Folks drive from far and wide to feast on the top-class food served at this rickety hillside joint. While its specialities such as stir-fried pig intestines with dried prawn and chilli, braised terrapin, or Marmite crab may not appeal to all, we can vouch for the delicious baked spare ribs in honey sauce and stir-fried udon noodles in black pepper sauce.

Bangsar

★BANGSAR SUNDAY MARKET HAWKER $

Map p262 (Pasar Malam; car park east of Jln Telawi 2; hawker food RM4-6; ⏰1-9pm Sun; 🚇Bank Rakyat-Bangsar) This weekly market, though mostly for fresh produce, is also a fine hawker food-grazing zone. Stalls sell satay and a variety of noodles including *asam laksa* (laksa with a prawn paste and tamarind-flavoured gravy), *chee cheong fun* (rice noodles) and fried *kway teow* (noodles fried in chilli and black-bean sauce).

You'll also find *popiah* (similar to spring rolls, but not fried) and dim sum stalls as well as traditionally prepared *putu bambu* – rice flour with pandan and *gula melaka* (palm sugar) steamed inside hollow bamboo and covered with desiccated coconut.

★SRI NIRWANA MAJU INDIAN $

Map p262 (☎03-2287 8445; 43 Jln Telawi 3; meals RM5-16; ⏰10am-2am; 🚇Bank Rakyat-Bangsar) There are far flashier Indian restaurants in Bangsar, but who cares about the decor when you can tuck into food this good and cheap? It serves it all, from roti for breakfast to banana-leaf curries throughout the day.

CHAWAN MALAYSIAN $

Map p262 (☎03-2287 5507; 69g Jln Telawi 3; mains RM13-24; ⏰8am-1am Sun-Thu, to 2am Fri & Sat; 🚇Bank Rakyat-Bangsar) A contemporary take on a *kopitiam* (coffee shop) offering megastrength coffees from all of the country's states to wash down dishes such as beef rendang and brown-paper-wrapped *nasi lemak*. There's also a branch in Publika (p110).

RESTAURANT MAHBUB INDIAN $

Map p262 (☎03-2095 5382; www.restoranmahbub.com; 17 Lg Ara Kiri 1; mains RM7-15; ⏰7am-2am; 🚇Bank Rakyat-Bangsar) Tables spill out on to the street from this long-running operation famous for its luscious honey chicken biryani.

NASI KANDAR PELITA MALAYSIAN $

Map p262 (☎03-2282 5532; www.pelita.com.my; 2 Jln Telawi 5; mains RM10-25; ⏰24hrs; 🚇Bank Rakyat-Bangsar) Serves *mamak* (Muslim Indian-Malay) food, including *roti canai* and *hariyali tikka* (spiced chicken with mint, cooked in the tandoor).

JASLYN CAKES BAKERY $

Map p262 (☎03-2202 2868; www.jaslyncakes.com; 7a Jln Telawi 2; cakes per portion RM3-10; ⏰11am-7pm Tue-Fri, to 8pm Sat & Sun; 🚇Bank Rakyat-Bangsar) This tiny bakery is justifiably popular for its exquisite cakes made with free-range eggs and organic flour. Also sells delicious pastries, breads and biscuits.

★SOUTHERN ROCK SEAFOOD SEAFOOD $$

Map p260 (☎03-2856 2016; www.southernrockseafood.com; 34 Jln Kemuja; mains RM28-65; ⏰10am-10pm; 📶; 🚇Bank Rakyat-Bangsar) The fishmonger to some of KL's top restaurants has opened its own operation and it's a corker. The fish and seafood – in particular the wide range of oysters – is top quality, simply prepared to allow the flavours to sing. The blue-and-white decor suggests nights spent on the sparkling Med rather than the muddy Sungai Klang.

ASHLEY'S BY LIVING FOOD INTERNATIONAL $$

Map p262 (☎017-325 3663; www.ashleys.my; 11 Jln Telawi 3; mains RM18-78; ⏰10.30am-11.30pm Mon-Fri, 8.30am-midnight Sat & Sun; 🌱; 🚇Bank Rakyat-Bangsar) Although not exclusively vegetarian, this arty, rustic place is where you can sample inventive and well-prepared veg-only dishes such as vegan laksa. They take care to use organic ingredients where possible and serve other rarities (for KL) such as gluten-free chocolate cake and 'raw food' cooked at under 40°C to preserve nutrients, texture and taste.

LOCAL KNOWLEDGE

LUCKY GARDENS

South of Jln Ara, **Lucky Gardens** (Map p262; Lg Ara Kiri; Bank Rakyat-Bangsar) may not be as ritzy as the grid of Telawis, but locals love to hit the morning fruit-and-veg market here and it is blessed with some delicious and inexpensive dining options. Time your visit to the **Nam Chuan Coffee Shop** (hawker dishes RM5-8; 7am-10pm), a busy, no-frills food court, so that you can enjoy a bowl of Christina Jong's fantastic Sarawak laksa (RM5; from 8.30am to 2.30pm Thursday to Tuesday) or Ah Mun's *kueh* (rice cakes; RM1; from 2pm) – his *onde onde* (glutinous rice balls filled with palm sugar) are flavoured with real pandan and are considered the best in KL.

There's also a fantastic strip of outdoor hawker stalls along Lg Ara Kiri: sample Indian vegan delights at **Chelo's Appam Stall** (snacks RM5; 7am-10pm Mon-Sat;); more vegetarian food at **Poomy's** (RM5; 3-9pm;), including the sweet *appam* (coconut-milk pancakes); and the taste-bud explosion of **Bangsar Fish Head Corner** (mains RM3-20; 9am-6pm Mon-Sat;), where if you don't fancy the actual fish head you can still get the curry sauce poured over rice along with delicious fried chicken.

NUTMEG — INTERNATIONAL $$

Map p262 (03-2201 3663; www.facebook.com/nutmegkl; Bangsar Village II, 2 Jln Telawi 1; mains RM18-55; 9.30am-10pm; ; Bank Rakyat-Bangsar) The closest thing you're going to get to a Jewish deli in KL, this popular cafe makes an impression with its bagel and lox and salt beef hash, as well as other comfort foods and cakes.

YEAST BISTRONOMY — FRENCH $$

Map p262 (03-2282 0118; www.yeastbistronomy.com; 24g Jln Telawi 2; mains lunch RM15-45, dinner RM32-118; 8am-10pm Sun-Thu, to 10.30pm Fri & Sat; ; Bank Rakyat-Bangsar) Justifiably popular for its range of breads, croissants and tarts, Yeast is the best place in town for French-style baked goods. As well as selling pastries, loaves and sandwiches to take away, the bistro serves breakfasts, lunches of salads and savoury tarts, and dinners of seafood stews, boeuf bourguignon and steak tartare. There is also a branch at Mid Valley Megamall (p108).

WONDERMAMA — MALAYSIAN $$

Map p262 (03-2284 9821; http://wondermama.co; Bangsar Village I, 1 Jln Telawi 1; mains RM13-27; 9am-10.30pm Mon-Thu, to 11.30pm Fri-Sun; ; Bank Rakyat-Bangsar) Traditional meets contemporary at this family-friendly two-level restaurant serving Malaysian food with a modern twist. There's also a branch in Avenue K (p65) at the KLCC.

G3 KITCHEN & BAR — INTERNATIONAL $$

Map p262 (19 Jln Telawi 3; mains RM29-35; 10.30am-10.30pm Mon-Fri, 8.30am-11.30pm Sat & Sun; ; Bank Rakyat-Bangsar) A casual indoor vibe, deck seating, excellent wood-fired pizzas, and made-from-scratch burgers and sandwiches make this bistro a popular hangout on one of Bangsar's busier strips.

HOUSE+CO KITCHEN — INTERNATIONAL $$

(03-2094 3139; www.houseandco.com.my; Bangsar Shopping Centre, 285 Jln Maarof; mains RM20; 11am-11pm; ; Bank Rakyat-Bangsar) One of the best places to eat if you're at the Bangsar Shopping Centre mall, this laid-back cafe makes great local dishes – try the delicious *kway teow* soup or the spicy *mee hoon kerabu* (rice noodle salad), and come hungry as the portions are huge.

ALEXIS BISTRO — INTERNATIONAL $$

Map p262 (03-2284 2880; www.alexis.com.my; 29 Jln Telawi 3; mains RM30-50; noon-midnight Sun-Thu, to 1am Fri & Sat; ; Bank Rakyat-Bangsar) Consistently good food is delivered at this Bangsar stalwart where Asian favourites such as Sarawak laksa (the owner is originally from this Malaysian state) mix it up with European fare. After your meal, move on to the ultrasmooth Sino The Bar Upstairs (p107).

FIERCE CURRY HOUSE — INDIAN $$

Map p260 (03-2202 3456; www.facebook.com/FierceCurryHouse; 16 Jln Kemuja; mains RM8-20; 10.30am-10.30pm; Bank Rakyat-Bangsar) There's outdoor and indoor seating at this biryani speciality restaurant just west of Little India in Bangsar. Choose from mutton, chicken, or even lobster biryanis (order the day before), and good-value veggie thali sets (RM10) and banana-leaf meals.

LOCAL KNOWLEDGE

LORONG KURAU

Tucked away from the bustle of Bangsar Baru is this quiet leafy lane of cafes, bars and restaurants that's worth exploring. The pick of the bunch is **Ganga Cafe** (Map p262; 03-2284 2119; www.theganga.com.my; 19 Lg Kurau; mains RM8.50-10.50, Sun brunch buffet RM21; 8.30am-9.30pm Mon-Sat, 10am-3pm Sun; ; Bank Rakyat-Bangsar), a sunny little cafe with an excellent Sunday brunch buffet.

DELICIOUS INTERNATIONAL **$$**

Map p262 (03-2287 1554; www.delicious.com.my; ground fl, Bangsar Village II, Jln Telawi 1; mains RM19.50-31.50; 11am-10.30pm Mon-Wed, to 11pm Thu & Fri, 9am-11pm Sat & Sun; Bank Rakyat-Bangsar) Serving brunches, healthy salads, pasta, sandwiches and pies (among many other things) in a contemporary setting. It's worth dropping by for the afternoon teas.

DRINKING & NIGHTLIFE

Lake Gardens & Brickfields

MAI BAR COCKTAIL BAR

Map p260 (www.aloftkualalumpursentral.com; Aloft Kuala Lumpur Sentral, 5 Jln Stesen Sentral; noon-midnight Sun-Thu, to 2am Fri & Sat; ; KL Sentral, KL Sentral) This Polynesian-style tiki bar, which goes a little too heavy on the red lights, is another addition to KL's growing band of high-rise bars with panoramic city views. DJs spin Wednesday to Saturday after 10pm. For a more casual atmosphere, and live music Friday nights, try the hotel's W XYZ bar.

KIA KLEMENZ COFFEE

Map p260 (www.kiaklemenz.com; 2 Kedai Cenderamata 1, Jln Cenderawasih, Perdana Botanical Garden; 9am-6.30pm; Masjid Jamek) In the small cafe attached to this boutique and gift shop, owner Rokiah prepares coffee from her native Borneo that's worth searching out, as well as a few pastries and snacks. The shop has a good range of handicrafts and textiles such as hand-printed batik and artwork from Sabah. Take a taxi from Masjid Jamek.

Bangsar & Around

★**COLEY** COCKTAIL BAR

Map p260 (www.facebook.com/LongLiveColey; 8 Jln Kemuja; 5pm-1am Tue-Sat, 3-9pm Sun; Bank Rakyat-Bangsar) Named after Ada Coleman, a female bartender in 1920s London and creator of the Hanky Panky cocktail, this tiny bar at the back of DR.Inc (p109) is the place to come for a seriously well-mixed drink. Legendary local mixologist CK Kho works the bar, serving a selection of classic cocktails with a contemporary twist.

MANTRA BAR KL ROOFTOP BAR

Map p262 (www.mantrabarkl.com; Bangsar Village II, Jln Telawi Satu; 4.30pm-1.30am Sun & Tue-Thu, to 3am Fri & Sat; Bank Rakyat-Bangsar) This sophisticated bar on the rooftop of Bangsar Village II has an indoor lounge and outdoor deck with spectacular views over the leafy, low-rise suburbs to the city skyline beyond. A dress code applies on Friday and Saturday nights, when DJs play to a fashionable crowd. There are happy-hour prices until 7pm (cocktails RM15 to RM22).

PULP BY PAPA PALHETA CAFE

Map p262 (www.facebook.com/PULPbyPapaPalheta; 29-01 Jln Riong; 7.30am-10pm Tue-Fri, 9am-11pm Sat & Sun; ; Bank Rakyat-Bangsar) Expect top-quality brews from this premium coffee roaster from Singapore. Its contemporary shed-like cafe is in the grounds of the media printers APW (www.apw.my/home), where exhibitions and various events are held. Apart from coffee, it also serves craft beer from Japan and tasty snacks such as truffle popcorn and croissant sandwiches.

RIL'S BAR COCKTAIL BAR

Map p262 (03-2201 3846; www.rils.com.my; 30 Jln Telawi 5; 6pm-1am Sun-Thu, to 3am Fri & Sat; ; Bank Rakyat-Bangsar) There's a premium-grade steak restaurant downstairs, but the main action happens at the Prohibition-era-style cocktail bar upstairs, where the mixologists get creative and there's live music (jazz, blues, soul) on the weekends. On Wednesdays there are free drinks for women from 9pm to 11pm at its tiki-inspired night.

COFFEA COFFEE CAFE
Map p262 (http://coffea.my; 8 Jln Telawi 2; ⏲8am-midnight Mon-Thu, to 2am Fri, 9am-2am Sat, to midnight Sun; 📶; 🚇Bank Rakyat-Bangsar) Now one of many branches of this Korean speciality coffee franchise, which gets rave reviews for its single-origin bean drinks and expert baristas.

PLAN B CAFE
Map p262 (☎03-2287 2630; www.thebiggroup.co/planb; G5, ground fl, Bangsar Village 1, 1 Jln Telawi Satu; ⏲9am-11pm; 📶; 🚇Bank Rakyat-Bangsar) The BIG Group successfully clones the sophisticated Melbourne-look cafe-bar at several locations around town, including this one on the ground floor of Bangsar Village. Handy for a latte, a light meal or something more substantial.

SINO THE BAR UPSTAIRS BAR
Map p262 (☎03-2284 2880; www.alexis.com.my; 29 Jln Telawi 3; ⏲6pm-1am Sun-Thu, to 2am Fri & Sat; 📶; 🚇Bank Rakyat-Bangsar) Above the popular Alexis Bistro, this chilled-out drinking spot offers comfortable chairs and soothing sounds on the decks. The first Monday of the month it hosts a jazz jam session that gives you a chance to catch some top local jazz talents.

SOCIAL BAR
Map p262 (☎03-2282 2260; http://thesocial.com.my/wp; 57-59 Jln Telawi 3; ⏲11.30am-2am; 🚇Bank Rakyat-Bangsar) This popular meeting spot has pool tables, good food and cheap happy-hour draught beer.

BILIQUE BANGSAR BAR
Map p262 (www.facebook.com/biliquekl; 34a & 36a Jln Telawi; ⏲6pm-2am; 🚇Bank Rakyat-Bangsar) Table football, darts, a pool table and an outdoor terrace are the main draws of this Bangsar bar.

☆ ENTERTAINMENT

TEMPLE OF FINE ARTS THEATRE
Map p260 (☎03-2274 3709; www.tfa.org.my; 116 Jln Berhala; ⏲closed Mon; 🚇KL Sentral, KL Sentral) Classical Indian dance and music shows take place here throughout the year. The centre also runs performing-arts courses; see the website for schedules.

SHOPPING

Brickfields

WEI-LING GALLERY ART
Map p260 (www.weiling-gallery.com; 8 Jln Scott; ⏲10am-6pm Mon, 11am-7pm Tue-Fri, 10am-5pm Sat, by appointment only Sun; 🚇KL Sentral, KL Sentral) The top two floors of this old shophouse have been imaginatively turned into a contemporary gallery to showcase local artists. Note the artwork covering the metal security gate in front of the shophouse next door.

Its sister gallery Wei-Ling Contemporary is on the 6th floor of the Gardens Mall (p108), part of the Mid Valley complex.

LAVANYA ARTS ARTS & CRAFTS
Map p260 (www.facebook.com/lavanyaarts; Temple of Fine Arts, 114-116 Jln Berhala; ⏲10am-9.30pm Tue-Sat, to 3pm Sun; 🚇KL Sentral) Lavanya, inside the Temple of Fine Arts (p107), sells colourful craft goods including adorable kids' and adults' clothes and home decorations. Come the week around Deepavali for a festive range of beautiful Indian tribal arts, as well as handsome painted wooden dolls, brass sculpture, and colourful furniture from Rajasthan.

SONALI FASHION & ACCESSORIES
Map p260 (www.sonali.com.my; 67a Jln Scott; ⏲10am-7pm Mon-Sat; Tun Sambanthan) Sequins, silks, filigree patterns and tie-dye – all the elements of the flash Bollywood look are present in this boutique. It's mainly for women but also has some fancy tops for men.

NU SENTRAL MALL
Map p260 (www.nusentral.com; 201 Jln Tun Sambanthan; ⏲10am-10pm; 🚇KL Sentral, KL Sentral) Providing the connection between the monorail and the main station at KL Sentral is this shiny, multilevel mall. Among many shops there's a branch of Parkson department store, a MPH bookshop, a GSC multiplex and a food court, as well as the escape-game complex Breakout (www.breakout.com.my).

WORTH A DETOUR

MID VALLEY

Like a fortress island surrounded by concentric moats of highways and rail tracks, Mid Valley is a two-tower complex anchored by two giant malls: **Mid Valley Megamall** (Map p262; www.midvalley.com.my; Lingkaran Syed Putra; ⏲10am-10pm; Ⓡ Mid Valley) and its luxe sibling **Gardens Mall** (Map p262; www.thegardensmall.com.my; ⏲10am-10pm; Ⓡ Mid Valley), which also offers a good top-end hotel and serviced apartments. The KL Komuter Mid Valley station makes getting here a cinch.

Shopping

Mega is the only way to describe this complex, where you could easily lose yourself for a day or two: it's an ideal place to head if there's a tropical downpour or you just need to escape the heat for a few hours of air-con shopping, but do avoid it on the weekends and holidays if you're not into crowds.

Mid Valley Megamall alone has some 430 shops and restaurants as well as an 18-screen cinema, a bowling alley, a huge food court and even a colourful Hindu temple. For street-style unisex T-shirts and accessories head to **Fabspy** (https://store.fabspy.com; 3rd fl, north mall; ⏲10am-10pm), which is well stocked with local labels such as Kozo, Supercrew, Nerd Unit and Medium Rare. Specialist shops include **Cap City** (www.facebook.com/TheCapCity; 3rd fl, north mall; ⏲10am-10pm) for headgear and **World of Feng Shui** (www.wofs.com; 3rd fl; ⏲10am-10pm).

If the Megamall is proving too plebeian for your shopping tastes, luxury brands are in abundance in the connected Gardens Mall. Anchored by Isetan and Robinsons department stores, here you'll also find many lovely fashion emporiums, an art gallery, another multiplex and the spa and beauty floor.

Eating & Drinking

There are food courts and a multitude of cafes and restaurants in both malls. Should the enclosed mall environment start getting to you, take a breather on the road separating the Megamall from Gardens Mall where there are several restaurants and cafes with outdoor seating, including the **Library** (☎03-2282 6001; ⏲10am-2am Sun-Wed, to 3am Thu-Sat), which has live music in the evenings.

The Gardens' most classy restaurant and wine bar is **Sage** (Map p262; ☎03-2268 1328; www.sagekl.com; level 6, Gardens Residences, Mid Valley, Jln Syed Putra; set lunches/dinners RM120/220; ⏲noon-2pm Mon-Fri, 6-10.30pm Mon-Sat), offering inventive cuisine using high-quality ingredients, and there's also a swanky oyster and seafood bar, **Shucked** (www.shuckedoysterbars.com; 3rd fl; mains RM28-50; ⏲10am-10pm) – oyster happy hour runs from 3pm to 6pm. Another option is the Japanese restaurant **Yuzu** (☎03-2284 7663; http://yuzu.com.my/gardens; 3rd fl; sets RM36-78; ⏲11.30am-10pm). The pictures in the menu do look better than what you get but portions are large and the prices are right.

Activities

Apart from going to the movies, there's a bowling alley in Megamall. **Dive Station Explorer** (☎03-2282 1948; www.divestation.com.my; 3rd fl; ⏲10am-10pm) is an experienced operator and dive shop through which you can arrange three-day/two-night PADI open-water courses and other dive courses.

Entertainment

GSC Mid Valley (www.gsc.com.my; 3rd fl; tickets RM11-20) The recently revamped Mid Valley branch of the GSC cinema chain includes a 277-seater screening room.

Bangsar

★DR.INC HOMEWARES

Map p260 (03-2283 4698; www.facebook.com/thincacademykl; 8 Jln Kemuja; 9am-7pm; ; Bank Rakyat-Bangsar) Lisette Scheers is the creative force behind the Nala brand of homewares, stationery, accessories and other arty items. All her products embody a contemporary but distinctly local design aesthetic and are beautifully displayed at this Instagram dream of a concept shop and cafe.

★PUCUK REBUNG ART

Map p262 (03-2094 9969; prebung@gmail.com; 18 Lg Ara Kiri 2; 10.30am-6.30pm Mon-Fri, to 7pm Sat & Sun; Bank Rakyat-Bangsar) Specialising in antiques and fine arts, this is one of the best places in KL to find quality pieces of local craft as well as pricier Malay ethnological items. It's worth dropping by for a browse and a chat with the affable owner, ex-banker Henry Bong.

TRIBECA FASHION & ACCESSORIES

Map p262 (03-2287 6760; 1st fl, Bangsar Village II; 10am-10pm; Bank Rakyat-Bangsar) This little shop is packed with treasures made mostly by small independent designers. You could easily lose an hour here looking through the gorgeous children's clothes by local labels Meor and Kooshoo and the Japanese-made bags and accessories by Malaysian designer Beatrice, as well as original artwork, patchwork furniture and vintage posters.

COMODDITY CLOTHING

Map p262.(www.thecomoddity.com; upper ground fl, Bangsar Village II, cnr Jln Telawi 1 & Jln Telawi 2; 10am-10pm; Bank Rakyat-Bangsar) Up-and-coming Malaysian menswear designer Vincent Siow has shown at KL Fashion Week as well as at street shows in Paris and Shanghai. His label Comoddity specialises in unique pieces such as hand-painted trousers, suit jackets adorned with cityscape motifs, and purple PVC bomber jackets. The boutique also acts as a gallery for Siow's artwork.

I LOVE SNACKFOOD VINTAGE

Map p262 (03-2201 7513; www.ilovesnackfood.com; 17a Jln Telawi 3; 11am-7pm; Bank Rakyat-Bangsar) Snackfood specialises in kitsch interior decor, vintage collectables (think typewriters, trunks and globes), books and stationery.

NEVER FOLLOW SUIT FASHION & ACCESSORIES

Map p262 (www.facebook.com/Never.Follow.Suit.Bangsar; 28-2, Jln Telawi 2; 11am-9pm; Bank Rakyat-Bangsar) You're guaranteed to find a unique piece at this extraordinary boutique hidden away on the 2nd floor. New and up-cycled clothes and accessories are displayed like artworks in a hipster, shabby-chic gallery. Note that at the time of research the shop was closed for renovations.

SHOES SHOES SHOES SHOES

Map p262 (www.shoesshoesshoes.com.my; 22 Jln Telawi 3; 11am-9pm; Bank Rakyat-Bangsar) The lifelong dream of a shoe fanatic is realised in this bright 2nd-floor shop selling a range of home-grown and imported shoes as well as a great selection of jewellery, sunglasses and other accessories. Also has branches at Publika (p110) and Bangsar Shopping Centre (p111).

★THISAPPEAR FASHION & ACCESSORIES

Map p262 (03-2201 2290; www.thisappearplus.com; 1st fl, 51 Jln Telawi 3; noon-8pm; Bank Rakyat-Bangsar) Co-owned by four young local designers, Thisappear is a gallery-like space selling runway fashion by Joe Chia, Kozo and Alia Bastaman, handmade leather bags by Producthief and unisex streetwear by Justin Chew.

MIMPIKITA FASHION & ACCESSORIES

Map p262 (www.mimpikita.com.my; 1st fl, 15 Jln Telawi 2; 11am-7pm Mon-Sat; Bank Rakya-Bangsar) High-end local fashion made with gorgeous printed fabrics, as well as jewellery by Dipped Row.

D.D.COLLECTIVE FASHION & ACCESSORIES

Map p262 (dd-collective.com; Bangsar Village II, cnr Jln Telawi 1 & Jln Telawi 2; 10am-10pm; Bank Rakyat-Bangsar) Contemporary, high-end fashion for men and women by Paris-based Malaysian designer Jonathan Liang.

LONELY DREAM FASHION & ACCESSORIES

Map p262 (www.facebook.com/lonelydreamstore; lot 11, 2nd fl, Telawi Sq, 39 & 41 Jln Telawi 3; noon-10pm; Bank Rakyat-Bangsar) Cookie H stocks her own label, Replay, as well as pieces by other designers from Malaysia and elsewhere at her cutting-edge boutique.

WORTH A DETOUR

PUBLIKA

Art, shopping, dining and social life are all in harmony at **Publika** (www.facebook.com/PublikaGallery; 1 Jln Dutamas, Solaris Dutamas; ⏲10am-9pm), a forward-thinking retail and residential development less than 10 minutes' drive north of Bangsar. Dazzling murals, quirky themes for the toilets and a fun kids' playground all add to Publika's visual interest and point to a liberal vibe that's in striking contrast to the conservative Islamic high court, the giant mosque and the Istana Negara (National Palace) that are the complex's neighbours.

Galleries & Events

Contemporary art is fostered at several independent galleries at Publika, with **MAP** (☎03-6207 9732; www.facebook.com/mapkl; ⏲10am-9pm) acting as the cultural anchor with a wide variety of performances, talks and art exhibitions held in its White and Black Box spaces – everything from Malaysian death-metal bands to major public events and product launches. Free films are screened each Monday in the central square and a handicrafts market is held on the last Sunday of the month. MAP's and Publika's Facebook pages list up-to-date details of all events.

Eating & Drinking

There are two good food courts: EAT and Made in Malaysia; the former includes an outlet of Kin Kin where you can sample supremely tasty *pan mee* ('dry' noodles). Other good places to eat and drink include the following:

Bee (☎03-6201 8577; thebee.com.my; 36b, level G2; mains RM16-38; ⏲10am-midnight Mon-Thu, to 1.30am Fri, 9am-1am Sat, 9am-midnight Sun; ❄📶) A happening cafe-bar serving burgers, sandwiches, salads and fine coffee, and hosting events including live music, film screenings and open-mic nights.

Nathalie's Gourmet Studio (☎03-6207 9572; www.nathaliegourmetstudio.com; Unit A4-1-5; mains lunch RM22-28, dinner RM60-95; ⏲11.30am-3.30pm & 6.30-11pm Thu-Sat; ❄) For delicious nouvelle cuisine and melting macarons. It also runs cooking classes.

Journal by Plan b (http://thebiggroup.co/planb; Lot 65, Level G2; mains RM10-33; ⏲8am-11pm) A pile of chairs hanging from the ceiling and an old TV screening P Ramlee movies are part of the quirky decor at this upmarket branch of cafe-bar Plan b.

There are also branches of reliable chains Ben's, The Social, Chawan and Wondermilk. For a caffeine fix, head to **Coffee Stain by Joseph** (www.coffeestain.my; ⏲8am-11pm; 📶).

Shopping

Rents are kept low to encourage new talents and retail ideas – look out for pop-up shops on the Level G2 Art Row. **Ben's Independent Grocer** (BIG; www.thebiggroup.co/BIG; Lot 1A, 83-95, Level UG; ⏲9am-10pm) is a huge and creatively designed supermarket. There's a particularly good section of shops for children, including the arts-and-crafts workshop **Artis Kids Store** (☎03-1233 1233; www.artisworkshop.com; 48, Level G3; per 45min weekday RM45, weekend RM50; ⏲10.30am-8pm).

Fashionistas are well served by a good range of small boutiques, as well as major fashion retailer **British India** (Lot 20-22, Level G2; ⏲11am-8pm Mon-Thu, to 9pm Fri-Sun) and its youth-oriented offshoot **Just B**. Also check out **White Elephant**, where old British India stock is sold for knock-down prices, with the proceeds going to charity. Don't miss **Shoes Shoes Shoes** (http://shoesshoesshoes.com.my; Lot 16, G2; ⏲10am-10pm), a footwear emporium that also sells gorgeous accessories and bags as well as clothing by Malaysian designer Jonathan Liang's label **d.d.collective.**

Browse **Arcadia** (www.facebook.com/arcadiakualalumpur; 10, Level 3; ⏲10am-10pm) for retro knick-knacks and furnishings.

Getting There & Away

A taxi to Publika from Sentral KL/Bangsar should cost no more than RM12/7 on the meter.

BANGSAR SHOPPING CENTRE MALL

(BSC; www.bsc.com.my; 285 Jln Maarof; ⊙10am-10pm; Bank Rakyat-Bangsar) BSC has carved a niche with KL's gourmets thanks to its fabulous food hall, Jason's, and its collection of restaurants, cafes and bars. Other retail reasons for heading here are to get a new outfit at British India, homewares at House & Co or fancy footwear from Shoes Shoes Shoes. There are also some very pukka tailors should you need a dress shirt or suit.

SILVERFISH BOOKS BOOKS

Map p262 (03-2284 4837; www.silverfishbooks.com; 2nd fl, Bangsar Village II, Jln Telawi 1; ⊙10am-10pm; Bank Rakyat-Bangsar) This local bookshop and publisher of contemporary Malaysian literature and writings has a good selection of English-language books and hosts regular talks.

NURITA HARITH FASHION & ACCESSORIES

Map p262 (www.nuritaharith.com; 2nd fl, Jln Telawi 3, beside Alexis Bistro; ⊙10am-6pm Tue-Sun; Bank Rakyat-Bangsar) A boutique specialising in bridal wear by one of KL's top designers.

SPORTS & ACTIVITIES

★HAMMAM SPA SPA

Map p262 (03-2282 2180; www.hammamspas.com; 3rd fl, Bangsar Village II, Jln Telawi 1; treatments RM116-398; ⊙10am-10.30pm; Bank Rakyat-Bangsar) The Moroccan steam bath comes to KL at this small and beautiful mosaic-tiled spa. Couples and singles packages are available with sumptuous titles such as the Royal Couple (RM730) and the Sultan's Daughter's Wedding (RM456), or you can go for a simple steam and scrub *(gommage)*. There's also a branch at Publika (p110).

OLD KL & NATURE WALK WALKING

Map p260 (03-2698 0332; www.visitkl.gov.my; ⊙9-11.30am Tue & Thu; Masjid Jamek) FREE The latest of the free walking tours offered by Visit KL is a 2½-hour stroll from the Loke Chow Kit mansion (p85; home to the KL Tourism Bureau) through Chinatown to the KL Forest Eco Park, with stops at Masjid Jamek, the Sin Sze Si Ya Temple and the Muzium Telekom. The guide's stories and old photographs bring the history of the city to life.

MAJESTIC SPA SPA

Map p260 (03-2785 8070; www.majestickl.com; Majestic Hotel, 5 Jln Sultan Hishamuddin; treatments RM410-995; ⊙10am-10pm; Kuala Lumpur) Charles Rennie Mackintosh's Willow Tea Rooms in Glasgow are the inspiration for the Majestic's delightful spa, where treatments are preceded by a refreshing tea or Pimm's cocktail. After your pampering, there's a pool for a dip and sunbathe.

TUGU DRUM CIRCLE PERFORMING ARTS

Map p260 (⊙5.30-8.30pm Sun; Masjid Jamek) This open group for drummers meets at Plaza Tugu Negara in the Tun Abdul Razak Heritage Park (p95) on Sundays from 5.30pm till 8.30pm. Beginners are welcome. See the Facebook page for details. Get a taxi from Masjid Jamek.

YMCA LANGUAGE

Map p260 (03-2274 1439; www.ymcakl.com; 95 Jln Padang Belia; KL Sentral) Become a member, then you can join the Bahasa Malaysia classes as well as courses studying Thai, Mandarin, Cantonese and Japanese.

KIZSPORTS & GYM HEALTH & FITNESS

Map p262 (03-2284 6313; www.kizsports.com.my; 3rd fl, Bangsar Village II, Jln Telawi 1; child RM40; ⊙10am-7pm; Bank Rakyat-Bangsar) This large soft play area for under-12s is a great place for little ones to blow off steam, and there's a 'drop and shop' service for over-threes (RM42 per hour). Children must wear socks.

KOMPLEKS SUKAN BANGSAR GYM

Map p262 (Bangsar Sports Complex; 03-2284 1150; 3 Jln Terasek 3; RM3; ⊙9.30am-noon, 2-4.30pm & 6-8.30pm Mon-Sat; Bank Rakyat-Bangsar) Entry fee includes a swimming session at the 25m outdoor pool. You can also rent courts for badminton (per hour RM8) and tennis (per hour RM10).

Day Trips from Kuala Lumpur

Batu Caves (p113)

This dramatic limestone crag riddled with caverns is both a natural marvel and religious site with its holy Hindu shrines and colourful dioramas.

Forest Research Institute Malaysia (FRIM; p115)

Switch track from the drone of city traffic and air-conditioning to bird-song and all-encompassing greenery at this jungle park.

Bukit Fraser (Fraser's Hill; p116)

Breathe easy at this classic, colonial-era, high-altitude resort on the Selangor–Pahang border; it's also a top bird-spotting destination.

Klang Valley (p118)

Travel from city to coast, pausing at a range of fun attractions and sights including a giant water theme park, a mega-mosque and Klang's vibrant Little India.

Putrajaya (p122)

Malaysia's administrative hub is a showboat of daring contemporary and Islamic heritage architecture arranged around a pretty, artificial lake.

JAREL REMICK/500PX ©

TOP SIGHT
BATU CAVES

One of Malaysia's most iconic sights and holiest Hindu shrines, this complex of giant limestone caves houses temples that have been drawing pilgrims for more than 120 years. Home to a troop of cheeky macaques, the caves are always a colourful and fascinating place to visit, especially during the festival of Thaipusam when hundreds of thousands of pilgrims converge here.

DON'T MISS

- Temple Cave
- Golden statue of Lord Murugan
- Dark Cave
- Ramayana Cave

PRACTICALITIES

- Batu Caves

Temple Cave

The so-called **Temple Cave** (8am-8.30pm) FREE, actually two enormous caverns joined by a short flight of stairs, sits atop 272 steps populated by scampering macaque monkeys and is guarded by an impressive, 42.7m golden statue of Hindu God Lord Murugan, erected in 2006 and said to be the largest in the world. The dome-shaped cavern has been a Hindu shrine since K Thambusamy Pillai, founder of the Sri Mahamariamman Temple (p72) in KL, placed a statue of Lord Murugan here in 1890.

Inside the first cavern, at the top of the stairs, Murugan's six abodes are carved into the walls. The second cavern holds the temple of Valli Devanai, Murugan's wife. Murugan, son of Shiva and Hindu god of war, is widely worshipped in Hindu Tamil communities. Prayers are held at 8.30am and 4.30pm.

Dark Cave

At step 204 on the way up to the Temple Cave, branch off to the **Dark Cave** (012-371 5001; www.darkcavemalaysia.com; adult/child RM35/25; 10am-5pm Tue-Fri, 10.30am-5.30pm Sat & Sun) to join an excellent, 45-minute guided tour along 850m of the 2km of surveyed passageways within the cave complex. The tour takes you through seven different chambers where you can witness dramatic limestone formations, including gorgeous flowstones, see pits used for guano extraction, and possibly spot two species of bat and hundreds of other life forms, including the rare trapdoor spider.

TOP TIPS

To visit the Temple Cave, women must wear skirts or trousers that come below the knee. Sarongs are available to rent at the cave entrance for RM3.

Bring water for the climb up to the Temple Cave, but keep any bottles or food out of sight of the monkeys.

TAKE A BREAK

The best of the restaurants and food stalls on the strip to the right of the Temple Cave is **Restoran Rani** (mains RM6-12; ⌚8am-9pm; 🌿); head there for good-value vegetarian thali sets, rotis and *dosas* washed down with a refreshing coconut juice served straight from the nut.

MONKEYS

Loitering in gangs on the steps up to the Temple Cave, the macaques of Batu Caves can seem by turn both adorable and menacing. Give them their space and you'll be fine. Feeding the monkeys is a bad idea, since it encourages aggressive behaviour. Avoid eating or carrying food as it might be stolen.

Tours run every 20 minutes and are organised by the Malaysian Nature Society. To get further into the cave on the three- to four-hour Adventure Tour you need a minimum of 10 people (RM80 per person); bookings must be made at least one week in advance.

There is an interesting natural history gallery outside the cave with informative displays on the formation of the cave and its unique flora and fauna.

Ramayana Cave

Perhaps no cave at Batu is more spectacularly embellished and enjoyable to visit than the **Ramayana Cave** (RM5; ⌚8.30am-6pm), which boasts psychedelic dioramas of the Indian epic Ramayana. This cave is on the left as you come out of the train station.

Near the entrance, look for the giant statue of Kumbhakarna, brother of Ravana and a deep sleeper (he once snoozed for six months). At the top of the towering cave interior is a shrine to a naturally occurring lingam, a stalagmite that is a symbol of Shiva.

Muzium Orang Asli

A trip to Batu Caves can easily be combined with a visit to the nearby **Muzium Orang Asli** (www.jakao.gov.my; 24 Jln Pahang, Gombak; ⌚9am-5pm Sat-Thu) FREE in the village of Gombak, 25km north of KL and around 9km from Batu Caves. This excellent museum is dedicated to Peninsular Malaysia's indigenous peoples, the Orang Asli. Exhibits over two floors highlight the 18 tribes' different traditions, beliefs and cultures, including their musical instruments, the importance of dreams and the distinct death rituals of the various groups. A gallery upstairs examines the Orang Asli's place in modern-day Malaysian politics and society.

A taxi from the caves to the museum costs RM50; it's best to do the trip in this direction and ask the driver to wait as it's difficult to find a taxi at the museum.

Zoo Negara

Laid out over 62 hectares around a central lake, **Zoo Negara** (National Zoo; ☎03-4108 3422; www.zoonegaramalaysia.my; Jln Ulu Kelang; adult/child RM85/43; ⌚9am-5pm; Ⓜ Wangsa Maju), 13km northeast of KL and 11km southeast of Batu Caves, is home to a wide variety of native wildlife, including tigers and other animals from other parts of Asia and Africa. One of the most popular new exhibits is the giant pandas. Although some of the enclosures could definitely be bigger, this is one of Asia's better zoos.

TOP SIGHT
FOREST RESEARCH INSTITUTE MALAYSIA (FRIM)

Covering nearly 600 hectares, the Forest Research Institute Malaysia (FRIM) was established in 1929 to research the sustainable management of the country's forests. As well as being an active centre for scientific research, FRIM also functions as a giant park, with quiet roads for cycling and established trails through the jungle landscape. The highlight is a fabulous canopy walkway.

DON'T MISS

- Canopy walkway
- Forest trails
- Museum

PRACTICALITIES

- FRIM
- ☎03-6279 7592
- www.frim.gov.my
- adult/child RM5/1
- ⏲8.30am-7.30pm
- 🚉Kepong Sentral

Canopy Walkway

Hanging a vertigo-inducing 30m above the forest floor, the 150m long **canopy walkway** (adult/child RM10/3; ⏲9.30am-1.30pm Tue-Thu, Sat & Sun) takes you right into the trees, offering views of the rainforest and the towers of KL in the distance. It's reached by a steep, 900m trail from the **tourist information office** (☎03-6279 7649; ⏲9am-1pm & 2-5pm Mon-Thu, 9am-12.15pm & 2.45-5pm Fri, 9am-1.30pm & 2-3pm Sat & Sun), on the right off the main road 1km from the entrance gate.

As you head down from the walkway, the trail picks its way through the jungle to a shady picnic area where you can cool off in a series of shallow waterfalls. The return hike, incorporating the walkway, takes around two hours.

Forest Trails

If you can get a group together, it's well worth hiring one of the park's experienced and knowledgeable **guides** (☎03-6279 7045; per group RM120) for a one- to two-hour tour of the three forest trails: the Salleh, Keruing and Engkabang trails.

Because the forest is planned, it has some unusual quirks; the same species of trees were usually planted together, leading to the phenomenon of 'crown shyness' (certain species of tree never touch the leaves of another tree of the same species). On the Salleh trail look up for the *National Geographic* shot of the canopy of kapur trees and the maze of channel-like gaps between them.

Museum & Cafe

The oldest building at FRIM houses an interesting **museum** (⏲9am-noon & 2-4pm Sat-Thu, 9am-noon & 3-4pm Fri) FREE with displays explaining the five forest types endemic to Malaysia, their different wood types and how they are used. Among the assorted items on display is a 60-year-old boat from Kelantan once used by the royal family. Upstairs a gallery highlights the forest-related research carried out by FRIM. In the section on the park's fauna, check out the gallery of forest bugs containing stick insects the length of your forearm.

More than a hundred scientists are employed at FRIM, researching uses for the forest's flora. The products developed by the institute are displayed in the museum and a few of them, such as lemongrass soap and natural insect repellent, can be bought in the shop at the One Stop Centre.

Head to **Cafe Kasah** (Sungai Kroh picnic area; mains RM5-6; ⏲7am-5pm) for *nasi goreng* (fried rice) and other local fare. Otherwise, bring your own picnic to enjoy by the Sungai Kroh waterfalls.

Bukit Fraser (Fraser's Hill)

Explore

Of all Malaysia's hill stations, Bukit Fraser (Fraser's Hill) retains the most colonial-era charm. Spread across seven densely forested hills in the Titiwangsa Range at an altitude ranging from 1220m to 1524m, this cool, quiet and relatively undeveloped station offers hiking and birdwatching within a short stroll of the village centre. With some excellent old-world accommodation options, Bukit Fraser is one of the best overnight retreats close to KL.

The Best...

- **Activity** Bird-spotting
- **Place to Eat** Scott's Pub & Restaurant (p117)
- **Place to Stay** Ye Olde Smokehouse Fraser's Hill

Top Tip

In May or June Bukit Fraser hosts an International Bird Race, in which teams of birdwatchers compete to observe and record the highest number of species in a set time period.

Getting There & Away

- **Taxi** The route to Bukit Fraser is via Chiling Waterfalls and Kuala Kubu Bharu (KKB). You can take a KTM Komuter train to KKB and then a taxi (one way RM100). There are few taxis at KKB, however, so rather than showing up and hoping for the best have your hotel arrange one for you. From Kuala Lumpur a taxi will cost around RM250.
- **Car** If driving yourself, note there's no petrol station in Bukit Fraser; the nearest ones are found at Raub and KKB.

Need to Know

- **Area Code** ☎09
- **Location** On the Selangor–Pahang border, 100km north of KL.
- **Fraser's Hill Tourist Information** (☎09-517 1623; www.pkbf.gov.my; Puncak Inn, Jln Genting)

SIGHTS

BIRD INTERPRETIVE CENTRE MUSEUM

(☎09-3622 007; ⏰10am-5pm Sat & Sun) FREE For an overview of the birding scene, visit the Bird Interpretive Centre on the 2nd floor of the golf course clubhouse, across the village square. To access the centre during the week, ask at the Puncak Inn.

SLEEPING IN FRASER'S HILL

If you plan to stay overnight, schedule your visit for midweek. Accommodation rates increase steeply at weekends and on public holidays.

Ye Olde Smokehouse Fraser's Hill (☎09-362 2226; www.thesmokehouse.my; Jln Jeriau; d/ste incl breakfast from RM280/400; wi-fi) Exposed beams, log fires, four-poster beds and chintz – the Smokehouse goes for broke on its English-charm offensive. Even if you don't stay here, drop by for a pint at the bar, or a well-made pie or roast at lunch (mains RM28 to RM70). Afternoon tea (RM28) is from 3pm to 6pm on the garden terrace, overlooking a wooded valley.

Puncak Inn (☎09-362 2007; puncakinn2@yahoo.com; Jln Genting; d incl breakfast from RM110, apt/cottages from RM150/300; @ wi-fi) This place offers the best-value rooms in Bukit Fraser and a handy central location. Apart from the hotel, it also offers studios, two- and three-bedroom apartments, and four cottages which can sleep between four and 15 people.

Shahzan Inn Fraser's Hill (☎09-362 3300; shahzan7@yahoo.com; Jln Lady Guillemard; d/apt incl breakfast from RM200/660; wi-fi) Overlooking the **golf course** (p118) – where guests receive a 20% discount – this is the most contemporary accommodation in Bukit Fraser.

WORTH A DETOUR

GENTING HIGHLANDS

Though referred to as a hill station, **Genting** (www.rwgenting.com) is a modern and heavily developed resort 2000m above sea level. About 50km north of KL, it's in stark contrast to the Old English style of other Malaysian upland resorts. There are no walks here, no quaint stone village, and in general little public space to stroll about and enjoy the mountain scenery.

Genting's raison d'être is **Resort World Genting** (☎03-2718 1888; ⊙casino open 24hrs), a glitzy casino billed as the only one in Malaysia, plus – coming soon – **20th Century Fox World**, a vast theme park slated to open in 2017.

Bird lovers should note that Genting is a prime location for birdwatching, with around 254 species seen here. The 3.4km-long **Genting Skyway** (one way RM6.40; ⊙7.30am-midnight) is a gentle 11-minute cable-car glide above the dense rainforest. Kids will also enjoy the various theme-park attractions here including those at the **First World Indoor Theme Park** (adult/child RM29.70/31.80; ⊙10am-midnight Mon-Fri, 9am-midnight Sat & Sun).

Genting is an easy day trip from KL but, if you'd prefer to stay, the resort has a choice of six hotels (sleeping a total of 10,000 people). Rates vary enormously, the most expensive nights generally being Saturday and public holidays; check the website. There's no shortage of places to eat, including cheap fast-food outlets and noisy food courts.

Genting Express buses leave at 7.30am and then on the hour from 9am to 7pm from KL's Pudu Sentral bus station (adult/child RM11/9.90, 1½ hours). The same service is offered on the hour from 8am to 8pm from KL Sentral (RM10.70/9.60). The price includes the return trip on the Skyway cable car. At these locations you can also join the **Go Genting Package Day Tour** (RM78), which includes return transport from KL, the Skyway transfer and either a theme-park pass or a combo meal. A taxi from KL to the Skyway costs at least RM100.

JERIAU WATERFALL WATERFALL

About 4km northwest of the town centre, along Jln Air Terjun, is Jeriau Waterfall, where you can swim. It's a 20-minute climb up from the road to reach the falls.

EATING & DRINKING

SCOTT'S PUB & RESTAURANT PUB

(www.thesmokehouse.my; Jln Genting; ⊙noon-10pm Thu-Tue) A slice of olde England is recreated at this pub where you can sink a pint of Fuller's London Pride and indulge in all-day breakfasts, stuffed chicken, steak or sandwiches (mains RM15 to RM30).

RESTORAN ARZED MALAYSIAN $

(☎09-326 2299; 5 Food Garden, Pine Tree Rd; mains RM6.50-16.50; ⊙noon-10pm) A friendly, family-run place at the Food Garden hawker centre, a 10-minute walk uphill from the clock tower. Come here for nasi goreng, *roti canai* and chicken and beef sets.

HILL VIEW CHINESE $$

(3 Food Garden, Pine Tree Rd; mains RM16-30; ⊙10am-9pm; 🖉) The family that has run this stall for a couple of generations serves up simple dishes. Find it in a hawker food court, a 10-minute walk uphill from the village square.

ACTIVITIES

MR DURAI BIRDWATCHING

(☎013-983 1633; durefh@hotmail.com; Shahzan Inn Fraser's Hill, Jln Lady Guillemard; per group half-/full day RM200/600) For one of Malaysia's top birding guides, contact the eagle-eyed Mr Durai, who has been taking people birdwatching for 28 years.

PINE TREE TRAIL HIKING

The best-known trail in the Bukit Fraser area is the 5km Pine Tree Trail, which takes about eight to 10 hours return. You don't need a guide, but you must register at the **police station** in the village first. Note that it's a long walk to the trailhead for those without a vehicle.

HEMMANT TRAIL HIKING

This relatively flat and wide path runs above the golf course for 1km. The trailhead is a few minutes' walk up from the village square.

WORTH A DETOUR

KUALA KUBU BHARU

Most travellers zip through Kuala Kubu Bharu, 70km north of KL, on their way to Bukit Fraser. However, the pretty town, known as KKB, is the jumping-off point for a number of outdoor activities including cycling, as it's the start point for a gruelling 40km pedal up to Bukit Fraser. For rafting and other water activities on local rivers and dams, a recommended outfitter is **Pierose Swiftwater** (☎013-361 3991; www.raftmalaysia.com; 11 Jln Damai 7; rafting per person from RM180; ⏲8am-6pm).

Thirteen kilometres after KKB on Federal Rte 55, just a short distance past the Selangor Dam, look right for the entrance to the Santuari Ikan Sungai Chiling (Chiling River Fish Reserve). On weekends you can't miss the spot as dozens of cars will be parked outside. Within the reserve you'll find a rough camping ground and a highly popular trail up to the 20m-tall Chiling Waterfalls on the Sungai Chiling (Chiling River). It's a 1½-hour walk starting from the small pedestrian bridge across the lot from the camping area. Register at the ranger's cabin by the bridge before you cross.

The route up is clearly marked, but it's a good idea to go with a group or guide, since you have to cross the river five times and there is a risk of flash flooding. **Happy Yen** (☎017-369 7831; www.happyyen.com; tours per person RM400) organises tours to the falls from KL, or join one of the many hiking groups.

KKB is connected to KL by the KTM Komuter train (RM8.70); you'll need to change at Rawang. A taxi from the station into town costs RM5 to RM10. Sleeping options in KKB are limited since most visitors continue on to Bukit Fraser. On the road back to KL near the town of Serendah (35km from KKB), the designer self-catering accommodation at **Sekeping Serendah** (☎012-324 6552; www.sekeping.com; 2-/4-/6-/10-person cabins from RM300/500/630/1160; ❄) makes for a blissfully peaceful rainforest retreat.

PADDOCK HORSE RIDING

(short rides adult/child RM9/6.50; ⏲9am-noon & 2-4.30pm Mon-Fri, to 7pm Sat & Sun) This small but charming paddock east of the golf course offers very short rides on gentle retired horses.

FRASER'S HILL GOLF CLUB GOLF

(☎09-362 2129; Jln Genting; green fees/clubs RM40/40; ⏲8am-6.30pm) East of the village square is this picturesque nine-hole golf course, one of the oldest in the country. A 20% discount is often available for guests of hotels in the area.

Klang Valley

Explore

Heading southwest of Kuala Lumpur along the Klang Hwy, the Kota Darul Ehsan ceremonial arch marks the transition between the city and Selangor. Just over the boundary, the mall-heavy suburb of Petaling Jaya (known locally as PJ) blends into Shah Alam, the state capital.

Next along is Klang, Selangor's former royal capital. The town makes for a pleasant diversion and, if combined with a trip to nearby Pulau Carey and a sumptuous feast in the vibrant Little India, a good day out.

Efficient public transport makes for easy day trips along the Klang Valley to see the scattered sights. For a complete escape from urbanised Malaysia, journey to the end of the rail line and hop on a ferry to Pulau Ketam, an island with a picturesque fishing village surrounded by mangroves.

The Best...

- **Cool-Down Spot** Sunway Lagoon (p121)
- **Mosque** Masjid Sultan Salahuddin Abdul Aziz Shah (p119)
- **Secret Garden** 1 Utama (p120)

Top Tip

Check out the Klang Valley's contemporary-music pulse at **Merdekarya** (☎016-2071 553, 016-2020 529; www.merdekarya.com; 1st fl, 352 Jln 5/57, Petaling Garden; ⏲7pm-1am Tue-Thu, to 2am Fri & Sat; Ⓜ Bank Rakyat-Bangsar), which hosts concerts and open-mic nights and sells local-interest books and CDs.

Getting There & Away

➡**Bus** From Pasir Seni in KL, frequent buses fan out to PJ, Shah Alam and Klang.

➡**LTR** The Sri Petaling and Kelana Jaya LRT lines connect Putra Heights with central KL, passing numerous stations in Petaling Jaya on the way.

➡**Train** KTM Komuter trains run from KL Sentral to Shah Alam (RM2.50, 30 minutes, every 20 to 30 minutes) and Klang (RM5.40, one hour, every 20 to 30 minutes)

Need to Know

➡**Area Code** 03

➡**Location** PJ is 10km, Shah Alam 20km and Klang 32km southwest of KL

➡**Tourist Information** www.tourismselangor.my/

SIGHTS

Shah Alam

MASJID SULTAN SALAHUDDIN ABDUL AZIZ SHAH MOSQUE

(Blue Mosque; 03-5159 9988; 9am-noon, 2-4pm & 5-6.30pm, closed 11.30am-3pm Fri; Shah Alam) FREE Known as the Blue Mosque, this is Southeast Asia's second-biggest mosque (it can hold up to 24,000 worshippers), and has the distinction of sporting the world's largest dome (for a religious building) and the tallest cluster of minarets, each more than 140m. Note that at research time the mosque was undergoing renovations and was closed to visitors. Get a taxi from Shah Alam.

LAMAN SENI 7 PUBLIC ART

(Lorong Belakang; www.facebook.com/khznhstudio; Jln Plumbum Q7/Q) FREE The works on display in this fun street-art project in a hidden alley include an intricately painted mural of a jungle scene and a Picasso-style abstract 3D piece incorporating plates. The project is a collaboration between Shah Alam City Council and artists from the KHZNH studio.

CITY OF DIGITAL LIGHTS AT I-CITY AMUSEMENT PARK

(03-5521 8800; www.i-city.my; Jln Multimedia; water park/other attractions RM30/52; City of Digital Lights 5pm-midnight, water park 11am-7pm Mon & Wed-Fri, 10am-7pm Sat & Sun; Padang Jawa) This amusement park built around the theme of lighting, with forests of multicoloured trees, flamingos and peacocks, will appeal to kids and lovers of kitsch experiences alike. Among the attractions are a **snowalk**, where the air-con is cranked up to keep the fairy-lit snowmen happy, an outdoor funfair and a water park. Note that each attraction has a separate entrance fee. Take a taxi from Padang Jawa.

Klang

GALERI DIRAJA SULTAN ABDUL AZIZ MUSEUM

(03-3373 6500; www.galeridiraja.com; Jln Stesen; 10am-5pm Tue-Sun) FREE This handsome, whitewashed colonial-era building designed by AB Hubback and built in 1909 was first used as a British administrative centre. It now houses a mildly interesting royal gallery devoted to the history of the Selangor Sultanate, which dates back to 1766. Inside there's a wide array of royal regalia, gifts and artefacts, including replicas of the crown jewels. The museum is three blocks from the train station on Jln Stesen.

MASJID DI RAJA SULTAN SULEIMAN MOSQUE

(Jln Kota Raja) This former state mosque, opened in 1934, is a striking blend of art deco and Middle Eastern influences. Several sultans are buried here. Note that at research time it was not possible to go inside the mosque because of ongoing repairs; once it's open, step inside to admire the stained-glass dome.

KLANG FIRE STATION MUSEUM

(Jln Gedung Raja Abdullah; 8am-6pm) FREE This working fire station has occupied the same Victorian-style building since 1890 and now also houses a small museum dedicated to the history of the Klang's fire service. If you're lucky, the fire station chief himself might be on hand to show you the exhibits, which include a wind-up siren from 1945, historic fire extinguishers, uniforms, hoses and nozzles.

ISTANA ALAM SHAH PALACE

(Jln Istana) This was the Selangor sultan's palace before the capital was moved to Shah Alam. You can't enter, but the park opposite offers a decent view.

Head out of the train station along Jln Stesen and continue walking as the road heads up the hill. The Istana Alam Shah is on the left across from a park.

EATING & DRINKING

Shah Alam

★DEWAKAN MALAYSIAN $$$

(03-5565 0767; www.dewakan.my; lower ground fl, KDU University College, Jln Kontraktor U1/14, Shah Alam; 5/10 courses RM180/240; 6.30-10pm Mon-Sat; Batu Tiga) Darren Teoh heads a team of exciting young chefs at this innovative restaurant based at the KDU University College in Shah Alam. It's worth making the journey out here to taste the impeccably presented fine-dining dishes with local flashes, such as cured mackerel with local flowers, braised aubergine with jackfruit seeds, and *gula melaka* (palm sugar) marquise. Book in advance.

The sublime mango curry mousse is based on Teoh's grandmother's recipe and made using mangoes from the chef's own garden. Get a taxi from Batu Tiga.

Klang

★YAP KEE MALAYSIAN $

(20 Jln Besar; mains RM7.50; 10.30am-4pm) This banana-leaf restaurant in an old shophouse two blocks to the right as you come out of the station usually has just a couple of choices available. But go with what's on offer and you won't regret it; the expert cooking of simple curry and rice meals is what gives Klang its reputation as a foodie town.

SRI BARATHAN MATHA VILAS INDIAN $

(34-36 Jln Tengku Kelana; mains RM6-10; 7am-10.30pm) It's hard to resist a bowl of this restaurant's signature dish of spicy mee goreng (fried noodles). The chef prepares them in a giant wok beside the entrance.

SENG HUAT BAK KUT TEH MALAYSIAN $$

(012-309 8303; http://senghuatbakkutteh.com; 9 Jln Besar; mains RM11-20; 7.30am-noon & 5.30-8.30pm;) Klang is famous for *bak kut teh* (pork stew made by simmering ribs in a broth of herbs and spices). If you like yours fragrant but not overpowering, sample it at Seng Huat, two blocks to the right as you exit the train station, beneath Klang Bridge. Get here early before the meat sells out.

★SERAPH AWAKEN COFFEE

(www.facebook.com/seraphawaken; 28 Jln Stesen 1; noon-7pm Mon & Thu-Fri, 10am-6pm Sat & Sun) Coffee-making is approached with scientific precision at Seraph Awaken, where owners Cheau See and Chun Hoong serve hand-brewed drip coffee from a counter of beakers and rubber tubes that wouldn't look out of place in a chemistry lab. The couple started out with a roadside coffee stall before moving into a beautiful, plant-filled *kopitiam* dating from 1928. Try the signature Hibiscus or Roselle coffees.

SHOPPING

Petaling Jaya

SUNWAY PYRAMID MALL

(03-7494 3100; www.sunwaypyramid.com; skating rink admission incl skate hire Mon-Fri RM17, Sat & Sun RM22; skating rink 9am-8pm; Setia Jaya) The vast Sunway Pyramid mall is distinguished by its giant lion gateway, faux Egyptian walls and crowning pyramid. Inside is a skating rink, bowling alley, multiplex cinema and the usual plethora of shops and dining outlets. Take a taxi from Setia Jaya.

CURVE MALL

(03-7710 6868; www.thecurve.com.my; 6 Jln PJU 7/3; 10am-10pm; M Mutiara Damansara) This sprawling shopping complex has an Ikea, a Tesco and plenty more shops and restaurants. It's about 15km west of the centre in Petaling Jaya.

JAYA ONE MALL

(http://jayaone.com.my; 72A Jln Universiti; 10am-10pm; M Asia Jaya) Home to the performing arts centre **PJ Live Arts** and a branch of the cafe, bar and live-music venue the **Bee**, Jaya One also hosts **Markets**, a huge bazaar of more than 80 vendors selling new and old items as well as handicrafts, held once every three months. Take a taxi from Asia Jaya station.

1 UTAMA MALL

(www.1utama.com.my; 1 Lebuh Bandar Utama, Bandar Utama; 10am-10pm Sun-Thu, to

WORTH A DETOUR

ISLAND ESCAPES

The islands of **Pulau Ketam** (Crab Island; www.pulauketam.com) and **Pulau Carey** – one reached by ferry, the other by road – are ideal antidotes to the Klang Valley's urban sprawl.

Ketam means 'crab' and an abundance of these creatures is what first brought Chinese settlers to the island, a 30-minute ferry trip (return RM14) through the mangroves from Pelabuhan Klang. On arrival you'll find a rickety yet charming fishing village built on stilts over the mudflats. Wander around the wooden buildings then enjoy a Chinese seafood lunch at one of several restaurants. Ferries depart roughly every hour starting at 8.45am; the last ferry back from Pulau Ketam is at 5.30pm (6pm at weekends).

On Pulau Carey, the **Mah Meri Cultural Village** (010-2522 800, 03-2282 3035; http://mmcv.org.my; Kampung Orang Asli Sungai Bumbun; RM7, with guide RM10; 9am-6pm Tue-Sun) is well worth a visit to learn about the distinct culture and traditions of the Mah Meri, a subgroup of the Senoi people who live along the coast of Selangor. The Mah Meri are renowned for their masterful woodcarving and expressive masks worn during dance rituals to represent ancestral spirits. Call or email to make an appointment before making the journey out here since the villagers are not always around.

The village museum has excellent displays of Mah Meri art with accompanying texts explaining the mythologies and local legends informing each piece. You are likely to see villagers weaving origami, used to decorate houses and please the spirits. It's also possible to arrange demonstrations of dance and wedding rituals.

You can order woodcarvings at the village centre, or pick up less expensive, but still wonderfully pretty, woven baskets and mats made from pandanus leaves, or palm leaf origami. You can also rent rickety bikes (RM15 per hour) to explore the rest of the island.

The Mah Meri Cultural Village is well signposted. If you don't have your own wheels, there are a couple of options for getting to the island. Check out the tour packages available on the website (minimum two people) or hire a taxi to Pulau Carey from Klang (return with a couple of hours on the island RM160).

10.30pm Fri & Sat; Kelana Jaya) The main reason for visiting this mall is for its 30,000-sq-ft **Secret Garden**, one of the largest roof gardens in the world with more than 500 varieties of plants. There's also a mini-rainforest in the mall's atrium and the climbing centre Camp5. Take a taxi from Kelana Jaya.

AMCORP MALL MALL

(www.facebook.com/amcorpmallofficial; 18 Jln Persiaran Barat; 10am-10pm; Taman Jaya) Amcorp might not fare well against the area's newer, shinier malls, but it's worth visiting at weekends for its popular **flea market**. Browse the stalls for secondhand clothes, antiques, old movie posters and other collectables every Saturday and Sunday.

Klang

AJUNTHA TEXTILE FASHION & ACCESSORIES

(03-3371 7571; 20 Jln Tengku Kelana; 9am-10pm) Behind an elaborate carved wooden shopfront is this Indian textiles and jewellery emporium. Come here for silk scarves, saris, jewellery and gorgeous children's outfits.

ACTIVITIES

Petaling Jaya

SUNWAY LAGOON AMUSEMENT PARK

(03-5639 0182; http://sunwaylagoon.com; 3 Jln PJS, 11/11 Bandar Sunway; adult/child RM150/120; 10am-6pm; Setia Jaya) Built on the site of a former tin mine and quarry, this multi-zone theme park has 80 attractions, including the world's largest artificial surf beach and an array of water slides (don't miss riding a dinghy down into a giant funnel on the Vuvuzela). It's a great place to cool off on a hot, sticky day. Get a taxi from Setia Jaya.

CAMP5 CLIMBING

(03-7726 0410; www.camp5.com; 5th fl, 1 Utama Shopping Centre, Bandar Utama Damansara; day passes adult/child RM33/16, 1hr taster sessions incl equipment RM55; ⏲2-11pm Mon-Fri, 10am-8pm Sat & Sun; Ⓜ Kelana Jaya) The 5th floor of the 1 Utama mall (p120) has been transformed into a state-of-the-art indoor climbing facility. One great advantage of climbing in this 24m-high space is that it's air-conditioned. Grab a taxi from Kelana Jaya.

Klang

ROYAL KLANG HERITAGE WALK WALKING

(☎03-5513 2000; www.tourismselangor.my; ⏲10am-12.30pm Sat & Sun) FREE This free guided walk from Tourism Selangor meets at the Galeri Diraja Sultan Abdul Aziz (p119) every Saturday and Sunday at 10am and covers nine of the town's heritage sights.

Putrajaya

Explore

An eye-catching array of monumental architecture amid lush, manicured greenery is on display in Putrajaya, 25km south of KL and 20km north of Kuala Lumpur International Airport (KLIA). Covering 49.32 sq km of former rubber and oil-palm plantations, the federal government's administrative hub (almost exclusively Muslim in population) was but a twinkle in the eye of its principal visionary – former prime minister Dr Mahathir – as late as the early 1990s.

As a showcase of urban planning and vaulting architectural ambition, Putrajaya is impressive, but it's still a long way off its envisioned population of over 300,000 and a strange place to visit. At its heart is a 6-sq-km artificial lake fringed by landscaped parks and an eclectic mix of buildings and bridges, best viewed when illuminated at night.

The Best...

➜**Lakeside Mosque** Putra Mosque (p123)

➜**Botanical Garden** Taman Botani (p123)

➜**Place to Eat** Alamanda (p123)

Top Tip

Just over 97% of Putrajaya's population is Muslim – something to be aware of when choosing how to dress and behave while visiting the city's mosques.

Getting There & Away

➜**Train** KLIA transit trains from KL Sentral (one way RM14, 20 minutes) and KLIA (one way RM9.40, 18 minutes) stop at Putrajaya Sentral (Putrajaya & Cyberjaya).

Getting Around

➜**Bus & taxi** The 502 bus runs from the train station to close to Dataran Putra. A taxi is RM15.

➜**Electric vehicles & bicycles** Both can be hired from the Tourist Information Booth (p122). The two-seater electric cars are RM100 per hour. At weekends bicycles are also available to rent (RM6 per hour).

Need to Know

➜**Area Code** ☎03

➜**Location** 25km south of KL and 20km north of KLIA

➜**Tourist Information Booth** (Dataran Putra; ⏲9am-1pm & 2-5pm, closed 12.45-2.45pm Fri)

SLEEPING IN PUTRAJAYA

Putrajaya Shangri-la (☎03-8887 8888; www.shangri-la.com; Taman Putra Perdana, Presint 1; d from RM320; ❄@🛜🏊) This elegant hotel has spacious rooms with Malay-style wooden furnishings and great hillside views across to Putrajaya Lake. Good-value weekend packages are available, and there are frequent online promotions.

Pullman Putrajaya Lakeside (☎03-8890 0000; www.pullmanputrajaya.com; 2 Jln P5/5, Presint 5; d from RM230; ❄@🛜🏊) Close to the Convention Centre and beside Putrajaya Lake, this large resort complex incorporates traditional Malaysian architectural elements into its design. The best rooms are the ones with balconies and lake views. Resort facilities include a good-sized pool and an al fresco seafood restaurant built over the lake.

SIGHTS

Monumental buildings designed in an array of architectural styles line the main boulevard of Persiaran Perdana, which runs from the circular **Dataran Putra** (Putra Sq) to the elevated, spaceship-like **Putrajaya Convention Centre** (03-8887 6000; Presint 5), worth visiting for the views. In between, check out the Mogul-esque **Istana Kehakiman** (Palace of Justice); the striking modernist Islamic gateway (composed of a lattice of steel blades) fronting the **Kompleks Perdadanan Putrajaya** (Putrajaya Corporation Complex); and the **Tuanku Mizan Zainal Abidin Mosque** (Iron Mosque), which can be seen through the gateway across the **Kiblat Walk** skyway.

On opposite edges of Dataran Putra are **Perdana Putra**, housing the offices of the prime minister, and the handsome **Putra Mosque** (9am-12.30pm, 2-4pm & 5.30-6pm Sat-Thu, 3-4pm & 5.30-6pm Fri) FREE, with space for 15,000 worshippers and an ornate pink-and-white-patterned dome, influenced by Safavid architecture from Iran. Non-Muslim visitors are welcome outside prayer times.

There are nine bridges in Putrajaya, all in different styles. The longest, at 435m, is the **Putra Bridge**, which mimics the Khaju Bridge in Esfahan, Iran. Also worthy of a photo is the futuristic, sail-like **Seri Wawasan Bridge** connecting Precinct 2 and 8. The bridges and buildings look their best viewed from **Putrajaya Lake**.

TAMAN BOTANI — GARDENS

(Botanical Gardens; 03-8888 9090; Presint 1; 9am-1pm & 2-6pm Sat-Thu, 9am-noon & 3-6pm Fri) FREE This 93-hectare site just north of town features attractive tropical gardens, a visitor centre, a lakeside restaurant and a beautifully tiled **Moroccan Pavilion** (admission adult/child RM3/1). A tourist tram (RM4) trundles between the flower beds and trestles, and you can hire bicycles (RM4 per hour). You'll need to take a taxi to get here.

TAMAN WETLAND — PARK

(03-8887 7773; Presint 13; 9am-5.30pm Mon-Fri, to 6.30pm Sat & Sun) A short taxi ride from Dataran Putra, this serene space has peaceful nature trails, aquatic animals and waterbirds, fluttering butterflies and picnic tables overlooking the lake. Canoes, kayaks and bikes can be rented at the boathouse (from 9am to 7pm), which is about 1km from the Nature Interpretative Centre (open 9am to 5pm Tuesday to Sunday) by road or walkway.

CHINA-MALAYSIA FRIENDSHIP GARDEN — GARDENS

(Anjung Floria; Precinct 4) FREE It's worth dropping by this peaceful Chinese-style garden, located next to the **Seri Saujana Bridge** in Precinct 4. The design of the garden incorporates elements of Lingnan architecture, a style originating in Guangdong and nearby provinces of China, and includes a pretty pagoda, rockery and pond. Plants are labelled in English.

EATING

SELERA PUTRA — FOOD HALL $

(mains RM7-10; 9am-7pm Mon-Fri, to 9pm Sat & Sun) Head to this food court beneath Dataran Putra and enjoy the lakeside view while enjoying a wide range of inexpensive Malaysian dishes.

ALAMANDA — FOOD HALL $$

(www.alamanda.com.my; Jln Alamanda, Presint 1; meals RM20; 10am-10pm) Putrajaya's shopping mall is home to several restaurants as well as an excellent food court where you can join the local bureaucrats for a meal. You'll need to take a taxi or your own wheels to get here.

ACTIVITIES

CRUISE TASIK PUTRAJAYA — BOATING

(03-8888 5539; www.cruisetasikputrajaya.com; adult/child Perahu Dondang Sayang boat RM42/27, Belimbing cruise RM53/37; 10am-7.15pm Mon-Fri, to 9.30pm Sat & Sun) Located just beneath Dataran Putra underneath Putra Bridge, this outfit offers two basic options for cruising Putrajaya Lake: the gondola-like Perahu Dondang Sayang boats, which depart any time for a 25-minute trip, and a 45-minute air-con cruise on the Belimbing boat, which leaves about every hour. There are also shorter early-bird air-conditioned cruises before 1pm (25 minutes in duration).

PUTRAJAYA SIGHTSEEING — TOURS

(03-8890 4788; Putrajaya Sentral; adult/child RM20/10; 3pm Fri, 11am & 1pm Sat-Thu) These tours stop at 12 sights in town. Tickets can be purchased on the spot (just after you exit the platform area) but call ahead to confirm departure times as they are changeable.

Sleeping

KLites' love of brands is reflected in the city's many international hotel chains. You can often grab great online deals for top-end accommodation, and there are also some excellent new boutique-style midrange options. Budget sleeps are plentiful, too, but the best places fill up quickly, so book ahead – especially over public holidays.

Hostels & Guesthouses

Kuala Lumpur has plenty of inexpensive hostels and guesthouses. Most offer dorm beds as well as basic rooms with shared or private bathrooms. Even the cheapest accommodation usually has air-con; fan-only rooms are rare.

If your budget is really tight, there are several cramped and musty hostels appealing only for their rock-bottom rates. For those who are more flush, however, there are some very appealing 'flashpacker' hostels and guesthouses. A preferable option to zero-personality budget business hotels, these offer spacious, comfy dorms and private rooms with bells and whistles that are several steps up from the norm in quality.

Hotels

As a rule, the cheapest budget hotels offer poky box rooms, often with thin plywood partition walls and no windows; there may be a choice of private or shared bathrooms. In cheaper hotels, 'single' normally means one double bed, and 'double' means two double beds. To aid ventilation, the walls of cheaper rooms may not meet the ceiling, which is terrible for acoustics and privacy - bring earplugs.

At midrange hotels air-con is standard, and rooms typically come with TVs, phones, proper wardrobes and private bathrooms. Many midrange hotels also have restaurants, business centres and swimming pools. Some boutique properties offer stylish rooms for very reasonable rates.

With stiff competition at the top end of the market, KL's best hotels pull out all the stops. Rooms have every conceivable amenity, including fast wi-fi, safes, minibars, slippers and robes, and even prayer mats for Muslim guests. Look online for discount rates and also for news about several pending international openings, including the Four Seasons and the Banyan Tree.

Homestays

Staying with a Malaysian family in KL is possible, although few homestays will be centrally located. Contact local offices of Tourism Malaysia (www.tourismmalaysia.gov.my) for more information and also check sites such as iBilik (www.ibilik.my) and Asia Homestay (asiahomestay.com).

Serviced Apartments & Longer-Term Rentals

Some of KL's best accommodation deals, particularly for longer stays, are offered by serviced apartments. Studios and suites tend to be far larger and better equipped than you'd get for a similar price at top-end hotels. There are usually pools and gyms within the complexes, too. There are quite a few of these complexes scattered across the city. For short stays, breakfast is usually included.

Lonely Planet's Top Choices

BackHome (p129) Chic pit stop for flashpackers with a cool cafe and a tree-studded courtyard.

Sekeping Tenggiri (p131) Rough-luxe guesthouse plus top contemporary art gallery.

Villa Samadhi (p128) Asian-chic style at a gorgeous villa in the embassy district.

Best by Budget

$

BackHome (p129) Stripped-back concrete-chic dorms and rooms, plus a great cafe.

Lantern Hotel (p129) Slick, contemporary hotel in the heart of Chinatown.

Reggae Mansion (p129) Cool crash pad for the modern backpacker.

$$

Sekeping Tenggiri (p131) Lovely guesthouse combining art, greenery and a plunge pool.

Kuala Lumpur Journal (p127) Hip new boutique hotel in Bukit Bintang with a fantastic rooftop pool.

Aloft Kuala Lumpur Sentral (p131) Playful, relaxed concept hotel steps from the KLIA Ekspres.

$$$

Majestic Hotel (p132) Heritage hotel with a modern tower wing and a gorgeous spa.

G Tower Hotel (p128) Slick, modern luxury accommodation on the upper floors of the G Tower.

Villa Samadhi (p128) Beautiful Asian-chic bolthole with gorgeous tree-shaded pool.

Best Heritage Hotels

Majestic Hotel (p132) Soak up the colonial style and take tea in the orchid room.

Anggun Boutique Hotel (p128) Antique-style charmer with four-poster beds and patterned tile floors.

Sarang Vacation Homes (p130) Friendly B&B operation in a variety of centrally located heritage homes.

Best Designer Stays

Sekeping Sin Chew Kee (p130) Swoon-worthy pair of contemporary-art-decorated rooms and apartments.

Chaos Hotel (p127) Concrete and exposed brick abound at this minimalist designer joint.

Container Hotel (p127) Stacked shipping containers have been turned into cosy en-suite rooms.

Best Flashpacker Hostels

BackHome (p129) Zen simple decoration, fab rain showers and a blissful central courtyard.

Reggae Mansion (p129) Lively rooftop bar, mini cinema and cafe-bar.

Paper Plane Hostel (p130) Exposed brick and original artwork in a restored 90-year-old shophouse.

Best Serviced Apartments

E&O Residences Kuala Lumpur (p128) Live the life of a high-rolling expat at these gorgeous serviced apartments.

Fraser Place Kuala Lumpur (p129) Functional, fashionable and facility-packed complex.

NEED TO KNOW

Prices

The following price ranges refer to a double room with bathroom.

$ less than RM100

$$ RM100–RM400

$$$ more than RM400

Discounts

Practically all midrange and top-end places offer promotions that substantially slash rack rates; booking online will almost always bring the price down. Room discounts will not apply during public holidays.

Taxes & Service Charges

At all budget places prices will be net, but at many others 10% service and 6% tax (expressed as ++) will be added to the bill.

Tipping

Not expected.

Wi-Fi

Usually free but sometimes only in the hotel lobby.

Useful Websites

iBilik (www.ibilik.my) Room rentals in Malaysia.

Asia Homestay (http://asiahomestay.com) Malaysian homestay booking site.

Lonely Planet (www.lonelyplanet.com/malaysia/kuala-lumpur/hotels) Recommendations and bookings.

Where to Stay

NEIGHBOURHOOD	FOR	AGAINST
BUKIT BINTANG & KLCC	Kuala Lumpur's top shopping, dining and nightlife are all within easy walking access. There's good public transport, too, with the many hotels near a monorail or LRT station.	Bring earplugs if you're staying in properties around Changkat Bukit Bintang, as it gets very noisy at night.
CHINATOWN, MERDEKA SQUARE & BUKIT NANAS	Best location for quality hostels and hanging out with other budget travellers. Good public transport and great food and local atmosphere on the doorstep.	The cheapest places to stay range from very basic to down-right awful.
MASJID INDIA, KAMPUNG BARU & NORTHERN KL	Worth looking online for home-stay options in Kampung Baru. Reasonably good public transport links as well as excellent eating options.	Many budget and midrange hotels are scruffy and have little character. The nearby Chow Kit red-light district is seedy.
LAKE GARDENS, BRICKFIELDS & BANGSAR	Prime access to Kuala Lumpur International Airport (KLIA) and the rest of the city from KL Sentral. Interesting and lively Brickfields area a short walk away, as well as Lake Gardens.	Not as much street life as in Chinatown or Bukit Bintang.

Bukit Bintang & KLCC

DORMS KL HOSTEL $

Map p252 (03-2110 1221; www.dormskl.com; 5 Tengkat Tong Shin; dm incl breakfast RM30; ; Imbi) This sociable, dorm-only hostel in a renovated shophouse is within stumbling distance of the bars and eateries of Changkat Bukit Bintang and Jln Alor. There is a comfy lounge area where travellers congregate to swig beers and watch movies. The spotless bathrooms have rain showers.

CONTAINER HOTEL DESIGN HOTEL $

Map p253 (03-2110 4388; http://containerhotel.my; 1 Jln Delima; d RM60-169; ; AirAsia-Bukit Bintang) Stacked shipping containers turned into cosy en-suite rooms are the basis of this inventive place. Deviating from the industrial design theme, a number of containers house safari-style tents for an indoor 'camping' experience; we preferred the beds in giant concrete cylinders. The concrete and campsite rooms share bathrooms.

★**KUALA LUMPUR JOURNAL** BOUTIQUE HOTEL $$

Map p252 (03-2110 2211; www.kljournalhotel.com; 30 Jln Beremi; d from RM275; ; Air Asia-Bukit Bintang) This sleek new boutique hotel with a hip, urban vibe and appealing retro design is located steps away from Bukit Bintang's shopping and nightlife. Rooms feature blown-up prints of KL street life by local photographer Che Mat and floor-to-ceiling windows to take in the city views. The rooftop saltwater pool and bar is a plus.

D'MAJESTIC PLACE HOTEL $$

Map p252 (03-2148 9988; www.swissgarden.com; 376 Jln Pudu; d/ste from RM280/350; ; MPudu) The rooms and one- and two-bedroom suites at this slick new hotel are spacious and well designed with contemporary furnishings and splashes of colour, but D'Majestic Place's biggest draw is its rooftop infinity pool and deck, with spectacular city views. It's located close to Pudu LRT station, about 1.5km from Bukit Bintang.

WOLO BUKIT BINTANG BOUTIQUE HOTEL $$

Map p252 (03-2719 1333; www.thewolo.com; cnr Jln Bukit Bintang & Jln Sultan Ismail; d from RM200; ; AirAsia-Bukit Bintang) Neon and mirror-clad elevators whisk you to dark corridors, the walls rippled with fabric, and on into rooms where the mattress sits on a blonde-wood floor base, like a futon, and the shower and toilet are hidden behind faux padded-leather doors. The vibe is rock-star-glam and a change from the midrange norm.

MELANGE BOUTIQUE HOTEL HOTEL $$

Map p252 (03-2141 8828; www.melangehotel.com.my; 14 Jln Rembia; s/d from RM80/120; ; AirAsia-Bukit Bintang) The Melange's small, well-equipped rooms are decorated in one of three themes: *tampan* (handsome) rooms have a masculine feel with plenty of wood and gold and black marble; *ayu* (elegant) rooms are minimalist and white; while *manja* (fun) rooms are brightly coloured with insect-shaped lamps and dragonflies on the ceiling. A good-value option with some fun design touches.

CHAOS HOTEL HOTEL $$

Map p252 (03-2148 6688; www.chaos-hotel.com; lot B1, Fahrenheit 88, 179 Jln Bukit Bintang; s/d from RM135/168; ; AirAsia-Bukit Bintang) It might seem like tempting fate to call your hotel Chaos, but this place is actually well run with compact, smart, minimalist rooms with concrete and exposed brick walls, wooden fixtures and snazzy graphic art. Standard rooms are windowless.

CERIA HOTEL HOTEL $$

Map p252 (03-2143 1111; www.ceriahotel.com; 270 Jln Changkat Thambi Dollah; s/d RM98/138; ; Imbi) An old shophouse has been cleverly converted into this 44-room hotel with exposed brick walls and some cool retro design features. Not all the rooms have windows but they're of a reasonable size with slightly better quality features than similar hotels at this price point. Plus there's a nice attached cafe for breakfast.

MESUI HOTEL BOUTIQUE HOTEL $$

Map p253 (03-2144 8188; www.themesuihotel.com; 9 Jln Mesui; d from RM170; ; Raja Chulan) This low-scale gem is crafted from an old building that looks like it was made from a giant's set of building blocks. The Luxe rooms allow you to peer out of the large signature circular windows on to the street. Other compact, functional rooms gain their light from the interior courtyard, one wall of which is covered in lush greenery.

Plans are in the works to create a rooftop garden.

ANGGUN BOUTIQUE HOTEL HOTEL $$

Map p252 (03-2145 8003; www.anggunkl.com; 7-9 Tengkat Tong Shin; d incl breakfast from RM250; Imbi) Two 1920s shophouses have been combined to create this antique-style, boutique property, which oozes tropical charm with four-poster beds, dark-wood floors and local crafts. A restaurant on the 1st-floor terrace serves breakfast and dinner, and there is a new spa up in the eaves (one-hour massage costs RM60). Avoid rooms facing the noisy street though – or bring earplugs.

SAHABAT GUEST HOUSE GUESTHOUSE $$

Map p253 (03-2142 0689; www.sahabatguesthouse.com; 39-41 Jln Sahabat; d incl breakfast from RM115; Raja Chulan) This blue-painted guesthouse is well run, offering 14 tidy bedrooms with tiny en-suite bathrooms and a feature wall plastered in vivid patterned wallpaper. There's a grassy front garden in which to relax and a small kitchen for preparing food. Rates are slightly higher from Friday to Sunday.

CLASSIC INN HOSTEL $$

Map p252 (03-2148 8648; www.classicinn.com.my; 36 & 52 Lg 1/77a; dm/s/d incl breakfast RM38/118/148; Imbi) Check-in is at the newer, more upmarket branch of Classic Inn at No 36, where there's spotless rooms all with private bathrooms and a pleasant verandah cafe. The original yellow-painted shophouse at No 52 continues to be a retro-charming choice with dorms and private rooms, a small grassy garden and welcoming staff. Rates are slightly higher at weekends.

YY38 HOTEL HOTEL $$

Map p252 (03-2148 8838; www.yy38hotel.com.my; 38 Tengkat Tong Shin; s/d/loft room from RM130/150/360; AirAsia-Bukit Bintang) The bulk of the rooms here are fine but no-frills. However, the 7th floor offers 17 creatively designed duplexes, each sleeping three, with fun themes ranging from Marilyn Monroe to circus and tree house – a good one if you're travelling with kids.

RAINFOREST BED & BREAKFAST GUESTHOUSE $$

Map p253 (03-2145 3525; www.rainforestbnbhotel.com; 27 Jln Mesui; dm/d/tw incl breakfast RM37/115/130; Raja Chulan) The lush foliage sprouting around and tumbling off the tiered balconies of this guesthouse is eye-catching and apt given its name. Inside, bright-red walls and timber-lined rooms (some without windows) are visually distinctive and there is a small kitchen for preparing food. The location couldn't be better for nightlife, cafes and restaurants.

★**G TOWER HOTEL** HOTEL $$$

Map p250 (03-2168 1919; www.gtowerhotel.com; 199 Jln Tun Razak; r from RM400; Ampang Park) There's an exclusive atmosphere at this slickly designed property atop an office complex, where the facilities include a gym, infinity pools and a top-floor lounge, restaurant and bar. Arty black-and-white prints set a sophisticated tone in the bedrooms. Ask for one of the slightly bigger corner rooms, preferably with a view of Tabung Haji.

★**E&O RESIDENCES KUALA LUMPUR** APARTMENT $$$

Map p251 (03-2023 2188; www.eoresidences.com; 1 Jln Tengah; 1-bed apt from RM600; Raja Chulan) Chances are once you spend a night in these elegantly designed apartments, with their clean-line furnishings and striking contemporary art, you will not want to leave. There's a good gym and large outdoor pool in the landscaped courtyard garden.

★**VILLA SAMADHI** HOTEL $$$

Map p250 (03-2143 2300; www.villasamadhi.com.my; 8 Persiaran Madge; d from RM700; Ampang Park) It's hard to believe you're in the heart of KL when staying at this gorgeous boutique property that epitomises Southeast Asian chic. The black polished concrete, bamboo and reclaimed-timber rooms combine with luxurious light fixtures, idyllic central pool, lush foliage, poolside bar (serving complimentary cocktails) and intimate modern Malay restaurant Mandi Mandi to conjure an antidote to urban stress.

The recent addition of a Thai-style spa in the roof space is set to raise bliss levels even higher.

INVITO APARTMENT $$$

Map p253 (03-2386 9288; www.invitohotelsuites.com.my; 1 Lg Ceylon; studio/2-bed apt from RM370/550; Raja Chulan) A lively location and good facilities, including a decent-sized pool, Jacuzzi and gym, mark out this stylish hotel of self-catering studios and apartments. All units have balconies, and the purple and silver decor is reasonably classy.

MICASA ALL SUITE HOTEL APARTMENT $$$
Map p250 (03-2179 8000; www.micasahotel.com; 368b Jln Tun Razak; apt from RM425; ; Ampang Park) A choice of one-, two- or three-bedroom suites – all reasonably priced, with wood floors and well-equipped kitchens. Relax beside the large, palm-tree-fringed pool, or enjoy the small spa and the gourmet restaurant Cilantro (p57). Facilities include a gym and coin-operated laundry.

RITZ CARLTON HOTEL $$$
Map p253 (03-2142 8000; www.ritzcarlton.com; 168 Jln Imbi; d/ste incl breakfast from RM932/1550; ; AirAsia-Bukit Bintang) Recent renovations have revamped the Ritz, where the gleaming new lobby sports contemporary gold light fixtures and a mirrored reception desk. Dark wood and marble create a nostalgic old-world atmosphere, and rooms are extravagantly appointed, if conservative in taste. The on-site Spa Village (p66) is highly recommended.

FRASER PLACE KUALA LUMPUR APARTMENT $$$
Map p250 (03-2118 6288; http://kualalumpur.frasershospitality.com; lot 163, 10 Jln Perak; apt from RM380; ; Bukit Nanas) Good workspaces and walk-in closets feature in these colourfully designed apartments. The facilities, including an outdoor infinity pool, gym, sauna and games room, are top-notch.

MANDARIN ORIENTAL HOTEL $$$
Map p250 (03-2380 8888; www.mandarin-oriental.com/kualalumpur; Jln Pinang; d from RM720; ; KLCC) Backing on to the greenery of KLCC Park, the Mandarin is one for sybarites. Silks and batiks lend an Asian feel to the rooms, which have every conceivable amenity. The club rooms are the ones to pick, allowing access to a lounge overlooking the Petronas Towers. There's a spa and an infinity pool that seems to merge into the parkland beyond.

GRAND HYATT KUALA LUMPUR HOTEL $$$
Map p250 (03-2182 1234; www.kualalumpur.grand.hyatt.com; 12 Jln Pinang; d from RM600; ; Raja Chulan) Elevators whisk you up to a panoramic entrance lobby that pits you eye to eye with the upper levels of the Petronas Towers. All the marble- and wood-clad rooms provide great city views, and together with the top-class facilities are what you'd expect from this international brand.

PARKROYAL SERVICED SUITES APARTMENT $$$
Map p251 (03-2084 1000; www.parkroyalhotels.com; 1 Jln Nagasari; studio/1-bed/2-bed apt from RM380/410/990; ; Raja Chulan) In a great location with designer studios and one- and two-bedroom suites; the Parkroyal's facilities include two outdoor pools (one on the roof).

TRADERS HOTEL KUALA LUMPUR HOTEL $$$
Map p250 (03-2332 9888; www.shangri-la.com; KLCC, off Jln Kia Peng; d without/with towers view from RM480/605; ; KLCC) Perched on the edge of the KLCC Park, this contemporary design hotel offers a superb vantage point for Petronas Towers gazing; it's worth paying the supplement for a room facing the iconic landmark. Its rooftop pool and Sky Bar (p62) is a famous hang-out.

Chinatown, Merdeka Square & Bukit Nanas

★**BACKHOME** HOSTEL $
Map p248 (03-2022 0788; www.backhome.com.my; 30 Jln Tun HS Lee; dm/d/tr incl breakfast from RM56/138/192; ; Masjid Jamek) This chic pit stop for flashpackers offers polished-concrete finishes, Zen simple decoration, fab rain showers (all rooms share bathrooms) and a blissful central courtyard sprouting spindly trees. Also check out its cool cafe, LOKL (p77).

★**REGGAE MANSION** HOSTEL $
Map p248 (03-2072 6877; www.reggaehostelsmalaysia.com/mansion; 49-59 Jln Tun HS Lee; dm/d from RM55/130; ; Masjid Jamek) Grooving to a beat that's superior to that of most backpacker places, this is one cool operation. The decor is whitewashed faux colonial with contemporary touches, including a lively rooftop bar, a mini cinema and a flash cafe-bar where a free meal is served in the evenings. Ask for a quieter room away from the bar if you're not a night owl.

LANTERN HOTEL HOTEL $
Map p249 (03-2020 1648; www.lanternhotel.com; 38 Jln Petaling; d incl breakfast RM95-115; ; Pasar Seni) You can't get more cen-

tral to Chinatown than this slickly designed, contemporary hotel. The simple, whitewashed rooms with feature walls in lime or tangerine all have their own bathrooms – the cheapest ones have no windows, others have small balconies. A huge plus is the terrace with a cityscape mural, creeper plants and a bird's-eye view of Petaling Street Market.

PALOMA INN HOTEL $

Map p249 (☎03-2110 6677; www.hotelpalomainn.com.my; 12-14 Jln Sin Chew Kee; dm/s/d incl breakfast from RM48/95/128; ❄@📶; 🚝Hang Tuah) Set on a backstreet of painted pre-war shophouses, Paloma is a great hang-out that's well run and quiet, but also super central. VCR cafe (p79) is just around the corner for superb espresso, while the nightlife of Changkat Bukit Bintang is a 10-minute walk away. Rates are slightly higher Friday to Sunday.

EXPLORERS GUESTHOUSE HOSTEL $

Map p249 (☎03-2022 2928; www.theexplorersguesthouse.com; 128-130 Jln Tun HS Lee; dm/d incl breakfast from RM38/97; ❄@📶; Ⓜ Pasar Seni) One of Chinatown's more appealing hostels, the Explorers is comfortable and well run. The spacious lobby leads on to clean rooms with colourfully painted walls and a few arty touches, and there's a roof terrace. All rooms share bathrooms.

★SARANG VACATION HOMES GUESTHOUSE $$

Map p249 (☎012-333 5666; www.sarangvacationhomes.com; 6 Jln Galloway; s/d incl breakfast from RM120/150; ❄📶; 🚝Hang Tuah) This appealing bed-and-breakfast operation is run by Michael and Christina. They have houses, apartments and rooms in five nearby locations and can accommodate single travellers and families alike. The furnishings are simple, the vibe is relaxed and welcoming and the location is excellent. It's a skip away from Jln Alor in a residential shophouse enclave. The couple also runs an excellent cafe, and cooking classes through Sarang Cookery (p81).

PAPER PLANE HOSTEL HOSTEL $$

Map p249 (☎03-2110 1676; www.paperplanehostel.com; 15 Jln Sin Chew Kee; dm/d RM74/170; ❄📶; 🚝Hang Tuah) A 90-year-old shophouse on photogenic Jln Sin Chew Kee has been converted into this spotlessly clean, hipstertastic hostel with original features and exposed brick walls. The space doubles as a gallery for boss Sam's artworks and murals. Loft-room dorms have dizzying three-tier bunks. Bathrooms are shared.

HOTEL 1000 MILES HOTEL $$

Map p248 (☎03-2022 3333; http://1000mileskl.com; 17 & 19 Jln Tun HS Lee; d incl breakfast from RM115; ❄@📶; Ⓜ Masjid Jamek) Channelling a vague 1960s feel (black-and-white photos of KL, a few modish pieces of mid-century modern furniture), this bright hotel has kerb appeal and friendly management. The rooms are all en suite and fine, and the roof terrace has good views of the Menara KL. Rates increase slightly at weekends.

SEKEPING SIN CHEW KEE APARTMENT $$

Map p249 (www.sekeping.com; 3 Jln Sin Chew Kee; d/apt RM250/800; ❄📶; 🚝Hang Tuah) Architect Ng Seksan's pared-back, quirky style is in full evidence at this rough-luxe accommodation tucked away on Jln Sin Chew Kee, one of the last pre-war shophouse rows in the city. Raw yet beautiful and decorated with fab local art, the upstairs apartment sleeps up to eight and has a kitchen and outdoor relaxation space. Barlai (p79) is on the ground floor, so it can be a bit noisy.

ANCASA HOTEL & SPA KUALA LUMPUR HOTEL $$

Map p249 (☎03-2026 6060; www.ancasa-hotel.com; Jln Tun Tan Cheng Lock; d incl breakfast from RM258; ❄@; Ⓜ Plaza Rakyat) Promotional rates (including Friday to Sunday rates of RM160) make this one of Chinatown's best midrange options. The comfortable rooms are well equipped and there's an in-house Balinese-style spa.

5 ELEMENTS HOTEL HOTEL $$

Map p249 (☎03-2031 6888; www.the5-elementshotel.com.my; lot 243 Jln Sultan; s/tw/d incl breakfast from RM150/180/190; ❄@📶; Ⓜ Pasar Seni) Offering a good range of rooms, some with views towards Menara KL, this reasonable midrange hotel makes a credible stab at boutique styling with a sensuous design motif snaking its way across the corridor and bedroom walls.

PACIFIC REGENCY HOTEL SUITES APARTMENT $$$

Map p248 (☎03-2332 7777; www.pacific-regency.com; Jln Punchak, Menara Panglobal; apt incl breakfast from RM465; ❄@📶🏊; 🚝Bukit Nanas) These upmarket self-catering studios and serviced apartments are good value compared with the rooms of a similar standard at KL's other five-star properties. Head up top to enjoy the rooftop pool and bar, **Luna** (⌚5pm-1am Sun-Thu, to 3am Fri & Sat).

Masjid India, Kampung Baru & Northern KL

TUNE HOTEL DOWNTOWN HOTEL $

Map p256 (☎03-2694 3301; www.tunehotels.com; 316 Jln TAR; s/d from RM69/79; ❄@📶; 🚝Medan Tuanku) This clean and well-run place offers excellent value if you book online in advance: a double including all the usual amenities starts at RM79. Rooms have TVs and attached bathrooms with rain showers.

REEDS BOUTIQUE HOTEL $$

Map p256 (☎03-2602 0330; www.thereeds-hotel.com; 9 Jln Yap Ah Shak; dm/s/d from RM45/98/120; ❄📶; 🚝Medan Tuanku) Handy for the dining and nightlife on Jln Doraisamy and exploring nearby Kampung Baru, teal-painted Reeds has boutique stylings and a wide range of rooms of varying quality. Interesting decorative touches include old Chinese posters, patterned wallpaper on feature walls, and a very comfy lounge/lobby area with a cafe bar. Not all rooms have windows.

VISTANA HOTEL $$

Map p256 (☎03-4042 8000; www.vistanahotels.com; 9 Jln Lumut; d from RM265; ❄@📶🏊; MTitiwangsa, 🚝Titiwangsa) Steps from the Titiwangsa stations and a pleasant riverside food court is this fine upper-midrange choice with decently proportioned and decorated rooms and public areas. The small swimming pool is a plus.

BAGASTA BOUTIQUE GUESTHOUSE BOUTIQUE HOTEL $$

Map p259 (☎03-2698 9988; www.bagasta.com.my; 56 Jln Raja Alang; d from RM180; ❄📶; MKampung Baru) Even though it's not in one of the old wooden mansions of Kampung Baru, there are good views of the area from this small hotel in a modern block. The spacious, simple rooms incorporate local crafts and a sprinkling of Malay design (wood from old *kampung* houses was used to make headboards), giving it more character than other midrange options.

Lake Gardens, Brickfields & Bangsar

PODS HOSTEL $

Map p260 (☎03-2276 0858; www.podsbackpacker.com; 1-6, 30 Jln Thambipillay; dm/s/d with shared bathroom RM35/65/85; ❄📶; 🚆KL Sentral, 🚝KL Sentral) This basic backpackers offers some of the cheapest beds in town. Note partitions between the rooms are flimsy and mattresses are on the floor. There's a pleasant cafe on the ground floor for breakfast and bikes can be rented for RM30 per day.

★ALOFT KUALA LUMPUR SENTRAL HOTEL $$

Map p260 (☎03-2723 1188; www.starwoodhotels.com/alofthotels; 5 Jln Stesen Sentral; d RM330-600; ❄@📶🏊; 🚆KL Sentral, 🚝KL Sentral) Designed for the Google generation of young creatives, Aloft is industrial chic meets plastic fantastic. Staff are super friendly and you have to smile at the witty cartoon art in each of the spacious, well-designed rooms. Place a big tick against its infinity rooftop pool and bar with one of the best views in KL.

★SEKEPING TENGGIRI GUESTHOUSE $$

Map p262 (☎017-207 5977; www.sekeping.com; 48 Jln Tenggiri; d RM220-330; ❄📶🏊; MBank Rakyat-Bangsar) Providing access to architect Ng Seksan's superlative private collection of contemporary Malaysian art – displayed in the rooms of the adjoining house (p101) – this is a lovely place to stay. The rough-luxe mix of concrete, wood and wire decor (with cleverly recycled materials making up lamp fixtures) is softened by abundant garden greenery and a cooling plunge pool.

YMCA HOTEL $$

Map p260 (☎03-2274 1439; www.ymcakl.com; 95 Jln Padang Belia; d & tw RM111, tr with shared bathroom RM111; ❄📶; 🚆KL Sentral, 🚝KL Sentral) Handy for KL Sentral, the Y has spick-and-span (if a little old-fashioned) rooms. There are laundry facilities and a shop and cafe, as well as tennis courts for hire if you become a member, which will also give you 10% off the hotel rates.

★MAJESTIC HOTEL HISTORIC HOTEL $$$

Map p260 (☎03-2785 8000; www.majestickl.com; 5 Jln Sultan Hishamuddin; d/ste incl breakfast from

KLIA TRANSIT HOTELS

If all you need to do is freshen up before or after your flight, KL has a number of decent transit-accommodation options.

Capsule by Container Hotel (03-7610 2020; www.capsulecontainer.com; L1-2 & 3, Gateway, KLIA2; s for 6/9/12hr RM80/100/110, d for 6/9/12hr RM160/200/220; ; KLIA) Grab forty winks at this contemporary crash pad, where the capsule rooms are housed in cleverly adapted transportation containers. During the day a bed for up to six hours costs RM55. Use of a shower (no bed) costs RM20. Located next to KLIA2.

Sama-Sama Express KLIA (03-8787 4848; www.samasamaexpress.com; Mezzanine Level, Satellite A Bldg, KLIA, Gate C; d for 6/12hr RM280/560; ; KLIA) Located inside the terminal (air side), this hotel offers rooms with private bathrooms and TVs. A stay of 12 hours or longer includes a buffet breakfast. Use of a shower only (no room stay) costs RM45. The company also runs a **branch** (03-8787 3333; www.samasamahotels.com; r from RM500; ; KLIA) at KLIA2.

Tune Hotel KLIA2 (1300 88 8863; www.tunehotels.com; Lot PT 13, Jln KLIA 2/2; r from RM200; ; KLIA2) A decent option if you have an early flight, the Tune Hotel is connected to the airport terminal via a covered walkway. There is a cafe-bar and a convenience store on the ground floor. Book online in advance for the best rates.

RM360/860; ; Kuala Lumpur) Originally opened in 1932 and the pre-WWII KL equivalent of Raffles in Singapore, the impeccably restored Majestic is one of the city's top luxury hotels. Appealing features include an orchid-filled conservatory, two swimming pools and a fine spa (p111) with Charles Rennie Mackintosh–inspired decor. Its website provides the best booking deals.

ST REGIS KUALA LUMPUR HOTEL **$$$**

Map p260 (03-2727 1111; www.stregiskualalumpur.com; 6 Jln Stesen Sentral 2; d/ste from RM1084/3800; ; KL Sentral) KL's newest luxury hotel is the extravagantly appointed St Regis. In the lobby, a 2.5-ton bronze horse by Colombian sculptor Fernando Botero sets the tone. Rooms are decorated in old Hollywood glamour style with darkwood and pale-grey furnishings adorned with plenty of bling, and come with dressing tables and bespoke illuminated mirrors fit for a movie star.

GARDENS HOTEL & RESIDENCES HOTEL **$$$**

Map p262 (03-2268 1111; www.stgiles.com; Gardens, Lingkaran Syed Putra; d/apt with breakfast from RM330/694; ; Mid Valley) Attached to the swanky Gardens Mall (p108), this luxury hotel and serviced residences are very appealing. Wood panelling with lattice details and striking flower prints on the walls make the rooms' decor pop; the apartments are even better.

HILTON KUALA LUMPUR HOTEL **$$$**

Map p260 (03-2264 2264; www.hilton.com; 3 Jln Stesen Sentral; d/ste from RM519/919; ; KL Sentral, KL Sentral) Sharing a fabulous landscaped pool and spa with the Meridien next door, the Hilton offers beautiful contemporary design. Sliding doors open to join the bathroom to the bedroom, picture windows present soaring city views, and rooms are decked out from floor to ceiling in eye-catching materials.

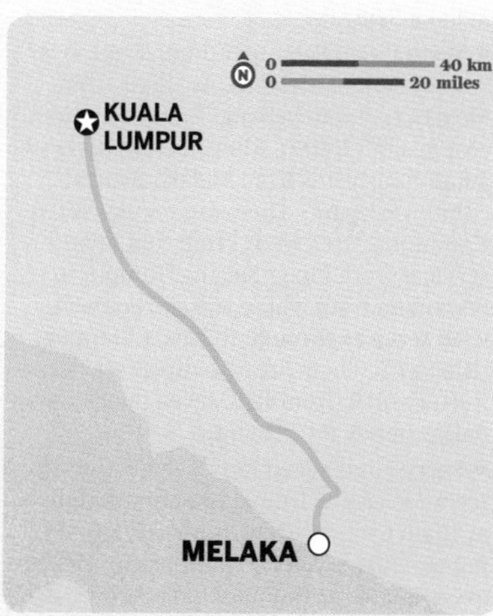

Melaka City

Melaka's remarkable restaurants and cafes p144
Feasting on Peranakan curries, Portuguese seafood, Indian banana-leaf spreads and good coffee.

Chinatown p139
Strolling or cycling around this historic area, discovering galleries, craft workshops and the murals along the Melaka River.

Jonker Walk Night Market p148
Experiencing the razzle-dazzle and street food of Melaka City's week-end night market.

Trishaws p135
Going for a spin around the historic centre in one of these kitschy contraptions.

Baba & Nyonya Heritage Museum p139
Embracing nostalgia at this atmospheric museum in a gorgeously decorated old home.

Explore

Like a peacock, Melaka City is bright and loud and preens with its wealth of home-grown galleries, crimson colonial buildings and showy trishaws.

Since the city's historic centre achieved Unesco World Heritage status in 2008, many old shophouses and mansions have enjoyed makeovers as galleries and hotels. The city's kaleidoscope of architectural styles – spanning Peranakan, Portuguese, Dutch and British elements – is well preserved. Tourism has boomed, particularly on weekends when the vibrant Jonker Walk Night Market provides music, shopping and street food galore.

Inevitably, a strong whiff of commercialism has accompanied this success. However, it's easy to feel the town's old magic (and get a seat at popular restaurants) on quiet weekdays. And Melaka City, as it has for centuries, continues to exude tolerance and welcomes cultural exchange.

The Best...

- **Sight** Chinatown (p139)
- **Place to Eat** Nancy's Kitchen (p144)
- **Place to Drink** Daily Fix (p147)

Top Tip

Avoid visiting on the weekends when there are so many photo-snapping tourists that the whole heritage district can feel like front row at a rock concert.

Getting There & Away

- **Air Melaka International Airport** (☎06-317 5860; Lapangan Terbang Batu Berendam), 12km north of Melaka City, has daily flights from Melaka to Penang and Pekanbaru (Indonesia).
- **Bus Melaka Sentral** (Jln Tun Razak), the huge, modern long-distance bus station, is 5km north of the city. A medley of privately run bus companies makes checking timetables a herculean feat; scout popular routes at www.expressbusmalaysia.com/coach-from-melaka. You can buy bus tickets in advance (not a bad idea on busy weekends or if you have a plane to catch) at Discovery Cafe (p147) in downtown Melaka City – there's a small commission, dependent on the ticket fare.
- **Taxi** Taxis to KL (RM184) leave from Melaka Sentral.
- **Train** Pulau Sebang/Tampin Station is 38km north of Melaka City. Taxis from Melaka to Pulau Sebang/Tampin Station cost around RM80. Alternatively, there's a half-hourly bus from Melaka Sentral (RM5, 1½ hours). There are regular KTM Komuter (http://www.ktmb.com.my) services from Pulau Sebang/Tampin to Seremban from where you can connect with services through to Kuala Lumpur (RM13.70). There are also direct services to Butterworth (from R42, seven hours, two daily), handy for Penang.
- **Ferry** High-speed ferries make the trip from Melaka to Dumai in Sumatra daily at 10am (one way/return RM110/170, 1¾ hours; child tickets are half-price). Tickets are available at Indomal Express (Map p137) and Tunas Rupat Follow Me Express (Map p137) near the wharf.

Getting Around

- **Walking/Bicycling** Melaka City is small enough to walk around or, for the traffic fearless, you can rent a bike for between RM5 and RM10 per day from guesthouses.
- **Bus** Bus 17 runs every 15 minutes from Melaka Sentral to the centre of town, past the huge Mahkota Parade shopping complex, to Taman Melaka Raya and on to Medan Portugis. Find local bus route information at www.panoramamelaka.com.my/routes.
- **Trishaw** Taking to Melaka City's streets by trishaw is a must – they should cost RM40 by the hour or RM20 for any one-way trip within town, but you'll have to bargain.
- **Taxis** Charge around RM15 for a trip anywhere around town.
- **Car** To visit other parts of Melaka state you will find it handy to hire a car. Centrally based Hawk (www.hawkrentacar.com.my) has good rates.

Need to Know

- **Area Code** ☎06
- **Location** Melaka City is 149km from Kuala Lumpur
- **Tourism Malaysia** (www.tourismmalaysia.gov.my)

HISTORY

The modern city-state of Melaka bloomed from a simple 14th-century fishing village founded by Parameswara, a Hindu prince or pirate (take your pick) from Sumatra. According to legend, Parameswara was inspired to build Melaka after seeing a plucky mouse deer fend off a dog attack.

Melaka's location halfway between China and India, with easy access to the spice islands of Indonesia, soon attracted merchants from all over the East and it became a favoured port. In 1405, the Chinese Muslim Admiral Cheng Ho arrived in Melaka bearing gifts from the Ming emperor and the promise of protection from Siamese enemies. Chinese settlers followed, who mixed with the local Malays to become known as the Baba and Nonya, Peranakans or Straits Chinese. By the time of Parameswara's death in 1414, Melaka was a powerful trading state. Its position was consolidated by the state's adoption of Islam in the mid-15th century.

In 1509 the Portuguese came seeking spice wealth and in 1511 Alfonso de Albuquerque forcibly took the city. Under the Portuguese, the fortress of A'Famosa was constructed. While Portuguese cannons could easily conquer Melaka, they could not force Muslim merchants from Arabia and India to continue trading there, and other ports in the area, such as Islamic Demak on Java, grew to overshadow Melaka.

Suffering attacks from neighbouring Johor and Negeri Sembilan, as well as from the Islamic power of Aceh in Sumatra, Melaka declined further. The city passed into Dutch hands after an eight-month siege in 1641 and the Dutch ruled Melaka for about 150 years. Melaka again became the centre for peninsular trade, but the Dutch directed more energy into their possessions in Indonesia.

When the French occupied Holland in 1795, the British (as allies of the Dutch) temporarily assumed administration of the Dutch colonies. In 1824 Melaka was permanently ceded to the British.

Melaka, together with Penang and Singapore, formed the Straits settlements, the three British territories that were the bases for later expansion into the peninsula. However, under British rule Melaka was eclipsed by other Straits settlements and then superseded by the rapidly growing commercial importance of Singapore. Apart from a brief upturn in the early 20th century when rubber was an important crop, Melaka returned again to being a quiet backwater, patiently awaiting its renaissance as a tourist drawcard.

SIGHTS

Historic Town Centre

Striking blood-red-painted buildings and a multitude of museums dominate Melaka City's historic centre. Many of the museums are small, with a niche focus and an uninspiring diorama format. Start with more developed attractions like the Stadthuys (p135) and the Maritime Museum (p138) complex.

STADTHUYS HISTORIC BUILDING

Map p140 (☎06-282 6526; Dutch Sq; foreign/local visitor RM10/5; ⌚9am-5.30pm Sat-Thu, 9am-12.15pm & 2.45-5.30pm Fri) Melaka's most unmistakable landmark and favourite trishaw pick-up spot is the Stadthuys. This cerise town hall and governor's residence dates to 1650 and is believed to be the oldest Dutch building in the East. The building was erected after Melaka was captured by the

TRICKED-OUT TRISHAWS

First you hear a distant blare of horn honking and hip-hop. Then, suddenly, a convoy of three-wheeled vehicles is careening your way in a blur of fairy lights and cartoon cut-outs. Melaka City's trishaws are the glitziest you'll see anywhere in Malaysia, decorated with paraphernalia from papier mâché models of colonial buildings to Disney princesses and Christmas trees. Local opinion is divided over whether Melaka City's blinged-up trishaws help preserve this historic mode of transport or hideously distort it. But it's hard to imagine a trip to Melaka City without at least one ride. And it's impossible not to raise a smile when tourist groups hire them en masse, forming a carnivalesque, cycle-powered conga line.

Melaka City

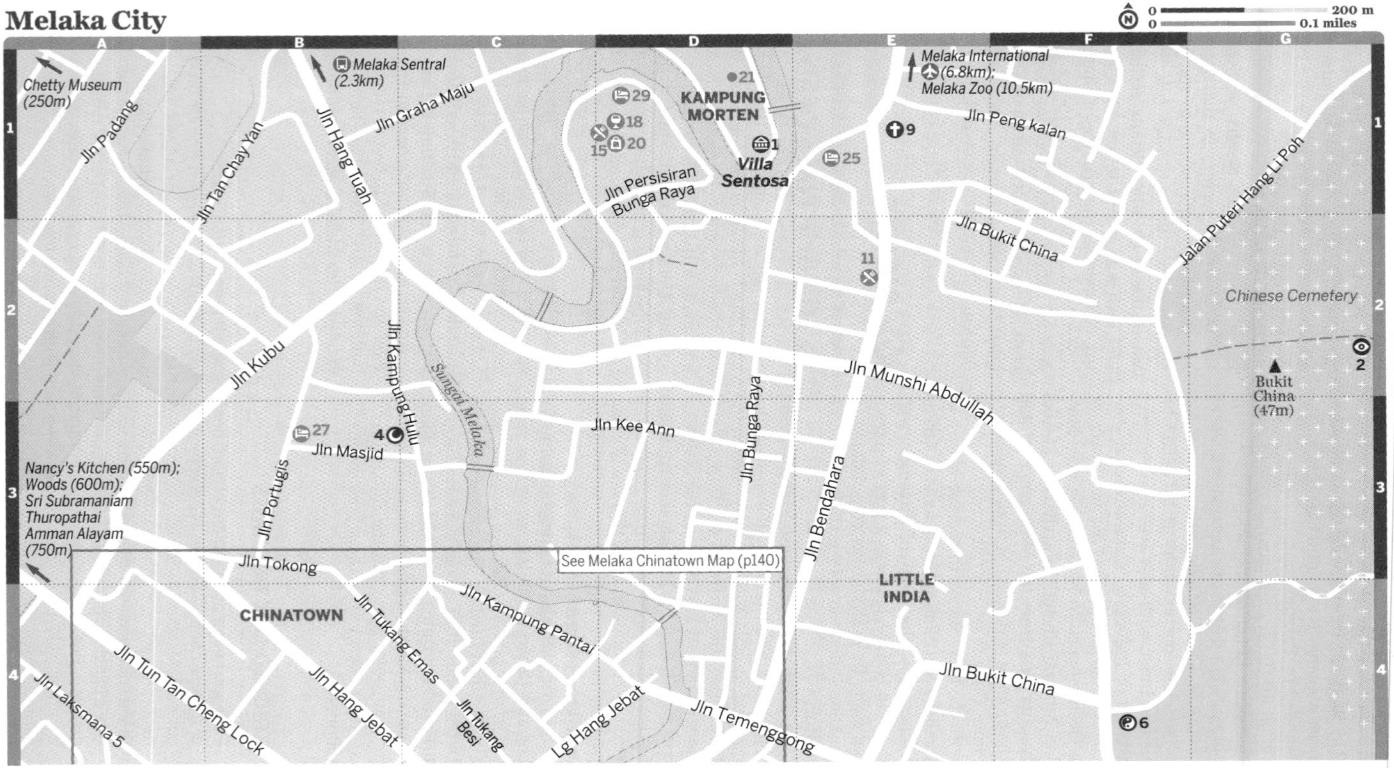

0 200 m
0 0.1 miles
A
B
C
D
E
F
G
1
2
3
4
Chetty Museum (250m)
Melaka Sentral (2.3km)
Melaka International (6.8km); Melaka Zoo (10.5km)
Jln Padang
Jln Tan Chay Yan
Jln Hang Tuah
Jln Graha Maju
KAMPUNG MORTEN
Villa Sentosa
Jln Persisiran Bunga Raya
Jln Peng kalan
Jln Bukit China
Jalan Puteri Hang Li Poh
Chinese Cemetery
Bukit China (47m)
Jln Kubu
Jln Kampung Hulu
Sungai Melaka
Jln Munshi Abdullah
Jln Kee Ann
Jln Bunga Raya
Jln Bendahara
Jln Masjid
Jln Portugis
Nancy's Kitchen (550m); Woods (600m); Sri Subramaniam Thuropathai Amman Alayam (750m)
Jln Tokong
See Melaka Chinatown Map (p140)
CHINATOWN
LITTLE INDIA
Jln Kampung Pantai
Jln Tukang Emas
Jln Tukang Besi
Jln Tun Tan Cheng Lock
Jln Hang Jebat
Lg Hang Jebat
Jln Temenggong
Jln Laksmana 5
1
2
4
6
9
11
15
18
20
21
25
27
29

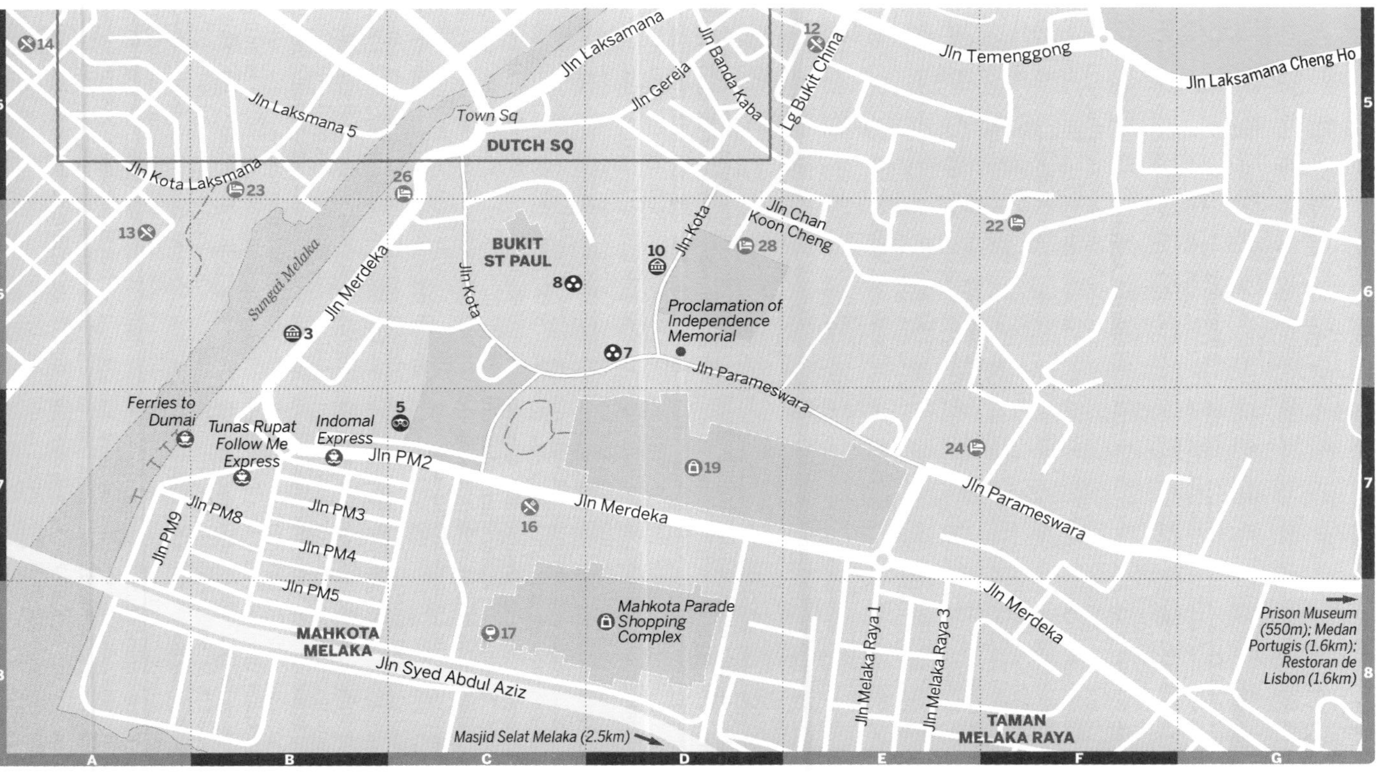

Jln Laksamana
Jln Gereja
Jln Banda Kaba
Lg Bukit China
12
Jln Temenggong
Jln Laksamana Cheng Ho
14
Jln Laksmana 5
Town Sq
DUTCH SQ
Jln Kota Laksmana
23
26
13
Sungai Melaka
Jln Merdeka
3
Jln Kota
BUKIT ST PAUL
8
10
Jln Kota
Jln Chan Koon Cheng
28
22
Proclamation of Independence Memorial
7
Jln Parameswara
Ferries to Dumai
Tunas Rupat Follow Me Express
Indomal Express
5
Jln PM2
19
24
Jln Parameswara
Jln PM9
Jln PM8
Jln PM3
Jln PM4
Jln PM5
16
Jln Merdeka
Jln Merdeka
MAHKOTA MELAKA
17
Mahkota Parade Shopping Complex
Jln Syed Abdul Aziz
Jln Melaka Raya 1
Jln Melaka Raya 3
Prison Museum (550m); Medan Portugis (1.6km); Restoran de Lisbon (1.6km)
Masjid Selat Melaka (2.5km)
TAMAN MELAKA RAYA

Melaka City

Top Sights
1 Villa Sentosa D1

Sights
2 Bukit China G2
3 Maritime Museum & Naval Museum B6
4 Masjid Kampung Hulu B3
5 Menara Taming Sari C7
6 Poh San Teng Temple F4
7 Porta de Santiago D6
8 St Paul's Church C6
9 St Peter's Church E1
10 Sultanate Palace D6

Eating
11 Bulldog E2
12 Capitol Satay E5
13 Green House Vegetarian Restaurant A6
14 Pak Putra Restaurant A5
15 Purple Cane Tea Restaurant D1
16 Restoran Nyonya Suan C7

Drinking & Nightlife
17 Mixx C8
18 Pampas Sky Bar D1

Shopping
19 Dataran Pahlawan D7
20 Shore Shopping Gallery D1

Sports & Activities
21 Kampung Morten Walking Tour D1
Malacca Night Cycling .... (see 27)
Nonya Culinary Journey .... (see 24)
Peranakan Culinary Journey .... (see 25)

Sleeping
22 Apa Kaba Home & Stay F6
23 Casa Del Rio B5
24 Hotel Equatorial E7
25 Majestic Malacca E1
26 Quayside Hotel C5
27 Ringo's Foyer B3
28 Rucksack Caratel D6
29 Swiss-Garden Hotel & Residences D1

Dutch in 1641 and is a reproduction of the former Stadhuis (town hall) of the Frisian town of Hoorn in the Netherlands. Today it's a museum complex, with the **History & Ethnography Museum** as the highlight. Admission covers all the museums. There is no fee for guided tours.

For in-depth acquaintance with Melaka past and present, you can also peruse the **Governor's House**, **Democratic Government Museum**, a **Literature Museum** focusing on Malaysian writers, **Cheng Ho Gallery** and the **Education Museum**.

ST PAUL'S CHURCH — RUINS

Map p136 (Jln Kota; 24hr) FREE The evocative ruin of St Paul's Church crowns the summit of Bukit St Paul overlooking central Melaka. Steep stairs from Jln Kota or Jln Chang Koon Cheng lead up to this faded sanctuary, originally built by a Portuguese captain in 1521. The church was regularly visited by St Francis Xavier, whose marble statue – minus his right hand and a few toes – stands in front of the ruin.

Following his death in China, the saint's body was temporarily interred here for nine months before being transferred to Goa. You can look into St Francis' ancient tomb (surrounded by a wire fence) inside the church.

When the Dutch completed their own Christ Church at the base of the hill in 1590, St Paul's fell into disuse. Under the British, a lighthouse was built and the church was used as a storehouse for gunpowder.

MARITIME MUSEUM & NAVAL MUSEUM — MUSEUM

Map p137 (06-283 0926; Jln Merdeka; adult/child RM10/6; 9am-5pm Mon-Thu, 9am-8.30pm Fri-Sun) Embark on a voyage through Melaka's maritime history at these linked museums. The most enjoyable of the museum's three sections (one ticket covers them all) is housed in a huge re-creation of the *Flor de la Mar*, a Portuguese ship that sank off the coast of Melaka. The fun of posing on the deck and clambering between floors rather eclipses the displays and dioramas.

The museum continues in the building next door (follow the signs) with exhibits featuring local vessels, including the striking *kepala burung* (a boat carved like a feathered bird) plus an assortment of nautical devices. Across the road from here, the **Naval Museum** has uniforms and informative displays, but the highlight is an atrium packed with boats and a helicopter.

DUTCH SQUARE SQUARE

Map p140 (Jln Gereja) The focal point of the Unesco Heritage zone, this attractive square is surrounded by Dutch-era buildings that have been painted blood-red, shady trees and a mass of kitschly decorated trishaws waiting for customers. Take a moment to admire the pretty fountain erected in 1904 in memory of Queen Victoria and decorated with four bas-relief images of the monarch.

MENARA TAMING SARI VIEWPOINT

Map p137 (☎06-288 1100; www.menaratamingsari.com; Jln Merdeka; adult/child RM23/15; ⏲10am-11pm) Melaka's revolving viewing deck looks worryingly like a theme-park ride without the seatbelts. Luckily, this is a leisurely thrill ride and one with air-con. The UFO-shaped chamber atop this 80m-high tower slowly rotates as it ascends and descends, allowing panoramic views of Melaka City. Binoculars are provided. Tickets are on sale in the adjacent building.

PORTA DE SANTIAGO RUINS

Map p137 (A'Famosa; Jln Kota; ⏲24hr) FREE Most visitors pause for a photo at Porta de Santiago before hiking to the ruined church on Bukit St Paul. It was built as a Portuguese fortress in 1511; the British took over in 1641 and destroyed it in 1806 to prevent it falling into Napoleon's hands. Fortunately Sir Stamford Raffles arrived in 1810 and saved what remains today.

SULTANATE PALACE MUSEUM

Map p137 (☎06-282 6526; Jln Kota; adult/child RM5/2; ⏲9am-5.30pm Tue-Sun) This wooden replica of the palace of Sultan Mansur Shah, who ruled Melaka from 1456 to 1477, houses an open-air cultural museum and lovely gardens. The fine buildings were crafted without the use of nails and closely follow descriptions of the original palace from *Sejarah Melayu (Malay Annals)*, a chronicle of the establishment of the Malay sultanate and 600 years of Malay history.

MELAKA MALAY SULTANATE WATER WHEEL MONUMENT

Map p140 (Jln Merdeka) In 2006, work on the Menara Taming Sari revolving tower uncovered another part of the city's fortress walls. The revolving tower was relocated further inland; the remains of the fortress walls were reconstructed and are now home to the 13m-high Melaka Malay Sultanate Water Wheel replica. The original wheel would have been used to channel the river waters for the large number of traders swarming Melaka during the 15th and 16th centuries.

⊙ Chinatown

Chinatown is Melaka City's most interesting area to explore. Jln Tun Tan Cheng Lock, formerly called Heeren St, was the preferred address for wealthy Peranakan (also known as Straits Chinese) traders. Jln Hang Jebat, formerly known as Jonker St, is dominated by souvenir shops and restaurants; every weekend it hosts the Jonker Walk Night Market (p148). Jln Tokong, which changes name to Jln Tukang Emas and Jln Tukang Besi as you head from north to south, is home to several Chinese temples, a mosque and an Indian temple – the reason it is also known as Harmony St.

★BABA & NYONYA HERITAGE MUSEUM MUSEUM

Map p140 (☎06-283 1273; http://babanyonyamuseum.com; 48-50 Jln Tun Tan Cheng Lock; adult/child RM16/11; ⏲10am-1pm & 2-5pm Wed-Mon) Touring this traditional Baba-Nonya (Peranakan) townhouse transports you to a time when women peered at guests through elaborate partitions and every social situation had its specific location within the

LOCAL KNOWLEDGE

SUNGAI MELAKA & CHINATOWN STREET ART

Some efforts have been made by the Melaka authorities to create pleasant walkways alongside the Sungai Melaka between Chinatown and Kampung Morten. Along the route you'll pass many colourful and creative murals on building walls. Images include those of Parameswara, Melaka's founder and Ming dynasty princess Hang Li Po. The alley leading to the river at the end of Jln Tukang Besi in Chinatown looks like a child's picture book come to life, while on the corner of Jln Hang Kasturi and Jln Kampung Pantai you'll find horses galloping up the street in the style of classical Chinese painting.

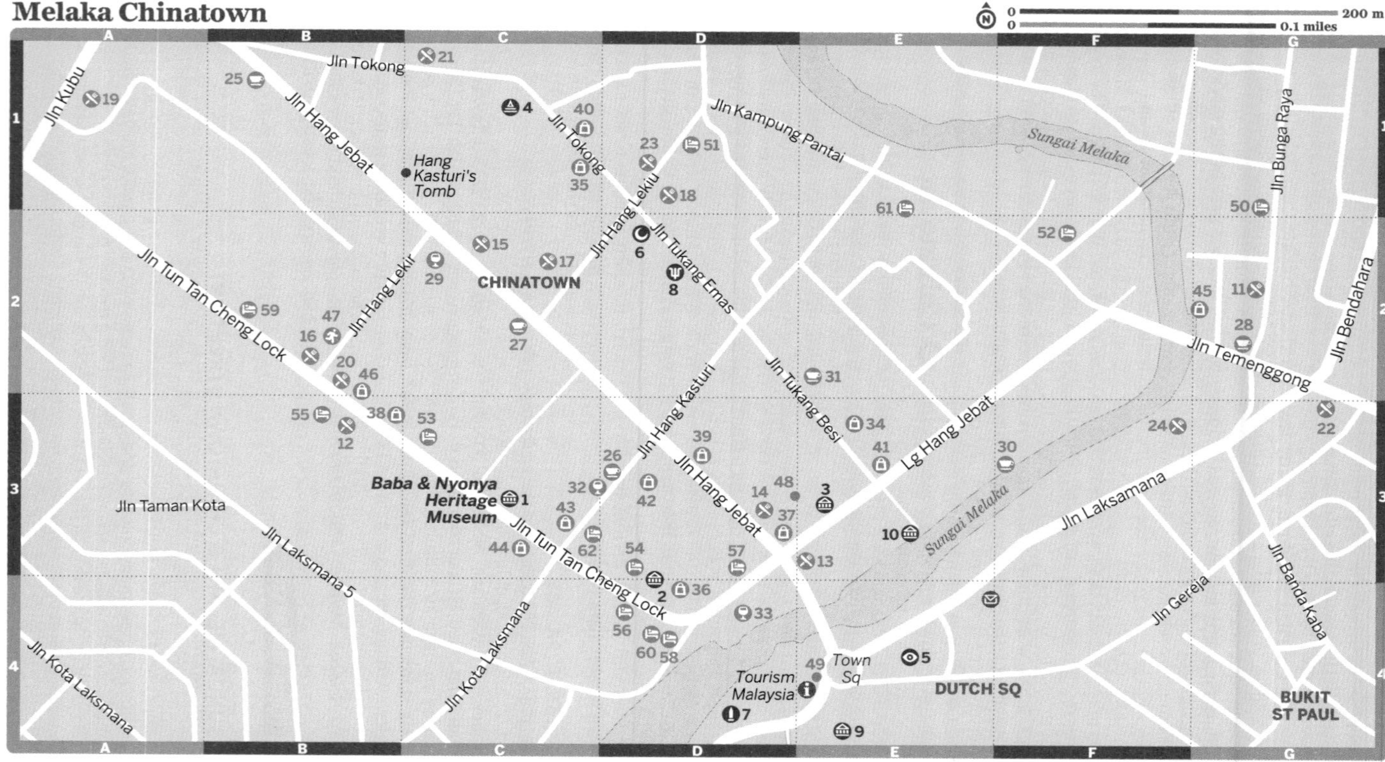
Melaka Chinatown
200 m
0.1 miles
Jln Kubu
Jln Tokong
Jln Hang Jebat
Hang Kasturi's Tomb
Jln Tokong
Jln Hang Lekiu
Jln Tukang Emas
Jln Kampung Pantai
Sungai Melaka
Jln Bunga Raya
Jln Bendahara
Jln Temenggong
CHINATOWN
Jln Hang Lekir
Jln Tun Tan Cheng Lock
Jln Hang Kasturi
Jln Tukang Besi
Lg Hang Jebat
Jln Hang Jebat
Baba & Nyonya Heritage Museum
Jln Taman Kota
Jln Laksmana 5
Jln Tun Tan Cheng Lock
Jln Kota Laksmana
Jln Kota Laksmana
Jln Laksamana
Jln Gereja
Jln Banda Kaba
Town Sq
Tourism Malaysia
DUTCH SQ
BUKIT ST PAUL

Melaka Chinatown

Top Sights
1 Baba & Nyonya Heritage Museum ... C3

Sights
2 8 Heeren Street ... D4
3 Cheng Ho Cultural Museum ... E3
4 Cheng Hoon Teng Temple ... C1
5 Dutch Square ... E4
6 Masjid Kampung Kling ... D2
7 Melaka Malay Sultanate Water Wheel ... D4
8 Sri Poyatha Venayagar Moorthi Temple ... D2
9 Stadthuys ... E4
10 Zheng He Duo Yun Zuan ... E3

Eating
11 13 Hibiscus Vintage Art Cafe ... G2
12 Baboon House ... B3
13 Chung Wah ... E3
14 Hoe Kee Chicken Rice Ball ... D3
15 Jonker 88 ... C2
16 Kocik Kitchen ... B2
17 Limau-Limau Cafe ... C2
18 Low Yong Moh ... D1
19 Poh Piah Lwee ... A1
20 Salud Tapas ... B2
21 Seeds Garden ... C1
22 Selvam ... G3
23 Shui Xian Vegetarian ... D1
24 Street Kitchen ... F3

Drinking & Nightlife
25 Backlane Coffee ... B1
26 Calanthe Art Cafe ... D3
27 Daily Fix ... C2
28 Discovery Cafe & Guest House ... G2
29 Geographér Cafe ... C2
30 Idlers Corner ... F3
31 Kaya Kaya Cafe ... E2
32 Me & Mrs Jones ... C3
33 Sid's Pub @ Jonkers ... D4

Shopping
34 Clay House ... E3
35 Hueman Studio ... C1
36 Joe's Design ... D4
37 Jonker Walk Night Market ... D3
38 Malaqa House ... B3
39 Orangutan House ... D3
40 Orangutan House ... C1
41 Orangutan House ... E3
42 Puri Padi ... D3
43 Red Handicrafts ... C3
44 Tham Siew Inn Artist Gallery ... C3
45 Trash & Treasure ... G2
Umyang Batik ... (see 62)
46 Wah Aik Shoemaker ... B2

Sports & Activities
Biossentials Puri Spa ... (see 59)
47 Huolong Foot Reflexology & Massage ... B2
48 Melaka River Cruise ... D3
49 Old Melaka Heritage Tour ... E4

Sleeping
50 1825 Gallery Hotel ... G1
51 45 Lekiu ... D1
52 Bridge Loft ... F2
53 Cafe 1511 Guesthouse ... C3
54 Calanthe Artisan Loft ... D3
55 Courtyard@Heeren ... B3
56 Gingerflower ... D4
57 Hangout@Jonker ... D3
58 Heeren House ... D4
59 Hotel Puri ... B2
60 Nomaps ... D4
Opposite Place ... (see 51)
61 Rooftop Guesthouse ... E1
62 Stables ... C3

house. The captivating museum is arranged to look like a typical 19th-century Baba-Nonya residence. Tour guides enliven the setting with their arch sense of humour.

Book ahead or arrive just before the strike of the hour. Last tour of the day is an hour before closing time.

ZHENG HE DUO YUN ZUAN GALLERY

Map p140 (☎06-282 6966; 42A & 44A Lg Hang Jebat; ⏲9am-6pm) FREE A Shanghai-based auction house has funded this impressive gallery split between two converted warehouses facing onto the Melaka River and entered from the path running alongside the water. Exhibitions (at which some of the works are for sale) change roughly every three weeks and focus mainly on Chinese arts and culture. The alley separating the two buildings has a wall painted with one of the most colourful of Melaka City's street-art murals.

CHENG HOON TENG TEMPLE BUDDHIST TEMPLE

Map p140 (Qing Yun Ting or Green Clouds Temple; ☎06-282 9343; www.chenghoonteng.org.my; 25

Jln Tokong; ⏲7am-7pm) FREE Malaysia's oldest traditional Chinese temple, constructed in 1673, remains a central place of worship for the Buddhist community in Melaka City. Notable for its carved woodwork, the temple is dedicated to Kuan Yin, the goddess of mercy.

MASJID KAMPUNG KLING MOSQUE

Map p140 (cnr Jln Hang Lekiu & Jln Tukang Emas) FREE Originally dating back to 1748, the 19th-century rebuild of the mosque you see today mingles a number of styles. Its multitiered meru roof (a stacked form similar to that seen in Balinese Hindu architecture) owes its inspiration to Hindu temples, the Moorish watchtower minaret is typical of early mosques in Sumatra, while English and Dutch tiles bedeck its interior. Admission times to go inside vary; dress modestly and, if you're female, bring a scarf.

The proximity of Kampung Kling mosque to Cheng Hoon Teng temple and Hindu temple Sri Poyatha Venayagar Moorthi has prompted locals to dub this area 'Harmony St'.

SRI POYATHA VENAYAGAR MOORTHI TEMPLE HINDU TEMPLE

Map p140 (Jln Tukang Emas) FREE One of the first Hindu temples built in Malaysia, this temple was constructed in 1781 on a plot donated by the religiously tolerant Dutch and dedicated to the Hindu deity Venayagar. The building adds a dash of Indian colour and spiritual variety to 'Harmony St'.

MASJID KAMPUNG HULU MOSQUE

Map p136 (cnr Jln Masjid & Jln Kampung Hulu) This is the oldest functioning mosque in Malaysia and was, surprisingly, commissioned by the Dutch in 1728. The mosque is made up of predominantly Javanese architecture with a multitiered roof in place of the standard dome (at the time of construction, domes and minarets had not yet come into fashion). It's not particularly well set up for visitors, but this Chinatown icon is worth admiring from outside.

8 HEEREN STREET HISTORIC BUILDING

Map p140 (8 Jln Tun Tan Cheng Lock; by donation; ⏲11am-4pm) FREE This 18th-century, Dutch-period residential house was restored as a model conservation project. Guides are on hand to explain various aspects of the house. Pick up an *Endangered Trades: A Walking Tour of Malacca's Living Heritage* (RM5) booklet and map for an excellent self-guided tour of the city centre. Entry is free, but donations are appreciated.

The restoration project was partially chronicled in the beautifully designed coffee-table book *Voices from the Street,* which is for sale at the house, along with other titles.

CHENG HO CULTURAL MUSEUM MUSEUM

Map p140 (☎06-283 1135; www.chengho.org/museum; 51 Lg Hang Jebat; adult/child RM20/10; ⏲9am-6pm) The impressive exploits of Chinese-Muslim seafarer Ming Admiral Cheng Ho (Zheng He) are celebrated through this museum's dioramas, maritime miscellany and enormous giraffe, a model of the rather inconvenient animal gift brought overseas by the adventurer. Cheng Ho's tremendous voyages make for interesting reading, though the level of detail in this multifloor museum wearies after a while.

The museum is a good excuse to wander through a creaky old Chinese mansion, complete with swaying lanterns and mother-of-pearl-embossed furnishings.

⊙ North of the City Centre

East of Chinatown on the opposite side of the river is Melaka City's surprisingly plain Little India. While it's not nearly as charming as the historic centre or Chinatown, this busy area along Jln Bendahara and Jln Temenggong is a worthwhile place to soak up some Indian influence and grab a banana-leaf meal.

★VILLA SENTOSA HISTORIC BUILDING

Map p136 (Peaceful Villa; ☎06-282 3988; Jln Kampung Morten; entry by donation; ⏲hours vary, usually 9am-1pm & 2-5pm) The highlight of visiting the charming Malay village of Kampung Morten (p150) is this living museum within a 1920s *kampung* house. Visitors (or rather, guests) are welcomed by a member of the household who points out period objects, including photographs of family members, Ming dynasty ceramics and a century-old Quran. You're unlikely to leave without a photo-op on plush velvet furniture or a few strikes of the lucky gong.

BUKIT CHINA CEMETERY

Map p136 (Jln Puteri Hang Li Poh) More than 12,500 graves, including about 20 Muslim tombs, cover the 25 grassy hectares of serene 'Chinese Hill'. In the middle of the 15th century, the sultan of Melaka imported the Ming emperor's daughter from China as his bride in a move to seal relations between the two countries. She brought with her a vast retinue, including 500 handmaidens, who settled around Bukit China. It has been a Chinese area ever since.

Since the times of British rule, there have been several attempts to acquire Bukit China for road widening, land reclamation or development purposes. Fortunately, Cheng Hoon Teng Temple (p141), with strong community support, has thwarted these attempts.

At the base of the hill is the **Poh San Teng Temple**. 'Precious Hill Temple' was built around 1795 and is dedicated to the guardian deity Tua Pek Kong. To the right of the temple is the King's Well, a 15th-century well built by Sultan Mansur Shah.

ST PETER'S CHURCH CHURCH

Map p136 (☎06-282 2950; 166 Jln Bendahara) FREE This is the oldest functioning Catholic church in Malaysia, built in 1710 by descendants of early Portuguese settlers. It has recently been given a repaint in cream and green and houses some colourful statues.

Kampung Chetti

As well as the Peranakan community, Melaka City also has a small contingent of Chetti – Straits-born Indians, offspring of the Indian traders who intermarried with Malay women. Arriving in the 1400s, the Chetties are regarded as older than the Chinese-Malay Peranakan community.

Their traditional village, Kampung Chetti, lies west of Jln Gajah Berang, about 1km northwest of Chinatown; look for the archway with elephant sculptures opposite where Jln Gajah Berang meets Jln Kampong Empat. The best time to visit this colourful neighbourhood is during Hindu festivals such as the Mariamman Festival (Pesta Datuk Charchar) in late April or early May.

CHETTI MUSEUM MUSEUM

(☎06-281 1289; Jln Gajah Berang; adult/child RM2/1; ⏲9am-1pm & 2-5pm Tue-Sun) This small museum is a community effort with a collection of artefacts, including antique *cendol* (shaved ice) makers and embroidered wedding garb. There are excellent English-language explanations about the Chetti language and rites of passage, plus news clippings about local efforts to preserve Chetti heritage.

SRI SUBRAMANIAM THUROPATHAI AMMAN ALAYAM TEMPLE

(Jln Gajah Berang, Kampung Chetti; ⏲7.30am-10pm) FREE A huge *gopuram* (tower), as elaborate and pink as a tiered wedding cake, erupts from this temple. Few visitors come here, but if you shed your shoes you can marvel at exterior statues of Surya with his chariot pulled by seven horses, and at a rainbow of enamelled decorations inside.

Southeast of the City Centre

MASJID SELAT MELAKA MOSQUE

(off Jln Baiduri 8; ⏲7am-7pm) Especially beautiful during morning or dusk light, this gold-domed mosque gazes dreamily at the Strait of Melaka from its shoreside perch on an artificial island a short taxi ride or bicycle pedal from central Melaka City. Completed in 2006, the mosque's grand archways are panelled with stained glass. When water levels are high, it appears to float.

Non-Muslim visitors are permitted provided they dress modestly and heed the 'no shoe' signs around different parts of this large complex. Women must bring a scarf or use a rental shawl to cover their head.

There are few attractions nearby and taxis don't always ply this part of town. If you don't have your own wheels, ask a taxi driver for a return trip (RM15 each way) plus waiting time.

MEDAN PORTUGIS SQUARE

(Portuguese Square) Roughly 4km east of the city centre, this seaside square populated by seafood restaurants is the focal point of Melaka City's Eurasian community. Many of the residents are descended from marriages between the colonial Portuguese and Malays some 400 years ago and many of them speak Kristang, a Creole language that mixes Malay with archaic Portuguese. The square, styled after a typical Portuguese *mercado*, wasn't completed until the late 1980s.

The *kampung* (village) is unexceptional and the square is often empty, except in the evenings when people come here to down a beer and scoff seafood. The sea breeze is lovely even if the views are being marred by construction of the new Harbour City development. Bus 17 from Dutch Sq will get you here.

PRISON MUSEUM MUSEUM

(FIB Muzium Penjara Malaysia; ☎06-281 3548; cnr Jln Parameswara & Jln Melati; adult/child RM6/3; ⏰9am-5pm Tue-Sun) Fixing an unflinching gaze on Malaysian prisons, past and present, this museum occupies – naturally enough – a former prison. There is interesting detail on the 18th-century beginnings of the Malaysian prison system, how it was shaped under British rule, and on famous jails like Pulau Jerjak, Malaysia's version of Alcatraz. Things get more disturbing with interactive displays on corporal punishment and the insides of lonely prison cells. Definitely not one for the kids.

The museum is isolated 2.5km east of Chinatown; a taxi should cost around RM10.

EATING

Peranakan cuisine is Melaka City's most famous type of cooking. It's also known as Nonya (or Nyonya), an affectionate term for a Peranakan wife (often the family chef). You'll also find Portuguese Eurasian food, Indian, Chinese and more.

Chinatown & Around

★**NANCY'S KITCHEN** MALAYSIAN $

(☎06-283 6099; www.eatatnancyskit.com; 13 Jln KL 3/8, Taman Kota Laksamana; mains RM10; ⏰11am-5pm Sun, Mon, Wed & Thu, 11am-9pm Fri & Sat) The mouth-watering meals stirred up in this Peranakan (Nonya) restaurant are revered in Melaka and Nancy's Kitchen lives up to the hype. Local diners crowd this small restaurant, especially at weekends, their bellies rumbling for a taste of signature dishes like candlenut chicken (succulent meat simmered in a nutty sauce, fragrant with lemongrass).

If you want to take some Peranakan home-cooking flair away with you, call to arrange cooking courses (p150) with Nancy herself.

★**PAK PUTRA RESTAURANT** PAKISTANI $

Map p137 (☎012-601 5876; 58 Jln Kota Laksmana 4; mains RM9-12; ⏰5.30pm-1am, closed alternate Mon; ✎) Scarlet tikka chickens rotate hypnotically on skewers, luring diners to this excellent Pakistani restaurant. With aromatic vegetarian dishes, seafood and piquant curries, there's no shortage of choice (try the masala fish). The unchallenged highlights are oven-puffed naan bread and chicken fresh from the clay tandoor. Portions are generous and service is speedy.

LOW YONG MOH CHINESE $

Map p140 (☎06-282 1235; 32 Jln Tukang Emas; dim sum RM2.40-3.70; ⏰5.30am-noon Wed-Mon) Famous across Melaka for its large and delectably well-stuffed *pao* (steamed pork buns), this place is Chinatown's biggest breakfast treat. With high ceilings, plenty of fans running and a view of Masjid Kampung Kling, the atmosphere oozes charm. It's usually packed with talkative, newspaper-reading locals by around 7am. Food offerings thin out by 11am, so arrive early.

POH PIAH LWEE MALAYSIAN $

Map p140 (14 Jln Kubu; mains RM3-5; ⏰9am-5pm) This lively hole in the wall has one specialist cook preparing delicious Hokkien-style *popiah* (lettuce, bean sprouts, egg and chilli paste in a soft sleeve), another making near-perfect *rojak* (fruit and vegetable salad in a shrimp paste, lime juice, sugar and peanut dressing), while the third whips up laksa.

JONKER 88 DESSERTS $

Map p140 (88 Jln Hang Jebat; mains RM6-10.50; ⏰11am-10pm Tue-Thu, to 11pm Fri & Sat, to 9pm Sun) Slurp-worthy laksa and decent Peranakan fare are served up at this efficient and busy canteen. But the highlight is its *cendol,* which comes in a fabulous selection of flavours and toppings. This frosty dessert, a mountain of shaved ice, coconut, pandan noodles, red beans and jaggery syrup, is as rainbow-coloured (and wacky) as it sounds.

SHUI XIAN VEGETARIAN CHINESE $

Map p140 (☎012-635 8052; 43 Jln Hang Lekiu; mains RM2.80-6; ⏰7.30am-2.30pm Mon-Sat; ✎) In a city where vegetable dishes so often arrive strewn with shrimp or pork, vegetarians can breathe a sigh of relief here. This no-frills canteen whips up meat-free versions of *nasi lemak*, laksa and even 'chicken' rice balls.

LOCAL KNOWLEDGE

JONKER WALK'S HAWKER CRAWL

The best reason for elbowing your way through the crowds that descend on the Jonker Walk Night Market (p148) is to graze on its lip-smacking range of local hawker food treats. Look out for the following items.

Kuih nonya Coconut milk and sticky-rice sweets, too colourful to resist.

Dodol Jellies made from the seaweed agar agar in *gua melaka* (palm sugar), pandan and durian flavours.

Pineapple tarts Buttery pastries with a chewy jam filling.

Popiah Spring rolls without the crunch, stuffed with shredded veggies, prawns, garlic and more.

Watermelon slushies Whole watermelons are punctured with two big holes, the contents mushed up with an electric whisk and ice added for a portable refresher.

GREEN HOUSE VEGETARIAN RESTAURANT — VEGETARIAN $

Map p137 (011-1073 1188; www.facebook.com/greenhousemalacca; 4 Jln Kota Laksamana 1; mains RM10; 11.30am-3.30pm & 5.30-9.30pm;) Serving decent veggie versions of classic Malay dishes such as the fragrant soup *bah-kut-teh* (usually made with pork) and sweet-and-sour *assam* fish. If you don't fancy these mock-meat dishes, there are plenty of vegetables that can be cooked just to your liking.

LIMAU-LIMAU CAFE — INTERNATIONAL $

Map p140 (9 Jln Hang Lekiu; mains from RM7; 9am-5pm Thu-Mon;) Choose from healthy granolas or towering sandwiches and wash it all down with tempting smoothies like dragonfruit or a papaya-lime blend (RM10 to RM12).

SEEDS GARDEN — VEGETARIAN $

Map p140 (017-363 9626; www.seedsgarden.com.my; 60 Jln Tokong; mains RM13-15; 11.30am-3.30pm & 6-9pm Thu-Tue;) Among the spate of veggie restaurants that appear to be blooming across Melaka, this one is certainly the trendiest looking. It's also probably the only one that's inspired by the principles of phytotherapy – eating healthily to improve personal, social and environmental wellness.

CHUNG WAH — SOUTHEAST ASIAN $$

Map p140 (18 Jln Hang Jebat; chicken half/whole RM22.30/44.60; 8.30am-3pm Mon-Fri, until 4pm Sat & Sun) As you'll see from the queue outside, this is one of Melaka City's top spots for juicy poached chicken served with wadded balls of rice, themselves sticky with chicken stock. That's the only dish on offer, but it's done perfectly and served with cooling beakers of freshly squeezed lime juice.

HOE KEE CHICKEN RICE BALL — CHINESE $$

Map p140 (4 Jln Hang Jebat; mains from RM14; 9.30am-4.30pm) A popular pilgrimage place for Hainanese chicken rice; don't expect a menu or deferential service. The queue allows plenty of time to decide if you're hungry enough for a quarter chicken (RM14) or a whole one (RM42).

★KOCIK KITCHEN — PERANAKAN $$

Map p140 (016-929 6605; 100 Jln Tun Tan Cheng Lock; mains RM20-30; 11am-6.30pm Mon, Tue & Thu, 11am-5pm & 6-9pm Fri & Sat, 11am-7.30pm Sun) This unassuming little restaurant is hot on the heels of Melaka City's other Peranakan (Nonya) specialists; try the creamy *lemak nenas* prawns, swimming in fragrant coconut milk with fresh chunks of pineapple. The set lunch (RM12 to RM15) is a bargain.

★SALUD TAPAS — SPANISH $$

Map p140 (06-282 9881; www.facebook.com/SALUDTAPAS; 94 Jln Tun Tan Cheng Lock; tapas/mains from RM12/46; 12.30pm-1am Wed-Mon;) 'Small bites, big flavours' is the tag line for this sophisticated new tapas bar that really delivers. It helps that the chef is Spanish and that the ingredients and recipes are authentic. It's a lovely spot for a glass of wine and a few appetisers but equally tempting for a full meal such as paella.

BABOON HOUSE — BURGERS $$

Map p140 (012-938 6013; 89 Jln Tun Tan Cheng Lock; burgers RM15; 10am-5pm Mon, Wed & Thu, to 7pm Fri-Sun;) If gourmet burgers, such as Greek-style spicy lamb or the signature Baboon pork belly, sound like a pleasant change from tastebud-searing Indian or Peranakan cuisine, settle in for a meal here. The setting in a time-worn shophouse with a plant-filled courtyard is delightful, though the signs forbidding photography and urging quiet somewhat tarnish the mood.

STREET KITCHEN FUSION **$$**

Map p140 (017-329 8331; www.facebook.com/thestreetkitchenmlk; 47 Jln Laksamana; mains RM9-22; 5pm-2am Wed-Mon) Dishes such as sweet-and-sour pomfret, homemade popcorn chicken and Thai-style spaghetti are among the Asian-fusion dishes that this youthful and friendly operation turns out. With seats beside the Melaka River, it's also a great spot to sip one of the tropical mocktails and juices.

Jalan Merdeka & Around

Restaurants in the shopping mall district are mostly unexciting chains, but a lively food court just west of Mahkota Pde serves Malay and Chinese fare. East of the centre, Medan Portugis (Portuguese Sq) has food stalls serving seafood dishes beside the sea.

RESTORAN NYONYA SUAN MALAYSIAN **$$**

Map p137 (06-286 4252; 1336D Jln Merdeka; mains RM17-30; 11am-2.30pm & 5-9.30pm) Fiery Peranakan specialities are served up at this large and pleasant restaurant, with *ikan gerang asam* (fish in a spicy tamarind sauce) and chicken rendang the stand-out dishes. A couple of swaying lanterns and some stained-glass panelling give you something to admire while awaiting your towering *cendol* (shaved-ice dessert).

RESTORAN DE LISBON PORTUGUESE **$$**

(Medan Portugis; mains RM16-50; 1pm-midnight) The main reason to head to the Portuguese Sq is the food that you can enjoy at outdoor tables with a sea view. This laid-back outlet to the rear of the complex, away from the throng of touts in the car park, serves delicious local specialities: chilli crab (RM50 for two crabs) or Eurasian chicken *debal* ('devil's curry', from RM25).

Little India to Bukit China

★**SELVAM** INDIAN **$**

Map p140 (06-281 9223; 2 Jln Temenggong; mains RM5-11; 7am-10pm;) This classic banana-leaf restaurant is excellent value, with efficient and amiable staff. Generous servings of aromatic chicken biryani are eclipsed by the vegetarian offerings, in particular the Friday-afternoon veggie special.

★**BULLDOG** MALAYSIAN **$**

Map p136 (016-303 3970; www.facebook.com/bulldogmalacca; 145 Jln Bendahara; mains RM10-15; 11.30am-2pm & 6-11pm Mon-Sat) Specialising in Peranakan cuisine, Bulldog is a contemporary, monochrome-decorated space that serves its excellent food with a spicy edge that's very appealing. Don't miss the chilli-paste-slavered aubergine or the *otak otak* (fish-paste patties). Live music sets toes tapping Friday and Saturday night from 9.30pm.

13 HIBISCUS VINTAGE ART CAFE MALAYSIAN **$**

Map p140 (011-1073 1188; www.facebook.com/13hibiscus; 13 Jln Bunga Raya; mains RM7; 9am-5pm Sat & Sun;) For its quirky retro decor alone, which includes the giant letters from an old cinema hung on the wall plus engaging street art, this weekend-only cafe is well worth a visit. It serves simple dishes such as *nasi lemak* (rice boiled in coconut milk, served with fried *ikan bilis*, peanuts and a curry dish) and nonya laksa (noodles in spicy coconut broth).

Upstairs is a wonderful rental apartment sleeping up to five people (weekdays/weekends RM380/550); it also has another very cute two-person apartment for rent (weekdays/weekends RM280/400) nearby with the perfect view over the Sungai Melaka.

CAPITOL SATAY MALAYSIAN **$**

Map p137 (06-283 5508; 41 Lg Bukit China; sticks from RM1.10-10; 4pm-midnight Wed-Mon;) Famous for its *satay celup* (a Melaka adaptation of steamboat with satay sauce), this place is usually packed and is one of the cheapest outfits in town. Stainless-steel tables have bubbling vats of soup in the middle where you dunk skewers of okra stuffed with tofu, sausages, chicken, prawns, bok choy and the like.

PURPLE CANE TEA RESTAURANT CHINESE $$

Map p136 (☎06-283 3090; www.tearestaurant.com.my; Lot 1F-06 Level 1, The Shore Shopping Gallery, 193 Pinggiran @ Sungai Melaka, Jln Persisiran Bunga Raya; meals RM27; ⊙10am-10pm) Many of the dishes involve tea at this pleasant restaurant, one of the more interesting and, crucially, local chains in the new Shore shopping mall. The four-course set meal deals are a steal. It also sells all its teas and snacks in nice packaging, making it a good place for gifts.

DRINKING & NIGHTLIFE

Unlike much of Malaysia, there is no shortage of spots to cool down with a beer in Melaka City. On Friday, Saturday and Sunday nights, Jonker Walk Night Market (p148) in Chinatown closes Jln Heng Lekir to traffic and the handful of bars along the lane become a mini street party with live music and tables spilling beyond the sidewalks. Karaoke enthusiasts take over the stage at the apex of Jln Hang Jebat and Jln Tokong.

★DAILY FIX CAFE

Map p140 (☎06-283 4858; www.facebook.com/thedailyfixcafe; 55 Jln Hang Jebat; ⊙10am-5pm Mon-Fri, 8.30am-5.30 Sat & Sun) Our favourite Melaka City cafe is a secret oasis tucked behind an otherwise identikit souvenir shop in Chinatown. Soy milk for coffees and shakes is a great plus and you won't want to miss out on the delicious *gua melaka* (brown palm sugar) cake. There's a fab range of other things to eat too, but it's the tranquil atmosphere here that's the draw.

★CALANTHE ART CAFE COFFEE

Map p140 (13 States Coffee; ☎06-292 2960; www.facebook.com/calanthe.melaka; 11 Jln Hang Kasturi; ⊙10am-11pm Fri-Wed; 📶) Full-bodied Johor or classic Perak white? Choose a Malaysian state's favourite coffee and this perky place will have it blended with ice and jelly cubes for a refreshing caffeine kick. Breakfasts are served here too (10am to 11.45am) and it's worth dropping by just to admire the creative decor.

★BACKLANE COFFEE CAFE

Map p140 (☎06-282 0542; www.facebook.com/Backlane-Coffee-574343952693116; 129 Jln Hang Jebat; ⊙11am-midnight Sun-Thu, until 1am Fri & Sat; 📶) Ace chill-out space that's an ideal retreat from all the tourist and karaoke craziness at this end of the Jonker Walk Night Market. There's a good range of coffee, tea and other beverages as well as a tempting range of professionally made cakes.

★GEOGRAPHÉR CAFE BAR

Map p140 (☎06-281 6813; www.geographer.com.my; 83 Jln Hang Jebat; ⊙10am-1am Sun-Thu, until 2am Fri & Sat; 📶) A swinging soundtrack of Eurotrash, jazz and classic pop keeps the beers flowing at this traveller magnet. It's a well-ventilated cafe-bar, strewn with greenery and feeling like a haven despite bordering busy Jonker St. Monday nights have live jazz while Fridays and Saturdays bring a father-daughter vocal-keyboard duet (both 8.30pm).

Geographér also serves decent food (mains RM15); watch out for the chilli kick of the *kampung* fried rice.

★PAMPAS SKY BAR BAR

Map p136 (☎017-707 2731; www.pampas.com.my; Level 41, The Shore Shopping Gallery, 193 Pinggiran @ Sungai Melaka, Jln Persisiran Bunga Raya; ⊙4pm-1am Sun-Thu, until 2am Fri & Sat) The views of Melaka from the 41st floor of the Shore complex are impressive, but this bar and restaurant goes one further with a leafy outdoor area to relax in and enjoy a cocktail or beer.

DISCOVERY CAFE & GUEST HOUSE CAFE

Map p140 (☎06-292 5606, 012-683 5606; www.discovery-malacca.com; 3 Jln Bunga Raya; @) Owner Bob Teng offers nearly everything that caters to travellers' needs here, from budget rooms, bicycle and scooter rental to bus tickets, tours and cafe food. At the very least drop by for a beer – they get cheaper the more of them you drink, with the best deals being for the party-sized 3L towers (RM75.90).

There's live music most nights and the nearby riverside setting is pleasant.

IDLERS CORNER CAFE

Map p140 (☎06-282 1748; www.facebook.com/malaccaidlerscorner; Lg Hang Jebat; ⊙noon-midnight) Snap open a beer or sip on soft drinks away from the Chinatown chaos at this simple but friendly bar with cane chairs and tables overlooking the water. Enter either through the clothing store on Lg Hang Jebat or find it along the riverside walkway.

KAYA KAYA CAFE CAFE

Map p140 (☎06-281 4089; www.facebook.com/kayakayacafelol; 32 Jln Tukang Besi; ⏱8am-6pm; 📶) Good spot if you're hankering for an early morning coffee or a spot of breakfast: try the yummy Melaka Elvis banana pancakes with peanut butter and chocolate sauce. The bare brick walls, street art and retro, mismatched furniture all add to the hipster vibe.

ME & MRS JONES PUB

Map p140 (☎016-234 4292; 3 Jln Hang Kasturi; ⏱7pm-midnight Tue-Sun) This cosy pub is staunchly unhip and all the more enjoyable for it. At weekends there is live blues and rock, often with retired co-owner Mr Tan leading a jam session. Relax into the atmosphere and grab a beer or juice (long menus are not the Jones' style).

SID'S PUB @ JONKERS PUB

Map p140 (☎06-283 7437; www.sidspubs.com; 2 Lrg Hang Jebat; ⏱11am-midnight Sun-Thu, until 1am Fri & Sat) Sid's has been a fixture on the KL bar scene for years. He's now set up a branch in Melaka City, bagging a convivial, multilevel spot in a prime riverside position. Happy hour runs until 8pm and all day Sunday.

WOODS CAFE

(☎016 622 7770; www.facebook.com/thewoodsbookstore; 35 Jln Gajah Berang; ⏱11am-8pm Thu-Tue; 📶) Over near Kampung Chetti, this charmingly rustic cafe and secondhand bookshop is worth searching out. The owner takes his time making his hand-dripped coffee and herbal teas.

MIXX CLUB

Map p136 (2nd fl, Mahkota Arcade, Jln Syed Abdul Aziz; ⏱10pm-late Tue-Sat) In a city where nightclubs are thin on the ground, Mixx dominates the scene with Paradox, a laser-lit, warehouse-style venue where international DJs spin techno and electronica; and Arris, which has a garden area and live bands. It's definitely Melaka's best place to pound a dance floor. Cover (RM10) is charged on Friday and Saturday nights and includes one drink.

SHOPPING

★JONKER WALK NIGHT MARKET MARKET

Map p140 (Jln Hang Jebat; ⏱6-11pm Fri-Sun) Melaka City's weekly shopping extravaganza keeps the shops along Jln Hang Jebat open late, while trinket sellers, food hawkers and the occasional fortune teller close the street to traffic. Unashamedly commercial and attracting hordes of tourists, it is nevertheless an undeniably colourful way to spend an evening shopping and grazing.

★ORANGUTAN HOUSE ART

Map p140 (☎06-282 6872; www.absolutearts.com/charlescham; 59 Lg Hang Jebat; ⏱10am-6pm Thu-Tue) It's impossible to miss the giant orangutan mural above artist Charles Cham's gallery and T-shirt store. His colourful, primitive-style paintings sell for US$525 upwards, while his cheeky range of T-shirts (RM39) are a more affordable, wearable art for all. Designs range from Chinese astrology animals to uplifting slogans and 'play safe' banners above condoms.

There are two smaller branches elsewhere in Chinatown on Jln Hang Jebat and Jln Tokong Emas.

★THAM SIEW INN ARTIST GALLERY ART

Map p140 (☎06-281 2112; www.thamsiewinn.com; 49 Jln Tun Tan Teng Lock; ⏱10am-6pm Thu-Tue) Vibrant watercolours of sunsets, street scenes and temples fill this lovely art gallery spanning the entire length of a shophouse along with its inner courtyard garden. Also here, the artist's son carves traditional Chinese stone seals to your choice of design and is a very able artist in his own right.

★TRASH & TREASURE MARKET

Map p140 (☎012-298 3834; 3 Jln Bunga Raya; ⏱10am-5pm Sat & Sun) It's great fun rooting around this excellent new flea market in a riverside warehouse behind Discovery Cafe. All kinds of gifts and collectables are on offer, from vintage signs and bicycles to handmade jewellery, art and old magazines. The vibe is very relaxed.

RED HANDICRAFTS ARTS & CRAFTS

Map p140 (30C Jln Hang Kasturi; ⏱11am-6pm Thu-Tue) Ray Tan draws Japanese- and Chinese-inspired designs that range from flowing organic patterns to quirky cartoons. Watch him hand-print your favourite onto a 100%

cotton T-shirt or peruse his intricate paper-cutting art. Also for sale are colourful Chinese baby toys.

HUEMAN STUDIO ART

Map p140 (☎06-288 1795; 9 Jln Tokong; ⏰10.30am-6pm) Woodblock prints, many with themes such as astrology and calligraphy, take centre stage in this art studio-gift shop. Portable souvenirs include hand-painted rosewood jewellery (from RM16), buffalo-horn pendants (RM45) and more.

CLAY HOUSE ARTS & CRAFTS

Map p140 (☎06-292 6916; 18 Jln Tukang Besi; ⏰10am-6pm Thu-Tue) Perforated pottery tea-light holders, bowls and ornaments are made here by the clay craftsman, Leong Chee Hsiung. For RM60 he will also teach you how to make your own pot and post the finished product back to you in a month's time.

PURI PADI HOMEWARES

Map p140 (☎06-283 2116; http://puripadi.blogspot.co.uk; 16 Jln Hang Kasturi) One of the more sophisticated gift shops in Chinatown, Puri Padi stocks everything you could need to turn your home into an old-world Asian oasis, from stone buddha heads and batik wall hangings to carved wood and pottery ornaments.

JOE'S DESIGN JEWELLERY

Map p140 (☎06-281 2960; www.facebook.com/joedesignhandcrafted; 6 Jln Tun Tan Cheng Lock; ⏰10am-5pm) Owl-shaped ornaments, iridescent floral necklaces and beautifully curled copper-wire creations are some of the stock at this lovely craft-jewellery shop.

MALAQA HOUSE ANTIQUES

Map p140 (☎06-281 4770; 70 Jln Tun Tan Cheng Lock; ⏰10am-6pm) A huge museum-like shop in an elegant building stuffed to the gills with antiques and replicas – it's not cheap, but it bursts with character.

UMYANG BATIK CLOTHING

Map p140 (☎06-292 6569; 6 Jln Hang Kasturi) The cat-and-mouse designs on Ha Mi Seon's hand-painted, batik-print T-shirts and other clothing are undeniably cute. It's a great place to pick up something for a child to wear. She uses all natural colours for her dyes.

LOCAL KNOWLEDGE

MELAKA'S ART GALLERIES

With its potent cocktail of cultures and pretty urbanscapes, Melaka City inspires many an artist. Chinatown has an impressive concentration of independent galleries and craft workshops. Some are a delight for serious art collectors, such as Tham Siew Inn Artist Gallery and Zheng He Duo Yun Zuan, with paintings and sculptures to browse and buy. Others, like Orangutan House and Hueman Studio, place their unique designs on handmade souvenirs and T-shirts.

WAH AIK SHOEMAKER SHOES

Map p140 (☎06-284 9726; http://wahaikshoemakermelaka.webs.com; 92 Jln Tun Tan Cheng Lock) The three Yeo brothers continue the shoemaking tradition begun by their grandfather. Their beaded Peranakan shoes are considered Melaka's finest and begin at a steep but merited RM350. The most unusual souvenirs are tiny bound-feet shoes (from RM95).

This minute footwear harks back to China's now-defunct tradition of foot binding, where women endured lifelong pain and deformity to attain the 'golden lotus' ideal of feet no longer than 4in.

SHORE SHOPPING GALLERY MALL

Map p136 (www.theshoreshoppinggallery.com; 193 Pinggiran @ Sungai Melaka, Jln Persisran Bunga Raya; ⏰10am-10pm) Anchored by upmarket Singaporean department store Tangs, this is Melaka City's newest mall. It's a pleasant spot for a browse of around 100 shops if you're in this part of town, and it houses several other attractions, including an aquarium and the Sky Tower viewing platform.

DATARAN PAHLAWAN MALL

Map p137 (☎06-281 2898; www.dataranpahlawan.com; Jln Merdeka; ⏰10am-10pm) Melaka's largest mall has a collection of upscale designer shops and restaurants in the western half and an underground craft-and-souvenir market in the eastern portion, which is beneath a grassy square where events are held.

ACTIVITIES

Reflexology centres are plentiful in Chinatown. A half-hour foot massage costs around RM25, but it's often worth paying a few extra ringgit for a quality experience.

KAMPUNG MORTEN WALKING TOUR WALKING

Map p136 (Jln Kampung Morten; ⏰4pm Mon, Wed & Fri) FREE Protected by a bend in the Melaka River, Kampung Morten is a charming village of 85 homes, including 52 in traditional Melakan style. These free guided tours leave from Villa Sentosa (p142); as long as you don't arrive at the same time as a tour bus, walking around is a relaxing experience and you'll meet plenty of welcoming people.

MELAKA RIVER CRUISE CRUISE

Map p140 (☎06-281 4322, 06-286 5468; www.melakarivercruise.com; Jln Laksamana; adult/child RM15/7; ⏰9am-11.30pm) The most convenient place to board this 40-minute riverboat cruise along Sungai Melaka is at the quay near the Maritime Museum. Cruises go 9km upriver past Kampung Morten and old *godown* (river warehouses) with a recorded narration explaining the riverfront's history.

OLD MELAKA HERITAGE TOUR WALKING

Map p140 (Tourism Malaysia, Jln Kota; ⏰9am Tue, Thu & Sat) FREE Lasting around 2½ hours, this guided walk sets off from Tourism Malaysia's office beside Dutch Sq and takes in the key sights of the Unesco Heritage area, including Bukit St Paul and Chinatown.

NANCY'S KITCHEN COOKING

(☎06-283 6099; www.eatatnancyskit.com; 13 Jln KL 3/8, Taman Kota Laksamana Seksyen 3; per person RM180) Nancy of this near-legendary Peranakan restaurant (p144) teaches cookery classes by request. Reserve well in advance.

NONYA CULINARY JOURNEY COOKING

Map p136 (☎Hotel Equatorial 06-282 8333; Hotel Equatorial, Jln Parameswara; per person RM115) These two-hour cooking classes include a set lunch and a certificate of completion. You'll cook three Peranakan (Nonya) dishes, including specialities such as *ayam pong teh* (miso soy chicken) and *udang lemak nenas* (prawns with pineapple and spicy coconut), hands-on with the chef. Advanced booking required.

PERANAKAN CULINARY JOURNEY COOKING

Map p136 (☎06-289 8000; www.majestic-malacca.com; Majestic Malacca Hotel, 188 Jln Bunga Raya; per person RM290) Learn about each ingredient and the history of each dish with a master Peranakan chef who does most of the cooking at the Majestic Malacca Hotel. Book one week in advance. A minimum of two people and a maximum of four keeps things intimate.

MALACCA NIGHT CYCLING CYCLING

Map p136 (☎016-668 8898; 46A Jln Portugis; per person RM35) Operating out of Ringo's Foyer hostel, these guided cycling tours through Melaka City will test your trishaw-dodging skills. Evening, when the temperature drops, is the most pleasant time to tour the city. Tours leave by arrangement at 8.30pm and last 90 minutes (or longer, if you like). Call a day or two in advance to book.

ECO BIKE TOUR CYCLING

(☎019-652 5029; www.melakaonbike.com; per person RM100) Explore the fascinating landscape around Melaka City with Alias on his three-hour bike tour (minimum two people) through 20km of oil-palm and rubber-tree plantations and delightful *kampung* communities surrounding town. Flag your level of fitness when you book. Pickups are from your accommodation.

BIOSSENTIALS PURI SPA SPA

Map p140 (☎06-282 5588; www.hotelpuri.com/spa.html; Hotel Puri, 118 Jln Tun Tan Cheng Lock; ⏰10am-7pm) This spa in a sensual garden isn't a walk-in like Jonker St's casual reflexology outlets. The reward for booking ahead is the delicious menu of treatments, including steams, scrubs, facials and milk baths. Aromatherapy foot treatments (45 minutes) start at RM65, while body wraps and deep-tissue massages (one hour) cost around RM145.

HUOLONG FOOT REFLEXOLOGY & MASSAGE MASSAGE

Map p140 (☎017-602 5717; 5 Jln Hang Lekir; ⏰11am-11pm) This centrally located massage place offers good value to have your toes reset with a satisfying snap. A half-hour reflexology session costs RM30, while a full hour treating your shoulders and feet is RM45.

SLEEPING

Melaka City has a dynamic accommodation scene with new places frequently popping up. The quality is the best it's been in years and there's a good range of rental properties in characterful heritage buildings should you wish to have your private Melaka City space. Chinatown is the best area to be based in or near, although it can get both busy and noisy, particularly at weekends.

Chinatown

★NOMAPS HOSTEL $

Map p140 (06-283 8311; www.thenomaps.com; 11 Jln Tun Tan Cheng Lock; dm/r incl breakfast from RM80/270;) A real step up for Melaka's hostel options. The attractive street art of Kenji Chai decorates the walls of this otherwise minimalist flashpackers in a key Chinatown location. Six- and four-bed dorms are tiny but have colourful duvets and quality mattresses. A laundry and comfy TV room are other pluses.

RINGO'S FOYER GUESTHOUSE $

Map p136 (06-281 6393, 016-668 8898; www.ringosfoyer.com; 46A Jln Portugis; s/d/q incl breakfast from RM25/60/100;) Travellers will find a warm welcome at this super convivial hostel. The friendly owners do a great job of keeping the atmosphere sociable, particularly in the rooftop cafe and hang-out area. With bike rental, laundry (RM8) and guitars, this place has everything a weary backpacker could want. Howard, the owner, also runs Malacca Night Cycling (p150).

CAFE 1511 GUESTHOUSE GUESTHOUSE $

Map p140 (06-286 0150; 52 Jln Tun Tan Cheng Lock; s/d incl breakfast from RM60/90;) As well as operating a cafe, this old Peranakan mansion has six small, simple, spotless rooms for overnight stays. The place has an old-style feeling accompanied by the music of a water fountain in the light well that extends from the restaurant below.

ROOFTOP GUESTHOUSE HOSTEL $

Map p140 (012-327 7746, 012-380 7211; rooftopguesthouse@yahoo.com; 39 Jln Kampung Pantai; d RM93, dm/d/tr with shared bathroom RM28/63/84;) This hostel is simple but hits the spot with decent air-con, a choice of dorm room or private accommodation, and a bird's-eye view from the roof terrace. Minimum two nights' stay.

GINGERFLOWER BOUTIQUE HOTEL $$

Map p140 (06-288 1331; www.gingerflower-boutiquehotel.com; 13 Jln Tun Tan Cheng Lock; d from RM210;) Rooms are small, but period fittings and immaculate housekeeping make this restored Peranakan townhouse a very pleasant place to stay. It's a few paces from the Jonker St hubbub and well placed for gallery and museum visits along Jln Tun Tan Cheng Lock.

HEEREN HOUSE GUESTHOUSE $$

Map p140 (06-281 4241; www.heerenhouse.com; 1 Jln Tun Tan Cheng Lock; s/d/q incl breakfast from RM139/159/269;) The traditional furnishings of this prime-location hotel have a nostalgic air, while the family-run vibe and hearty breakfasts infuse the place with a homely feel. The six airy and clean rooms in this former warehouse largely overlook the river. Not all rooms pick up the wi-fi signal from the lobby. The hotel also has a good cafe.

COURTYARD@HEEREN BOUTIQUE HOTEL $$

Map p140 (06-281 0088; www.courtyard-atheeren.com; 91 Jln Tun Tan Cheng Lock; d or tw/ste incl breakfast from RM200/300;) Each room here is decorated with an individual touch, with light and bright decor paired with antique wood furniture. Some rooms have minimalist stained-glass details, modern takes on Chinese latticework or luxuriant drapes, but not all have windows. It's professionally run with great service.

HANGOUT@JONKER HOTEL $$

Map p140 (06-282 8318; www.hangouthotels.com; 19-21 Jln Hang Jebat; s/d/tr/q incl breakfast from RM90/120/150/180;) While its sparse contemporary decor is at odds with the glitzy Peranakan mansions elsewhere in Chinatown, rooms here are surgically clean. There's also a roof terrace from which to ogle Chinatown's skyline.

HOTEL PURI HOTEL $$

Map p140 (06-282 5588; www.hotelpuri.com; 118 Jln Tun Tan Cheng Lock; d/tr/q/ste incl breakfast from RM188/310/380/408;) One of Chinatown's gems, Hotel Puri is an elegant creation in a superbly renovated Peranakan mansion dating to 1822. Its elaborate lobby, decked out with beautiful old cane and inlaid furniture, opens to a gorgeous courtyard garden where breakfast is served. Standard rooms have butter-yellow walls, crisp sheets, wi-fi and shuttered windows. There's also an on-site spa.

★**45 LEKIU** RENTAL HOUSE **$$$**
Map p140 (☎016-274 9686, 012-698 4917; www.45lekiu.com; 45 Jln Hang Lekiu; weekdays/weekends RM1299/1499;) Sleeping four, this gorgeous restoration project of a shophouse has kept the big old beams and original exposed brickwork but has updated with stylish contemporary decor. There are cooking facilities. Highlights include a bougainvillea-filled courtyard with a dipping pool and a roof terrace overlooking the city.

The same company also rents out the similar luxe restorations **Stables** (Map p140; ☎012-698 4917, 016-274 9686; http://thestable-malacca.com; No D Jln Hang Kasturi; r weekdays/weekends RM380/480;) and **Opposite Place** (Map p140; http://opposite-place.com; 18 Jln Hang Lekiu; r weekday/weekend incl breakfast from RM499/599;).

CALANTHE ARTISAN LOFT RENTAL HOUSE **$$$**
Map p140 (☎06-281 2960; http://calantheartisan-loft.wixsite.com/calantheartisanloft; 16 Jln Tun Tan Cheng Lock; house RM500;) You won't fail to miss the technicolour entrance to this rental house run by the owners of Calanthe Art Cafe. It's not the fanciest home in Chinatown, but it has plenty of charm and comfortably sleeps four with a maximum of seven (RM50 for each extra person) if you use the beanbags in the TV room downstairs.

CASA DEL RIO HOTEL **$$$**
Map p137 (☎06-289 6888; www.casadelrio-melaka.com; 88 Jln Kota Laksmana; r/ste incl breakfast from RM665/1574;) With a fabulous location right on the river and steps from Chinatown, Case Del Rio has palatial architecture that blends Portuguese/Mediterranean with Malaysian for a result that's airy and grand. Rooms are massive, with bathrooms fit for a Portuguese princess, and river-view rooms capture the feel of Asia and Venice combined.

There's a rooftop infinity pool that overlooks the river and common areas are strewn with loungable couches and tons of cushions.

Jalan Merdeka & Around

★**RUCKSACK CARATEL** BOUTIQUE HOTEL **$**
Map p137 (☎06-292 2107; http://therucksack-group.com/caratel; 107 Jln Banda Kaba; r incl breakfast from RM90;) There's a fun flashpacker vibe at this great addition to central Melaka City's budget options. The cheapest rooms are in mock 'caravans' on the ground floor, each given a famous star's name and decorated with their portrait. More-pricey rooms offer heavenly king-sized beds and views of the neighbouring lush gardens of Sultanate Palace.

★**APA KABA HOME & STAY** GUESTHOUSE **$**
Map p137 (☎06-283 8196, 012-798 1232; www.apa-kaba.com; 28 Kg Banda Kaba; d/tr with shared bathroom from RM45/60, tw/tr RM85/95;) This tranquil homestay has rooms as low-key and relaxing as its *kampung* (village) setting, despite being within walking distance of central Melaka City. Rooms are simple (the more expensive have air-con) and there's a large garden to lounge in, complete with chickens and dangling mango trees. The 1912 building is a mishmash of Malay and Chinese styles.

The owners are long-term residents who treat guests like family. They are more than happy to impart the secrets of perfect chicken rice and where to find the best *cendol* in town.

QUAYSIDE HOTEL HOTEL **$$**
Map p137 (☎06-284 1001; www.quaysidehotel.com.my; 1 Jln Merdeka; r/ste inc breakfast from RM195/230;) Occupying an airy, warehouse-like building in a key location, the Quay combines contemporary style with great value. Rooms are spacious and modern, with wooden floors and big beds. The best ones have riverside balconies. Breakfast is served in the attached Halia Inc restaurant.

HOTEL EQUATORIAL HOTEL **$$**
Map p137 (☎06-282 8333; http://melaka.equatorial.com; Jln Bandar Hilir; r/ste from RM237/611;) The Equatorial has a refined air, elegantly decorated rooms, quality on-site restaurants and a decent-sized swimming pool. Good discounts are available online. Service is well mannered and the overall presentation is crisp.

WORTH A DETOUR

AYER KEROH

Ayer Keroh (also spelt Air Keroh) has a handful of kid-friendly attractions that are largely deserted on weekdays. Some feel a little contrived, but there's no denying this area, about 13km northeast of Melaka City, is a fine family day trip.

Ayer Keroh's attractions are all clustered either side of a main highway. Bus 19 from Melaka Sentral (RM2, 30 minutes) stops at both the zoo and Taman Mini Malaysia. A taxi to the area will cost around RM45.

Having your own wheels – either a car or scooter – will make it far easier to travel between each attraction as they are fairly spread out. Bicycles (RM5 per hour) can be rented at the entrance to Melaka Botanical Garden.

Melaka Botanical Garden (Taman Botanikal Melaka; ☎06-231 4343; Lebuh Ayer Keroh) A good place for an easy ramble, this lush green enclave is part jungle and part landscaped park with paved trails along which you can walk, cycle or ride an electric buggy – both the buggies and bikes can be rented at the entrance.

Skytrex Melaka (☎018-909 5679; www.skytrex-adventure.com; Melaka Botanical Garden, Lebuh Ayer Keroh; RM55-65; ⌚9am-3pm) There are two adventurous circuits strung between the trees to be tackled here – you'll get to do some climbing, zip-lining and general making out like Tarzan. Bookings for time slots between 9am and 3pm should be made online and it's a good idea to pay the extra RM20 for gloves and water.

Melaka Bird Park (☎06-233 0330; www.melakabirdpark.com; off Lebuh Ayer Keroh; adult/child RM23.70/17.80, with Melaka Wonderland RM65.20/53.30; ⌚9am-6pm) At this well-set-up bird park, a short drive from the Melaka Botanical Garden, you can view around 450 local and international species and get a bird's-eye view from along a canopy walkway.

Melaka Wonderland (☎06-231 3333; www.melakawonderland.com.my; off Lebuh Ayer Keroh; adult/child RM45/37.90, with Melaka Bird Park RM65.20/53.30; ⌚11am-7pm Tue-Fri, 9am-7pm Sat & Sun) When it gets too steamy in Melaka, this water park, close to the Melaka Bird Park, is a great spot to head to cool off and have some fun. There are plenty of different slides to slosh down and pools to splash about in.

Melaka Butterfly & Reptile Sanctuary (Taman Rama Rama; ☎06-232 0033; www.butterflyreptile.com; Lebuh Ayer Keroh; adult/child RM22/16; ⌚8.30am-5.30pm) Your chance to get up close and personal with more than 20 species of butterflies as well as a collection of exotic creepy-crawlies, snakes and some crocodiles.

Melaka Zoo (☎06-232 4054; www.melakazoo.com; Lebuh Ayer Keroh; adult/child RM23.70/17.80; ⌚9am-6pm, night zoo 8-11pm Fri & Sat; P) Melaka's zoo has been going for more than 50 years and is home to more than 200 species of animal, from tigers and lions to less ferocious critters like capybaras, monkeys and mouse deer. The zoo takes pride in its conservation focus and most enclosures are large, though cages for some birds and smaller animals are still rather poky. The night safari allows visitors the chance to spot nocturnal animals at their most active but gets mixed reviews about the wildlife-spotting and live shows during this time.

Taman Mini Malaysia (☎06-234 9988; www.pknm.gov.my; Lebuh Ayer Keroh; adult/child RM24/18; ⌚9am-6pm; P) This open-air museum exhibits traditional houses from all 13 Malaysian states. Visitors can tiptoe through a long-roofed fishing house from Perlis and peruse rice-pounding equipment from Langkawi at numerous re-creations across the site. It's family-focused and a little twee, but the houses are beautifully decorated with plenty of explanations about local traditions, foods and languages.

Giant B (Leboh Ayer Keroh; ⌚9am-6pm) While visiting the Botanical Garden, it's worth dropping by this showroom for a local bee-breeding and honey-making demonstration. In the showroom, which is surrounded outside by stingless and Italian beehives, you can learn all about bees and sample various delicious honeys before you buy.

Little India to Bukit China

★1825 GALLERY HOTEL BOUTIQUE HOTEL **$$**
Map p140 (06-288 2868; http://1825galleryhotel.com; 27-31 Jln Bunga Raya; r from RM151;) Three 1825 vintage shophouses have been combined to create this classy boutique hotel. Original features such as lofty ceilings, brick walls and wood beams harmonise with contemporary art, reclaimed-wood furniture and a waterfall splashing into a fish-filled pond in the lobby. Opt for a river suite with balcony overlooking the Melaka River.

BRIDGE LOFT RENTAL HOUSE **$$**
Map p140 (012-681 2719; www.thebridgeloft.com; 5 Lrg Jambatan; house RM180-380;) One of the more affordable house-rental options in Melaka City is the Bridge Loft, which rents out rooms in three cosy shophouses steps from the Melaka River. Each are simply but tastefully furnished and sleep between two and six people. You can grab breakfast in the cute cafe beneath the unit at number 5.

★MAJESTIC MALACCA BOUTIQUE HOTEL **$$$**
Map p136 (06-289 8000; www.majesticmalacca.com; 188 Jln Bunga Raya; r incl breakfast from RM568;) Claw-foot tubs and polished four-poster beds are just some of the trappings at this regal modern hotel. The bar, library and dining areas groan with nostalgia (think ornate Peranakan screens and gleaming teak furniture), while a small pool and richly endowed spa area add to the opulent feel.

Majestic Malacca is mere steps away from Kampung Morten and a five-minute walk takes you to Little India.

SWISS-GARDEN HOTEL & RESIDENCES HOTEL **$$**
Map p136 (06-288 3131; www.swissgarden.com; T2, The Shore @ Melaka River, Jln Persisiran Bunga Raya; r from RM218;) The Swiss-Garden occupies part of the swanky new Shore development. Rooms are slickly designed and spacious with all the amenities you could wish for. It also manages some of the residency units in the attached apartment block; both the hotel and the units have access to a large central pool and gym facilities.

Penang

George Town p159
Exploring the World Heritage Zone, staying in a boutique heritage hotel and digging into delicious hawker food.

Penang National Park p179
Hiking through rainforest to beaches where monkeys scamper.

Tropical Spice Garden p173
Becoming familiar with the contents of your spice rack at this wonderful hillside garden.

The Habitat p182
Encountering nature and enjoying cool breezes and fantastic views of the island from atop Penang Hill.

Art & Garden by Fuan Wong p179
Marvelling at this outdoor gallery of incredible plants, glass sculptures and contemporary art.

Explore

If there's a better microcosm of the exotic east than Penang, we've yet to find it. Located at the intersection of Asia's great kingdoms and Europe's powerful colonial empires, Penang has long served as the link between Asia's two halves and an important outlet to the markets of Europe and the Middle East.

This is one of Malaysia's most diverse, cosmopolitan and exciting cultures. It culminates in George Town, Penang Island's main city and an urban centre that delivers old-world Asia in spades; think trishaws pedalling past watermarked Chinese shophouses and blue joss smoke perfuming the air.

Yet it would be a shame to neglect the rest of the island's tropical abundance, its palm-fringed beaches and fishing villages, its mountainous jungle and farms growing exotic produce such as nutmeg and durian.

The Best...

➡**Temple** Kek Lok Si Temple (p183)

➡**Beach** Pantai Pasir Panjang (p184)

Top Tip

Penang is best visited during the major festivals and events such as Chinese New Year and the George Town Festival, but book accommodation well in advance.

Getting There & Away

➡**Air Penang International Airport** (Map p158; ☎04-252 0252; www.malaysiaairports.com.my; 11900 Bayan Lepas; 🚌401), 18km south of George Town.

➡**Boat** There are two daily **ferries** (LFS; ☎04-264 2088, 016-419 5008; www.langkawi-ferry.com; PPC Bldg, Lebuh King Edward; adult/child one way RM70/51.30; ⏲7am; 5.30pm Mon-Sat, 7am-3pm Sun) connecting George Town with the beach resort island of Langkawi in Kedah, 120km north of Penang.

➡**Bus** There are plenty of long distance buses to both Butterworth on the mainland and **Sungai Nibong Bus Station** (Map p158; ☎04-659 2099; www.rapidpg.com.my; Jln Sultan Azlan Shah, Kampung Dua Bukit; 🚌401, 303) on Penang Island.

➡**Train** Penang's train station, next to the ferry terminal and bus and taxi station in Butterworth, has services to and from Kuala Lumpur and Hat Yai in Thailand. Check with www.ktmb.com.my for fares and schedules.

Getting Around

➡**To/From the Airport** Bus 401 runs to and from the airport (RM4) every half-hour between 6am and 11pm daily, and stops at KOMTAR and Weld Quay, taking at least an hour. The fixed taxi fare to central George Town is RM44.70; expect the journey to take around 30 minutes depending on traffic.

➡**Bus Rapid Penang** (☎04-238 1313; www.rapidpg.com.my) runs public transport buses around the state. Fares range from RM1.40 to RM4. Most routes originate at Weld

ℹ GETTING TO & FROM BUTTERWORTH

Butterworth, the city on the mainland bit of Penang state (known as Seberang Perai), is home to Penang's main train station and is the departure point for ferries to Penang Island. Unless you're taking the train or your bus has pulled into Butterworth's busy bus station from elsewhere, you'll probably not need to spend any time here.

The cheapest way to get to George Town is via the **ferry** (Map p158; foot passenger/bicycle/motorbike/car RM1.20/1.40/2/7.70; ⏲5.20am-0.40am); the Pangkalan Sultan Abdul Halim Ferry Terminal is linked by walkway to Butterworth's bus and train stations. Ferries take passengers and cars every 10 minutes from 5.20am to 9.30pm, every 20 minutes until 11.15pm, and hourly after that. The journey takes 10 minutes and fares are charged only for the journey from Butterworth to Penang; returning to the mainland is free.

Taxis to/from Butterworth (approximately RM50) cross the 13km Penang Bridge. There's a RM7 toll payable at the toll plaza on the mainland, but no charge to return. If self-driving to or from Kuala Lumpur, the 24km Sultan Abdul Halim Muadzam Shah Bridge, joining Batu Maung at the southeastern tip of Penang Island to Batu Kawan on the mainland, is a more convenient route. The toll here is RM8.50.

Quay Bus Terminal and most also stop at KOMTAR and along Jln Chulia. There are no public bus services connecting Butterworth and Penang Island.

➡**Car & Motorcycle Hire Hawk** (☎016-207 6535; www.hawkrentacar.com; 53-01-A Mbf Tower, Jln Sultan Ahmad Shah) and **La Belle** (☎04-264 2717, 016-416 0617; www.labelle.net.my; 440B Lebuh Chulia; motorcycle/car per 24hr from RM30/100; ⏰9am-1pm & 2-10pm) operate out of George Town. There are also several companies based at Penang International Airport, including **Avis** (☎04-643 9633; www.avis.com; Penang International Airport; ⏰7.30am-9.30pm) and **Hertz** (☎04-643 0208; www.hertz.com; Penang International Airport; ⏰7.30am-10pm Mon-Sat, 8am-4pm Sun). You can hire motorcycles and scooters from many places, including guesthouses and shops along Lebuh Chulia. Manual bikes start at about RM30 and automatic about RM40, for 24 hours. A good alternative are the electric scooters of **DAE Motors** (☎04-263 8286; www.daemotors.com; 132 Jln Dr)

➡Lim Chwee Leong; per 24hr RM50; h9am-6pm).

➡**Bicycle** There are plenty of places that rent bicycles in George Town, although few of them have robust enough bikes for long-distance pedalling around the island (which is hilly).

➡**Trishaw** Bicycle rickshaws are a fun, if touristy, way to negotiate George Town's backstreets and cost between RM20 and RM40 per hour depending on your negotiating skills. As with taxis, it's important to agree on the fare before departure.

Need to Know

➡**Area Code** ☎04

➡**Location** Penang is 370km northwest of KL

➡**Penang Global Tourism** (☎04-264 3456; www.mypenang.gov.my; Whiteways Arcade, Lebuh Pantai; ⏰9am-5pm Mon-Fri, to 3pm Sat, to 1pm Sun) The visitor centre of the state tourism agency is the best all-round place to go for maps, brochures and local information.

HISTORY

Little is known of Penang's early history. Chinese seafarers were aware of the island, which they called Betelnut Island, as far back as the 15th century, but it appears to have been uninhabited. It wasn't until the early 1700s that colonists arrived from Sumatra and established settlements at Batu Uban and the area now covered by southern George Town. The island came under the control of the sultan of Kedah, but in 1771 the sultan signed the first agreement with the British East India Company, handing them trading rights in exchange for military assistance against Siam (present-day Thailand).

Fifteen years later Captain Francis Light, on behalf of the East India Company, took possession of Penang, which was formally signed over in 1791. Light renamed it Prince of Wales Island, as the acquisition date fell on the prince's birthday. Light permitted new arrivals to claim as much land as they could clear and this, together with a duty-free port and an atmosphere of liberal tolerance, quickly attracted settlers from all over Asia. By the turn of the 18th century, Penang was home to over 10,000 people.

In 1800, a slice of the peninsula opposite Penang Island, today known as Seberang Perai, was ceded to the British by the sultan of Kedah. It was named Province Wellesley after Richard Wellesley, then Governor of Madras and Governor General of Bengal.

Penang briefly became the capital of the Straits Settlements (which included Melaka and Singapore) in 1826, until it was superseded by Singapore. By the middle of the 19th century, Penang had become a major player in the Chinese opium trade, which provided more than half of the colony's revenue. It was a dangerous, rough-edged place, notorious for its brothels and gambling dens, all run by Chinese secret societies.

There was little action in Penang during WWI, but WWII was a different story. When it became evident that the Japanese would attack, Penang's Europeans were immediately evacuated, leaving behind a largely defenceless population. Japan took over the island on 19 December 1941, only 12 days after the attack on Pearl Harbour in the US. The following 3½ years were the darkest of Penang's history.

Things were not the same after the war. The local impression of the invincibility of the British had been irrevocably tainted and the end of British imperialism seemed imminent. The Straits Settlements were dissolved in 1946; Penang became a state of the Federation of Malaya in 1948 and one of independent Malaysia's 13 states in 1963.

Penang

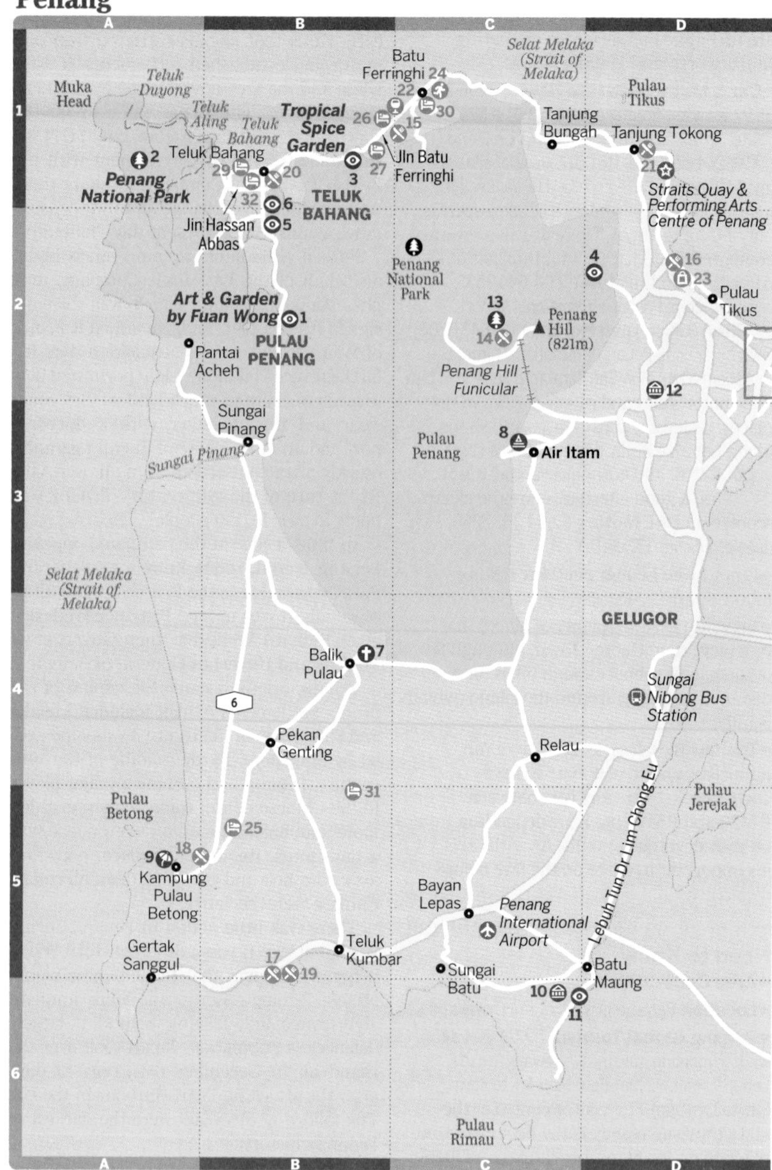

With its free-port status withdrawn in 1969, Penang went through several years of decline and high unemployment. Over the next 20 years, the island was able to build itself up as one of the largest electronics manufacturing centres of Asia and is now sometimes dubbed the 'Silicon Valley of the East'.

Today, Penang is the only state in Malaysia that has elected an ethnic Chinese chief minister since independence, something that has caused relations with the Malay-led federal government to be, at times, less than

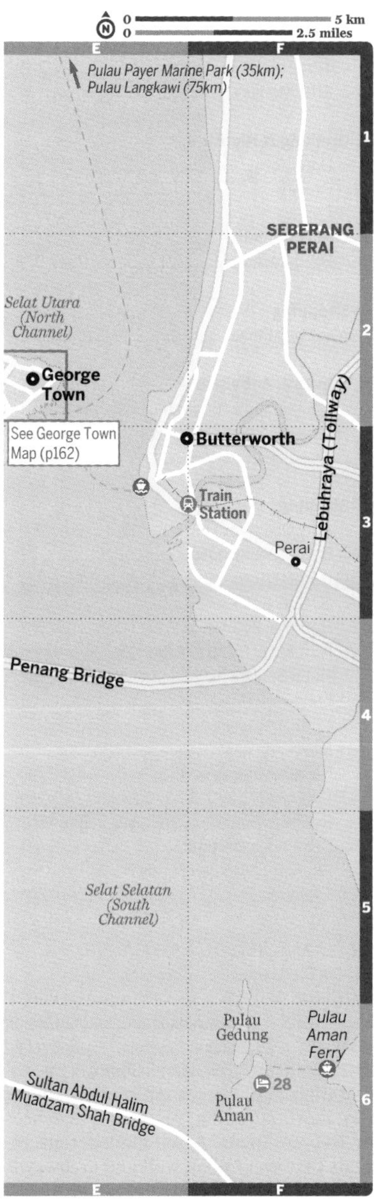

accommodating. In June 2016, Penang chief minister Lim Guan Eng was charged with two counts of corruption, a turn of events that is widely seen as politically motivated.

George Town

Explore

Combine three distinct and ancient cultures, indigenous and colonial architecture, shake for a few centuries, and garnish with some of the best food in Southeast Asia, and you've got the irresistible urban cocktail that is George Town.

Alongside the time-worn shophouses of the Unesco World Heritage Zone, you'll find Chinese temples in Little India and mosques in Chinatown, and Western-style skyscrapers and shopping complexes gleaming high above British Raj–era architecture.

The eclectic jumble makes this a city that rewards explorers. Get lost in the maze of chaotic streets and narrow lanes, past shrines decorated with strings of paper lanterns and fragrant shops selling Indian spices; or enjoy George Town's burgeoning street-art scene, its modern cafes and fun bars.

The Best...

➡ **Sight** Blue Mansion (p159)

➡ **Place to Eat** Lg Baru (New Lane) Hawker Stalls (p171)

➡ **Place to Drink** Kopi C (p170)

Top Tip

There are no specific LGBT bars or clubs in George Town, although **Seventy7** (Map p162; www.facebook.com/Seventy7cafe; 34 Jln Nagore; ⌚7.30pm-1.30am) is certainly gay-friendly. All the GHT properties (www.georgetownheritage.com) are LGBT-friendly too.

SIGHTS

Inside the Unesco Protected Zone

★**BLUE MANSION** HISTORIC BUILDING

Map p162 (Cheong Fatt Tze Mansion; www.thebluemansion.com.my; 14 Lebuh Leith; adult/child RM16/8; ⌚tours 11am, 2pm & 3.30pm) Now one of Penang's most authentic heritage hotels, the magnificent 38-room, 220-window 'Blue Mansion' was built in the 1880s and rescued from ruin in the 1990s. It blends Eastern and Western designs with louvred

Penang

Top Sights

1 Art & Garden by Fuan Wong B2
2 Penang National Park A1
3 Tropical Spice Garden B1

Sights

Ban Po Thar .... (see 8)
4 Botanical Gardens D2
5 Entopia by Penang Butterfly Farm B2
6 Escape B1
7 Holy Name of Jesus Catholic Church B4
8 Kek Lok Si Temple C3
9 Pantai Pasir Panjang A5
10 Penang War Museum C6
11 Sam Poh Footprint Temple C6
12 Suffolk House D2
13 The Habitat C2

Eating

Bungalow .... (see 30)
Cafe Ko Cha Bi Balik Pulau .... (see 7)
14 David Brown's C2
15 Ferringhi Garden C1
16 Gurney Drive Hawker Stalls D2
17 Hai Boey Seafood B5
18 Jia Siang Cafe A5
Kek Lok Si Temple Restaurant .... (see 8)
19 Khunthai B5
20 Restoran K-Haleel B1
21 Sea Pearl Lagoon Cafe D1
Suffolk House .... (see 12)
Tarbush .... (see 15)
Terapung Pulau Aman .... (see 28)
Tree Monkey .... (see 3)

Drinking & Nightlife

22 Bora Bora C1
Gravity .... (see 23)

Entertainment

Hard Rock Cafe .... (see 27)

Shopping

23 Gurney Plaza D2

Sports & Activities

24 Chi the Spa at Shangri-la C1
Tropical Spice Garden Cooking Courses .... (see 3)

Sleeping

25 Audi Guesthouse B5
26 Baba Guest House B1
G Hotel Gurney .... (see 23)
G Hotel Kelawai .... (see 23)
27 Hard Rock Hotel B1
28 Homestay Pulau Aman F6
29 Hotel Sportfishing B1
30 Lone Pine Hotel C1
LZB .... (see 15)
31 Malihom B5
Rasa Sayang Resort .... (see 24)
Roomies .... (see 15)
Roomies Suites .... (see 30)
32 Sea Princess Hotel B1
Shangri-La Golden Sands Resort .... (see 30)

windows, art nouveau stained glass and beautiful floor tiles, and is a rare surviving example of the eclectic architectural style preferred by wealthy Straits Chinese.

Hour-long guided tours (included in the admission fee) provide a glimpse of the interior as well as an insight into traditional Chinese architecture.

The mansion was commissioned by Cheong Fatt Tze, a Hakka merchant-trader who left China as a penniless teenager and eventually established a vast financial empire throughout east Asia, earning himself the dual sobriquets 'Rockefeller of the East' and the 'Last Mandarin'. Its distinctive (and once-common in George Town) blue-hued exterior is the result of an indigo-based limewash.

★PINANG PERANAKAN MANSION & STRAITS CHINESE JEWELRY MUSEUM MUSEUM

Map p163 (www.pinangperanakanmansion.com.my; 29 Lebuh Gereja; adult/child RM21.20/10.60; ⏲9.30am-5.30pm) This ostentatious, mint-green structure is among the most stunning restored residences in George Town. A self-guided tour reveals that every door, wall and archway is carved and often painted in gold leaf; the grand rooms are furnished with majestic wood furniture with intricate mother-of-pearl inlay; there are displays of charming antiques; and bright-coloured paintings and fascinating black-and-white photos of the family in regal Chinese dress grace the walls.

The house belonged to Chung Keng Quee, a 19th-century merchant, clan leader and community pillar as well as being one of the wealthiest Peranakan of that era.

After visiting the main house, be sure to also check out Chung Keng Kwi Temple, the adjacent ancestral hall and the attached **Straits Chinese Jewelry Museum** with its dazzling collection of vintage bling and glittery ornamentation.

PENANG MUSEUM MUSEUM

Map p163 (☎04-263 1942; www.penangmuseum.gov.my; Lebuh Farquhar; RM1; ⊙9am-5pm Sat-Thu) Penang's state-run museum includes exhibits on the history, customs and traditions of the island's various ethnic groups, with photos, videos, documents, costumes, furniture and other well-labelled, engaging displays. Upstairs is the history gallery, with a collection of early-19th-century watercolours by Captain Robert Smith, an engineer with the East India Company, and prints showing landscapes of old Penang.

CHEW JETTY AREA

Map p163 (Pengkalan Weld) The largest and most intact of the clan jetties, Chew Jetty consists of 75 elevated houses, several Chinese temples, a community hall and lots of tourist facilities, all linked by elevated wooden walkways. It's a fun place to wander around with docked fishing boats, folk cooking in their homes and kids running around. There is also a **homestay option** (Map p162; ☎013-438 1217; www.mychewjetty.com; 59A Chew Jetty; r incl breakfast from RM148; ❄📶) here.

KUAN YIN TENG BUDDHIST TEMPLE

Map p163 (Temple of the Goddess of Mercy; Jln Masjid Kapital Keling; ⊙24hr) FREE This atmospheric and photogenic temple is dedicated to Kuan Yin – the goddess of mercy, good fortune, peace and fertility. Built in the early 19th century by the first Hokkien and Cantonese settlers in Penang, the temple is popular with the Chinese community, and seems to be forever swathed in smoke from the outside furnaces where worshippers burn paper money, and from the incense sticks waved around inside.

PROTESTANT CEMETERY CEMETERY

Map p162 (Jln Sultan Ahmad Shah; ⊙24hr) FREE Under a canopy of magnolia trees you'll find the graves of Captain Francis Light and many others, including governors, merchants, sailors and Chinese Christians who fled the Boxer Rebellion in China (a movement opposing Western imperialism and evangelism), only to die of fever in Penang. Also here is the tomb of Thomas Leonowens, the young officer who married Anna – the schoolmistress to the King of Siam, made famous by *The King and I*.

SRI MARIAMMAN TEMPLE HINDU TEMPLE

Map p163 (Lebuh Queen; ⊙6am-noon, 4.30-9pm) FREE Sri Mariamman was built in 1883 and is George Town's oldest Hindu house of worship. For local south Indians, the temple fulfils the purpose of a Chinese clanhouse; it's a reminder of the motherland and the community bonds forged within the diaspora. It is a typically south Indian temple, dominated by the *gopuram* (entrance tower).

GEORGE TOWN STREET NAMES

Finding your way around George Town can be slightly complicated since many roads have both a Malay and an English name; while many street signs list both, it can still be confusing. To make matters worse, Jln Penang may also be referred to as Jln Pinang or Penang Rd – but there's also a Penang St, which may also be called Lebuh Pinang! Similarly, Chulia St is Lebuh Chulia but there's also a Lorong Chulia, and this confuses even taxi drivers.

We use primarily the Malay name. Below are the two names of some of the main roads:

MALAY	ENGLISH
Lebuh Gereja	Church St
Jln Masjid Kapitan Keling	Pitt St
Jln Tun Syed Sheh Barakbah	The Esplanade
Lebuh Pantai	Beach St
Lebuh Pasar	Market St

George Town

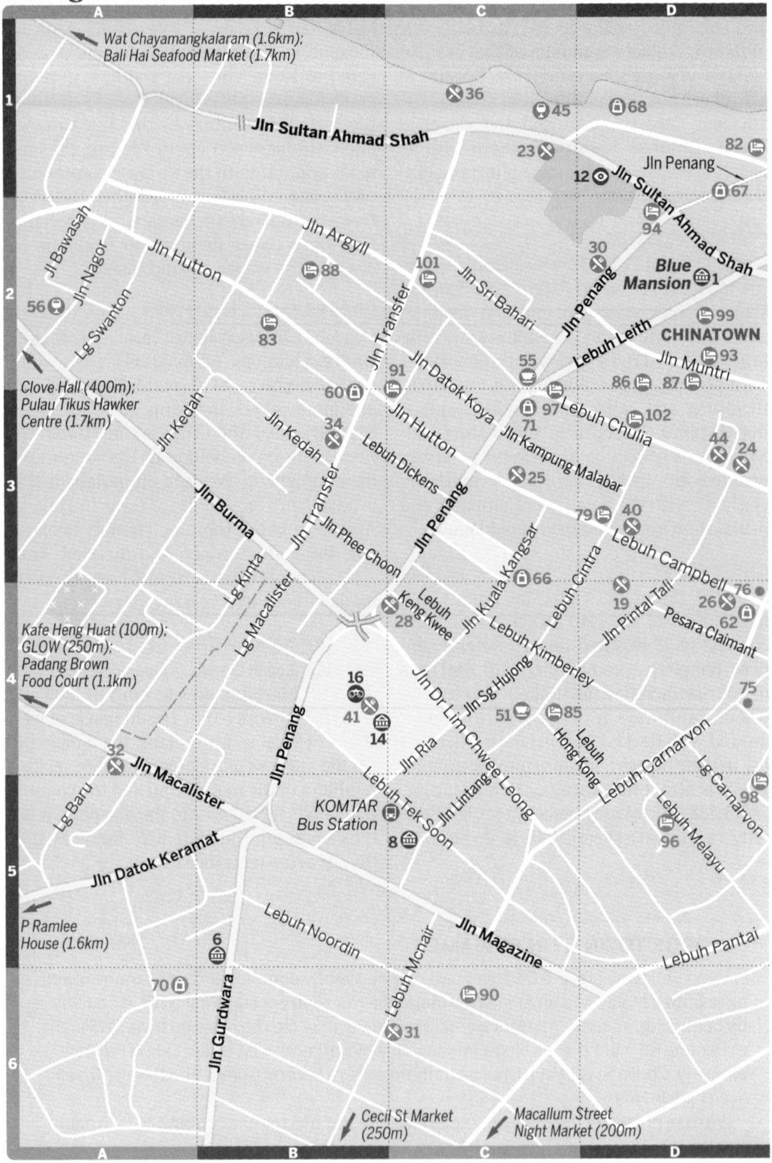

Outside the Unesco Protected Zone

HIN BUS DEPOT ART CENTRE GALLERY

Map p162 (http://hinbusdepot.com/index.html; 31A Jln Gurdwara; noon-7pm) FREE The elegant remains of this former bus station have become a vibrant hub for George Town's burgeoning contemporary art scene, hosting exhibitions, events, a regular arts and crafts market every Sunday, and art-house movies and documentaries on Tuesdays. The open-air areas are bedecked with street art.

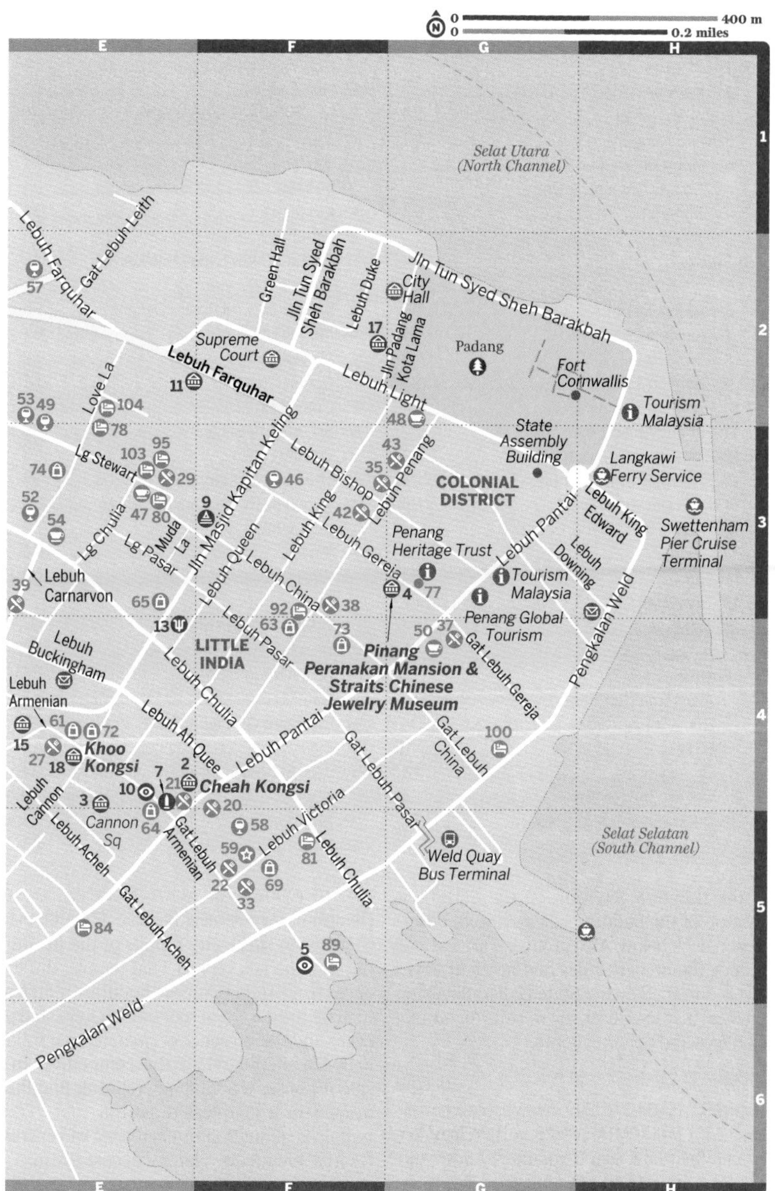

Within the grounds there are also a couple of cafes, workshops and the **Run Amok** (Map p162; http://runamok.my/wordpress; 59A Jln Timah; ⌚noon-7pm Tue-Sun) gallery.

THE TOP AT KOMTAR VIEWPOINT

Map p162 (☎04-262 3800; http://thetop.com.my; Jln Penang) There are all kinds of attractions promised in this major revamp of part of George Town's iconic KOMTAR tower, which was well under way during our latest research visit. Likely to have the widest appeal

George Town

Top Sights

1 Blue Mansion ... D2
2 Cheah Kongsi ... E4
3 Khoo Kongsi ... E4
4 Pinang Peranakan Mansion & Straits Chinese Jewelry Museum ... G3

Sights

5 Chew Jetty ... F5
6 Hin Bus Depot Art Centre ... B5
7 Kids on a Bicycle ... E4
8 Komik Asia ... C5
9 Kuan Yin Teng ... F3
10 Lebuh Armenian ... E4
11 Penang Museum ... E2
12 Protestant Cemetery ... D1
13 Sri Mariamman Temple ... E4
14 Tech Dome Penang ... B4
15 Teochew Puppet & Opera House ... E4
16 The Top at KOMTAR ... B4
17 Town Hall ... F2
18 Yap Kongsi ... E4

Eating

Awesome Canteen ... (see 69)
19 Boey Chong Kee ... D4
BTB ... (see 20)
20 China House ... F4
21 Cozy in the Rocket ... E4
22 Da Shu Xia Seafood House ... F5
23 Fu Er Dai ... C1
24 Goh Thew Chik ... D3
25 Hameediyah ... C3
26 Hong Kee Bamboo Noodle ... D4
27 Jawi House ... E4
28 Joo Hooi Cafe ... C4
29 Kebaya ... E3
30 Kirishima ... D2
31 Lebuh Presgrave Hawker Stalls ... C6
32 Lg Baru (New Lane) Hawker Stalls ... A4
33 Ming Xiang Tai Pastry Delights ... F5
34 Moody Cow ... B3
35 My Nonya Favourites ... F3
36 Ocean Green ... C1
37 Quay Café ... G4
38 Sri Ananda Bahwan ... F3
39 Teksen ... E3
40 Tho Yuen Restaurant ... D3
41 Top View Restaurant & Lounge ... B4
42 Veloo Villas ... F3
43 Via Pre ... G3
44 Wai Kei ... D3

Drinking & Nightlife

45 Beach Blanket Babylon ... C1
46 C&J Alabama Shake ... F3
47 Café 55 ... E3
48 Constant Gardener ... G2
49 Inch ... E2
50 Jing-Si Books & Cafe ... G4
Kopi C ... (see 20)
51 Métisser ... C4
52 Micke's Place ... E3

is the Rainbow Skywalk on the 68th-floor rooftop of the building along with an observation deck below. Also promised are various indoor theme-park rides and areas at lower levels and the Penang State Gallery focusing on local history. Check the website for admission fees and opening hours.

KOMIK ASIA MUSEUM

Map p162 (04-371 5512; www.paccm.com.my; Level 2, ICT Mall KOMTAR; RM20; 11am-7pm Mon-Fri, until 9pm Sat & Sun) If you don't know your Lat from your Tezuka Osamu, then this is the place to discover the dynamic art of comic-book artists from across the region. Kids and not a few adults will love this remarkable collection from nine Asian countries, including Malaysia, China, Japan and Korea. There's a good gift shop, too. To find the museum, enter the mall from Lebuh Lintang and take the lift to the 2nd floor.

WAT CHAYAMANGKALARAM BUDDHIST TEMPLE

(Temple of the Reclining Buddha; 17 Lg Burma; 7am-6pm) FREE The Temple of the Reclining Buddha is a typical Thai temple; differences from Malay Chinese Buddhist temples include the design of roofs which have sharp eaves and the presence of *chedi* (stupa; solid bell-shaped pillars) in the compound. Inside it houses a 33m-long reclining Buddha draped in a gold-leafed saffron robe. The temple is about 2.5km northwest of central George Town; a taxi here will cost RM15.

EATING

You'll soon realise why locals are so passionate about the food here. The diversity of George Town's food scene is breathtaking. Whether you choose to dine at hawker

53 Mish Mash E2
54 Mugshot Cafe E3
55 Odeon Trick Art Cafe & Restaurant C2
56 Seventy7 .... A2
57 Three Sixty Revolving Restaurant & Sky Bar E2
58 Vine & Single F5

Entertainment
59 Canteen F5

Shopping
60 Batek-Lah B3
61 Bon Ton E4
62 Campbell St Market D4
63 Chop Kongsi F4
64 Fuan Wong E5
65 Gerak Budaya E3
66 Kuala Kangsar Market C3
67 Little Penang Street Market D1
68 Moon Shop D1
69 ottokedai F5
70 Run Amok A6
71 Sam's Batik House C3
72 Shop Howard E4
Sunday Pop-Up Market .... (see 6)
73 Tropical Spice Garden In Town F4
74 Unique Penang E3

Sports & Activities
75 George Town World Heritage Incorporated D4
76 Nazlina Spice Station D4
77 Penang Heritage Trust G3

Sleeping
78 23 Love Lane E3
Blue Mansion .... (see 1)
79 Campbell House D3
80 Coffee Atelier E3
81 Container Hotel F5
82 Eastern & Oriental Hotel D1
83 Jawi Peranakan Mansion B2
84 Lang Hoose E5
85 Le Dream C4
86 Muntri Grove D2
87 Muntri Mews D2
88 Museum Hotel B2
89 My Chew Jetty F5
90 Noordin Mews C6
91 Penaga Hotel C2
92 Ren i Tang F3
93 Ryokan Muntri D2
94 Segara Ninda D2
95 Seven Terraces E3
96 Sinkeh D5
97 Siok Hostel C3
98 Spices Hotel D5
99 The Edison D2
100 The Rice Miller Hotel G4
101 Tido Penang Hostel C2
102 Time Capsule Hotel D3
103 Tipsy Tiger Party Hostel E3
104 You Le Yuen E2

stalls or the finest white-tablecloth restaurants, you're sure to find quality food.

Inside the Heritage Zone

★THO YUEN RESTAURANT CHINESE $

Map p162 (92 Lebuh Campbell; dim sum RM1.60-8; ⏲6am-3pm Wed-Mon) Our favourite place for dim sum. It's packed with newspaper-reading loners and chattering groups of locals all morning long, but you can usually squeeze in somewhere. Servers speak minimal English but do their best to explain the contents of their carts.

SRI ANANDA BAHWAN INDIAN $

Map p163 (☎04-264 4204; http://sriananda-bahwan.com.my/53.html; 53-55 Lebuh Penang; mains from RM3; ⏲7am-11.30pm; 🅥) The local version of fast food – but so much better. This place is busy and buzzy, and whips up everything from tandoori chicken to vegetarian Indian dishes. Its vegetarian-only outlet is a few doors along the street at No 25.

WAI KEI CHINESE $

Map p162 (Lebuh Chulia; mains RM7; ⏲11am-2pm) This gem sits in the middle of the greatest concentration of travellers in George Town, yet is somehow almost exclusively patronised (in enthusiastic numbers) by locals. Come on the early side of the three-hour open window for *char siew* (barbequed pork) and *siew yoke* (pork belly) that are considered among the best in town.

HAMEEDIYAH MALAYSIAN $

Map p162 (☎04-261 1095; 164 Lebuh Campbell; mains RM5.50-25; ⏲10am-10pm) Dating back to 1907 and allegedly the oldest *nasi*

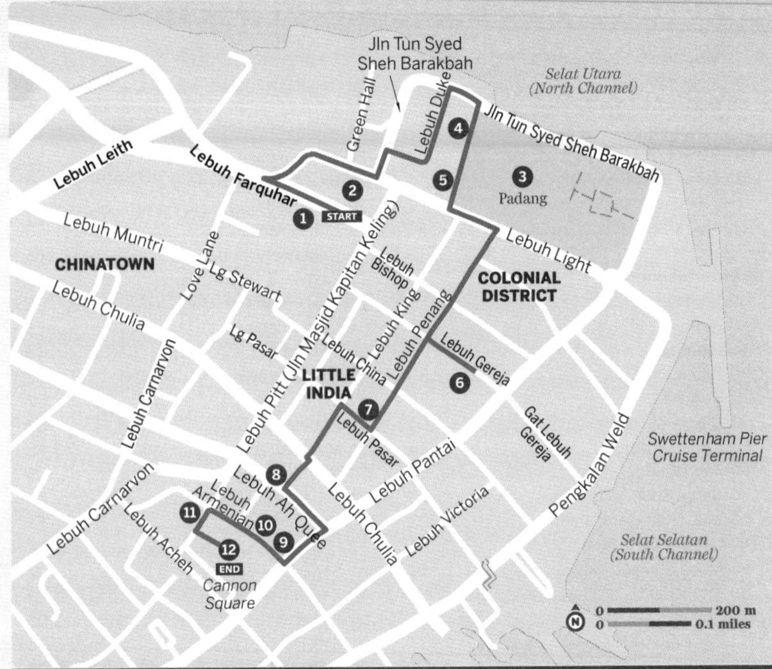

Neighbourhood Walk
Five Cultures on Two Feet

START PENANG MUSEUM
END KHOO KONGSI
LENGTH 2.25KM; THREE TO FOUR HOURS

This walk will give you a glimpse of George Town's cultural mix: English, Indian, Malay, Peranakan and Chinese.

Starting at 1 **Penang Museum** (p161), head west and then north towards the waterfront, passing the 2 **Supreme Court**. Note the statue of James Richardson Logan, advocate for non-whites during the colonial era. Walk north along Lebuh Duke to the waterfront, then south along Jln Padang Kota Lama past the vast 3 **Padang** (field) and grandiose architecture of 4 **City Hall** and 5 **Town Hall**. Proceed east along Lebuh Light, then south on Lebuh Penang. A detour east along Lebuh Gereja finds the impressive 6 **Pinang Peranakan Mansion** (p160), the old digs of one of George Town's great Peranakan merchant barons.

Returning to Lebuh Penang, head south into 7 **Little India** and take a deep breath of all that spice. At Lebuh Pasar, head west past shops selling milky South Asian sweets, then south at Lebuh King to the intersection of 8 **Lebuh King and Lebuh Ah Quee**, a literal example of Penang's cultural crossroads.

Head east along Lebuh Ah Quee, then south along Jln Pantai; you're now at 9 **Lebuh Armenian**. Among George Town's most gentrified streets today, it was formerly a centre for Chinese secret societies and was one of the main fighting stages of the 1867 riots. Stroll east along restored shophouses until you reach 10 **Cheah Kongsi** (p168), home to the oldest Straits Chinese clan association in Penang.

Cross the street to the corner of Jln Masjid Kapitan Keling and the bright green 1924 Hokkien clanhouse 11 **Yap Kongsi**. Head south on Lebuh Cannon and duck into the magnificently ornate 12 **Khoo Kongsi** (p168), the most impressive *kongsi* (clan meeting house) in the city.

kandar (rice with curries and veggies) place in Malaysia, Hameediyah looked it until its recent facelift. In addition to rich curries served over rice, try the *murtabak*, a *roti prata* (flaky, flat bread) stuffed with minced mutton, chicken or vegetables, egg and spices.

HONG KEE BAMBOO NOODLE NOODLES $

Map p162 (☎04-261 9875; 37 Lebuh Campbell; noodles from RM6; ⏰6.30am-10pm) Known for its high-quality *wan thun mee* (noodle soup with dumplings), and at this shop you can see the noodles being handmade and prepared while you slurp. Good side dishes, too.

GOH THEW CHIK CHINESE $

Map p162 (338A Lebuh Chulia; mains RM4.50-6; ⏰11am-5pm Wed-Mon) This simple cafe draws in the crowds for its lunchtime servings of Hainanese chicken rice, so you may have to wait for a table. The meat is well cooked and juicy and comes with the traditional bowl of stock as well as a mound of rice.

FU ER DAI DIM SUM $

Map p162 (☎04-251 9289; 7 Jln Sultan Ahmad Shah; dim sum RM1.70-6; ⏰6.30am-2pm) There's a wide range of tasty steamed and fried small Chinese dishes served under this black-painted open shed with sea views across the busy road.

MING XIANG TAI PASTRY DELIGHTS CHINESE $

Map p163 (www.facebook.com/MingXiangTai1979; 166 Lebuh Victoria; pastries from RM2; ⏰9am-9pm) What started as a Chinese egg tart business run from a trishaw in the 1970s has blossomed into a mini-empire of pastry shops around George Town. You can watch the sweet and savoury tarts and buns being made on one side of the shop, and take your pick of the produce along with refreshing herbal tea drinks from the other. Other branches of Ming Xiang Tai can be found at 475A Jln Penang and 133 Jln Burma.

QUAY CAFÉ VEGETARIAN $

Map p163 (2 Gat Lebuh Gereja; mains RM5-15; ⏰11am-2pm Mon-Sat; ❄✍) A modern-feeling cafeteria serving Asian-style meat-free dishes. Expect set meals, an emphasis on noodle dishes, fresh juices and herbal teas.

VELOO VILLAS INDIAN $

Map p163 (☎04-262 4369; 22 Lebuh Penang; set meals RM5-9.50; ⏰7am-10pm; ✍) For one meal, set aside notions of service – and ambience – and instead focus on the vibrant, fun southern Indian cuisine. Come from approximately 11am to 4pm for hearty and

UNESCO & GEORGE TOWN

In 2008, the historic centre of George Town was designated a Unesco World Heritage site for having 'a unique architectural and cultural townscape without parallel anywhere in East and Southeast Asia'. A 'core' area comprising 1700 buildings and a 'buffer', which together span east from the waterfront as far west as Jln Transfer and Jln Dr Lim Chwee Leong, were drawn up, and the structures within these areas have been thoroughly catalogued and are protected by strict zoning laws. Details about the Unesco designation can be seen at **George Town World Heritage Incorporated** (p174) where you can also pick up informative free guides about George Town's architecture.

The general consensus is that the Unesco listing has been a good thing for George Town, having helped the city safeguard its age-old feel while also reaping the benefits of a facelift. The designation seems to have sparked an interest in local culture among residents, and some claim that it has also had the effect of drawing younger locals back to the city, which suffered from a debilitating 'brain drain' during the 1980s and 1990s.

However, there's no arguing that the listing has also been a double-edged sword. Many once-abandoned buildings have been snatched up by developers hoping to cash in, and property values have skyrocketed. Today, some shophouses can easily sell for more than US$1 million, and 'heritage' hotels and cutesy cafes can be found on just about every street in George Town. Not all of them have been renovated according to strict heritage rules. Uncontrolled rents haven't helped either, with some landlords hiking rates to over RM10,000 a month. The consequence is that the traditional shops and trades that gave the area much of its unique flavour are being forced to close down or move out to less pricey areas of the city.

LOCAL KNOWLEDGE

CLANHOUSES

Between the mid-1800s and the mid-1900s Penang welcomed a huge influx of Chinese immigrants, primarily from China's Fujian province. To help introduce uncles, aunties, cousins, old neighbourhood buddies and so on to their new home, the Chinese formed clan associations and built clanhouses, known locally as *kongsi*, to create a sense of community, provide lodging and help find employment for newcomers. In addition to functioning as 'embassies' of sorts, clanhouses also served as a deeper social link between an extended clan, its ancestors and its social obligations. As time went on, many clan associations became extremely prosperous and their buildings became more ornate. Clans – called 'secret societies' by the British – began to compete with each other over the decadence and number of their temples. Due to this rivalry, today Penang has one of the densest concentrations of clan architecture found outside China.

Khoo Kongsi (Map p163; www.khookongsi.com.my; 18 Cannon Sq; adult/child RM10/1; 9am-5pm) This spectacular clanhouse is one of the most impressive in George Town. Guided tours begin at the stone carvings that dance across the entrance hall and pavilions, many of which symbolise or are meant to attract good luck and wealth. The interior is dominated by incredible murals depicting birthdays, weddings and, most impressively, the 36 celestial guardians. Gorgeous ceramic sculptures of immortals, carp, dragons, and carp becoming dragons dance across the roof ridges.

Cheah Kongsi (Map p163; 04-261 3837; www.cheahkongsi.com.my; 8 Lebuh Armenian; adult/child RM10/5; 9am-5pm) Looking splendid after a recent major restoration, Cheah Kongsi is home to the oldest Straits Chinese clan association in Penang. The ornate front of the clanhouse can be seen clearly across a grassy lawn from Lebuh Pantai, but the official entrance where you need to buy a ticket is on Lebuh Armenian. Besides serving as a temple and assembly hall, this building has also been the registered headquarters of several clans.

diverse rice-based set meals, or outside of these hours for *dosa* (paper-thin rice-and-lentil crepes) and other snacks.

★TEKSEN — CHINESE $$

Map p163 (012-981 5117; 18 Lebuh Carnarvon; mains RM10-30; noon-3pm & 6-9pm Wed-Mon) There's a reason this place is always packed: it's one of the tastiest, most consistent restaurants in town (and in a place like George Town that's saying a lot). You almost can't go wrong here, but don't miss the favourites – the 'double roasted pork with chilli padi' is obligatory and delicious – and be sure to ask about the daily specials.

★MY NONYA FAVOURITES — MALAYSIAN $$

Map p163 (04-262 6696; 20F Lebuh Penang; mains RM15-30; 11.30am-2.30pm & 6-9pm Fri-Wed) Nothing to look at, this humble restaurant rightly gets the thumbs up from in-the-know locals for its tasty, authentic Peranakan (Nonya) dishes such as *cincalok cher bak* (stir-fried belly pork) and eggs *belanda* (eggs in tamarind gravy). The set lunch (RM6.90 to RM11.90) is a steal.

JAWI HOUSE — MALAYSIAN $$

Map p163 (www.jawihouse.com; 85 Lebuh Armenian; mains RM18-32; 11am-10pm Wed-Mon;) This cosy, shophouse restaurant specialises in the type of unique Muslim dishes you'd be hard-pressed to find outside of a local home or celebration. The fragrant biryani comes with prawns, chicken, lamb or beef and there are four different types of rice to choose from including 'lemuni rice', which is seasoned with flower petals.

BOEY CHONG KEE — CHINESE $$

Map p162 (04-261 7672; People's Court, off Lebuh Campbell; mains RM5-15; 6.30-10pm) Crowd-pleasing dishes such as stir-fried noodles, ginger stewed duck and sweet-and-sour pork are very competently done here, but it's primarily the courtyard setting – outdoor tables surrounded by the comings and goings from the surrounding low-rise public housing block – that is the clincher. It feels like dining in the Penang version of *Rear Window*.

DA SHU XIA SEAFOOD HOUSE — CHINESE $$

Map p163 (Tree Shade Seafood Restaurant; 012-474 5566; 177C Lebuh Victoria; mains RM10-50;

⌚11am-3.30pm & 5-10pm Thu-Tue) This open-air shack has lost the shade of the tree it was originally named after, but it remains a place where locals go for cheap and tasty seafood. Pick your aquatic protein from the trays out front, and the staff will fry, steam, soup or grill it up for you.

VIA PRE ITALIAN **$$**

Map p163 (☎04-262 0560; www.facebook.com/viapre; 20 Lebuh Penang; mains RM19-36; ⌚11am-11pm Mon-Thu, noon-1am Fri & Sat, noon-10pm Sun) Expect traditional Italian dishes, tasty pizzas and superb desserts at this well-respected restaurant that has a new, intimate home on the edge of Little India.

AWESOME CANTEEN INTERNATIONAL **$$**

Map p163 (☎04-261 3707; www.facebook.com/awesomecanteenpg; 164 Lebuh Victoria; mains RM20-25; ⌚11am-11pm Mon & Wed-Fri, 10am-11pm Sat & Sun) Although this relaxed bistro and cafe offers a paleo menu (no processed food and grains), it's the other options – such as Japanese rice bowls topped with grilled chicken, and peanut-butter-filled beef burgers – that catch the eye and nicely fill the stomach. If you like the look of the place, with its airy courtyard of skinny trees and industrial-chic furnishings, consider booking a stay in the suites via www.sekeping.com.

KIRISHIMA JAPANESE **$$**

Map p162 (☎04-370 0108; Cititel, 66 Jln Penang; set meals from RM35; ⌚noon-2pm & 6-10pm; ❄📶) Japanese living in or visiting Penang head straight here for the well-prepared sushi and other authentic dishes. Sake bottles line the walls, and there's a counter by the kitchen that's great for single diners. Set menus offer the best deal.

COZY IN THE ROCKET ITALIAN **$$**

Map p163 (262-264 Lebuh Pantai; mains RM25-40; ⌚9.30am-3pm Tue-Sun; 📶) Named after the favourite song of owners Hong and Yen, this arty, airy place offers a winning combo of a courtyard garden, good coffee, refreshing drinks and some of the best artisan pasta dishes Penang has to offer. However, it can get very busy at lunch, when orders can take up to an hour to arrive on your table.

MOODY COW DESSERTS **$$**

Map p162 (☎04-226 2646; www.facebook.com/moodycowpenang; 170 Jln Transfer; cheesecakes RM20-26; ⌚11am-midnight; 📶) Lovers of cheesecake and other sweet treats rejoice. There are scores of flavours of the dessert available, including locally inspired ones such as salted egg, durian and jackfruit (chempadak) at this super kitschy cafe in a black-and-yellow-painted building.

GEORGE TOWN'S STREET ART

The current craze for street art in George Town shows no sign of abating. It's a trend that goes back to 2010, when Penang's state government commissioned the studio **Sculpture At Work** (http://sculptureatwork.com) to do a series of cartoon steel art pieces across town. Affixed to George Town street walls, these 3D artworks detail local customs and heritage with humour, while also providing a quirky counterpoint to the natural urban beauty of the historic core.

It was in 2012, however, when George Town's street-art scene really took off. For that year's George Town Festival, Lithuanian artist **Ernest Zacharevic** (www.ernestzacharevic.com) was commissioned to do a series of public paintings in the city centre, some of which he chose to combine with objects such as bicycles, motorcycles and architectural features. The art has been a smash hit, with his **Kids on a Bicycle** (Map p163; Lebuh Armenian) piece on Lebuh Armenian having become a major tourist attraction, complete with long lines and souvenir stalls.

Zacharevic's success led to the '101 Lost Kittens' series of murals commissioned for the 2013 George Town Festival, with the intent of bringing attention to the issue of stray animals, as well as many examples of privately funded public art. Other major street artists' works to look out for include Russian arist Julia Volchkova's striking pieces (you'll see one off an alley on Lg Stewart) and UK artist Thomas Powell (www.thomaspowell-artist.com), whose works are at the **Hin Bus Depot Art Centre** (p162).

'Marking George Town', a free map showing the location of pieces by Ernest Zacharevic and some of the other artists mentioned above, is available at **Penang Global Tourism** (p157).

★KEBAYA PERANAKAN $$$

Map p163 (☎04-264 2333; http://kebaya.com.my; Seven Terraces, 8 Lg Stewart; set dinner RM120; ⏱6-10pm Tue-Sun; ❄) This is your chance to sample superb, subtly flavoured Peranakan-influenced cuisine. The stately dining room, part of the Seven Terraces hotel (p177), is decorated with a gorgeous collection of antiques, set to a soundtrack of live piano. Set four-course dinners are served at two sittings (either starting at 6pm or 8pm).

Outside the Heritage Zone

OCEAN GREEN SEAFOOD $$

Map p162 (☎04-227 4530; www.paramounthotel.com.my/restaurant.html; 48F Jln Sultan Ahmad Shah; dishes from RM10; ⏱noon-11pm) There's a menu at this waterfront seafood smorgasbord, but talk to your server about what's fresh. The dining hall is invariably packed – if it's too busy or hot, ask about the air-con rooms in the adjacent Paramount Hotel. It's a good idea to reserve. We loved the crab *bee hoon* (glass noodles) and prawns with chilli dipping sauce.

BALI HAI SEAFOOD MARKET SEAFOOD $$

(☎04-228 8272; www.balihaiseafood.com; 90 Persiaran Gurney; mains RM20-100; ⏱9am-10pm) A massive, always-packed seafood joint with big round tables inside and a few thatched huts outside, across from the waterfront promenade. The restaurant's motto is 'if it swims, we have it' – and they do, in a mind-boggling array of tanks where you can pick out your critters. You can also come here for dim sum in the mornings.

SUFFOLK HOUSE INTERNATIONAL $$

Map p158 (www.suffolkhouse.com.my; 250 Jln Ayer Itam; set lunch/dinner from RM40/65; ⏱noon-10.30pm) Dishes such as beef pot pie and prawn crusted sea bass are on the main menu, but the best reason for heading to this beautifully restored 200-year-old Georgian-style mansion is to indulge in its traditional afternoon tea (RM45 per person), featuring freshly baked scones, dainty cakes and neatly cut sandwiches. Entry to **Suffolk House** (adult/child RM20/free; ⏱10am-6pm) is deducted from your bill. A taxi here from central George Town will cost around RM15.

DRINKING & NIGHTLIFE

★MISH MASH COCKTAIL BAR

Map p163 (☎017-536 5128; www.mishmashpg.com; 24 Jln Muntri; ⏱2pm-midnight Tue-Sun) Mish Mash has brought some unique booze – not to mention some much-needed panache – to George Town's drinking scene. Come for the city's most well-stocked bar, clever cocktails and some great non-alcoholic drinks (try the 'traditional ginger soda'), as well as a full tobacco counter.

★CONSTANT GARDENER CAFE

Map p163 (☎04-251 9070; www.constantgardener.coffee; 9 Lebuh Light; ⏱9am-midnight Tue-Sun) A serious venue for serious coffee drinkers, this attractive place brews its lattes with coveted beans from Malaysia and beyond, and serves some pristine-looking pastries and cakes.

LOCAL KNOWLEDGE

CHINA HOUSE

You can't really say you've been to George Town unless you've stepped inside **China House** (Map p163; ☎04-263 7299; www.chinahouse.com.my; 153 & 155 Lebuh Pantai; ⏱9am-midnight). This block-wide amalgamation of shophouses is home to a variety of dining, drinking and shopping options. It all starts splendidly with the buzzy cafe-bakery, **Kopi C** (Map p162; www.chinahouse.com.my; China House, 153 & 155 Lebuh Pantai; mains from RM10; ⏱9am-midnight; 📶) serving scrumptious bakes, serious coffee and great light meals, and just gets better from there.

Return in the evening to experience the elegant yet relaxed restaurant **BTB** (Map p162; ☎04-262 7299; www.chinahouse.com.my/index-new.html; 155 Lebuh Pantai; mains RM44.52-76.32; ⏱6.30-10.30pm; ❄🍸), the cocktail and wine bar **Vine & Single** (Map p163; ☎04-263 7299; www.chinahouse.com.my; 153 & 155 Lebuh Pantai; ⏱5pm-midnight), the live-music venue **Canteen** (Map p163; www.chinahouse.com.my; 183B Lebuh Victoria; ⏱9am-11pm). And don't forget about the boutique shop and art gallery upstairs!

LOCAL KNOWLEDGE

HAWKER-STALL HEAVEN

Not eating at a hawker stall in George Town is like skipping the Louvre in Paris – unthinkable! There are tonnes of hawker centres and stalls in and around town, from shophouse-bound *kopitiam* (cafes) to open-air markets made up of mobile stalls.

Lg Baru (New Lane) Hawker Stalls (Map p162; cnr Jln Macalister & Lg Baru; mains from RM3; ⏲6-10.30pm Thu-Tue) Ask locals where their favourite hawker stalls are, and they'll generally mention this night-time street extravaganza. Just about everything's available here, but we like the stall serving *char koay kak* (a wok-fried dish of rice cakes, egg, crunchy pickled vegetables and bean sprouts); it also does great *otak otak* (a steamed fish curry). Lg Baru intersects with Jln Macalister about 250m northwest of the intersection with Jln Penang.

Pulau Tikus Hawker Centre (cnr Solok Moulmein & Jln Burma; ⏲6am-2pm) Before yet another bland guesthouse breakfast gets you down, consider a visit to this busy morning market area. A cluster of cafes sell Hokkien mee (yellow noodles fried with sliced meat, boiled squid, prawns and strips of fried egg), *mee goreng* (spicy fried noodles) and other dishes that have earned die-hard fans. The market is about 2.5km north of Jln Penang; a taxi here will set you back about RM20.

Lebuh Presgrave Hawker Stalls (Map p162; cnr Lebuh Presgrave & Lebuh Mcnair; ⏲5pm-midnight Fri-Wed) A famous Hokkien mee vendor draws most folks to this open-air hawker convocation, but there's lots to keep you around for a second course, from *lor bak* (deep-fried meats dipped in sauce) to a stall selling hard-to-find Peranakan dishes.

Sea Pearl Lagoon Cafe (Map p158; 338 Jln Tokong Thai Pak Koong, Tanjong Tokong; mains from RM8; ⏲5-10pm Thu-Tue) The unique location of this basic hawker centre – seemingly hidden in a Chinese temple complex looking out over the North Channel – and its excellent food make the Sea Pearl one of our favourite places to eat outside the city centre. Sea Pearl Lagoon is 7km northwest of George Town. A taxi here will set you back RM25.

Joo Hooi Cafe (Map p162; 475 Jln Penang; mains from RM3-5.50; ⏲11am-5pm) The hawker centre equivalent of one-stop shopping, this place has all of Penang's best dishes: laksa, *rojak* (a 'salad' of crispy fruits and vegetables in a thick, slightly sweet dressing), *char kway teow* (broad noodles, clams and eggs fried in chilli and black bean sauce) and *cendol* (a sweet snack of squiggly noodles in shaved ice with palm sugar and coconut milk).

Kafe Heng Huat (cnr Jl Macalister & Lg Selamat; mains RM10; ⏲10.30am-6.30pm Wed-Mon) Outside Kafe Heng Huat you'll find Soon Chuan Choo who, in her trademark red chefs hat, has been knocking up some of Penang's best *char kway teow* for more than 47 years. Adjacent stalls sell *won ton mee* (wheat-and-egg-noodle soup) and other Chinese Penang staples. Lg Selamat intersects with Jln Macalister about 500m northwest of the intersection with Jln Penang.

Gurney Drive Hawker Stalls (Map p158; Persiaran Gurney; mains from RM4; ⏲5pm-midnight) One of Penang's most famous hawker complexes sits amid modern high-rise buildings bordered by the sea. It's particularly known for its laksa stalls (try stall 11) and the delicious *rojak* at Ah Chye. Gurney Drive is about 3km west of George Town. A taxi here will set you back RM20.

★BEACH BLANKET BABYLON BAR

Map p162 (http://32mansion.com.my/beach-bar-penang; 32 Jln Sultan Ahmad Shah; ⏲noon-midnight) The open-air setting and relaxed vibe contrast with the rather grand building this bar is linked to. Pair your drink and al fresco views over the North Channel with tasty local dishes.

C&J ALABAMA SHAKE BAR

Map p163 (www.facebook.com/cjalabamashake; 92 Lebuh Gereja; ⏲2pm-late) Just your average American boozer – if your average American bar was located in Malaysia and was run by a gregarious Serbian and a local. Come to think of it, there's little that's ordinary about this bar, previously known as B@92, but it gets it right – from tasty

LOCAL KNOWLEDGE

DINING & DRINKING WITH A VIEW

If you thought George Town looked pretty good at ground level, just give yourself some elevation to get the bird's-eye view on how attractive the city really is. As well as the following favourites, the bar on the roof of **Le Dream** (p176) hotel is also worth a visit.

Three Sixty Revolving Restaurant & Sky Bar (Map p163; ☎04-261 3540; http://360rooftop.com.my; Bayview Hotel George Town, 25A Lebuh Farquhar; ⏰6.30-10.30pm; 📶) Although, as the name indicates, there's a revolving restaurant (buffet RM88), we prefer the adjacent open-air Sky Bar. For cocktails at sunset in central George Town it simply can't be beaten.

Gravity (Map p158; www.ghotelkelawai.com.my/dining-gravity.html; G Hotel Kelawei, 2 Persiaran Maktab; ⏰5pm-1am) Yes, it's a hotel pool bar. But the breezy rooftop location and spectacular views make Gravity one of the island's top sundowner destinations. Plus for RM55 you can enjoy free-flow house wines all night.

Top View Restaurant & Lounge (Map p162; ☎04-262 5960; http://thetop.com.my; Level 59 & 60 KOMTAR, Jln Penang; set lunch Mon-Sat RM48, Sun brunch adult/child RM78/48, dinner from RM88; ⏰10am-10pm Mon-Fri, 8am-10pm Sat & Sun; 📶) The impressive buffet spreads at the top of KOMTAR complement the panoramic city views. On weekends it also offers a sunrise breakfast (RM48) from 8am to 10am. Or you can drop by for a drink and a snack (RM28) anytime during opening hours.

American-themed cocktails to slow-cooked pulled-pork sandwiches.

MUGSHOT CAFE — CAFE

Map p163 (www.facebook.com/themugshotcafepenang; 302 Lebuh Chulia; ⏰8am-midnight; 📶) Chalk up your misdemeanour and make like one of the 'usual suspects' at this popular cafe serving a variety of bagel sandwiches and other baked goods from its neighbouring bakery. The homemade yoghurt with fruit and granola in glass jars is also luscious.

MICKE'S PLACE — BAR

Map p163 (www.facebook.com/mikesplacelovelane; 94 Love Lane; ⏰noon-3am) This eclectic bar/restaurant is both the longest-standing and most fun of the area's backpacker bars. Pull up a grafittied chair, bump to the vintage soundtrack, suck on a shisha and make a new friend.

MÉTISSER — TEAHOUSE

Map p162 (☎04-251 9739; www.facebook.com/metissermalaysia; 140-142 Jln Pintal Tali; ⏰noon-11pm Thu-Tue) Offering some 60 different types of fine and flavoured teas from around the world from RM15 a pot, this pristine new tea salon does things in a very pukka way, right down to white-gloved waiters serving your drink in china cups. There's also a very tempting range of pastries.

INCH — BAR

Map p163 (☎04-261 1693; http://inchfoodbar.com; 44 Jln Muntri; ⏰10am-midnight Wed-Mon) A heritage building has been gutted to create several different styled spaces that make up this restaurant and bar. It rarely fills up but is worth visiting as it's one of the few places in town that stocks a small range of international craft beers.

JING-SI BOOKS & CAFE — CAFE

Map p163 (31 Lebuh Pantai; ⏰10am-7pm Mon-Sat, 8am-6pm Sun) An oasis of spiritual calm, this outlet for a Taiwanese Buddhist group's teachings is a wonderful place to revive in hushed surroundings over a pot of interesting tea or coffee – all of which go for RM5.

ODEON TRICK ART CAFE & RESTAURANT — CAFE

Map p162 (☎04-251 9196; www.facebook.com/odeonpenang; 130 Jln Penang; ⏰noon-10pm) A defunct cinema in a lovely art deco building has been transformed into this new entertainment attraction. The best part is the cafe and restaurant that occupies the old auditorium, which has a spectacular central spiral ramp and stage where live-music shows can take place. Some great cartoon images by local artist Kim Jung Gi decorate the walls.

SHOPPING

★SHOP HOWARD — ARTS & CRAFTS

Map p163 (☎04-2611 917; www.studiohoward.com; 154 Jln Masjid Kapitan Keling; ⏰10am-6pm) Pick up one of Howard Tan's distinctive photographic prints at this compact gift boutique also selling unique postcards, art, handicrafts and books on local topics, all made by other local artists. There's a second branch at the rear of **Fuan Wong** (Map p162; ☎04-262 9079; www.fuanwong.com; 13 Lebuh Armenia; ⏰10am-6pm Mon-Sat).

★TROPICAL SPICE GARDEN IN TOWN — ARTS & CRAFTS

Map p163 (29 Lebuh China; ⏰9am-5pm) Linked with Batu Ferringhi's Tropical Spice Garden (p173), this fragrant shop sells soaps, essential oils, dried spice and other spice-related goods as well as artworks by owner Rebecca Duckett (http://rebeccaduckett.com).

★BON TON — ARTS & CRAFTS

Map p163 (China Joe's; 95 Lebuh Armenian; ⏰10am-7pm) Head here for fabrics – both new and antique – boxes, stationery, coffee-table books, art pieces, bags and other classy Asian bric-a-brac. There's also a branch above China House (p170), and for bigger pieces of furniture and more of its stock check out 179 The House (179 Lebuh Pantai).

★BATEK-LAH — FASHION & ACCESSORIES

Map p162 (☎04-228 2910; www.batek-lah.com; 158 Jln Transfer; ⏰11am-7pm Mon-Sat) Batik printed cloth, produced in Malaysia, is made up into a variety of men's and women's fashions and gift items here. Some of the more expensive designs are hand-drawn rather than block-printed, making them unique. Staff can also arrange for clothes tailored to your request using your choice of batik cloth.

★UNIQUE PENANG — ARTS & CRAFTS

Map p163 (www.uniquepenang.com; 62 Love Lane; ⏰5-11pm Mon-Fri, 6pm-midnight Sat & Sun) Be charmed by the colourful artworks, prints and postcards of friendly young owners Clovis and Joey, as well as the many images created by the young art students they train here. As the couple points out, paintings are hard to squeeze in a backpack, so nearly all of the gallery's art is available in postcard size, which they will even arrange to post for you at a time of your choosing.

★MOON SHOP — GIFTS & SOUVENIRS

Map p162 (www.facebook.com/moonshopgallery; 38/1 Lebuh Farquhar; ⏰11am-7pm Tue-Sun) Tan Wei Min creates lush and beautiful terrariums in everything from small glass jars to giant globes. Buying one is like taking home a piece of the tropics. Even if you're not in the market for a plant, the shop is well worth visiting for a hand-brewed artisan coffee or matcha (powdered green tea) drink.

★GERAK BUDAYA — BOOKS

Map p163 (☎04-261 0282; http://gerakbudaya-penang.com; 78 Jln Masjid Kapitan Keling; ⏰11am-8pm) If you're looking for books about Malaysia and the region, or books written by local authors, this is the place to come – the selection is unsurpassed.

CHOP KONGSI — ARTS & CRAFTS

Map p163 (www.etsy.com/people/ChopKongsi; 82C Lebuh Penang; ⏰10am-6pm) The charming artist Fu Mei Lin will likely list plenty of things in her cosy shop that she *doesn't* want to sell. Nevertheless stick with it and you're sure to find some lovely piece of jewellery or fabric art that she has created.

OTTOKEDAI — ARTS & CRAFTS

Map p163 (www.facebook.com/otto.kedai; 174 Lebuh Victoria; ⏰10am-7pm Mon-Thu, until 10pm Fri-Sun) This tiny, charming shop has a carefully curated selection of local items, from edibles to literature. Look out for the tote bags, stationery and T-shirts with prints inspired by George Town.

SAM'S BATIK HOUSE — CLOTHING

Map p162 (☎04-262 1095; http://samsbatikhouse.com; 183-185 Jln Penang; ⏰8am-7pm) Nicknamed 'Ali Baba's Cave', this deep shop of silky and cottony goodness is one of the best places in town to buy sarongs, batik shirts and Indian fashions.

GURNEY PLAZA — MALL

Map p158 (www.gurneyplaza.com.my/en; Persiaran Gurney; ⏰10am-10pm) In addition to more than 300 shops, including the department store Parkson, Penang's biggest and boldest mall includes tonnes of food and beverage outlets, a multiplex cinema, amusement theme park and fitness centre and beauty spa. A taxi here from central George Town costs about RM15.

LOCAL KNOWLEDGE

GEORGE TOWN'S MARKETS

George Town has some wonderful old-school markets, such as the ones on **Lebuh Campbell** (Map p162; cnr of Lebuh Campbell & Lebuh Carnarvon; ⏲6am-noon), **Jln Kuala Kangsar** (Map p162; Jln Kuala Kangsar; ⏲6am-noon) and **Lebuh Cecil** (Pasar Lebuh Cecil; 40-48 Lebuh Cecil; ⏲9am-7pm). You'll see butchers and fishmongers here in all their visceral glory alongside vendors of fresh fruit, vegetables and all kinds of daily goods as well as a smattering of crafts. Cecil St Market is a particularly good spot for grazing on hawker food, too, as is the **Macallum Street Night Market** (Lingtan Macallum 1; ⏲6-10.30pm Mon).

Modern George Town markets cater more for tourists and serve to showcase the up-and-coming talents of Penang's creative scene. The best of them is Hin Bus Depot's **Pop-Up Market** (Map p163; Hin Bus Depot, 31A Jln Gurdwara; ⏲11am-5pm Sun) every Sunday but you might also find something interesting at the **Occupy Beach Street (Legally)** (www.facebook.com/occupybeachstreet; Lebuh Pantai; ⏲7am-1pm Sun) event, also every Sunday, and the monthly **Little Penang Street Market** (Map p162; www.littlepenang.com.my; Jln Penang; ⏲10am-5pm last Sun of month).

ACTIVITIES & TOURS

There's a huge variety of self-guided tours of George Town, from food walks to those focusing on traditional trades or architecture – pick up a pamphlet of the routes at Penang Global Tourism (p157) or the Penang Heritage Trust (p174). Likewise, the **Penang Global Ethic Project** (www.globalethicpenang.net) has put together a World Religion Walk that takes you past the iconography and houses of worship of Christians, Muslims, Hindus, Sikhs, Buddhists and Chinese traditional religion.

If walking isn't your thing, consider the **Hop-On Hop-Off** (www.myhoponhopoff.com/pg; single trip adult/child RM20/10, 24hr pass adult/child RM40/19; ⏲9am-8pm) city bus route, which winds its way around the perimeter of the Unesco Protected Zone. It's a good way to get a quick overview of the town, and you can get on and off at one of 17 stops.

NAZLINA SPICE STATION — COOKING

Map p162 (☎012-453 8167; www.pickles-and-spices.com/cooking-traditional-food-class.html; 2 Lebuh Campbell; morning/afternoon classes RM225/180) The bubbly and enthusiastic Nazlina will teach you how to make those dishes you've fallen in love with while in Penang. A course begins with a visit to the Campbell St morning market and a local breakfast, followed by instruction on four to five dishes including dessert. Afternoon lessons are vegan/vegetarian with no market tour.

PENANG HERITAGE TRUST — WALKING

Map p163 (PHT; ☎04-264 2631; www.pht.org.my; 26 Lebuh Gereja; tours from RM160; ⏲9am-5pm Mon-Fri, 9am-1pm Sat) This conservation-minded entity leads well-regarded walking tours of George Town. There are four different walks, ranging from a religious-themed meander to an exploration of George Town's Little India, all led by experienced guides. Walks require at least two people, usually last around three hours, and must be booked three working days in advance.

GEORGE TOWN WORLD HERITAGE INCORPORATED — WALKING

Map p162 (www.gtwhi.com.my; 116-118 Lebuh Acheh; ⏲9.30am, second & last Sat of month) On the second Saturday of the month, the theme of this two-hour walking tour is George Town's traditional trades. On the last Saturday of the month, the focus is on clanhouses, secret societies and Penang's melting pot of cultures.

SLEEPING

George Town has all the accommodation options you would expect of an established and growing tourism destination, from the grungiest hostels to the swankiest hotels. In particular there are some really charming boutique places converted from former shophouses in the Heritage Zone. However, be wary that not everything advertised as a 'heritage hotel' truly fits that description.

In general, hotel prices increase on weekends and holidays. Just about everything fills up quickly, so be sure to book ahead – especially if a holiday, such as Chinese New Year, is approaching.

Inside the Unesco Protected Zone

★TIDO PENANG HOSTEL HOSTEL $

Map p162 (04-251 9266; www.tidopenanghostel.com; 106 Jln Argyll; dm/r incl breakfast from R40/90;) Malay for 'sleep', Tido is one of George Town's best-designed hostels. Just the right side of industrial chic, the polished concrete walls and floors are brightened up with colourful art and space. There's a lift, so no carting your backpack up five floors to the ace common room with great views. Friendly staff and bicycle and scooter rental round out the package.

SIOK HOSTEL HOSTEL $

Map p162 (04-263 2663; www.siokhostel.com; 458 Lebuh Chulia; dm/r incl breakfast from RM45/125;) Taking full advantage of its huge, colonial-era structure is this spacious, nicely decorated hostel that claims to be George Town's largest flashpackers. Dorms range from six to eight beds, and there's a great rooftop communal area.

TIME CAPSULE HOTEL HOSTEL $

Map p162 (04-263 0888; www.timecapsule.my; 418 Lebuh Chulia; dm from RM62;) If you aspire to feel like a Japanese salaryman – or just want to save some ringgit – consider a stay at this unique hostel. Upon checking in, you'll receive a bag of toiletries, slippers and, if needed, pyjamas, before being led to your bed: one of 80 futuristic pods equipped with TV, wi-fi, lights and a safe. There's an example of the pod at the hostel's entrance so you can see exactly what you'll be sleeping in.

RYOKAN MUNTRI HOSTEL $

Map p162 (04-250 0287; www.ryokanmuntri.com; 62 Jln Muntri; dm/r incl breakfast from RM39/158;) This flashpacker hostel boasts a minimalist feel – though not an especially Japanese one, despite the name. The dorms, ranging from four to six beds (and three women-only rooms), are almost entirely white, and the communal 'Chillax', TV and reading rooms are similarly chic. Private rooms with their own bathrooms have the same vibe – yet, lacking windows and space, are overpriced.

TIPSY TIGER PARTY HOSTEL HOSTEL $

Map p162 (04-261 2063; www.facebook.com/tipsytigerhostel; 20 Lrg Stewart; dm/r incl breakfast RM40/90;) The clue is in the hostel's name. This airy place's prime selling point is its bar, where guests can drink for half-price or go for an all-you-can-drink package starting at RM50. Whoever thought that *triple*-decker bunk beds were a cool idea might have had a few too many drinks themselves.

CONTAINER HOTEL HOSTEL $

Map p163 (04-251 9515; www.containerhotel.my/penang; 4 Gat Lebuh Chulia; dm/r from RM45/170) This hotel's concept rooms (crafted from old shipping containers) is a little fudged here in that there are no real

LOCAL KNOWLEDGE

PENANG FOR CHILDREN

Central George Town's busy streets and lack of broad pavements isn't the greatest place to stroll with kids, but there are plenty of diversions to entertain. Trishaw rides are always fun. The **Padang** (Map p163) and **Fort Cornwallis** (Map p163) both have lots of open space and food courts nearby with kid-friendly options. **Penang Museum** (p161) is educational, while other kid-friendly museums include **Teochew Puppet & Opera House** (Map p163; www.facebook.com/TeochewPuppetAndOpera; 122 Lebuh Armenian; adult/child RM10/free; 10am-6pm Tue-Sun), **Tech Dome Penang** (Map p162; 04-262 6663; www.techdomepenang.org; Level 4, Geodesic Dome, KOMTAR; adult/student/child RM40/32/24; 10am-6pm Wed-Mon) and **Komik Asia** (p164). The various indoor amusements at **The Top at KOMTAR** (p163) should also prove popular with both toddlers and teens.

The closest decent beaches are at Batu Ferringhi, while further afield at Telkuk Bahang, there's **Entopia by Penang Butterfly Farm** (p179) and the super adventure playground of **Escape** (p180). For more thrills in the rainforest, a hike through **The Habitat** (p182) on Penang Hill is sure to be a hit with its treetop walkways, giant swings and zip-lines.

containers used! Nonetheless, its dorms, which include female-only ones, are spotless and offer a smidgen more design style than similar backpackers. Private rooms are minimalist, compact and chic.

★CAMPBELL HOUSE HOTEL $$
Map p162 (☎04-261 8290; www.campbellhousepenang.com; 106 Lebuh Campbell; r incl breakfast from RM392; ❄@📶) Dating back to 1903, this once standard hotel is seeing a new life as a sumptuous boutique property. Thoughtful details, such as locally sourced toiletries, beautiful Peranakan tiles in the bathrooms, Nespresso machines and high-quality mattresses, make the difference – this in addition to excellent service and overwhelmingly positive feedback from guests.

★YOU LE YUEN GUESTHOUSE $$
Map p163 (☎04-261 1817; www.youleyuen.com; 7 Love Lane; r/ste incl breakfast from RM200/300; ❄📶) There are just four rooms at this boutique bed and breakfast, each making the most of this lovely antique shophouse with exposed brick walls, retro furnishings and a central courtyard (now used as a cafe). The duplex suites make full use of the building's height. As well as the cafe and bar there's also a fashion boutique to browse.

★REN I TANG HOTEL $$
Map p163 (☎04-250 8383; www.renitang.com; 82A Lebuh Penang; r incl breakfast from RM200; ❄📶) A careful restoration has transformed this former Chinese medicine wholesaler's into a warm, inviting small hotel. The 17 different-sized rooms, which carry charming reminders of the building's former life, span several layouts; we particularly liked the corner Tub Room, equipped with a wooden soaking tub and fragrant bath salts.

LANG HOOSE GUESTHOUSE $$
Map p163 (☎04-261 6616; www.langhoose.com; 269 Lebuh Pantai; s/d from RM119/199; ❄@📶) Badminton rackets and other sports memorabilia (including from Malaysia's Olympic medal winners) decorate the lobby of this appealing conversion of a colonial shophouse into a boutique guesthouse. The name is Gaelic for 'long house' which this certainly is, stretching the entire block and offering spacious rooms; cheaper ones share a bathroom.

SPICES HOTEL BOUTIQUE HOTEL $$
Map p162 (☎04-261 9986; www.spiceshotel.com; 5 Lorong Lumut; r from RM330) A 150-year-old bodhi tree sprouts from the wall in the courtyard of this appealing boutique hotel that has won an award for its architect owners. The eight rooms feature Malay, Islamic and Indian design influences. The neighbouring mosque will mean that you won't need an alarm clock for an early start.

SINKEH HOTEL $$
Map p162 (☎04-261 3966; www.sinkeh.com; 105 Lebuh Melayu; r incl breakfast from RM198; ❄📶) Yes, Sinkeh is located in an old shophouse, but inside modern concrete, glass and steel set the tone. Despite this, service is warm and the rooms are comfortable, if not particularly spacious.

LE DREAM BOUTIQUE HOTEL $$
Map p162 (☎04-251 9370; www.ledreamhotel.com; 139 Jln Pintal Tali; r incl breakfast from RM258; ❄📶) The eclectic decor mix of faux leather, galvanised metal and satin in gold and purple might not be everyone's idea of a dream, but there's undeniably a boldness about the place. Other appealing aspects include rooftop Jacuzzi pools with a view and the Sky Bar where guests can choose a movie to screen and are served free popcorn.

COFFEE ATELIER HOTEL $$
Map p163 (☎04-261 2261; www.coffeeatelier.com; 47-55 Lg Stewart; ste incl breakfast from RM380; ❄📶) Unlike the slick heritage hotels you'll find elsewhere, the renovation of this row of 1920s shophouses has left them feeling wonderfully rustic, and the peeling paint and quirky yet appropriate furnishings provide heaps of character. Each house is divided into two units, with a second smaller bedroom on the 1st floor and huge courtyard-style bathrooms in the ground-floor rooms.

Breakfast is served in attached **Café 55** (coffee from RM8; ⏲8.30am-5pm Tue-Sun), and there's also an art gallery on-site.

SEGARA NINDA HOTEL $$
Map p162 (☎04-262 8748; www.segaraninda.com; 20 Jln Penang; r RM100-180; ❄@📶) This elegant century-old villa was once the town residence of Ku Din Ku Meh, a wealthy timber merchant and colonial administrator. His home has been tastefully renovated, incorporating original features such as the carved wooden ventilation panels, staircase

and tiled floors. By contrast, the 16 rooms are simply furnished, but the place boasts an inviting, home-like atmosphere.

★23 LOVE LANE BOUTIQUE HOTEL **$$$**

Map p163 (☎04-262 1323; www.23lovelane.com; 23 Love Lane; d/ste incl breakfast from RM528/1208;) Occupying a former mansion, its kitchen and stables, 23 Love Lane tastefully combines antique furniture and fixtures with modern design touches and arty accents. There's lots of open spaces and high ceilings to catch the breezes, inviting communal areas, a peaceful aura, and service that complements the casual, homey vibe.

★BLUE MANSION HOTEL **$$$**

Map p163 (☎04-262 0006; www.thebluemansion.com.my; 14 Lebuh Leith; r incl breakfast RM498-1000;) Occupying one of George Town's most emblematic buildings, the Blue Mansion wrote the book on how to craft the ideal heritage hotel. The 18 spacious, high-ceiling guest rooms open onto airy courtyards and have octagonal terracotta tile floors. They're all decorated with antique and retro furniture and ooze authentic colonial-era atmosphere.

★EASTERN & ORIENTAL HOTEL HISTORIC HOTEL **$$$**

Map p162 (E&O; ☎04-222 2000; www.eohotels.com; 10 Lebuh Farquhar; ste incl breakfast RM960-3910;) Dating back to 1885, the E&O is one of those rare hotels for which historic opulence has gracefully moved into the present day. We fancy the suites in the original Heritage Wing, which seamlessly blend modern comfort with colonial-era style, using hardwood antiques and vintage-themed furnishings; those with a sea view are worth the extra outlay. Rooms in the more modern Victory Annexe are no less appealing.

★MUNTRI GROVE BOUTIQUE HOTEL **$$$**

Map p162 (☎04-261 8888; www.georgetownheritage.com/muntri-grove; 127-131 Jln Muntri; r incl breakfast RM400;) Tucked off a quiet street is this row of 19th-century servants houses that have been transformed into one of central George Town's loveliest boutique hotels. Large attractive rooms include huge four-poster beds and vintage furniture. The small pool and leafy surrounds are an added bonus, and rooms on the ground floor are pet-friendly.

SEVEN TERRACES BOUTIQUE HOTEL **$$$**

Map p163 (☎04-261 8888; www.georgetownheritage.com/seven-terraces-hotel; 8 Lg Stewart; ste incl breakfast from RM550;) Crafted from a row of seven joined shophouses, surrounding a beautiful central courtyard, Seven Terraces is one of the most luxurious place to stay in central George Town. The 16 two-storey suites (including two even larger multi-room 'apartments') are vast and regal-feeling, and have been decorated with a mix of original antiques, reproductions and contemporary pieces. Enormous bathrooms with monsoon-style showers and spacious balconies are also a plus.

MUNTRI MEWS HOTEL **$$$**

Map p162 (☎04-261 8888; www.georgetownheritage.com/muntri-mews; 77 Jln Muntri; r incl breakfast from RM400;) This building's original owners would no doubt be shocked to learn that their former stablehouse (mews) is today an attractive boutique hotel. The 13 rooms have a minimalist, studio-like vibe, with each boasting retro-themed furniture, an attractive black-and-white tiled bathroom, and vast 'double queen' beds.

THE EDISON BOUTIQUE HOTEL **$$$**

Map p162 (☎04-262 2990; http://theedisonhotels.com; 15 Lebuh Leith; d/ste from RM550/850;) Looking fabulous after a major overhaul, this spacious colonial building offers tastefully decorated rooms, a light-infused courtyard, high ceilings, latticed windows and a grand entrance. There are also cabanas to lounge in next to the pool.

Outside the Unesco Protected Zone

★NOORDIN MEWS HOTEL **$$**

Map p162 (☎04-263 7125; www.noordinmews.com; 53 Lebuh Noordin; s/d/ste incl breakfast RM368/396/593;) These two restored shophouses boast an attractive 1920s and '30s feel, down to the antique adverts and retro furniture. Very friendly service, a pool and a secluded-feeling location away from the main tourist drag are additional draws.

MUSEUM HOTEL HOTEL **$$**

Map p162 (☎04-226 6668; www.museumhotel.com.my; 72 Jln AS Mansor; r incl breakfast from RM160;) Attractive, comfortable, boasting great service and representing good value, the Museum Hotel is a gem in this price range. Located in a stately block of restored shophouses, the 24 rooms here range from tight-but-comfy singles to larger rooms, all tastefully decorated with antique- and vintage-themed design touches, and looked after by capable staff.

GLOW HOTEL **$$**

(☎04-226 0084; www.glowbyzinc.com/penang; 101 Jln Macalister; r incl breakfast from RM130; ❄@🛜🏊) A chain with charm. And lots of space. And a location near tonnes of street food. And it's great value. There's certainly a lot to like about this young-feeling hotel, located about 700m north of the intersection with Jln Penang.

JAWI PERANAKAN MANSION BOUTIQUE HOTEL **$$$**

Map p162 (☎04-261 8888; www.georgetownheritage.com/jawi-peranakan-mansion; 153 Jln Hutton; r incl breakfast from RM400; ❄🛜🏊) The latest in the GTH collection of boutique hotels in restored heritage buildings delivers Indian chic with its carved wooden doorways and wrought-iron details. It's a little bit of a walk from the main Heritage Zone but nothing too strenuous, and there's a good pool here to cool down in too.

★CLOVE HALL HOTEL **$$$**

(☎04-229 0818; www.clovehall.com; 11 Jln Clove Hall; ste incl breakfast RM575-675; ❄@🛜🏊) An Edwardian Anglo-Malay mansion housing six luxury suites, Clove Hall is the place to go if you want to feel and be treated like a mogul of the early 1900s – hardly surprising giving that the structure was originally the Sarkies brothers' (of the Eastern & Oriental Hotel (p177) fame) first Penang home. Jln Clove Hall intersects with Jln Burma about 1km north of Jln Transfer; a RM15 taxi ride from central George Town.

PENAGA HOTEL BOUTIQUE HOTEL **$$$**

Map p162 (☎04-261 1891; www.hotelpenaga.com; cnr Lg Hutton & Jln Transfer; r/ste from RM350/550; ❄@🛜🏊) This hotel takes up most of a city block and spans three sections: a row of two-storey family-friendly mini-homes, apartment-sized suites and spacious rooms. All are decorated with a mix of original art, vintage-themed furnishings, and some charming touches such as cowhide rugs and mid-century-modern furniture. The stack of amenities includes a pool, central gardens and a coffee shop.

G HOTEL KELAWAI BOUTIQUE HOTEL **$$$**

Map p158 (☎04-219 0000; www.ghotel.com.my; 2 Persiaran Maktab; r/ste from RM521/1453; ❄@🏊) The hipper sibling of the nearby G Hotel Gurney, this place is particularly popular with local visitors over the weekends, so book ahead if you wish to check in then. Rooms are all cool monochrome and elegance. The fab pool and superb rooftop bar are pluses.

Batu Ferringhi & Teluk Bahang

Explore

Batu Ferringhi is the best easy-access beach stop on Penang, and it makes a pleasant break from the city. However, the beach doesn't count among Malaysia's finest; the water isn't as clear as you might expect, swimming often means battling jellyfish, and the beach itself can be dirty. The majority of the area's accommodation and restaurants are located along Jln Batu Ferringhi, the main strip, a short walk from the beach.

Teluk Bahang is the quiet beach a few kilometres past Batu Ferringhi. The best reason for heading out this way is to spend time in Penang National Park, which also has deserted beaches you can hike to. Other attractions include a couple of gorgeous tropical gardens, Entopia by Penang Butterfly Farm and the Escape adventure park.

The Best...

➡ **Sight** Penang National Park (p179)

➡ **Place to Eat** Tree Monkey (p180)

➡ **Activity** Tropical Spice Garden Cooking Courses (p180)

Top Tip

Contact **Penang Nature Tourist Guide Association** (PNTGA; ☎04-881 4788; ⏲8am-6pm) to arrange a guide for Penang National Park (walks for up to five people from RM250).

Getting There & Away

Bus 101 runs from Weld Quay and KOMTAR in George Town and takes around 30 minutes to reach Batu Ferringhi and another 10 to Teluk Bahang (both destinations RM4). A taxi from George Town to Batu Ferringhi/Teluk Bahang will cost at least RM40/50.

SIGHTS

★PENANG NATIONAL PARK NATIONAL PARK

Map p158 (Taman Negara Pulau Pinang; 04-881 3500; 8am-5pm; 101) FREE At just 2300 hectares, Penang National Park is the smallest in Malaysia; it's also one of the newest, having attained national park status in 2003. It offers some interesting and challenging jungle trails, as well as some of the island's finest and quietest beaches.

Private guides and several boat operators can be found near the park entrance. Travel one way from Teluk Duyung (Monkey Beach) is RM50, from Pantai Kerachut is RM90 and from Teluk Kampi is RM100.

The park entrance is a short walk from Teluk Bahang's main bus stop. It's an easy 20-minute walk to the head of the canopy walkway (now permanently closed), from where you have the choice of two routes: bearing west towards Muka Head or south to Pantai Kerachut.

The easiest walk is the 15-minute stroll west to **Teluk Tukun beach** where Sungai Tukun flows into the ocean. There are some little pools to swim in here. Following this trail along the coast about 10 minutes more brings you to the private University of Malaysia Marine Research Station, where there is a supply jetty, as well as **Tanjung Aling**, a nice beach to stop at for a rest. From here it's another 45 minutes or so down the beach to **Teluk Duyung**, also called Monkey Beach (after the numerous primates who scamper about here). It's another 30 minutes to **Muka Head**, the isolated rocky promontory at the extreme northwestern corner of the island, where on the peak of the head is an off-limits lighthouse dating from 1883 and an Achenese-style graveyard. The views of the surrounding islands from up here are worth the sweaty uphill jaunt.

A longer and more difficult trail heads south from the suspension bridge towards **Pantai Kerachut**, a beautiful white-sand beach that is a popular spot for picnics and is a green turtle nesting ground. Count on about 1½ hours to walk to the beach on the clear and well-used trail. On your way is the unusual **meromictic lake**, a rare natural feature composed of two separate layers of unmixed freshwater on top and seawater below, supporting a unique mini-ecosystem. From Pantai Kerachut beach you can walk about 40 minutes onward to further-flung and isolated **Teluk Kampi**, which is the longest beach in the park; look for trenches along the coast that are remnants of the Japanese occupation in WWII.

★TROPICAL SPICE GARDEN GARDENS

Map p158 (04-881 1797; www.tropicalspicegarden.com; Jl Teluk Bahang; adult/child RM27.50/15.90, incl tour RM37.10/21.20; 9am-6pm; 101) This beautifully landscaped oasis of tropical, fragrant fecundity offers trails past more than 500 species of flora, with an emphasis on edible herbs and spices. You can explore the grounds on your own, or join one of four daily guided tours at 9am, 11.30am, 1.30pm and 3.30pm. Take bus 101 from George Town (RM4) and let the driver know that you want to get off here.

The garden offers well-regarded cooking courses (p180) and its restaurant (p180) is worth a visit. There's also a good shop, and just across the road from the gardens there's a beautiful white-sand beach.

★ART & GARDEN BY FUAN WONG GARDENS, GALLERY

Map p158 (013-533 1232; www.facebook.com/ArtandGardenbyFuanWong; adult/child RM30/15; 9am-6.30pm Thu-Mon; 501) Rising up a hillside on a part of the family's durian orchard is this amazing conceptual garden where glass artist Fuan Wong marries his superb collection of weird and wonderful plants with his sculptures and installations. Creative works by other artists are dotted throughout the garden, which also offers breathtaking views of Penang Hill.

ENTOPIA BY PENANG BUTTERFLY FARM GARDENS

Map p158 (04-888 8111; www.entopia.com; 830 Jln Teluk Bahang; adult/child RM49/29; 9am-7pm; 501) Entopia is about so much more than tropical butterflies – even though there's some 13,000 of these beauties from around 120 species fluttering around the well-designed attraction's outdoor gardens. You'll also be able to see and learn about all kinds of insects and invertebrates while wandering around this large maze-like environment. Count on spending at least a couple of hours here to see everything; there's a good cafe you can pause at half-way around.

ESCAPE AMUSEMENT PARK

Map p158 (04-881 1106; www.escape.my; 282 Jln Teluk Bahang; adult/child RM83/55; 9am-6pm Tue-Sun; 501) Fun for all the family here, but be warned: adults report being more challenged than their kids by the adventurous games and attractions at this eco-themed play park, some of which involve climbing and jumping. Escape is about 1km south of Teluk Bahang's roundabout.

EATING & DRINKING

Most of Batu Ferringhi's restaurants are strung along Jln Batu Ferringhi, close by the beach. There's plenty of budget options and hawker stalls as well as a preponderance of places serving Middle Eastern food, all aiming to capture the Arab visitors who favour the resort.

You can get a beer at most non-halal places, but outside of the hotels, toes-in-the-sand beach bars are few – **Bora Bora** (Map p158; 04-885 1313; www.facebook.com/boraborabysunset; Jln Batu Ferringhi; noon-1am Sun-Thu, until 3am Fri & Sat; 101), located roughly in the centre of the strip, is the exception.

The main shopping area along the road heading east to Batu Ferringhi has a few coffee shops where you'll find cheaper Chinese dishes and seafood, as well as a couple of places selling *nasi kandar* (standard rice with a choice of curry and vegetables), such as **Restoran K-Haleel** (Map p158; Jln Teluk Bahang; mains RM1.50-4; 24hr; 101).

TREE MONKEY THAI $$

Map p158 (04-881 3993; www.treemonkey.com.my; Tropical Spice Garden, Jln Teluk Bahang; mains RM18-80; 10.30am-10.30pm; ; 101) This is al fresco at its best, with a view of the sea and on the doorstep of the lush Tropical Spice Garden (p179). A Thai owner oversees a huge variety of tasty Thai dishes, including several 'tapas' sets (RM38 to RM168).

FERRINGHI GARDEN INTERNATIONAL $$

Map p158 (04-881 1193; Jln Batu Ferringhi; mains RM25-350; cafe 8am-5pm, restaurant 5-11pm; ; 101) Everyone falls in love with the outdoor setting with its terracotta tiles and hardwood surrounded by bamboo – not to mention the seafood-heavy menu. During the daytime hours, the neighbouring cafe serves good breakfast and real coffee – a relative rarity in Batu Ferringhi.

BUNGALOW INTERNATIONAL $$

Map p158 (04-886 8686; www.lonepinehotel.com; Lone Pine Hotel, 97 Jln Batu Ferringhi; mains RM28-40; ; 101) Back in the 1940s, the bungalow that this beachside restaurant partly occupies was the hub of the Lone Pine Hotel (p181), one of Batu Ferringhi's most historic properties. That period is evoked in dishes such as chicken chop – remnants of the era when Hainanese chefs, former colonial-era domestic servants, dominated restaurant kitchens. Other Malaysian and international dishes are available. On Sunday from 12.30pm to 3.30pm it serves a good-value buffet for RM65.

TARBUSH MIDDLE EASTERN $$

Map p158 (04-885 2558; www.tarbush.com.my; Jln Batu Ferringhi; mains RM15-60; noon-midnight; ; 101) Middle Eastern visitors have brought their cuisine to Batu Ferringhi, and Lebanese restaurants line the town's main strip. This branch of a KL restaurant empire is reliable. We fancy the two meze platters, which bring together everything from hummus to *kibbeh* (lamb meatballs with bulgur).

ACTIVITIES

There's plenty of water-sports rental outfits along the beach; options include **jet skis** (RM70 for 15 minutes), **banana-boating** (RM25 per person) and **parasailing** (RM150 per ride) trips. After which you might need a relaxing **massage**. All sorts of foot masseuses will offer you their services; expect to pay around RM40 for a 30-minute deep-tissue massage.

TROPICAL SPICE GARDEN COOKING COURSES COOKING

Map p158 (04-881 1797; http://tsgcookingschool.com; Jl Teluk Bahang; adult/child RM233.20/116.60; lessons 9am-1pm Mon-

Sat; 101) Hands-on cooking classes, of up to 10 people, provide all you need to know on how to prepare local dishes using ingredients that are grown just outside the door in the Tropical Spice Garden (p179). The half-day course begins with a guided tour of the garden and ends with lunch.

CHI THE SPA AT SHANGRI-LA SPA
Map p158 (04-888 8888; www.shangri-la.com; Rasa Sayang Resort, Jln Batu Ferringhi; treatments from RM150; 101) By a wide margin the most luxurious spa on Penang, Chi is its own little wonderland of pampering, with massages and other treatments taking place in one of 11 private villas in a lush beachside setting.

SLEEPING

There are lots of somewhat overpriced, chain-style resorts in Batu Ferringhi catering to families, and quite a few extremely overpriced, homestay budget places, but little in between. The vast majority of accommodation is along Jln Batu Ferringhi, the town's main strip, which runs parallel to the beach.

Teluk Bahang has mainly budget and midrange accommodation with nothing particularly outstanding. For top-end resorts, the closest option is to stay in nearby Batu Ferringhi. Alternatively you could sample Malaysian homelife by contacting the local **homestay collective** (019-412 4729; www.homestaytelukbahang.com; r full board from RM140).

ROOMIES HOSTEL $
Map p158 (04-881 1344; www.roomiespenang.com; 4th fl, 76C-4 Jln Batu Ferringhi; dm/r incl breakfast RM40/150; 101) If you don't mind sleeping communally, Roomies is by far the most appealing budget option in Batu Ferringhi. The dorm spans 10 beds, and is spacious, bright and clean. There are also two private rooms and all rooms share a clean set of bathrooms. The rooftop area with a hydroponic lettuce garden is a plus!

LZB GUESTHOUSE $
Map p158 (04-881 1252; 392 Jln Batu Ferringhi; dm RM30, r with/without bathroom RM70/60; 101) Located just off the main strip, behind a convenience store, LZB (formerly Lazy Boys) has smartened up since it was taken over by friendly Wan and her family. The dorms and rooms are clean and functional.

BABA GUEST HOUSE GUESTHOUSE $
Map p158 (04-881 1686; babaguesthouse2000@yahoo.com; 52 Batu Ferringhi; r from RM70; 101) A turquoise-painted domestic compound belonging to a friendly Chinese family houses large and spotless rooms – although bare. Half the rooms share bathrooms, while the more expensive air-con rooms come with a fridge and shower.

ROOMIES SUITES HOTEL $$
Map p158 (04-881 1378; www.roomiespenang.com; 4th fl, 1-9B Eden Parade, Lg Sungai Emas; r incl breakfast from RM150; 101) Despite being on the 4th floor of a shopping complex, Roomies Suites is easily Batu Ferringhi's best midrange option. The 13 rooms here are stylish and spacious, and are looked after by a friendly host.

SEA PRINCESS HOTEL HOTEL $$
Map p158 (04-346 0981; 811A Jln Hassan Abas; r from RM120; 101) You can't miss this brightly coloured, three-storey block, located along Teluk Bahang's main drag. The 18 rooms are clean and spacious, and have a dash of character thanks to feature wallpaper. The place is overseen by an enthusiastic owner.

HOTEL SPORTFISHING HOTEL $$
Map p158 (04-885 2728; Jln Nelayan; d/tr from RM120/125; 101) The two floors of plain-but-clean rooms are at the edge of the beach and look over the fishing pier. You'll pay about RM10 extra for a sea-view room.

★**LONE PINE HOTEL** RESORT $$$
Map p158 (04-886 8686; www.lonepinehotel.com; 97 Jln Batu Ferringhi; r/ste incl breakfast from RM644/1064; 101) Dating back to the 1940s, this is one of Batu Ferringhi's oldest – and best – resorts. The 90 rooms are spacious and bright; a few offer personal plunge pools or private gardens. The grounds have a stately, national-park-like feel, with hammocks suspended between the pines (actually casuarina trees), and a huge 'spa salt' pool as a centrepiece.

★**RASA SAYANG RESORT** RESORT $$$
Map p158 (04-881 1966; www.shangri-la.com; Jln Batu Ferringhi; r/ste incl breakfast from RM875/2290; 101) Spread across 30 acres, its beachside grounds shaded by historic raintrees, the Rasa Sayang is Batu Ferringhi's top resort. It's split into two wings, Garden and Rasa, with the latter

offering the more exclusive atmosphere. Rooms are large and pleasantly decorated; all have balconies and many have sea views.

SHANGRI-LA GOLDEN SANDS RESORT RESORT **$$$**

Map p158 (☎04-886 1191; www.shangri-la.com; Jln Batu Ferringhi; r from RM495; ❄@📶🏊; 🚌101) You can almost imagine Julie the cruise director leading you through the orderly array of blue, rubber-woven lawn chairs, sprawling cement walkways and mushroom-like thatched huts at this family-oriented resort. Rooms move into the modern age and are spacious with marble bathrooms.

HARD ROCK HOTEL RESORT **$$$**

Map p158 (☎04-881 1711; http://penang.hardrockhotels.net; Jln Batu Ferringhi; r/ste incl breakfast from RM464/1160; ❄@📶🏊; 🚌101) If you can stomach the corny, hyper-corporate vibe, this resort can be a fun place to stay. There's a particular emphasis on family-friendliness, with child-friendly pools, kid-friendly suites and teen-themed play areas (complete with pool table and video games). A branch of the **Hard Rock Cafe** (Map p158; ☎04-886 8050; http://penang.hardrockhotels.net; Jln Batu Ferringhi; ⏲11.30am-2am; 🚌101) is attached to the resort.

The Rest of Penang

Explore

Travelling around Penang, you'll find the same cultural mix as in George Town but in smaller doses and with a more paradisaical backdrop. There are hilltop views, quaint fishing villages, picturesque temples and smaller islands to discover.

While there are buses from George Town to specific destinations, there is no round-island bus route. So if you want to make the 70km circuit of the island, hire a car or motorcycle and plan to spend a minimum of five hours driving, including plenty of sightseeing and refreshment stops. If you are really fit, cycling is an option but you'll need to allow all day or – better still – consider scheduling a stop in Teluk Bahang for the night to rest the thighs. The north-coast road runs beside the beaches.

The Best...

➡ **Sight** Kek Lok Si Temple (p183)

➡ **Place to Eat** Khunthai (p184)

➡ **Beach** Pantai Pasir Panjang (p184)

Top Tip

To walk the 5km from the top of Penang Hill to the Botanical Gardens takes around 1½ hours; you'll see some experienced walkers going backwards to save the pounding on the knees.

Air Itam & Penang Hill

Sights

Penang's most spectacular Buddhist temple and the refreshing air, lush ancient rainforest and vistas from atop Penang Hill are all fine reasons for making time for this part of the island. This can easily be done as a day trip from George Town.

It's generally about 5°C cooler at the top of Penang Hill, 833m above sea level. The **funicular** (www.penanghill.gov.my; one-way adult/child RM15/5, fast lane adult/child RM45/5; ⏲6.30am-11pm; 🚌204) from Air Itam makes getting up the hill easy. Come for pleasant walks, including one through the treetops at the excellent new Habitat nature reserve, the exception to the generally tacky attractions clustered around the upper funicular station.

THE HABITAT NATURE RESERVE

Map p158 (☎04 -826 7677; http://thehabitat.my; Penang Hill; adult/child RM50/30; ⏲9.30am-6pm Wed-Mon) Bordering one of Penang's two virgin rainforest reserves, the spine of this fantastic addition to the Penang Hill experience is a finely crafted 1.6km nature trail. Along it you can access suspended walkways (thrillingly high up in the canopy), viewing platforms and pocket gardens featuring different species of tropical plants. You can explore on your own, but it's better to take one of the guided tours.

Canopy Discovery Tours (including short zip-lines and canopy bridge walks) and the Langur Tree Climb activity are set to debut in 2017, and each will incur separate charges. There are also plans for guided night walks.

KEK LOK SI TEMPLE BUDDHIST TEMPLE

Map p158 (Temple of Supreme Bliss; http://kekloksitemple.com; Jln Balik Pulau, Air Itam; 7am-6pm; 204) FREE Staggered on hillside terraces overlooking Air Itam, around 8km from the centre of George Town, Malaysia's largest Buddhist temple is a visual delight. Built between 1890 and 1905, Kek Lok Si is the cornerstone of the Malay-Chinese community, which provided the funding for its two-decade-long building (and ongoing additions). Its key features are the seven-tier **Ban Po Thar** (Ten Thousand Buddhas Pagoda; RM2; 8am-6pm) pagoda and an awesome 36.5m-high bronze statue of Kuan Yin, goddess of mercy.

To reach the temple's main entrance, you'll have to run the gauntlet of souvenir stalls on the uphill path. You'll also pass a pond packed with turtles and the complex's **vegetarian restaurant** (suggested donation RM8; 10am-6.30pm Tue-Sun;). There's a lot of climbing of stairs involved, but at least the final bit up to the statue of Kuan Yin is covered by a **funicular** (one-way/return RM3/6; 8.45am-5.30pm).

BOTANICAL GARDENS GARDENS

Map p158 (http://botanicalgardens.penang.gov.my/index.php/en; Waterfall Rd; 5am-8pm; 10) FREE Once a granite quarry, Penang's Botanical Gardens were founded in 1884 by Charles Curtis, a tireless British plant lover who collected the original specimens and became the first curator. Today, the 30-hectare grounds include a fern rockery, an orchidarium and a lily pond. Follow the 1.5km Curtis Trail, which dips into the jungle, or hike up to Penang Hill.

Eating

There's a vegetarian restaurant at Kek Lok Si and plenty of hawker stalls in the market at Air Itam. Up on Penang Hill, there's a good range of inexpensive hawker food at the food court, and Western food at **David Brown's** (Map p158; www.penanghillco.com.my; Penang Hill; mains from RM20; sky terrace 9am-11pm, restaurant 11am-10pm), the island's most atmospheric destination for colonial-style high tea (3pm to 6pm); the full deal for two people is RM88, or you can do just scones and tea for RM20.

Southeast Penang Island

A natural destination while making a clockwise round-island tour is the fishing port at **Batu Maung**. There are still some dilapidated, brightly painted boats along the coast, although the main sight to catch your eye will be the second bridge to the mainland. A good view of the bridge can be had from Sam Poh Footprint Temple, and while you're down here, you might also swing by hillside Penang War Museum. However, the best reason for heading south is to eat freshly cooked seafood beside the lovely beach at Teluk Kumbar.

You'll find both Penang International Airport (p156) and the Sungai Nibong Bus Station (p156), Penang's main interstate and international bus station, in the southeast of Penang Island. The area is also well connected with George Town by Rapid Penang (p156) buses, including the 307 to Batu Maung and the 401 and 401E to Teluk Kumbar. Taxis to both these destinations from George Town will cost at least RM50.

Sights

SAM POH FOOTPRINT TEMPLE TEMPLE

Map p158 (Jln Maung; 24 hours; 302) FREE This small seaside temple overlooking fishing boats and the second Penang bridge has a shrine dedicated to the legendary Admiral Zheng He. Also known as Sam Poh, his portrait is also painted on a giant boulder outside. The temple sanctifies a huge 'footprint' in the rock that's reputed to belong to the famous navigator.

PENANG WAR MUSEUM MUSEUM

Map p158 (04-626 5142; www.facebook.com/PenangWarMuseum; Bukit Batu Maung; adult/child RM37.10/18; 9am-5pm; 302) Perched on top of the steep Bukit Batu Maung, this former British fort, built in the 1930s, was used as a prison and torture camp by the Japanese during WWII. Today, the crumbling buildings have been restored as a memorial to those dark days. Barracks, ammunition stores, cookhouses, gun emplacements and other structures can be explored in this eerie, atmospheric place, and there are information boards in English all over the site.

Eating

★KHUNTHAI
THAI $$

Map p158 (04-625 1155; 1052 Mukim 9 Pasar Belanda, Teluk Kumbar; mains RM16-45; ⏲11am-11.30pm; 🚌401, 401E) A blissful beachside setting, intimate atmosphere and daytime dining gives Khunthai the edge over the neighbouring seafood restaurants at Teluk Kumbar. The steamed fish is excellent and you can choose from all the usual Thai dishes.

HAI BOEY SEAFOOD
SEAFOOD $$

Map p158 (☎04-649 3746; www.facebook.com/haiboeyseafoodpenang; 29 MK9 Pasir Belanda, Teluk Kumbar; mains from RM25-50; ⏲5.30-10.30pm; 🚌401, 401E) Right on the beach at Teluk Kumbar, this is one of Penang's most famous destinations for seafood. Choose what you'd like to eat from the tanks at the entrance. It's best to reserve a table on weekends or holidays when it can be very busy.

Balik Pulau & Kampung Pulau Betong

Meaning 'on the other side of the island', Balik Pulau is Penang Island's main inland outpost. It's a busy market town with a strip of charming old shophouses surrounded by rice fields, and durian, clove and nutmeg orchards. A short drive away in the southwest corner of the island is the sleepy fishing village Kampung Pulau Betong and one of Penang's loveliest beaches. Look out for striking murals by Julia Volchkova and Ernest Zacharevic along Balik Pulau's main street.

My Balik Pulau (RM2), a brochure available for purchase in George Town at ottokedai (p173), and *Discover Balik Pulau*, a map available at the various tourism offices, are great guides to the area's smaller attractions, culture and history. You can reach Balik Pulau via bus 502 and 401E from George Town and Bayan Lepas respectively (RM4), and bus 501 from Teluk Bahang (RM3.40).

Sights

PANTAI PASIR PANJANG
BEACH

Map p158 This empty, pristine beach with white sand the texture of raw sugar is one of the prettier spots on Penang for the few who make the effort to get here. The beach is backed by a National Service Training Centre for young graduates entering the army. Be vigilant if you go into the water – there's a heavy undertow. To get here, walk 1.5km over the hill from Kampung Pulau Betong village.

HOLY NAME OF JESUS CATHOLIC CHURCH
CHURCH

Map p158 (☎04-866 8545; Jln Bukit Penara; 🚌502, 401E, 501) FREE When this Catholic church was first established in 1854, it occupied a hut made of attap palm leaves; the handsome current structure dates from 1894. The floor tiles were designed by a French priest, the stained glass was imported from Belgium, the bell from France, and the church's twin spires stand impressively against the jungle behind.

Eating

Balik Pulau functions as a good lunch stop for anyone making a round-trip of the island. Locals have been known to cross the island for this town's signature dish: laksa Balik Pulau. Sample it at **Cafe Ko Cha Bi Balik Pulau** (Map p158; ☎012-474 5178; www.facebook.com/CafeKoChaBi; 110 Jln Balik Pulau; mains RM4; ⏲10am-6pm Fri-Wed; 🚌502, 401E, 501). In Kampung Pulau Betong you can buy fish and seafood at the village market stalls and bring them to **Jia Siang Cafe** (Map p158; 019-746 8465; 321 Mk 7 Kampung Pulau Betong; mains RM15-50; ⏲noon-7pm) to be cooked as you like, for around R14 per head.

Sleeping

AUDI GUESTHOUSE
GUESTHOUSE $

Map p158 (☎04-866 2569; www.audipenang.com; Jln Pulau Betung; dm/r from RM30/90; ❄📶) Roughly midway between Balik Pulau and the fishing village at Kampung Pulau Betong is this basic but appealing guesthouse. Rooms offer just mattresses on wooden floors or platforms, but it's all sparklingly clean and very spacious with a cafe and bicycle rental (RM20 per day).

MALIHOM
VILLA $$$

Map p158 (☎012-428 5191; www.malihom.com; Kiri N/t 168 Bukit Penara Mukim 6; villa incl breakfast from RM626; ❄@📶🏊) Accommodation at the top of this 518m peak takes the form of nine splendidly restored 100-year-old rice barns, united in a private retreat. Given its isolated location, you'll likely want to upgrade to full board. You'll need to be shuttled up in the resort's 4WD.

Understand Kuala Lumpur

KUALA LUMPUR TODAY 186
The government is pushing forward with the transformation of KL thanks to major transport and construction projects.

HISTORY 188
How a tin-mining outpost in the jungle of a British colony emerged as the capital of modern-day Malaysia.

LIFE IN KUALA LUMPUR 197
Insights into the daily routines of KLites, their work, family and social lives.

MULTICULTURALISM, RELIGION & CULTURE 200
Malaysia's three main ethnic groups bring a rich mix of religion and customs to the cultural table.

ARTS & ARCHITECTURE 207
Get a handle on the creative output and built environs of the city.

ENVIRONMENT 212
As the capital of a 'mega-diversity' country, how green is KL's environmental scorecard?

Kuala Lumpur Today

While KLites get on with day-to-day life with good cheer, tensions simmer beneath the surface of this modern, multicultural city. Prime Minister Najib Razak has tightened his grip on power in the face of ongoing allegations of corruption and a faltering economy. Meanwhile, it's full steam ahead on major infrastructure developments for the capital, including a new mass rapid transit (MRT) line and the River of Life urban-regeneration project.

Best on Film

Entrapment (1999) The climax of this Sean Connery and Catherine Zeta-Jones thriller takes place at KL's Petronas Towers.
Sepet (2004) Chinese boy falls for Malay girl in Yasmin Ahmad's romantic comedy.
Interchange (2016) Fantasy thriller set in KL that delves into the city's supernatural depths.

Best in Print

Urban Odysseys (edited by Janet Tay and Eric Forbes) Short stories that capture KL's multifaceted cultural flavour.
KL Noir Three volumes of short stories homing in on the city's sinister, spooky underbelly.
The Letter (Somerset Maugham) A short story and play based on the real-life scandal of a murder in KL in 1911.
My Life as a Fake (Peter Carey) This reworking of *Frankenstein* evokes the sultry side of KL.
Found in Malaysia (The Nut Graph) Compilation of 50 interviews with notable Malaysians.
The Consumption of Kuala Lumpur (Ziauddin Sardar) How the once sleepy capital has evolved into a modern economic marvel.

Najib Under Fire

Since July 2015 Malaysia's prime minister, Najib Razak, has been implicated in an ongoing corruption scandal involving the government's 1MBD sovereign investment fund that aims to turn Kuala Lumpur (KL) into a global financial hub. The fund racked up huge debts at the same time as it appears that nearly US$700 million had been transferred from it into Najib's personal bank accounts; subsequent news reports suggest the total may exceed US$1 billion.

In July 2016 the US Department of Justice moved to seize more than US$1 billion in assets connected to the 1MDB fund and in September it was claimed that Najib was personally implicated in the suit under the moniker 'Malaysian Official 1'. In the meantime, the prime minister – who claims the transfer was a political donation and denies any wrongdoing – has shut down Malaysian investigations, clamped down on media reporting and purged critics from his ruling party.

The public remains sceptical of Najib and the ruling Barisan Nasional (BN) coalition; for the past several years the Bersih movement (which calls for fair elections) has been organising protest rallies in KL and across the country. Tens of thousands have marched in the streets dressed in yellow T-shirts and tops, the colour of Bersih. At KL rallies in 2015 and 2016 they were joined by former prime minister Mahathir Mohamad, who has been vocal in his demands that Najib resign.

KL's Changing Skyline

At the southern end of Chinatown, the old Merdeka Park has been cleared and construction is under way on the controversial Merdeka PNB118 tower, which will rise up next to Stadium Merdeka and Stadium Negara by 2019 – at 682m, it will be Malaysia's tallest building. The estimated cost of the tower, slated to be the new headquarters of PNB (Malaysia's largest fund-management company and a key instrument in the government's pro-Malay affirmative-action policies), is RM5 billion, prompting accusations that the money would have been better spent on healthcare or education.

Meanwhile, the site of the former Pudu Prison is being redeveloped into the Bukit Bintang City Centre (BBCC) complex. The first phase, set to be complete by 2020, will include a mall (as if KL were short of them!) with a rooftop public park and concert hall, while plans to further develop the site involve the construction of an 80-storey signature tower by 2025.

Improving Public Transport

If one thing unites all KLites, it's their frustration with public transport. To address the problem the government is upgrading and integrating the mass rapid transit (MRT) system with the addition of three new lines, including a circular one that will span the KL–Klang Valley conurbation. The first new line – a link between Sungai Buloh and Kajang, 9.5km of which will be underground – will serve 400,000 passengers daily from early 2017.

River of Life

The MRT project is part of the government's expensive Economic Transformation Programme to make Malaysia a high-income nation by 2020. Another is the River of Life project, which involves transforming the Klang River from a polluted sinkhole into a clean and liveable waterfront, with parks and other beautification efforts.

The first phase of the project has centred on improvements in Chinatown, by widening pavements, brightening the streets with statues by local artists and improved signage, and pedestrianising Medan Pasar. The original steps down to the river behind Masjid Jamek have been uncovered and the area around the mosque and along the riverbank has been regenerated, with new pedestrian walkways, plazas and a bridge linking up to Merdeka Sq. Next up is the redevelopment of the riverbank south of Chinatown to Mid Valley, with pocket parks planned in the Brickfields area as well as cycle paths and bicycle-rental stations along the way.

if Kuala Lumpur were 100 people

46 would be Malay
43 would be Chinese
10 would be Indian
1 would be Other

belief systems
(% of population)

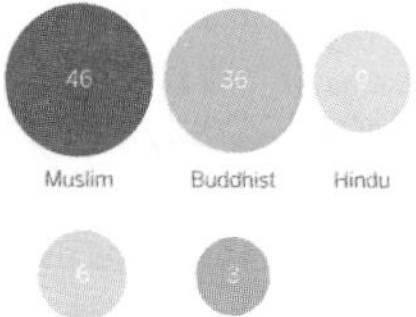

population per sq km

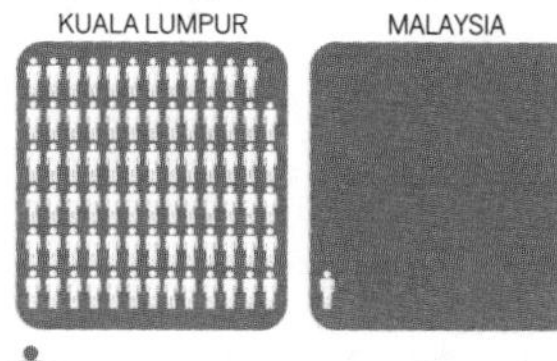

≈ 95 people

History

By the end of the 19th century, in less than 50 years Kuala Lumpur had grown from a jungle-bound mining settlement into the grand colonial capital of the Malay peninsula. It was here that British rule on the peninsula ended in 1957 and that the modern nation, Malaysia, was born in 1963. Though many government departments moved to Putrajaya in the 1990s, KL continues to function as the heart of Malaysia's economic, political and social life.

Compared with Indian Muslim traders, the Portuguese contributed little to Malay culture; attempts to introduce Christianity and the Portuguese language were never a big success, though a dialect of Portuguese, Kristang, is still spoken in Melaka and this is also where you'll find Malaysia's oldest functioning church.

The Melaka Empire

To understand how Kuala Lumpur came to be founded, it's important to go back four and a half centuries to when the seat of Malay power was Melaka. Legend has it that this great trading port was founded by Parameswara, a renegade Hindu prince-pirate from a little kingdom in southern Sumatra, who washed up around 1401 on the Malay coast. As a seafarer, Parameswara recognised a good port when he saw one and immediately lobbied the Ming emperor of China for protection from the Thais in exchange for generous trade deals. Thus the Chinese came to Malaysia.

Equidistant between India and China, Melaka became a major stop for freighters from India loaded with pepper and cloth, and junks from China loaded with porcelain and silks, which were traded for local metal and spices. Business boomed as regional ships and *perahu* (Malay-style sampans) arrived to take advantage of trading opportunities. The Melaka sultans soon ruled over the greatest empire in Malaysia's history, their territory including what is today Kuala Lumpur and the surrounding state of Selangor.

The Portuguese & Dutch Eras

In 1509, the death knell of the Melaka Sultanate was sounded by the arrival of the Portuguese. They laid siege to Melaka in 1511, capturing the city and driving the sultan and his forces back to Johor. Portuguese

TIMELINE

1826

Mohammed Shah becomes the third sultan of Selangor. During his reign, tin mines are opened at Ampang and the state is divided into five independently governed districts.

1857

Raja Abdullah and Raja Juma'at, nephews of Abdul Samad, fourth sultan of Selangor, sponsor an expedition of 87 Chinese miners up the Klang river to search for more tin.

1859

Chinese trader Hiu Siew is appointed the first Kapitan Cina (meaning Chinese captain) of the growing jungle settlement that had become known as Kuala Lumpur.

domination lasted 130 years, though the entire period was marked by skirmishes with local sultans.

Vying with the Portuguese for control of the spice trade, the Dutch formed an alliance with the sultans of Johor. A joint force of Dutch and Johor soldiers and sailors besieged Melaka in 1641 and wrested the city from the Portuguese.

Despite maintaining control of Melaka for about 150 years, the Dutch never fully realised the potential of the city. High taxes forced merchants to seek out other ports and the Dutch focused their main attention on Batavia (now Jakarta) as their regional headquarters.

It was the Dutch who brought in Muslim Bugis mercenaries from Sulawesi to establish the present hereditary sultanate in Selangor in 1740.

East India Company

British interest in the region began with the need for a halfway base for East India Company (EIC) ships plying the India–China maritime route. The first base was established on the island of Penang in 1786.

Meanwhile, events in Europe were conspiring to consolidate British interests on the Malay peninsula. When Napoleon overran the Netherlands in 1795, the British, fearing French influence in the region, took over Dutch Java and Melaka. When Napoleon was defeated in 1818, the British handed the Dutch colonies back.

The British lieutenant governor of Java, Stamford Raffles – yes, *that* Stamford Raffles – soon persuaded the EIC that a settlement south of the Malay peninsula was crucial to the India–China maritime route. In 1819 he landed in Singapore and negotiated a trade deal that saw the island ceded to Britain in perpetuity, in exchange for a significant cash tribute. In 1824, Britain and the Netherlands signed the Anglo-Dutch Treaty dividing the region into two distinct spheres of influence. The Dutch controlled what is now Indonesia, and the British controlled Penang, Melaka, Dinding and Singapore, which were soon combined to create the 'Straits Settlements'.

It's thought that the word Malay (or Melayu) is based on the ancient Tamil word *malia*, meaning hill. Other Malay words like *bahasa* (language), *raja* (ruler) and *jaya* (success) are Sanskrit terms imported to the area by Indian visitors as early as the 2nd century AD.

The Lure of Tin

Tin ore deposits had been mined in the interior of Selangor, certainly for decades and possibly for more than a century, before two nephews of the sultan of Selangor sponsored an expedition of 87 Chinese miners up the Klang river in 1857. Within a month all but 18 of the group were dead from malaria. However, sufficient tin was found around Ampang to encourage further parties of miners to follow. The jungle trading post where these prospectors alighted, at the meeting point of the Klang and Gombak rivers, was named Kuala Lumpur, meaning 'muddy confluence'.

1867

A war over the tax spoils of tin starts between Raja Abdullah, administrator of Klang, and Raja Mahadi. The war ends in 1874.

1869

Yap Ah Loy, commonly considered the founder of Kuala Lumpur, becomes third Kapitan Cina. When he dies in 1885 he owns a quarter of the city's buildings.

1880

Following the tin boom of 1879 and a swelling KL population, the British Resident in Selangor, Bloomfield Douglas, moves the state capital from Klang to Kuala Lumpur.

1882

Frank Swettenham becomes the new British Resident in KL and sets about rebuilding the city in brick following devastating fires and floods in 1881.

In 1858, traders Hiu Siew and Ah Sze set up shop in KL close to where the Central Market stands today. As more prospectors came to seek their fortunes, the backwater settlement quickly became a brawling, noisy, violent boom town, ruled by so-called 'secret societies', Chinese criminal gangs, and later *kongsi* (clan associations). In 1859, Hiu Siew, having proven himself adept in this fast-evolving world, was appointed by Raja Abdullah as the first Kapitan Cina (head of the Chinese community). Despite this precedent, it is Yap Ah Loy, the third of KL's six Kapitan Cinas, who is generally credited as the city's founder.

British Malaya

In Peninsular Malaya, Britain's policy of 'trade, not territory' was challenged when trade was disrupted by civil wars within the Malay sultanates of Negeri Sembilan, Selangor, Pahang and Perak. These wars were partly fought over the rights to collect export duties on the tin at Klang. In 1874 the British started to take political control by appointing British Residents in Perak and Selangor. The following year the same political expediency occurred in Negeri Sembilan and Pahang.

The civil wars laid waste to Kuala Lumpur, but thanks to Yap Ah Loy it soon bounced back: he reopened the shutdown tin mines and recruited thousands of miners to work them. By the end of the 1870s KL was back in business and booming to such an extent that the British were no longer content to leave its administration to the Kapitan Cina. In 1880, British Resident Bloomfield Douglas moved the state capital from

YAP AH LOY

He was only 17 when he left his village in southern China in search of work in Malaya. Fifteen years later, in 1868, Yap Ah Loy had shown sufficient political nous, organisational ability and street smarts to secure the role of KL's third Kapitan Cina. He took on the task with such ruthless relish that he's now credited as the founder of KL.

Yap's big break was being the friend of KL's second Kapitan Cina, Liu Ngim Kong. When Liu died in 1869, Yap took over and managed within a few years to gather enough power and respect to be considered the leader of the city's previously fractured Chinese community. According to legend, Yap was able to keep the peace with just six policemen, such was the respect for his authority.

Yap amassed great wealth through his control of the tin trade as well as more nefarious activities, such as opium trading and prostitution, which thrived in the mining boom town. He founded the city's first school in 1884 and, by the time he died a year later, was the richest man in KL. A short street in Chinatown is named after him and he is worshipped as a saint at the Sze Ya Temple, which he founded.

1888

State Treasurer Alfred Venning starts to lay out a botanical garden in the valley where a small stream is dammed to create a lake. Within a decade KL has its Lake Gardens.

1896

Perak, Selangor, Negeri Sembilan and Pahang join as Federated Malay States, with Kuala Lumpur as the capital. The sultans lose political power to British Residents.

1904

The rail link between KL and Port Swettenham (now Pelabuhan Klang) is completed. Lines are later extended to Ipoh, Penang and Singapore, making KL the region's rail hub.

1935

The British scrap the position of Resident General of the Federated States, decentralising its powers to the individual states, to discourage the creation of a united, self-governing country.

Klang to Kuala Lumpur and took up residence on the Bluff, the high ground west of the Klang river that flanked what was then a vegetable garden for the Chinese and which would later become the Padang, a sports field for the British.

F Spencer Chapman's memoir *The Jungle Is Neutral* relates the author's experience with a British guerrilla force based in the Malaysian jungles during the Japanese occupation of Malaya and Singapore.

Colonial KL

When Frank Swettenham, the third British Resident of Selangor, arrived to take up his post in 1882, KL was yet again in ruins following a major fire and a flood the previous year. He ruled that KL be rebuilt in brick, thus creating the Brickfields area, where the building blocks of the reborn colonial city were crafted. Swettenham also commissioned the country's first railway, linking the tin mines of KL with the port at Klang, later renamed Port Swettenham in his honour.

By 1886, scrappy, disease-ridden KL had morphed into one of the 'neatest and prettiest Chinese and Malay towns in the Colony or the States', according to Sir Frederick Weld, governor of the Straits Settlements. The city's most prestigious building – the Sultan Abdul Samad Building, housing the government offices – was completed in 1897, a year after KL had become the capital of the newly formed Federated Malay States of Negeri Sembilan, Pahang, Perak and Selangor.

The early 20th century saw the dawn of the age of the motorcar, and the subsequent global demand for rubber for tyres further improved KL's fortunes. Rubber plantations spread around the city and across the peninsula. City life improved, with amenities such as piped water and electricity coming online. Local Chinese millionaires such as Chua Cheng Bok and Loke Yew built grand mansions; the biggest would eventually become the old Istana Negara (National Palace) after WWII.

WWII

A few hours before the bombing of Pearl Harbor in December 1941, Japanese forces landed on the northeastern coast of Malaya. Within a few months they had taken over the entire peninsula and Singapore.

Although Britain quickly ceded Malaya and Singapore, this was more through poor strategy than through neglect. Many British soldiers were captured or killed and others stayed on and fought with the Malayan People's Anti-Japanese Army (MPAJA) in a jungle-based guerrilla war maintained throughout the occupation.

The Japanese achieved very little in Malaya. The British had destroyed most of the tin-mining equipment before their retreat, and the rubber plantations were neglected. However, Chinese Malaysians faced brutal persecution – the atrocities of the occupation were horrific even by the standards of WWII.

A History of Malaysia by Barbara and Leonard Andaya brilliantly explores the evolution of 'Malayness' in Malaysia's history and the challenges of building a multiracial, post-independence nation.

1941

Within a month of invading, the Japanese take KL and occupy the peninsula. The Chinese residents are badly treated and the city's economy stagnates for nearly four years.

1946

After public opposition to the proposed Malayan Union, the United Malays National Organisation (UMNO) forms, signalling a rising desire for political independence from Britain.

1948

Start of the Emergency, when the Malayan Communist Party (MCP) takes to the jungles and begins fighting a guerrilla war against the British that would last for 12 years.

1951

Sir Henry Gurney, British high commissioner to Malaya, is assassinated by MCP rebels, a terrorist act that alienates many moderate Chinese from the party.

The Japanese surrendered to the British in Singapore in 1945. Despite the eventual Allied victory, Britain had been humiliated by the easy loss of Malaya and Singapore to the Japanese, and it was clear that its days of controlling the region were numbered.

Revolusi '48 (http://revolusi48.blogspot.com, in Bahasa Malaysia), the sequel to Fahmi Reza's documentary *10 Tahun Sebelum Merdeka* (10 Years Before Merdeka), chronicles the largely forgotten armed revolution for national liberation launched against British colonial rule in Malaya in 1948.

Federation of Malaya

In 1946 the British persuaded the sultans to agree to the Malayan Union, which amalgamated all the Malay peninsula states into a central authority and came with the offer of citizenship for all residents regardless of race. In the process the sultans were reduced to the level of paid advisers, the system of special privileges for Malays was abandoned, and ultimate sovereignty passed to the king of England.

The normally acquiescent Malay population was less enthusiastic about the venture than the sultans. Rowdy protest meetings were held throughout the country, and the first Malay political party, the United Malays National Organisation (UMNO) was formed. This led to the dissolution of the Malayan Union and the creation of the Federation of Malaya in 1948, which reinstated the sovereignty of the sultans and the special privileges of the Malays.

The Emergency

While the creation of the Federation of Malaya appeased Malays, the Chinese felt betrayed, particularly after their massive contribution to the war effort. Many joined the Malayan Communist Party (MCP), which promised an equitable and just society. In 1948 the MCP took to the jungles and embarked on a 12-year guerrilla war against the British.

CREATING A MULTICULTURAL NATION

British rule radically altered the ethnic composition of Malaya. Chinese and Indian immigrant workers were brought into the country as they shared a similar economic agenda and had fewer nationalist grievances against the colonial administration than the native Malays, who were pushed from the cities to the countryside. The Chinese were encouraged to work the mines, the Tamil Indians to tap the rubber trees and build the railways, the Ceylonese to be clerks in the civil service, and the Sikhs to man the police force.

Even though 'better-bred' Malays were encouraged to join a separate arm of the civil service, there was growing resentment among the vast majority of Malays, who felt they were being marginalised in their own country. A 1931 census revealed that the Chinese numbered 1.7 million and the Malays 1.6 million. Malaya's economy was revolutionised, but the impact of this liberal immigration policy continues to reverberate today.

1953

Formation of Parti Perikatan (Alliance Party) between UMNO, the MCA and MIC. Two years later it wins 80% of the vote in Malaya's first national election.

1954

The Department of Aboriginal Affairs Malaysia is set up to protect the Orang Asli from modern encroachment and exploitation.

1957

On 31 August *merdeka* (independence) is declared in Malaya; Tunku Abdul Rahman becomes the first prime minister and the nine sultans agree to take turns as king.

1963

Malaysia comes into being in 1963 with the addition of Singapore and the British Borneo territories of Sabah and Sarawak; Brunei pulls out at the 11th hour, and Singapore is booted out in 1965.

Even though the insurrection was on par with the Malay civil wars of the 19th century, it was classified as an 'emergency' for insurance purposes.

The effects of the Emergency were felt most strongly in the countryside, where villages and plantation owners were repeatedly targeted by rebels. In 1951 the British high commissioner was assassinated on the road to Fraser's Hill. His successor, General Sir Gerald Templer, set out to win the hearts and minds of the people. Almost 500,000 rural Chinese were resettled into protected 'new villages', restrictions were lifted on guerrilla-free areas and the jungle-dwelling Orang Asli were brought into the fight to help the police track down the insurgents.

In 1960 the Emergency was declared over, although sporadic fighting continued and the formal surrender was signed only in 1989.

Noel Barber's *War of the Running Dogs* is a classic account of the 12-year Malayan Emergency. The title refers to what the communist fighters called the opposition who were loyal to the British.

Merdeka & Malaysia

Malaysia's march to independence from British rule was led by UMNO, which formed a strategic alliance with the Malayan Chinese Association (MCA) and the Malayan Indian Congress (MIC). The new Alliance Party, led by Tunku Abdul Rahman, won a landslide victory in the 1955 election. At midnight on 31 August 1957 *merdeka* (independence) was declared in a highly symbolic ceremony held at the Padang in KL; the Union flag was lowered and the Malayan flag hoisted.

In 1961 Tunku Abdul Rahman proposed a merger of Singapore, Malaya, Sabah and Sarawak. But when modern Malaysia was born in July 1963 it immediately faced a diplomatic crisis. The Philippines broke off relations, claiming that Sabah was part of its territory (a claim upheld to this day), while Indonesia laid claim to the whole of Borneo, invading parts of Sabah and Sarawak before finally giving up its claim in 1966.

The marriage between Singapore and Malaya was also doomed from the start. Ethnic Chinese outnumbered Malays in both Malaysia and Singapore and the new ruler of the island state, Lee Kuan Yew, refused to extend constitutional privileges to the Malays in Singapore. Riots broke out in Singapore in 1964 and in August 1965 Tunku Abdul Rahman was forced to boot Singapore out of the federation.

1957–2007 Chronicle of Malaysia, edited by Philip Mathews, is a beautifully designed book showcasing 50 years of the country's history in news stories and pictures.

13 May 1969

As the 1960s progressed, impoverished Malays became increasingly resentful of the economic success of Chinese Malaysians, while the Chinese grew resentful of the political privileges granted to Malays. The situation reached breaking point when the Malay-dominated government attempted to suppress all languages except Malay and introduced a national policy of education that ignored Chinese and Indian history, language and culture.

1969

Following the general election, on 13 March a race riot erupts in KL, killing hundreds. A national emergency is declared and parliament is suspended as KL is put under curfew.

1971

Parliament convenes and the New Economic Policy (NEP) is introduced, with the aim of putting 30% of Malaysia's corporate wealth in the hands of Malays within 20 years.

1974

After the sultan of Selangor cedes Kuala Lumpur to the state, making it a federal territory, KL citizens lose representation in the Selangor State Legislative Assembly.

1976

Hussein Onn becomes Malaysia's third prime minister following the death of Abdul Razak. His period of office is marked by efforts to foster unity between Malaysia's disparate communities.

In the 1969 general election, the Alliance Party lost its two-thirds majority in national parliament and tied for control of Selangor state with the opposition, made up of the Democratic Action Party (DAP) and Gerakan (The People's Movement). On 13 May, a black day etched in the city's collective memory, at an UMNO-organised post-election meeting in Kuala Lumpur, Chinese onlookers were said to have taunted those in attendance. The Malays retaliated and the situation quickly flared into a full-scale riot, which Malay gangs used as a pretext to loot Chinese businesses, killing hundreds of Chinese in the process.

Dr Mahathir Mohamad's first book, *The Malay Dilemma*, in which he postulated that Malay backwardness was due to hereditary and cultural factors, was banned in 1970.

A curfew was immediately imposed on KL and a state of emergency was announced; parliament was suspended for two years. Stunned by the savagery of the riots, the government decided that if there was ever going to be harmony between the races, the Malay community needed to achieve economic parity. To this end the New Economic Policy (NEP), a socio-economic affirmative-action plan, was introduced.

The Alliance Party invited opposition parties to join it and work from within. The expanded coalition was renamed the Barisan Nasional (BN; National Front), which continues to rule Malaysia to this day.

Enter Mahathir

In 1981 former UMNO member Mahathir Mohamad became prime minister. Under his watch Malaysia's economy went into overdrive, growing from one based on commodities such as rubber to one firmly rooted in industry and manufacturing. Government monopolies were privatised, and heavy industries such as steel manufacturing (a failure) and the Malaysian car (successful but heavily protected) were encouraged. Multinationals were successfully wooed to set up in Malaysia, and manufactured exports began to dominate the trade figures.

Amir Muhammad's 2009 documentary *Malaysian Gods* commemorates the decade since the *reformasi* movement began in 1998 with the sacking of Anwar Ibrahim as deputy prime minister.

During Mahathir's premiership the main media outlets became little more than government mouthpieces. The sultans lost their right to give final assent on legislation, and the once proudly independent judiciary appeared to become subservient to government wishes, the most notorious case being that of Mahathir's former heir apparent Anwar Ibrahim. Mahathir also permitted widespread use of the *Internal Security Act* (ISA) to silence opposition leaders and social activists, most famously in 1987's Operation Lalang, during which 106 people were arrested and the publishing licences of several newspapers were revoked.

Economic & Political Crisis

In 1997, after a decade of near-constant 10% growth, Malaysia was hit by the regional currency crisis. Characteristically, Mahathir blamed it all on unscrupulous Western speculators deliberately undermining the

1981

Dr Mahathir Mohamad becomes prime minister and introduces policies of 'Buy British Last' and 'Look East', in which the country strives to emulate Japan, South Korea and Taiwan.

1987

The police launch Operation Lalang (Operation Weeding), arresting 106 activists and opposition leaders under the *Internal Security Act* (ISA).

1995

Mahathir announces the construction of a new administrative capital, Putrajaya, as part of a Multimedia Super Corridor stretching from KL to the new international airport at Sepang.

1998

After six years of planning and construction, the Petronas Towers officially open. The twin towers hold the title of tallest building in the world until 2004.

BUMIPUTRA PRIVILEGES

When it was introduced in 1971, the aim of the New Economic Policy (NEP) was that 30% of Malaysia's corporate wealth should be in the hands of indigenous Malays – *bumiputra* ('princes of the land') – within 20 years. A massive campaign of positive discrimination began and handed majority control over the army, police, civil service and government to Malays. The rules extended to education, scholarships, share deals, corporate management and even the right to import a car.

By 1990 *bumiputra* corporate wealth had risen to 19% but was still 11% short of the original target. Poverty in general fell dramatically, a new Malay middle class emerged and nationalist violence by Malay extremists receded. However, cronyism and discrimination against Indians and Chinese increased, while Malays still account for three in four of the poorest people in the country.

Affirmative action in favour of *bumiputra* continues today, but there is growing recognition that it is hampering rather than helping Malaysia.

economies of the developing world for their personal gain. He pegged the Malaysian ringgit to the US dollar, implemented policies that were widely interpreted as bailing out politically connected companies, forced banks to merge and made it difficult for foreign investors to remove their money from Malaysia's stock exchange. Malaysia's subsequent recovery from the economic crisis, which was more rapid than that of many other Southeast Asian nations, further bolstered Mahathir's prestige.

At odds with Mahathir over how to deal with the economic crisis had been his deputy prime minister, Anwar Ibrahim. Their falling-out was so severe that in September 1998 Anwar was not only sacked but also charged with corruption and sodomy. Many Malaysians, feeling that Anwar had been falsely arrested, took to the streets chanting Anwar's call for '*reformasi*'. The demonstrations were harshly quelled and, in trials that were widely criticised as unfair, Anwar was sentenced to a total of 15 years' imprisonment. The international community rallied around Anwar, with Amnesty International proclaiming him a prisoner of conscience.

BN felt the impact in the following year's general election, when it suffered huge losses, particularly in the rural Malay areas. The gainers were the fundamentalist Islamic Parti Islam se-Malaysia (PAS), which had vociferously supported Anwar, and a new political party, Keadilan (People's Justice Party), headed by Anwar's wife, Wan Azizah.

Abdullah Badawi's Premiership

Mahathir's successor, Abdullah Badawi, led BN to a landslide victory in the 2004 election. In stark contrast to his feisty predecessor, the

2003

Having announced his resignation the previous year, Dr Mahathir steps down as prime minister in favour of Abdullah Badawi. He remains very outspoken on national policies.

2004

A month after the election in which BN takes 199 of 219 seats in the lower house of parliament, Anwar Ibrahim sees his sodomy conviction overturned and is released from prison.

2007

As the country celebrates 50 years since independence it is also shaken by two anti-government rallies in November, in which tens of thousands of protestors take to the streets of KL.

2009

In April, Najib Razak succeeds Abdullah Badawi as prime minister; the 1Malaysia policy is introduced to build respect and trust between the country's different races.

pious Abdullah impressed voters by taking a nonconfrontational, consensus-seeking approach. He set up a royal commission to investigate corruption in the police force and called time on several of the massively expensive mega-projects that had been the hallmark of the Mahathir era.

Released from jail in 2004, Anwar returned to national politics in August 2008 on winning the by-election for the seat vacated by his wife. However, sodomy charges were again laid against the politician in June and he was arrested in July.

In the March 2008 election, BN saw their parliamentary dominance slashed to less than the customary two-thirds majority. Pakatan Rakyat (PR), the opposition People's Alliance, led by Anwar Ibrahim, not only bagged 82 of parliament's 222 seats but also took control of four out of Malaysia's 13 states, including the key economic bases of Selangor and Penang. PR subsequently lost Perak following a complex power play between various defecting MPs.

Abdullah Badawi resigned in favour of his urbane deputy, Mohd Najib bin Tun Abdul Razak (typically referred to as Najib Razak), in April 2009. Son of Abdul Razak, Malaysia's second prime minister after independence, and nephew of Razak's successor Hussein Onn, Najib has been groomed for this role ever since he first entered national politics at the age of 23 in 1976.

MALAYSIA'S GOVERNMENT

Malaysia is made up of 13 states and three federal territories (Kuala Lumpur, Pulau Labuan and Putrajaya). Each state has an assembly and government headed by a *menteri besar* (chief minister). Nine states have hereditary rulers (sultans), while the remaining four have government-appointed governors, as do the federal territories. In a pre-established order, every five years one of the sultans takes his turn in the ceremonial position of Yang di-Pertuan Agong (king).

Malaysia's current prime minister is Najib Razak, who heads the Barisan Nasional (BN) coalition of the United Malays National Organisation (UMNO) and 13 other parties. The official opposition, Pakatan Rakyat (PR), is a coalition between Parti Keadilan Rakyat (PKR), the Democratic Action Party (DAP) and Parti Islam se-Malaysia (PAS); the opposition leader is Anwar Ibrahim. All sit in a two-house parliament: a 70-member Senate (Dewan Negara; 26 members are elected by the 13 state assemblies and 44 members are appointed by the king on the prime minister's recommendation) and a 222-member House of Representatives (Dewan Rakyat; elected from single-member districts). National and state elections are held every five years.

2011

The first of the rallies organised by the civil-rights organisation Bersih brings tens of thousands of people onto the streets of central KL in support of free and fair elections.

2012

In January a second set of sodomy charges against opposition leader Anwar Ibrahim are thrown out of court. In April, another Bersih rally in KL is violently broken up by police.

2013

General elections in May see BN hold onto power at the national level but fail to recapture Selangor from governance by the opposition coalition Pakatan Rakyat (PR).

2014

Malaysia suffers a double blow as Malaysia Airlines flight MH370 goes missing in March, and flight MH17 is shot down over Ukraine in July.

Life in Kuala Lumpur

The following provides an insight into how KLites go about their daily lives at work, home and play. Routines will differ slightly according to ethnicity and adherence to traditional cultural values, but these very differences – and the general acceptance of them – are what make KL such an appealing and cosmopolitan metropolis.

A City of Immigrants

The birth of KL coincided with an influx of Chinese immigrants, mainly Hakka and Hokien. They were followed by Cantonese, Swatow, Hainanese and, from India and the subcontinent, Tamils, Punjabis, Bengalis, Sikhs, Sinhalese and more, each bringing with them their own dialects and customs. What they all shared was a desire to build a new and more prosperous life.

That process is ongoing. KL continues to be a magnet for economic migrants from Malaysia and across the region (in particular Pakistan, Bangladesh, Indonesia, Nepal and Myanmar). Wander around Chinatown on a Sunday or Bukit Bintang on any night of the week and it's almost as if you've touched down in a convention of the United Nations.

For all the city's seeming harmony, underlying ethnic and religious tensions are a fact of life: many KLites openly acknowledge the lack of integration between the principal Malay, Chinese and Indian communities. There are also worries that Malaysia's tolerant brand of Islam is becoming more conservative, impacting the lives of KLites across the board.

Many of the people you'll encounter in KL don't actually live here: of the Greater KL/Klang Valley population of around six million, only 1.6 million live within the city boundaries; the rest are residents of satellite cities such as Petaling Jaya (PJ).

Daily Routine

Performance of religious rites – lighting incense sticks or a ghee candle for an altar, or kneeling in the direction of Mecca to pray – may be the individual response to the dawn of the day. Such differences aside, there are similarities that can be observed in the daily routines of all KLites.

Our average Mr or Ms KL, engaged in an office job, may leave their home (most likely in Petaling Jaya (PJ) or elsewhere in the Klang Valley) early – say around 7am – to avoid the worst of the morning rush of traffic into the city. Until public transport improves, they are wedded to their car as their primary means of transport.

Having reached the city, they will drop by a street stall to pick up a triangular packet of *nasi lemak* (rice boiled in coconut milk) for breakfast, along with a plastic bag filled with *teh tarik*, the milky sweet tea of choice. This can be consumed in the office but, should they prefer not to have crumbs on their desk, there's always a nearby *kopitiam* (coffee shop) serving a zingy *kopi-o* (black coffee with sugar) and *kaya* (coconut-cream jam) toast as a breakfast alternative or mid-morning snack.

While they may well flick through a daily newspaper such as the *Star*, most KLites approach the old-school, government-linked media with scepticism, preferring to get their news from trusted online sources

Expat Resources

Angloinfo (*http://kualalumpur.angloinfo.com*)

Expat Go (*www.expatgomalaysia.com*)

Expatriate Lifestyle (*www.expatriatelifestyle.com*)

such as Malaysiakini (www.malaysiakini.com). They love their blogs, too – both reading and writing them – so don't be surprised to find your neighbour at the *kopitiam* Instagramming their meal and adding a review for the online community.

If you're beginning to get the idea that eating drives the daily routine, then you're absolutely right. Every snacking opportunity is taken, right up to late-night supper with your mates at the local *mamak* (Indian Muslim food stall). And, if your average KLite is savvy, they'll hang on in the city until well after rush hour before attempting the commute home – especially if the heavens have opened, bringing traffic on the federal highways to a frustrating crawl.

'The Chinese do the work, the Malays take the credit, and the Indians get the blame.' A line from Huzir Sulaiman's satirical play *Atomic Jaya* sums up a commonly held belief among KLites.

Work

The most important change in the social structure of Malaysia (and by extension KL) has been the rise of the Malay community since independence. Following the riots of 1969, the New Economic Policy (NEP) was introduced. This program of positive discrimination was designed to bring marginalised Malays and Orang Asli – known collectively as *bumiputra* – into the political and economic mainstream. Although not wholly successful, after 40 years the result in KL is that the vast majority of government and government-affiliated jobs are held by Malays, who make up most of the police force, army, civil service and parliament.

With ambitious and talented Chinese and Indian Malaysians shut out of the best public-sector roles, these communities have tended to

TALKING THE TALK

As a federation of former British colonies, Malaysia is a fantastic country to visit for English speakers, but linguists will be pleased to tackle the region's multitude of other languages. Malaysia's national language is Bahasa Malaysia. This is often a cause of confusion for travellers, who logically give a literal translation to the two words and refer to the 'Malaysian language'. In fact you cannot speak 'Malaysian'; the language is Malay.

Other languages commonly spoken in the region include Tamil, Hokkien, Cantonese and Mandarin, but there are also Chinese dialects, various other Indian and Orang Asli languages and even, in Melaka, a form of 16th-century Portuguese known as Kristang. All Malaysians speak Malay, and many are fluent in at least two other languages.

Even if you stick to English, you'll have to get used to the local patois – Manglish – which includes plenty of Mandarin, Cantonese and Tamil words and phrases. Many words are used solely to add emphasis and have no formal meaning, which can make things a little confusing. Used incorrectly, Manglish can come across as quite rude, so listen carefully and take local advice before trying it out in polite company. To get you started, here are a few of the most common Manglish words and expressions:

Ah Suffix used for questions, eg 'Why late, ah?'

Got Used for all tenses of the verb 'to have' or in place of 'there is/are' eg 'Got money, ah?' and 'Got noodles in the soup.'

Lah Very common suffix used to affirm statements, eg 'Don't be stupid lah!'

Le Used to soften orders, eg 'Give le.'

Liao Used similarly to 'already', eg 'Finished liao.'

Lor Used for explanations, eg 'Just is lor.'

Meh An expression of skepticism, eg 'Really meh.'

One Adds emphasis to the end of a sentence, eg 'That car so fast one.'

Ready Another form of 'already', eg 'No thanks, eat ready.'

thrive in the private sector, in particular retail and property development. As it's the nation's capital, there's almost every other type of economic activity in KL, barring major heavy industry (which can still be found nearby in the Klang Valley). Finance, banking – KL is a major hub for Islamic financing – and the oil and gas business are all key, alongside tourism, education and healthcare.

The online community magazine Poskod (http://poskod.my) has interesting features on KL's cultural and social life. It also promotes grassroots campaigns and has its own project, BetterKL, to improve urban living.

Home Life

One of the most remarkable aspects of KL is the diversity of living areas that are crammed into its 243 sq km. The old heart of the city around Chinatown and Masjid Jamek is compact and relatively low-rise compared to the condominium tower blocks springing up across Bukit Bintang and around the KLCC mall. Further out of the centre are the affluent residential areas of Ampang, Bangsar, Damansara Heights, Mont Kiara and Sri Hartamas. Less-wealthy KLites might live in outlying areas such as Cheras or Setapak. There are even typical Malay *kampung* (villages) within the city limits, such as Sungai Penchala.

KL has the country's most expensive housing, with average house prices of more than RM700,000. The cost of renting a one-bedroom apartment in central KL is around RM2000 a month. With average monthly salaries around RM3000, it's easy to see why many young people have little choice but to remain living at home with their parents or to spend long hours commuting from more affordable areas in the Klang Valley.

Play

Eating out is *the* much-loved local pastime. Bar culture certainly exists, but Islam also means that an average KLite's night out on the town is as likely to be spent in a cafe nursing a bubble tea or cappuccino as quaffing beers and cocktails.

KL malls are popular one-stop destinations not just for their dining and shopping possibilities but also for leisure activities such as bowling, cinema-going, browsing art exhibitions, ice skating and even rock climbing.

For a weekend break, locals are likely to hop in their cars for a trip to the family *kampung*, Melaka or Ipoh for the food, or Port Dickson on the coast of Negeri Sembilan for the beach. Cheap flights with the likes of AirAsia and other budget carriers mean a quick trip to Penang or Singapore – other major foodie destinations – could also be on the agenda.

One of the aims of the federal government's Economic Transformation Programme is to have KL rank among the top 20 cities in the world in terms of economic growth and liveability by 2020.

Multiculturalism, Religion & Culture

Since the interracial riots of 1969, when distrust between the Malays and Chinese peaked, Malaysia has forged a more tolerant multicultural society. Though ethnic loyalties remain strong, the emergence of a single 'Malaysian' identity is now a much-discussed and lauded concept, even if it is far from being actually realised. Religious and ethnic tensions are a fact of life, particularly in KL, where the different communities coexist rather than mingle. Intermarriage is rare and education is still largely split along ethnic lines.

Government economic policies since the early 1970s have favoured Malays, thus helping defuse this community's fear and resentment of Chinese economic dominance. The cost has been Chinese and Indian Malaysians becoming second-class citizens in a country where they also have roots stretching back generations.

The Ethnic Mix

There are distinct cultural differences between Malaysia's three main ethnic communities – Malays, Chinese and Indians. There are also the Peranakan (Straits Chinese) and other mixed-race communities to take into account, alongside older aboriginal nations – the Orang Asli of Peninsular Malaysia – comprising scores of different tribal groups and speaking well over 100 languages and dialects.

KL has always been a city of immigrants, and it continues to be so: there are communities of Indonesians and Thais (many of whom live in the Kampung Baru), as well as Pakistanis, Bangladeshis, Nepalis and citizens of Myanmar (Burma), some of whom are refugees. People from the Middle East have also settled here. The Western expat population is relatively small in comparison.

The Malays

All Malays, Muslims by birth, are supposed to follow Islam, but many also adhere to older spiritual beliefs and adat. With its roots in the Hindu period, adat is customary law that places great emphasis on collective responsibility and maintaining harmony within the community – almost certainly a factor in the general goodwill between the different ethnic groups in Malaysia.

The enduring appeal of the communal *kampung* (village) spirit shouldn't be underestimated – many an urban Malay hankers after it, despite the affluent Western-style living conditions they enjoy at home. In principle, villagers are of equal status, though a headman is appointed on the basis of his wealth, greater experience or spiritual knowledge. Traditionally, the founder of the village was appointed village leader (*penghulu* or ketua kampung) and often members of the same family would also become leaders. A *penghulu* is usually a haji, one who has made the pilgrimage to Mecca.

The Muslim religious leader, the imam, holds a position of great importance in the community as the keeper of Islamic knowledge and the leader of prayer, but even educated urban Malaysians periodically turn to *pawang* (shamans who possess a supernatural knowledge of harvests and nature) or *bomoh* (spiritual healers with knowledge of curative plants and the ability to harness the power of the spirit world) for advice before making any life-changing decisions.

The Chinese

Religious customs govern much of the Chinese community's home life, from the moment of birth, which is carefully recorded for astrological consultations later in life, to funerals, which also have many rites and rituals. It is common to see Malaysian Chinese wafting sticks of incense outside their homes and businesses. There's also a strong attachment to the original area of China from where a family originated, seen in the attachment of families to specific temples or *kongsi* (clan houses).

The Chinese, who started arriving in the region in the early 15th century, came mostly from the southern Chinese province of Fujian and eventually formed one-half of the group known as Peranakans. They developed their own distinct hybrid culture, whereas later settlers, from Guangdong and Hainan provinces, stuck more closely to the culture of their homelands, including keeping their dialects.

If there's one cultural aspect that all Malaysian Chinese agree on it's the importance of education. It has been a very sensitive subject among the Malaysian Chinese community since the attempt in the 1960s to phase out secondary schools in which Chinese was the medium of teaching, and the introduction in the early 1970s of government policies that favour Malays. The constraining of educational opportunities within Malaysia for the ethnic Chinese has resulted in many families working doubly hard to afford the tuition fees needed to send their offspring to private schools within the country and to overseas institutions.

The Malay surname is the child's father's first name. This is why Malaysians will use your given name after Mr or Ms; to use your surname would be to address your father.

The Indians

Indians in Malaysia hail from many parts of the subcontinent and have different cultures depending on their religions – mainly Hinduism, Islam, Sikhism and Christianity. Most are Tamils, originally coming from the area now known as Tamil Nadu in southern India, where Hindu traditions are strong. Later, Muslim Indians from northern India followed, along with Sikhs. These religious affiliations dictate many of the home-life customs and practices of Malaysian Indians, although one celebration that all Hindus and much of Malaysia takes part in is Deepavali.

A small, English-educated Indian elite has always played a prominent role in Malaysian society, and a significant merchant class exists. However, a large percentage of Indians – imported as indentured labourers by the British – remain a poor working class.

The Orang Asli

The indigenous people of Malaysia – known collectively as Orang Asli – played an important role in early trade, teaching the colonialists about forest products and guiding prospectors to outcrops of tin and precious metals. They also acted as scouts and guides for anti-insurgent forces during the Emergency in the 1950s.

Despite this, the Orang Asli remain marginalised in Malaysia. According to the most recent government data, published in December 2004, Peninsular Malaysia has just under 150,000 Orang Asli (Original People), and 80% live below the poverty line – compared with an 8.5% national average. The tribes are generally classified into three groups: the Negrito, the Senoi, and the Proto-Malays, who are subdivided into 18 tribes, the smallest being the Orang Kanak, with just 87 members. There are dozens of tribal languages and most Orang Asli follow animist beliefs, though there are vigorous attempts to convert them to Islam.

Orang Asli Sights

Muzium Orang Asli (p114), Gombak

Orang Asli Craft Museum (p98), Kuala Lumpur

Mah Meri Cultural Village (p121), Pulau Carey

Since 1939 Orang Asli concerns have been represented and managed by a succession of government departments, the latest iteration being JAKOA, an acronym for Jabatan Kemajuan Orang Asli (Orang Asli Development Department), which came into being in 2011.

In the past, Orang Asli land rights have often not been recognised, and when logging, agricultural or infrastructure projects require their land, their claims are generally regarded as illegal. The current government has yet to adopt a different approach. Between 2010 and 2012 the Human Rights Commission of Malaysia (SUHAKAM) conducted a national enquiry into the land rights of indigenous peoples and made various recommendations. This was followed up by a government task force to study the findings and look at implementing the recommendations. The report was presented to government in September 2014, but two years later the government was yet to respond.

Religion

Peninsular Malaysia was Buddhist and Hindu for a thousand years before the local rulers adopted Islam. Today Islam is the state religion of Malaysia, and freedom of religion is guaranteed by the nation's constitution. The various Chinese religions are also strongly entrenched. Christianity has a presence, but it's never been strong in Peninsular Malaysia. About the only major religion you won't come across is Judaism.

Islam

The religion is believed to have spread through contact with Indian Muslim traders and it gained such respect that by the mid-15th century the third ruler of Melaka, Maharaja Mohammed Shah (r 1424–44), had converted. His son Mudzaffar Shah took the title of sultan and made Is-

THE PERANAKANS

Peranakan means 'half-caste' in Malay, which is exactly what the Peranakans are: descendants of Chinese immigrants who from the 16th century onwards settled principally in Singapore, Melaka and Penang and married Malay women.

The culture and language of the Peranakans is a fascinating melange of Chinese and Malay traditions. The Peranakans took the name and religion of their Chinese fathers, but the customs, language and dress of their Malay mothers. They also used the terms Straits-born or Straits Chinese to distinguish themselves from later arrivals from China.

Another name you may hear for these people is Baba-Nonyas, after the Peranakan words for men *(baba)* and women *(nonya)*. The Peranakans were often wealthy traders who could afford to indulge their passions for sumptuous furnishings, jewellery and brocades. Their terrace houses were brightly painted, with patterned tiles embedded in the walls for extra decoration. When it came to the interiors, Peranakan tastes favoured heavily carved and inlaid furniture.

Peranakan dress was similarly ornate. Women wore fabulously embroidered *kasot manek* (beaded slippers) and *kebaya* (blouses worn over a sarong), tied with beautiful *kerasong* (brooches), usually of fine filigree gold or silver. Men – who assumed Western dress in the 19th century, reflecting their wealth and their contacts with the British – saved their finery for important occasions such as the wedding ceremony, a highly stylised and intricate ritual dictated by adat (Malay customary law).

The Peranakan patois is a Malay dialect but one containing many Hokkien words – so much so that it is largely unintelligible to a Malay speaker. The Peranakans also included words and expressions from English and French, and occasionally used a form of backward Malay by reversing the syllables.

lam the state religion. With its global trade links, Melaka became a hub for the dissemination of Islam and the Malay language across the region.

The Malay strain of Islam is not like Arabia's more orthodox Islamic traditions. It absorbed rather than conquered existing beliefs, and was adopted peacefully by Malaysia's coastal trading ports. Islamic sultanates replaced Hindu kingdoms – though the Hindu concept of kings remained – and the Hindu traditions of adat continued despite the dominance of Islamic law. Malay ceremonies and beliefs still exhibit pre-Islamic traditions, but most Malays are ardent Muslims – to suggest otherwise would cause great offence.

With the rise of Islamic fundamentalism, calls to introduce Islamic law and purify the practices of Islam have increased; yet, while the federal government of Malaysia is keen to espouse Muslim ideals, it is wary of religious extremism.

Key Beliefs & Practices

Most Malaysian Muslims are Sunnis, but all Muslims share a common belief in the Five Pillars of Islam:

Shahadah (the declaration of faith) 'There is no God but Allah; Mohammed is his Prophet.'

Salat (prayer) Ideally five times a day, in which the muezzin (prayer leader) calls the faithful to prayer from the minarets of every mosque.

Zakat (tax) Usually taking the form of a charitable donation.

Sawm (fasting) Includes observing the fasting month of Ramadan.

Hajj (pilgrimage to Mecca) Every Muslim aspires to do the hajj at least once in their lifetime.

Muslim dietary laws forbid alcohol, pork and all pork-based products. Restaurants where it's OK for Muslims to dine will be clearly labelled 'halal'; this is a stricter definition than places that label themselves simply 'pork free'.

A radical Islamic movement has not taken serious root in Malaysia, but religious conservatism has grown over recent years. For foreign visitors, the most obvious sign of this is the national obsession with propriety, which extends to newspaper polemics on female modesty and raids by the police on 'immoral' public establishments, which can include clubs and bars where Muslims may be drinking.

More Muslim women wear the hijab (a head covering also known regionally as the *tudong*) today than, say, 20 years ago. In 2011 a young Muslim filmmaker, Norhayati Kaprawi, made the documentary *Siapa Aku?* (Who Am I?), which examines some of the reasons behind this, interviewing a spectrum of Malaysian women from across the country.

Islam in Malaysia: Perceptions & Facts, by Dr Mohd Asri Zainul Abidin, the former Mufti of Perlis, is a collection of articles on aspects of the faith as practised in Malaysia.

Islamic Festivals

Ramadan The high point of the Islamic festival calendar, Ramadan is when Muslims fast from sunrise to sunset. It always occurs in the ninth month of the Muslim calendar and lasts between 29 and 30 days, based on sightings of the moon. The start of Ramadan moves forward 11 days every year, in line with the Muslim lunar calendar. Fifteen days before the start of Ramadan, on Nisfu Night, it is believed the souls of the dead visit their homes. On Laylatul Qadr (Night of Grandeur), during Ramadan, Muslims celebrate the arrival of the Quran on earth, before its revelation by the Prophet Mohammed.

Hari Raya Aidilfitri Hari Raya marks the end of the month-long fast, with two days of joyful celebration and feasting – this is *the* major holiday of the Muslim calendar.

Mawlid al-Nabi Usually in March and celebrating the birth of the Prophet Mohammed.

Hari Raya Haji A two-day festival usually in November marking the successful completion of the hajj – the pilgrimage to Mecca – and commemorating the willingness of the Prophet Ibrahim (the biblical Abraham) to sacrifice his son. Many shops, offices and tourist attractions close and locals consume large amounts of cakes and sweets.

Awal Muharram The Muslim New Year, which falls in November or December.

Chinese Religions

The Chinese communities in Malaysia usually follow a mix of Buddhism, Confucianism and Taoism. Buddhism takes care of the afterlife, Confucianism looks after the political and moral aspects of life, and Taoism contributes animistic beliefs to teach people to maintain harmony with the universe.

But to say that the Chinese have three religions is too simplistic a view of their traditional religious life. At the first level Chinese religion is animistic, with a belief in the innate vital energy in rocks, trees, rivers and springs. At the second level people from the distant past, both real and mythological, are worshipped as gods. Overlaid on this are popular Taoist, Mahayana Buddhist and Confucian beliefs.

On a day-to-day level most Chinese are much less concerned with the high-minded philosophies and asceticism of the Buddha, Confucius or Lao Zi than they are with the pursuit of worldly success, the appeasement of the dead and the spirits, and seeking knowledge about the future. Chinese religion incorporates elements of what Westerners might call 'superstition' – if you want your fortune told, for instance, you go to a temple. The other thing to remember is that Chinese religion is polytheistic. Apart from the Buddha, Lao Zi and Confucius, there are many divinities, such as house gods, and gods and goddesses for particular professions.

The most popular Chinese gods and *shen* (local deities) are Kuan Yin, the goddess of mercy; Kuan Ti, the god of war and wealth; and Toh Peh Kong, a local deity representing the spirit of the pioneers and found only outside China.

Hinduism

Hinduism in the region dates back at least 1500 years, and there are Hindu influences in cultural traditions, such as *wayang kulit* (shadow-puppet theatre) and the wedding ceremony. However, it is only in the last 100 years or so, following the influx of Indian contract labourers and settlers, that it has again become widely practised. Hinduism has three basic practices: puja (worship), the cremation of the dead, and the rules and regulations of the caste system. Although still very strong in India, the caste system was never significant in Malaysia, mainly because the labourers brought here from India were mostly from the lower classes.

Hinduism has a vast pantheon of deities, although the one omnipresent god usually has three physical representations: Brahma, the creator; Vishnu, the preserver; and Shiva, the destroyer or reproducer. All three gods are usually shown with four arms, but Brahma has the added advantage of four heads to represent his all-seeing presence.

Animism

The animist religions of Malaysia's indigenous peoples are as diverse as the peoples themselves. While animism does not have a rigid system of tenets or codified beliefs, it can be said that animists perceive natural phenomena to be animated by various spirits or deities, and a complex system of practices is used to propitiate these spirits.

Ancestor worship is also a common feature of animist societies; departed souls are considered to be intermediaries between this world and the next.

Religious Issues

Freedom of Religion?

Islam is Malaysia's state religion, which has an impact on the cultural and social life of the country at several levels. Government institutions and banks, for example, are closed for two hours at lunchtime on Friday to allow Muslims to attend Friday prayers.

Government censors, with Islamic sensitivities in mind, dictate what can be performed on public stages or screened in cinemas. This has led to Beyoncé cancelling her shows when asked to adhere to strict guidelines on dress and performance style, and to the banning of movies such as *Schindler's List* and *Babe* – the themes of Jews being saved from the Holocaust and a cute pig star are not to Muslim tastes. In 2008, Malaysia's leading Islamic council issued an edict against yoga, fearing the exercises could corrupt Muslims.

Malaysian politicians have been known to call in a *bomoh* (a traditional spiritual healer and spirit medium) during election campaigns to assist in their strategy and provide some foresight.

Sharia law (Islamic law) is the preserve of state governments, as is the establishment of Muslim courts of law, which since 1988 cannot be overruled by secular courts. This has had a negative impact on Muslims wishing to change their religion and divorced parents who cannot agree on a religion by which to raise their children. The end result is that Malaysian Muslims who change their religion or practise no faith at all hardly ever make their choice public.

Those who do, such as Lina Joy, a Malay convert to Christianity, face insurmountable difficulties. After battling for nine years through the legal system, Ms Joy failed in 2007 to be allowed to have her choice of religion recognised on her identity card. Malaysia's high court ruled that she first needed permission from the *syariah* court – an institution that would treat her action as apostasy to be punished.

It's believed only one woman – 88-year-old Wong Ah Kui (legally known as Nyonya Tahir) – has ever been officially allowed to leave Islam in Malaysia, and then only after she had died in 2006 and her family wanted to have a Buddhist funeral.

THAIPUSAM

Each year in late January or early February, hundreds of thousands of pilgrims converge at Batu Caves for the Hindu festival of Thaipusam. This is at once a moving, raucous and sublime display of devotion and community spirit. Lord Murugan's silver chariot takes pride of place as it makes its way from the **Sri Mahamariamman Temple** (p72) in KL's Chinatown. The slow procession begins around midnight and arrives sometime in the early morning at the caves. Thousands of pilgrims follow the chariot, many in various states of trance.

As with Thaipusam festivals around the world, devotees of Murugan carry a *kavadi* (literally 'burden'). This burden, often a jug of milk, is an offering to Murugan for his blessings. On arrival, pilgrims carry their *kavadi* up the 272 steps to the Temple Cave where their burden is relieved by Hindu priests. Those who have pierced their flesh will have the barbs removed and the wounds treated with ash and lemon.

Tens of thousands may be at the site at any one time. It's crowded but not intolerably so, and you can easily move through the masses for a picture of the procession.

It's good to arrive at the cave area before 8am (best is to follow the whole procession from Chinatown). If you wish to see the activities within the Temple Cave, you should be there by 5am. Food and water are available outside the caves and from numerous stalls and shops (though if you are planning to be in the Temple Cave, bring your own).

The exact date of Thaipusam is usually announced in the local papers, and you can also contact the Sri Mahamariamman Temple.

Anti-Semitism

Penang once had a Jewish community large enough to support a synagogue (closed in 1976) and there's been a Jewish cemetery in George Town since 1805. Elsewhere in Malaysia, Jewish life is practically unknown.

Sadly, anti-Semitism, ostensibly tied to criticism of Israel, is a feature of Malaysia. In KL's bookshops it's not difficult to find anti-Semitic publications like *The Protocols of the Elders of Zion*. Former prime minister Mahathir is the most infamously outspoken Malaysian anti-Semite: in 2003 he made a speech to an Islamic leadership conference claiming the USA is a tool of Jewish overlords, and he once cancelled a planned tour of Malaysia by the New York Philharmonic because the program included work by a Jewish composer.

A 2014 survey by the US-based Anti-Defamation League (ADL) found that nearly two in three Malaysians admit to being prejudiced against Jews, the highest proportion by far in the region. Israeli passport holders are not permitted to enter Malaysia without clearance from the Ministry of Home Affairs, and very few local Muslims differentiate between Israelis and Jews generally – something worth noting if you're Jewish and travelling in the region.

Sisters in Islam (www.sistersinislam.org.my) is a website run by and for Malaysian Muslim women who refuse to be bullied by patriarchal interpretations of Islam.

Women in Malaysia

Malaysian women take part in all aspects of society, from politics and big business to academia and the judicial system; in 2010 Malaysia appointed its first two female Islamic-court judges. However, women in all communities, particularly those with conservative religious values, face restrictions on their behaviour despite the general openness of Malaysian society. Arranged marriage is common among Muslim and Hindu families, and the concept of 'honour' is still a powerful force in internal family politics.

Although the wearing of the *tudong* (headscarf) is encouraged, Muslim women are permitted to work, drive and go out unchaperoned, though the religious authorities frequently crack down on *khalwat* (close proximity, ie couples who get too intimate in public), which is considered immoral. Full *purdah* (the practice of screening women from men or strangers by means of all-enveloping clothes) is rare – if you do see this it's likely to be worn by women visiting from the Persian Gulf.

Recent changes to Islamic family law have made it easier for men to marry and divorce multiple wives and claim a share of their property. Muslim parties are also campaigning to remove the crime of marital rape from the statute books and bring in new laws requiring four male witnesses before a rape case can come to trial. In response to these moves, Marina Mahathir, the daughter of the former prime minister, compared the lot of Malaysia's Muslim women to that of blacks under apartheid in South Africa.

Arts & Architecture

The suggestion implicit in the naming of the Cooler Lumpur Festival is that the creativity of KLites in the arts and culture is not just 'cool' but 'cooler'. Take a close look at the city's contemporary art scenes and it's difficult not to agree. Mirroring the eclectic range of artistic pursuits is the city's built environment, which segues from elegant, traditional *kampung* houses to soaring, postmodern edifices endowed with Islamic flourishes.

Literature

A 1911 scandal involving the wife of a headmaster at a KL school who was convicted in a murder trial after shooting dead a male friend was the basis for Somerset Maugham's short story and play *The Letter*. Anthony Burgess picked up the thread of the dying days of British colonial rule in the region in *The Malayan Trilogy*, written in the 1950s when he was a school teacher in the country; it was Burgess who coined the phrase 'cooler lumpur'. *The Malayan Life of Ferdach O'Haney* is a fictionalised account of author Frederick Lees' experiences in 1950s Malaya; Lees was uniquely placed to observe mid-20th-century life in KL in his role as a top-ranking civil servant.

A snappy read is Amir Muhammad's *Rojak: Bite-Sized Stories*, in which the multi-talented artist and writer gathers a selection of the 350-word vignettes, many of them comic, that he penned as part of the creative-writing project City of Shared Stories, sponsored by the British Council

The literary baton has long since been passed to locally born writers such as Tash Aw (www.tash-aw.com), whose debut novel, *The Harmony Silk Factory,* won the 2005 Whitbread First Novel Award; Man Booker Prize–nominated author Tan Twan Eng (www.tantwaneng.com), whose literature fuses a fascination with Malaysia's past and an exploration of the impact of Japanese culture; and Preeta Samarasan (http://preetasamarasan.com), whose novel *Evening Is the Whole Day* shines a light on the experiences of an Indian immigrant family in the early 1980s.

Samarasan is one of the writers whose work features in *Urban Odysseys,* edited by Janet Tay and Eric Forbes, a mixed bag of short stories set in KL. An excellent collection of locally penned short stories about different aspects of sexuality is *Body 2 Body,* edited by Jerome Kugan and Pang Khee Teik. This anthology has a story by Brian Gomez, whose comedy-thriller *Devil's Place* is fun to read and very evocative of its KL setting. Kam Raslan's *Confessions of an Old Boy* is another comic tale, this time following the adventures both at home and abroad of politico Dato' Hamid.

Dance

There are several tourist-oriented dance shows in KL at which you can see traditional Malay dances from the peninsula; the main one is at the Malaysian Tourism Centre.

Traditional Indian dance is taught and performed at the Temple of Fine Arts in Brickfields. Malaysian dance legend Ramli Ibrahim founded Sutra Dance Theatre in 1983, a troupe that also takes Indian classical dance as the basis for its choreography. It has its own small dance theatre in Titiwangsa and also puts on shows at Kuala Lumpur

Performing Arts Centre (KLPAC). This is the venue at which you're most likely to catch other contemporary dance performances by local troupes such as Nyoba Kan (www.nyobakan.blogspot.com), which specialises in the Japanese dance form *buto*.

Drama

Local playwrights have to tread carefully when dealing with controversial topics such as race and religion, but you'd be surprised by how much they can get away with compared with what's acceptable in the cinema, on TV and for popular music performances.

Musicals, particularly about national heroes – from the sultanate-era warrior Hang Tuah to former prime minister Mahathir – are very popular; you'll likely find them staged at the Istana Budaya and KLPAC. There is also a strong interest in English-language theatre, as well as in Malay, Indian and Chinese languages.

The most interesting productions are generally staged by the Actors Studio (www.theactorsstudio.com.my), and at KLPAC and the Five Arts Centre (www.fiveartscentre.org), the latter based in the Taman Tun Dr Ismail neighbourhood of KL. The Black Box at Publika is another venue that's popular for alternative and cutting-edge performances.

Although traditional dramatic forms such as *wayang kulit* (shadow-puppet theatre) remain popular in Malaysia, it's rare for such shows to be performed in KL.

Music

Traditional & Classical

Traditional Malay music is based largely on *gendang* (drums), but other percussion instruments include the gong and various tribal instruments made from seashells, coconut shells and bamboo. The Indonesian-style *gamelan* (a traditional orchestra of drums, gongs and wooden xylophones) also crops up on ceremonial occasions. The Malay *nobat* uses a mixture of percussion and wind instruments to create formal court music.

For Western-style classical music, attend a performance by the Malaysian Philharmonic Orchestra at Dewan Filharmonik Petronas at the base of the Petronas Towers.

Chinese and Islamic influences are felt in the music of *dondang sayang* (Chinese-influenced romantic songs) and *hadrah* (Islamic chants, sometimes accompanied by dance and music). The KL-based Dama Orchestra (www.damaorchestra.com) combines modern and traditional Chinese instruments and plays songs that conjure up 1920s and '30s Malaysia.

Popular Music

Snapping at the high heels of demure Malaysian pop songstress Siti Nurhaliza are Zee Avi, who was signed by the US label Bushfire Records for her eponymous debut album, and Yuna, who has also cut a US record deal and is one of the talented vocalists and songwriters from the new generation of musicians. Also look out for Najwa, whose slickly produced album *Aurora* has garnered positive reviews; the MIA-style rapper Arabyrd; and the more retro guitar jingly pop stylings of Noh Salleh.

WAYANG

During important festivals for the Chinese community, such as Chinese New Year, there are street performances of *wayang* (Chinese opera) in KL. Shows feature dramatic music, high-pitched romantic songs and outrageous dances in spectacular costumes. Performances can go for an entire evening, but typically you don't have to understand Chinese to follow the simple plots.

In 2015 indie rock band Kyoto Protocol, which has been steadily building its reputation since forming in 2008, finally released a full album, *Catch These Men*. A great resource for catching up on other up-and-coming local bands and singers is The Wknd (http://the-wknd.com). Generally, though, KL's indie music scene is erratic, with artists not always able to go the distance to achieve local let alone international recognition.

Cinema

The heyday of Malaysia's film industry was the 1950s, when P Ramlee dominated the silver screen. This Malaysian icon acted in 66 films, recorded 300 songs and was also a successful film director. His directorial debut *Penarik Becha* (*The Trishaw Man*; 1955) is a classic of Malay cinema.

Yasmin Ahmad is considered to be the most important Malaysian filmmaker since Ramlee. Her film *Sepet* (2005), about a Chinese boy and Malay girl falling in love, cuts across the country's race and language barriers upsetting many devout Malays, as did her follow-up, *Gubra* (2006), which dared to take a sympathetic approach to prostitutes. Causing less of a stir were *Mukshin* (2007), a romantic tale about Malay village life, and *Talentime* (2009), about an inter-school performing arts contest, and what would be Yasmin's final film before her death from a stroke the same year.

Tsai Ming Liang's starkly beautiful but glacially slow interracial romance *I Don't Want to Sleep Alone* (2006) was filmed entirely on location in KL. Set in Kelantan, Dain Said's action-drama *Bunohan* (2012) did well at film festivals around the world, gaining it an international release – rare for a Malaysian movie. Said's follow-up *Interchange*, a film noir–style supernatural thriller set in KL, was released in Malaysia at the end of 2016.

Online Arts Resources

Arts.com.my *(www.arts.com.my)*

Malaysia Design Archive *(www.malaysiadesignarchive.org)*

MyDance Alliance *(www.mydancealliance.org)*

KL Dance Watch *(http://kldancewatch.wordpress.com)*

Visual Arts

Malaysia has a damned impressive contemporary art scene and KL is the best place to access it, both at public galleries and in several private collections that are open to visitors by appointment.

Among the most interesting and internationally successful contemporary Malaysian artists are Jalaini Abu Hassan ('Jai'), Wong Hoy Cheong, landscape painter Wong Perng Fey and Australian-trained multimedia artist Yee I-Lann. Amron Omar has focused for nearly 30 years on *silat* (a Malay martial art) as a source of inspiration for his paintings, a couple of which hang in the National Visual Arts Gallery in KL.

Latiff Mohidin, who is also a poet, is a Penang-based artist whose work spans several decades and has featured in a major retrospective at the National Visual Arts Gallery; he's considered a national treasure. One of his stainless-steel sculptures, *Kinetic 1*, is in the lobby of the Petronas Towers.

Abdul Multhalib Musa's sculptures have won awards; he created several pieces in Beijing for the 2008 Olympics. One of Musa's rippling steel-tube creations is in the garden at Rimbun Dahan, while another can be spotted outside Wisma Selangor Dredging, 142C Jln Ampang, in KL.

Kuala Lumpur: A Sketchbook showcases lovely watercolour paintings by Chin Kon Yit and text by Chen Voon Fee that together vividly capture the capital's rich architectural heritage.

Architecture

Traditional Malay

Vividly painted and handsomely proportioned, traditional wooden Malay houses are also perfectly adapted to the hot, humid conditions of the region. Built on stilts, with high, peaked roofs, they take advantage of even the slightest cooling breeze. Further ventilation is achieved by full-length windows, no internal partitions, and lattice-like grilles in the walls. The layout of a traditional Malay house reflects Muslim sensibilities. There are separate areas for men and women, as well as distinct areas where guests of either sex may be entertained.

In the grounds of Badan Warisan Malaysia, the National Museum and the Forest Research Institute Malaysia (FRIM), ornate examples of traditional wooden architecture have been transported from other parts of the country, reconstructed and opened for public inspection.

The best examples of this type of architecture in KL are found scattered across Kampung Baru, the most Malay part of the city.

Shophouses & Colonial

Thanks to fires and civil war, not to mention their own fragile nature, none of the wooden and *atap* (thatch) huts of the original settlers of KL have survived. However, from the 1880s onwards the city was built in brick, with tiled roofs and stucco facades. Grand civic buildings such as those around Merdeka Sq signalled the British desire to stamp its colonial mark on the city. It's also from this era that KL's first brick shophouses started appearing, some of which can still be found along Jln Tun HS Lee.

Shophouses are exactly what they sound like – a shop at the front with living quarters above and to the rear. Constructed in terraces, each unit is long and narrow, approximately 6m by 24m. An open courtyard in the middle of the building provides light and ventilation. Walkways sheltered by verandahs at the front provide protection from both rain and harsh sunlight. They are known as *kaki lima* ('five-foot ways') because they were supposed to be 5ft wide – not all are.

As KL became more prosperous so did the style of shophouse architecture. Look around Chinatown and the Masjid Jamek and Masjid India areas and you'll see shophouses with Grecian pediments and columns and fancy window frames – the neoclassical style of the 1910s; Dutch-inspired gables, a style from the 1920s known as Dutch Patrician; and the geometric art deco style of the 1930s. The wealthiest residents constructed palladian-style villas such as Loke Mansion and the former Istana Negara. Jln Ampang, the road leading out to the former tin mines of Ampang, used to be lined with these mansions – only a handful remain, among them the ones housing the Malaysian Tourism Centre and the Pakistan High Commission.

Postcolonial

Following independence there was a conscious effort to break with the florid architectural styles of the past, particularly when it came to public building works. This resulted in the elegant lines of the Masjid Negara (National Mosque), Stadium Merdeka (built for the declaration of independence in 1957) and neighbouring Stadium Negara.

TY Lee is the architect responsible for designing KL's art deco Central Market (1936) and Chin Woo Stadium (1953), an example of early modern style with stripped-back art deco elements.

Elaborate murals, with the Malaysian nation as their theme, were sometimes incorporated into these buildings: find them in Stadium Negara, the facades of the National Museum and Dewan Bahasa dan Pustaka (the Institute of Language and Literature) on the corner of Jln Wisma Putra.

Some projects, such as the National Parliament (built in 1963 and designed by William Ivor Shipley), the National Museum, Menara Maybank and Istana Budaya, incorporate distinctive motifs from traditional Malay architecture and art. Others, such as the beautiful Dayabumi Complex, and – later – the Petronas Towers, take their design references from Islam.

Among Malaysia's postcolonial architects of note is Hijjas Kasturi, who designed the Tabung Haji and Menara Maybank buildings; the giant shark fin of Menara Telekom, on the border between KL and Petaling Jaya and adorned with 22 outdoor 'sky gardens', one on every third

THE TWO ARTHURS

Arthur Benison Hubback (1871–1948) and Arthur Charles Norman (1858–1944) are the two colonial-era architects whose fanciful Indo-Saracenic style of buildings have lent distinction to Kuala Lumpur's cityscape since the late 19th century. Hubback is most famous for designing Masjid Jamek, the graceful mosque with its Mogul domes and scalloped horseshoe arches; the spectacular old KL Train Station; and the matching Malayan Railway Administration Building. Norman was responsible for the collection of buildings around Merdeka Sq, most notably the Sultan Abdul Samad Building; and Carcosa Seri Negara, home of British Resident Sir Frank Swettenham and now a luxury hotel.

floor; and the Bank Negara Malaysia Museum and Art Gallery. It's possible at certain times of the year to visit Kasturi's home, Rimbun Dahan, which is also a centre for developing traditional and contemporary art forms.

Contemporary & Future

Since the announcement of its planned construction in 2010, controversy over the use of state funds has surrounded Merdeka PNB118, a 118-storey tower under construction between Chinatown and Stadium Merdeka. The site of the former Pudu Prison is being redeveloped into the Bukit Bintang City Centre (BBCC) complex; plans include the construction of an 80-storey signature tower.

It's the River of Life project that has the most potential to transform the way residents and visitors see the city's architecture. With its focus on the rejuvenation and revitalisation of the Klang river, the project also includes establishing heritage routes through the most historic parts of KL, including Chinatown, where the Medan Pasar has been pedestrianised, pavements widened and surrounding buildings cleaned up.

Environment

These days, KL is very far from a city in the jungle (more like a city surrounded by oil-palm plantations). Still, there are pockets of old-growth forest to discover in and around KL that are havens for wildlife and sanctuaries for soaring tropical trees and plants. Easily accessible from KL are major national parks, such as Taman Negara, home to much of the amazing flora and fauna that once blanketed Peninsular Malaysia.

Wildlife

Apes & Monkeys

The Encyclopedia of Malaysia: The Environment by Professor Dato' Dr Sham Sani, one volume of an excellent series of illustrated encyclopedia, covers everything you need to know about Malaysia's environment.

The monkeys you're most likely to encounter living wild around KL are macaques, the stocky, aggressive monkeys that solicit snacks from tourists at nature reserves and rural temples such as those at Batu Caves. If you are carrying food, watch out for daring raids and be wary of bites as rabies is a potential hazard.

Leaf-eating langurs, such as the silvered leaf monkey whose fur is frosted with grey tips, are also quite common – spot them at the Forest Research Institute Malaysia (FRIM) swinging high through the trees.

To see Malaysia's signature animal, the orangutan, you'll have to drop by Zoo Negara; in Malaysia, these charismatic apes are found living wild only in the jungles of Sabah and Sarawak.

Dogs, Cats & Civets

The animals you're most likely to see in KL are domesticated dogs and cats. However, local Muslims consider dogs unclean, hence many have negative attitudes towards them. In 2009 villagers from Pulau Ketam in Selangor rounded up more than 300 strays and dumped them on two uninhabited islands. According to reports from animal-welfare agency SPCA Selangor, the starving dogs turned to cannibalism to survive.

Pangolins, also known as scaly anteaters, are the most traded species, even though they are protected under Malaysian law. Their scales, believed to have medicinal properties, can fetch up to RM800 per kilogram.

Cats hardly fare any better, with many local species of wild cats facing extinction because of hunting and the trade in body parts for traditional medicines. The Malayan tiger is now extremely rare on the peninsula, as are leopards and black panthers (actually black leopards). Smaller bay cats, leopard cats and marbled cats are slightly better off, in part because they need less territory and eat smaller prey (birds and small mammals). You may also spot various species of civet, a separate family of predators with vaguely catlike features but longer snouts and shaggier coats.

Bats & Birds

Malaysia has more than 100 species of bat, most of which are tiny, insectivorous species that live in caves and under eaves and bark. Fruit bats (flying foxes) are only distantly related; they have well-developed eyes and do not navigate by echolocation. They are often seen taking wing at dusk.

More than 650 species of bird live in Peninsular Malaysia. You can spot exotic species in many urban parks or aviaries such as Kuala Lumpur Bird Park, but for rarer birds you'll have to head to the jungle and the hillsides. The Malaysian Nature Society is helping to promote Genting Highlands as a prime birding location, and Fraser's Hill (Bukit Fraser) is already an established bird-spotting location.

If you see parts of or products made from endangered species for sale, call the 24-hour Wildlife Crime Hotline (☎019-356 4194).

Reptiles

Some 250 species of reptile have been recorded in Malaysia, including 140 species of snake. Cobras and vipers pose a potential risk to trekkers, although the chances of encountering them are low. Large pythons are sometimes seen in national parks and you may also encounter 'flying' snakes, lizards and frogs (all these species glide using wide flaps of skin). Even in city parks, you stand a chance of running into a monitor lizard, a primitive-looking carrion feeder notorious for consuming domestic cats.

Plants

The wet, tropical climate of this region produces an amazing range of trees, plants and flowers, including such signature species as the carnivorous pitcher plant, numerous orchids and the parasitic rafflesia (or 'corpse flower'), which produces the world's largest flower – a whopping 1m across when fully open. However, vast tracts of rainforest have been cleared to make way for plantations of cash crops such as rubber and oil palms. Just look out the window on the flight into Kuala Lumpur International Airport and you'll see endless rows of oil palms.

Malaysia's jungles support a staggering amount of life: around 14,500 species of flowering plant and tree, 210 species of mammal, 600 species of bird, 150 species of frog, 80 species of lizard and thousands of types of insect.

Oil-Palm Plantations

The oil palm, a native of West Africa that was introduced into Malaysia in the 1870s, is probably now the most common tree in Malaysia. The country's first oil-palm plantation was established in 1917; today, according to the Malaysian Palm Oil Council (www.mpoc.org.my), Malaysia is the world's leading producer of palm oil, accounting for over 40% of global production. The oil is extracted from the orange-coloured fruit, which grows in bunches just below the fronds. It is used primarily for cooking, although it can also be refined into biodiesel – an alternative to fossil fuels.

IMPROVING WILDLIFE CONSERVATION

Malaysia's Wildlife Conservation Act includes fines of up to RM100,000 and long prison sentences for poaching, smuggling animals and other wildlife-related crimes. Even so, smuggling of live animals and animal parts remains a particular problem in the region. In July 2010 police looking for stolen cars also uncovered an illegal 'mini zoo' in a KL warehouse containing 20 species of protected wildlife, including a pair of rare birds of paradise worth RM1 million.

After serving 17 months of a five-year sentence, Malaysia's most notorious animal smuggler Alvin Wong – described as 'the Pablo Escobar of wildlife trafficking' in Bryan Christy's book, *The Lizard King* – was allegedly back in business in 2013 according to a documentary screened by Al Jeezera in 2013.

It's not just live animals that are being smuggled. Malaysia has been fingered as a transit point for illegally traded ivory on its way to other parts of Asia. In August 2015 authorities busted a syndicate in KL that claimed to be trading in tiger and other wildlife parts.

For all the crop's benefits, there have been huge environmental consequences to the creation of vast plantations that have replaced the native jungle and previously logged forests; in 2003 Friends of the Earth reported that palm-oil production was responsible for 87% of deforestation in Malaysia. The use of polluting pesticides and fertilisers in palm-oil production also undermines the crop's eco credentials. Oil-palm plantations convert land into permanent monoculture, reducing the number of plant species by up to 90%. Oil palms require large quantities of herbicides and pesticides, which can seep into rivers; drainage may lower water tables, drying out nearby peat forests (and releasing huge quantities of greenhouse gases in the process). Plantations also fragment the natural habitats that are especially important to large mammals.

Iain Buchanan spent eight years creating the exquisite illustrations and text for *Fatimah's Kampung*, a parable about how Malaysia is in the process of sacrificing nature and traditional values for economic development.

The Palm Oil Action Group (www.palmoilaction.org.au) is an Australian pressure group raising awareness about palm oil and the need to use alternatives. Roundtable on Sustainable Palm Oil (RSPO) tries to look at the issue from all sides while seeking to develop and implement global standards. Proforest (www.proforest.net) has also been working with Wild Asia (www.wildasia.org) on the Stepwise Support Programme, designed to promote sustainability within the palm-oil industry.

National Parks & Other Protected Areas

Malaysia's jungles contain some of the world's oldest undisturbed areas of rainforest. It's estimated they've existed for about 100 million years, as they were largely unaffected by the far-reaching climatic changes brought on elsewhere by the last ice age.

Fortunately, quite large areas of some of the best and most spectacular of these rainforests have been made into national parks, in which all commercial activity is banned. The British established the first national park in Malaysia in 1938 and it is now included in Taman Negara, the crowning glory of Malaysia's network of national parks, which crosses the borders of Terengganu, Kelantan and Pahang; tour companies in KL run trips here.

In addition to this and the 27 other national and state parks across the country (23 of them in Malaysian Borneo), there are various government-protected reserves and sanctuaries for forests, birds, mammals and marine life. Right in the heart of KL you can visit the KL Forest Eco Park.

Sign up to be a voluntary forest monitor at Forest Watch (www.timalaysia-forestwatch.org.my), a Transparency International Malaysia project.

Environmental Issues

Malaysia's federal government maintains that it is doing its best to balance the benefits of economic development with environmental protection and conservation. However, many wildlife and environment protection agencies and pressure groups, beg to differ, pointing out how big business continues to have the ear of government when decision time rolls around.

Deforestation

Logging and palm-oil businesses provide hundreds of thousands of jobs, yet they also wreak untold ecological damage and have caused the displacement and consequent cultural erosion of many tribal peoples.

There's a disparity between government figures and those of environmental groups, but it's probable that more than 60% of Peninsular Malaysia's rainforests have been logged, with similar figures applying to Malaysian Borneo. Government initiatives such as the National

RESPONSIBLE TOURISM

- Tread lightly and buy locally, avoiding (and reporting) instances where you see parts of or products made from endangered species for sale. Call the 24-hour Wildlife Crime Hotline (019-356 4194) to report illegal activities.
- Visit nature sites, hire local trekking guides and provide custom for ecotourism initiatives. This puts cash in local pockets and lets you cast a vote for the economic (as opposed to the purely ecological) value of sustainability and habitat conservation.
- Sign up to be a voluntary forest monitor at Forest Watch (www.timalaysia-forest watch.org.my), a Transparency International Malaysia project.
- Check out projects sponsored and promoted by the Ecotourism & Conservation Society Malaysia (http://ecomy.org) and Wild Asia (www.wildasia.org) to learn more about responsible tourism in the region.
- Keep abreast of and support local campaigns by checking out the websites of organisations like WWF Malaysia (www.wwf.org.my) and the Malaysian Nature Society (www.mns.org.my).

Forestry Policy have led to deforestation being cut to 900 sq km a year, a third slower than previously. The aim is to reduce the timber harvest by 10% each year, but even this isn't sufficient to calm many critics, who remain alarmed at the rate at which Malaysia's primary forests are disappearing.

Close to KL, the Forest Research Institute Malaysia (FRIM) is pioneering new ways of preserving and regenerating Malaysia's rainforests. For more information on government forestry projects, visit the website of the Forestry Department (www.forestry.gov.my).

Environmental groups such as TrEES (www.trees.org.my) have also been campaigning for the protection of the rainforests and water catchment area along the eastern flank of Selangor. In 2010, 93,000 hectares of these uplands were gazetted as the Selangor State Park, making it the peninsula's third-largest protected area of forest after Taman Negara and Royal Belum State Park. Find out more about it at http://selangorstatepark.blogspot.com.

Environment Resources

Malaysian Nature Society *(www.mns.org.my)*

Orangutan Foundation *(www.orangutan.org.uk)*

Sahabat Alam Malaysia *(www.foe-malaysia.org)*

WWF Malaysia *(www.wwf.org.my)*

River of Life

Following successes in Melaka and Penang on cleaning up polluted rivers, the focus has now turned to KL and the Klang Valley. The literal translation of Kuala Lumpur is 'muddy estuary' and anyone gazing on any of the milky-coffee-coloured waterways that flow through the city would still find that name appropriate. Following moves in 2010 by the Selangor state government to clean up a 21km stretch of Sungai Klang around Klang, the federal government has stepped in to offer to coordinate the project. This makes sense, as the 120km-long, heavily polluted river flows through the capital on its way to the coast.

KL's RM4 billion River of Life project includes a plan to clean up a 110km stretch along the Klang river basin, shifting the water quality from its current Class III–Class V status (not suitable for body contact) to Class IIb (suitable for body-contact recreational usage) by 2020. Also part of the project are beautification proposals for the riverbanks, including new parks and walkways.

Cutting Carbon Emissions

At the 2014 UN Climate Summit, Prime Minister Najib confirmed that Malaysia was well on its way to achieving a 40% reduction in carbon emissions by 2020, a goal set by his government in 2009. Malaysia's average per capita carbon footprint remains around twice that of Thailand and four times higher than Indonesia, although it is just half of Singapore.

To reach its stated goal the federal government has added green technology to the portfolio of the Ministry of Energy & Water and announced the launch of a national green technology policy. Malaka is creating a smart electricity grid with the aim of becoming the country's first carbon-free city by 2020. The Carbon Trust (www.carbontrust.com) is also working with the local government of Petaling Jaya in Selangor to help develop its five-year carbon reduction strategy.

In the meantime, there's an ongoing air-quality threat in the region from 'haze' – smoke from fires set by Indonesian farmers and plantation companies to clear land for agricultural purposes. The haze is usually at its worst in Malaysia around March and just before September and October's rainy season.

Survival Guide

TRANSPORT 218

ARRIVING IN KL 218

KLIA 218

SkyPark Subang Airport . . 218

Boat 219

Bus 219

GETTING AROUND 219

Bicycle 219

Bus 220

Car & Motorcycle 220

KL's New MRT 220

Taxi 220

Train 221

TOURS 221

DIRECTORY A–Z 222

Customs Regulations 222

Electricity 222

Emergency 222

Gay & Lesbian Travellers . . 222

Health 223

Internet Access 225

Legal Matters 225

Medical Services 225

Money 226

Opening Hours 226

Post 226

Public Holidays 227

Safe Travel 227

Telephone 227

Time 228

Toilets 228

Tourist Information 228

Travellers with Disabilities 228

Visas 228

Women Travellers 228

LANGUAGE 229

Transport

ARRIVING IN KUALA LUMPUR

Most likely you'll arrive at Kuala Lumpur International Airport (KLIA), although a handful of flights land at SkyPark Subang Terminal. Coming overland, arrival points include KL Sentral for trains and Terminal Bersepadu Selatan (TBS) for buses. Ferries from Sumatra (Indonesia) dock at Pelabuhan Klang, which is connected by rail with KL Sentral.

Kuala Lumpur International Airport (KLIA) Trains RM55; every 15 minutes from 5am to 1am; 30 minutes to KL Sentral. Buses RM10; every hour from 5am to 1am; one hour to KL Sentral. Taxis from RM75; one hour to central KL.

KL Sentral Transport hub with train, light rail (LRT), monorail, bus and taxi links to rest of city.

Terminal Bersepadu Selatan (TBS) Long-distance buses from most destinations now arrive here. It's connected to KL by LRT.

KLIA

Kuala Lumpur International Airport (KLIA; ☎03-8777 7000; www.klia.com.my; 🚆KLIA), which comprises two terminals, is about 55km south of the city.

Bus

The **Airport Coach** (☎016-228 9070; www.airportcoach.com.my; one way/return RM10/18) takes an hour to KL Sentral; for RM18 it will take you to any central KL hotel from KLIA and pick you up for the return journey for RM25. The bus stand is clearly signposted inside the terminal. Other bus companies connecting KLIA to KL Sentral are **Skybus** (☎016-217 6950; www.skybus.com.my; one way RM10) and **Aerobus** (☎03-3344 8828; www.aerobus.my; one way RM9).

Taxi

Taxis from KLIA operate both on a fixed-fare coupon system and the meter. Buy your taxi coupon before you exit the arrivals hall; standard taxis cost RM75 (for up to three people), premier taxis for four people RM103 and family-sized minivans seating up to eight RM200. The journey will take around one hour. Given the extra charges on the metered taxis for tolls and pick-up at the airport (RM2), plus the unknown traffic factor, the fixed-fare coupon is the way to go.

Going to the airport by taxi, make sure that the agreed fare includes tolls; expect to pay RM65 from Chinatown or Jln Bukit Bintang.

Train

The fastest way to the city is on the comfortable **KLIA Ekspres** (☎03-2278 9009; www.kliaekspres.com; adult/child one way RM55/25), with departures every 15 to 20 minutes from 5am to 1am. From KL Sentral you can transfer to your final destination by monorail, light rail (LRT), KTM Komuter train or taxi.

The **KL Transit train** (☎03-2267 8000; www.kliaekspres.com; adult/child 1 way RM55/25) also connects KLIA with KL Sentral (35 minutes), stopping at three other stations en route (Salak Tinggi, Putrajaya and Cyberjaya, and Bandar Tasik Selatan).

If flying from KL on Malaysia Airlines, Cathay Pacific, Royal Brunei or Emirates, you can check your baggage in at KL Sentral before making your way to KLIA.

SkyPark Subang Airport

Firefly and Berjaya Air flights land at **SkyPark Subang Airport** (Sultan Abdul Aziz Shah Airport; ☎03-7842 2773; www.subangskypark.com; M17, Subang), around 20km west of the city centre.

Bus

Trans MVS Express (☎019-307 2521; www.facebook.com/Transmvsexpress) offers on-the-hour services from KL Sentral to SkyPark Subang (RM10, one hour) between 9am and 9pm; and from SkyPark Subang to KLIA and KLIA2 (RM10, one hour) roughly every two hours between 5am and 11pm.

Taxi

Taxis charge around RM40 to RM50 into the city, depending on traffic, which can be heavy during rush hour.

Boat

Ferries from Tanjung Balai (Asahan) and Dumai in Sumatra arrive at Pelabuhan Klang port. The KTM station is opposite the ferry terminal; trains to KL Sentral take just over an hour.

Bus

KL has several bus stations, but nearly all buses now leave from Terminal Bersepadu Selatan (TBS), 14.5km south of the city centre. Other long-distance bus services are operated by **Aeroline** (Map p250; ☎03-6258 8800; www.aeroline.com.my; Corus Hotel, Jln Ampang; Ⓜ KLCC) and **Transtar Travel** (Map p253; ☎03-2141 1771; http://transtar.travel; 135 Jln Imbi; Ⓜ Imbi).

Terminal Bersepadu Selatan

Connected to the Bandar Tasik Selatan train-station hub, about 15 minutes south of KL Sentral, is **Terminal Bersepadu Selatan** (TBS; ☎03-9051 2000; www.tbsbts.com.my; Jln Terminal Selatan, Bandar Tasik Selatan; Ⓜ Bandar Tasik Seletan, Ⓡ Bandar Tasik Seletan). Built to replace Pudu Sentral as KL's main long-distance bus station, TBS serves destinations to the south and northeast of KL. This vast, modern transport hub has a centralised ticketing service (CTS) selling tickets for nearly all bus companies – including services offered by major operator **Transnasional Express** (☎03-9051 2000; www.transnasional.com.my; Terminal Bersepadu Selatan, Jln Terminal Selatan, Bandar Tasik Selatan) – at counters on level 3 or online (up to three hours before departure).

Pekeliling Bus Station

Buses arrive at **Pekeliling** (Map p256; Jln Pekeliling; Ⓜ Titiwangsa, Ⓜ Titiwangsa) from central peninsula locations including Kuala Lipis, Raub and Jerantut. It's next to Titiwangsa LRT and monorail stations, just off Jln Tun Razak. Several companies, including **Plusliner** (www.plusliner.com), run services to Kuantan.

Pudu Sentral Bus Station

Steps from Chinatown and also close to Bukit Bintang, this **bus station** (Map p249; Jln Pudu; Ⓜ Plaza Rakyat) now serves only a few destinations, including the Genting Highlands, Seremban and Kuala Selangor.

GETTING AROUND KUALA LUMPUR

KL Sentral is the hub of a rail-based urban network consisting of the KTM Komuter, KLIA Ekspres, KLIA Transit, light rail (LRT) and monorail systems. Though the systems are poorly integrated, you can happily get around much of central KL on a combination of rail and monorail services. Buy the MyRapid card (www.myrapid.com.my; RM10) at monorail and LRT stations; it can also be used on Rapid KL buses.

- **Monorail** Stops in mostly convenient locations; gets very crowded during evening rush hour.
- **Light Rail Transit (LRT)** Handy for Chinatown, Kampung Baru and KLCC, but network is poorly integrated.
- **Bus** The GOKL City Bus has four free loop services connecting many city-centre destinations.
- **Taxi** Can be flagged down with metered fares. Some designated taxi ranks operate a prepaid coupon system for journeys.

Bicycle

Cycling Kuala Lumpur (cyclingkl.blogspot.com) is a great resource, with a map of bike routes and plenty of

CLIMATE CHANGE & TRAVEL

Every form of transport that relies on carbon-based fuel generates CO_2, the main cause of human-induced climate change. Modern travel is dependent on aeroplanes, which might use less fuel per kilometre per person than most cars but travel much greater distances. The altitude at which aircraft emit gases (including CO_2) and particles also contributes to their climate change impact. Many websites offer 'carbon calculators' that allow people to estimate the carbon emissions generated by their journey and, for those who wish to do so, to offset the impact of the greenhouse gases emitted with contributions to portfolios of climate-friendly initiatives throughout the world. Lonely Planet offsets the carbon footprint of all staff and author travel.

MYRAPID & TOUCH 'N GO CARDS

If you're staying for an extended period in KL or Malaysia, consider the prepaid **MyRapid** (www.myrapid.com.my) card, valid on Rapid KL buses, the monorail and the Ampang and Kelana Jaya LRT lines. It costs RM20 (including RM5 in credit) and can be bought at monorail and LRT stations. Just tap at the ticket gates or when you get on the bus and the correct fare will be deducted.

The **Touch 'n Go card** (www.touchngo.com.my) can be used on all public transport in the Klang Valley, at highway toll booths across Malaysia and at selected parking sites. The cards, which cost RM10.60 and can be reloaded with values from RM10 to RM500, can be purchased at KL Sentral and the central LRT stations KLCC, Masjid Jamek and Dang Wangi.

detail on how to stay safe on KL's roads. **KL By Cycle** (Map p248; ☎03-2691 1382; www.myhoponhopoff.com; Dataran Merdeka Underground Mall, Merdeka Sq; per hour RM10, deposit RM100; ⌚9am-6pm; Ⓜ Masjid Jamek) rents basic bikes at the information desk in the underground mall across from KL City Gallery. Rentals include a helmet. Rental bikes are also available at Titiwangsa Lake Gardens.

Bus

Most buses are provided by either **Rapid KL** (☎03-7885 2585; www.rapidkl.com.my; RM1-5; ⌚6am-11.30pm) or **Metrobus** (☎03-5635 3070). There's an **information booth** (Map p249; ⌚7am-9pm; Ⓜ Pasar Seni) at the Jln Sultan Mohammed bus stop in Chinatown. Rapid KL buses have their destinations clearly displayed. They are divided into four classes.

Bas Bandar (RM1) services run around the city centre.

Bas Utama (RM1 to RM3) buses run from the centre to the suburbs.

Bas Tempatan (RM1) buses run around the suburbs.

Bas Ekspres (RM3.80) are express buses to distant suburbs.

Local buses leave from half-a-dozen small bus stands around the city – useful stops in Chinatown include Jln Sultan Mohamed (by Pasar Seni), **Bangkok Bank** (on Lebuh Pudu) and Medan Pasar (on Lebuh Ampang).

The **GO-KL free city bus** (☎1800-887 723; www.facebook.com/goklcitybus; ⌚6am-11pm Mon-Thu, to 1am Sat, 7am-11pm Sun) has four circular routes around the city, with stops at KLCC, KL Tower, KL Sentral, the National Museum and Merdeka Sq. Buses run every five minutes during peak hours and every 10 to 15 minutes at other times.

Car & Motorcycle

KL is the best place to hire a car for touring the peninsula, though driving out of KL is complicated by a confusing one-way system and contradictory road signs that can throw off your sense of direction. All the major rental companies have offices at KLIA. City offices – generally open from 9am to 5.30pm weekdays and 9am to 1pm Saturday – include **Avis** (☎03-8776 6541; www.avis.com.my; counter C01, International Arrivals (Airside), Main Terminal Bldg, KLIA; ⌚7am-10pm) and **Hertz** (☎03-8787 4572; www.hertz.com; lot 16, ground fl, car park D, KLIA; ⌚7.30am-10pm Mon-Sat, to 7pm Sun).

Kuala Lumpur's New MRT

To give it its full title, the **Klang Valley Mass Rapid Transit (KVMRT) project** (www.mymrt.com.my) involves the construction of a rail-based public-transport network that, together with the existing light rail transit (LRT), monorail, KTM Komuter, KLIA Ekspres and KLIA Transit systems, aims to ease the road-traffic congestion that plagues the Greater Kuala Lumpur/Klang Valley region. The ambitious target is to make half of all journeys in the Klang Valley area taken by public transport.

The project involves the creation of three new commuter rail lines, the first of which is the 51km Sungai Buloh–Kajang line. Phase one, from Sungai Buloh to Semantan, was operational in December 2016. The remaining part of the line to Kajang will be finished during 2017.

Taxi

Kuala Lumpur has plenty of air-conditioned taxis, which queue up at designated taxi stops across the city. You can also flag down moving taxis, but drivers will stop only if there is a convenient place to pull over (these are harder to come by when it's raining and during peak hours). Fares start at RM3 for the first three minutes, with an additional 25 sen for each 36 seconds. From midnight to 6am there's a surcharge of 50% on the metered fare, and extra passengers (more than two) add 20 sen each to the starting fare. Blue taxis are newer and more comfortable and start at RM6 for the first three minutes and RM1 for each additional 36 seconds. Night surcharges of 50% also apply.

Unfortunately, some drivers have limited geographical knowledge of the city. Some also refuse to use the meter, even though this is a legal requirement. Taxi drivers lingering outside luxury hotels or tourist hotspots such as KL Bird Park are especially guilty of this behaviour. Note that KL Sentral and some large malls such as Pavilion and Suria KLCC have a coupon system for taxis where you pay in advance at a slightly higher fee than the meter.

One of the easiest ways to use taxis in KL is to download an app such as **Uber**, **Easy Taxi** or **Grab** (formally known as My Teksi) to your smartphone or tablet.

Train

Kuala Lumpur Monorail

The air-conditioned **monorail** (www.myrapid.com.my; RM1.20-4.10; ⌚6am-midnight) zips from KL Sentral to Titiwangsa, linking many of the city's sightseeing areas.

KTM Komuter Trains

KTM Komuter (www.ktmb.com.my; from RM1.40; ⌚6.45am-11.45pm) train services run every 15 to 20 minutes from 6am to 11.45pm and use KL Sentral as a hub. There are two lines: Tanjung Malim–Sungai Gadut and Batu Caves–Pelabuhan Klang.

Light Rail Transit

As well as the buses, Rapid KL runs the **Light Rail Transit** (LRT; ☎03-7885 2585; www.myrapid.com.my; from RM1.30; ⌚every 6-10min 6am-11.45pm Mon-Sat, to 11.30pm Sun) system. There are three lines: the Ampang line from Ampang to Sentul Timur; the Sri Petaling line from Sentul Timur to Putra Heights; and the Kelana Jaya line from Gombak to Putra Heights. The network is poorly integrated because the lines were constructed by different companies. As a result, you may have to follow a series of walkways, stairs and elevators, or walk several blocks down the street.

Buy single-journey tokens or MyRapid cards from the cashier or electronic ticket machines. An electronic control system checks tickets/tokens as you enter and exit via turnstiles (you tap the token on the way in and insert it in the gate on the way out).

TOURS

If you need a guide or assistance getting around, many local agencies offer various tours of the city and attractions around KL.

KL Hop-On Hop-Off (☎03-9282 2713; www.myhoponhopoff.com; adult/child 24hr ticket RM45/24; ⌚9am-7pm) This double-decker, air-con tourist bus makes a circuit of the main tourist sites half-hourly throughout the day and can be a handy way to get around, if you avoid rush hour. Stops include KLCC, Jln Bukit Bintang, Menara KL, Chinatown, Merdeka Sq and the attractions of Tun Abdul Razak Heritage Park. Tickets can be bought on the bus.

Going Places Tours (Map p249; ☎03-2078 4008; www.goingplaces-kl.com; 60a, 1st fl, Jln Sultan; Ⓜ Pasar Seni) Offers tours tailored to the backpacker market, including walking tours of Chinatown (RM130) and trips to see the fireflies in Kuala Selangor (RM220), to Putrajaya (RM160) and to Melaka (RM220).

Tour 51 Malaysia (Map p250; ☎03-2161 8830; www.tour51.com.my; 1st fl Wisma Central, Jln Ampang; ⌚7.30am-7pm; Ⓜ KLCC) Runs a decent selection of half-day city tours and day trips to places such as Putrajaya, Kuala Selangor and Pulau Ketam.

Travel Han (Map p248; ☎03-2031 0899; www.han-travel.com; ground Fl, Bangunan Mariamman, Jln Hang Kasturi; Ⓜ Pasar Seni) One of the many agents offering budget tours to Taman Negara, a 4343-sq-km reserve protecting one of the world's oldest tropical rainforests. Three-day, two-night packages from KL start from RM400 per person.

Directory A–Z

Customs Regulations

The following can be brought into Malaysia duty-free:

- 1L of alcohol
- 225g of tobacco (200 cigarettes or 50 cigars)
- souvenirs and gifts not exceeding RM400 (RM500 when coming from Labuan or Langkawi)

Cameras, portable radios, perfume, cosmetics and watches do not incur duty. Prohibited items include weapons (including imitations), fireworks, 'obscene and prejudicial articles' (pornography, for example, and items that may be considered inflammatory or religiously offensive) and drugs. Drug smuggling carries the death penalty in Malaysia.

Visitors can carry no more than the equivalent of US$10,000 in ringgit or any other currency into and out of Malaysia.

Electricity

230V/50Hz

Emergency

Police & Ambulance	999
Fire	994
Tourist Police	03-9235 4999

Gay & Lesbian Travellers

Malaysia is a predominantly Muslim country and the level of tolerance for homosexuality is vastly different from those of its neighbours. Sex between men is illegal at any age and sharia laws (which apply only to Muslims) forbid sodomy and cross-dressing. Outright persecution of gays and lesbians is rare.

Nonetheless, LGBT travellers should avoid behaviour that attracts unwanted attention. Malaysians are

PRACTICALITIES

- Connect to the reliable electricity supply (240V, 50Hz) with a UK-type three-square-pin plug.
- English-language newspapers include the New Straits Times (www.nst.com.my), the Star (www.thestar.com.my) and the Malay Mail (www.themalaymailonline.com).
- Listen to Traxx FM (90.3FM), HITZ FM (92.9FM) and MIX FM (94.5FM) for music, and BFM (89.9FM) or Fly FM (95.8FM) for news.
- Watch the two government TV channels, TV1 and TV2, and the four commercial stations, TV3, NTV7, 8TV and TV9, as well as a host of satellite channels.
- Use the metric system for weights and measures.

conservative about displays of public affection regardless of sexual orientation. Although same-sex handholding is quite common for men and women, this is rarely an indication of sexuality; an overtly gay couple doing the same would attract attention, though there is little risk of vocal or aggressive homophobia.

There's actually a fairly active gay scene in KL. The lesbian scene is more discreet, but it exists for those willing to seek it out. Start looking for information on www.utopia-asia.com or www.fridae.com, both of which provide good coverage of gay and lesbian events and activities across Asia.

The PT Foundation (www.ptfmalaysia.org) is a voluntary nonprofit organisation providing education on HIV/AIDS and sexuality, and care and support programs for marginalised communities in Malaysia.

Health

Before You Go

- Take out health insurance.
- Pack medications in their original, clearly labelled containers.
- Carry a signed and dated letter from your physician describing your medical conditions and medications, including their generic names.
- If you have a heart condition bring a copy of your ECG (taken just prior to travelling).
- Bring a double supply of any regular medication in case of loss or theft.

Recommended Vaccinations

Proof of yellow-fever vaccination will be required if you have visited a country in the yellow-fever zone (such as those in Africa or South America) within the six days prior to entering Malaysia.

DRINKING WATER

- Never drink tap water unless you've verified that it's safe. KL's water supply comes mostly from modern treatment plants and is usually safe to drink.
- Check bottled-water seals are intact at purchase.
- Avoid ice in places that look dubious.
- Avoid fresh juices if they have not been freshly squeezed or you suspect they may have been watered down.
- Boiling water is the most efficient method of purifying it.
- Iodine, the best chemical purifier, should not be used by pregnant women or those who suffer thyroid problems.

The World Health Organization (WHO) recommends the following vaccinations for travellers to Malaysia:

Adult diphtheria and tetanus Single booster recommended if none in the previous 10 years.

Hepatitis A Provides almost 100% protection for up to a year. A booster after 12 months provides at least another 20 years' protection.

Hepatitis B Now considered routine for most travellers. Given as three shots over six months. A rapid schedule is also available, as is a combined vaccination with hepatitis A.

Measles, mumps and rubella (MMR) Two doses of MMR are required unless you have had the diseases. Many young adults require a booster.

Polio There have been no reported cases of polio in Malaysia in recent years. Only one booster is required as an adult for lifetime protection.

Typhoid Recommended unless your trip is less than a week and only to developed cities. The vaccine offers around 70% protection, lasts for two to three years and is given as a single shot. Tablets are also available; however, the injection is usually recommended as it has fewer side effects.

Varicella If you haven't had chickenpox, discuss this vaccination with your doctor.

In Malaysia

AIR POLLUTION

If you're troubled by the air pollution, leave KL for a few days to get some fresh air. Consult the Air Pollutant Index of Malaysia (http://apims.doe.gov.my/v2) for the current situation.

AVAILABILITY OF HEALTHCARE

There are good clinics and international-standard hospitals in KL. Over-the-counter medicines and prescription drugs are widely available from reputable pharmacies across Malaysia.

HEAT

It can take up to two weeks to adapt to Malaysia's hot climate. Swelling of the feet and ankles is common, as are muscle cramps caused by excessive sweating. Prevent cramps by avoiding dehydration and excessive activity in the heat.

Dehydration is the main contributor to heat exhaustion. Symptoms include feeling weak, headache, irritability, nausea or vomiting, sweaty skin, a fast, weak pulse and a normal or slightly elevated body temperature. Treat by getting out of the heat, applying cool, wet cloths to the skin, lying flat with legs raised and rehydrating with water containing a quarter of a teaspoon of salt per litre.

Heatstroke is a serious medical emergency. Symptoms come on suddenly and include weakness, nausea, a hot, dry body with a body temperature of over 41°C, dizziness, confusion, loss of coordination, fits and eventually collapse and loss of consciousness. Seek medical help and commence cooling by getting the person out of the heat, removing their clothes and applying cool, wet cloths or ice to their body, especially to the groin and armpits.

Prickly heat – an itchy rash of tiny lumps – is caused by sweat being trapped under the skin. Treat by moving out of the heat and into an air-conditioned area for a few hours and by having cool showers. Creams and ointments clog the skin, so they should be avoided.

INFECTIOUS DISEASES

The following are the most common for travellers:

Dengue fever Increasingly common in cities. The mosquito that carries dengue bites day and night, so use insect-avoidance measures at all times. Symptoms can include high fever, severe headache, body ache, a rash and diarrhoea. There is no specific treatment, just rest and paracetamol – do not take aspirin, as it increases the likelihood of haemorrhaging.

Hepatitis A This food- and water-borne virus infects the liver, causing jaundice (yellow skin and eyes), nausea and lethargy. All travellers to Malaysia should be vaccinated against it.

Hepatitis B The only sexually transmitted disease (STD) that can be prevented by vaccination, hepatitis B is spread by body fluids.

Hepatitis E Transmitted through contaminated food and water and has similar symptoms to hepatitis A but is far less common. It is a severe problem in pregnant women and can result in the death of both mother and baby. There is currently no vaccine, and prevention is by following safe eating and drinking guidelines.

HIV Unprotected sex is the main method of transmission.

Influenza Can be very severe in people over the age of 65 or in those with underlying medical conditions such as heart disease or diabetes; vaccination is recommended for these individuals. There is no specific treatment, just rest and paracetamol.

Malaria Uncommon in Peninsular Malaysia and antimalarial drugs are rarely recommended for travellers. However, there may be a small risk in rural areas. Remember that malaria can be fatal. Before you travel, seek medical advice on the right medication and dosage for you.

Rabies A potential risk, and invariably fatal if untreated, rabies is spread by the bite or lick of an infected animal – most commonly a dog or monkey. Pretravel vaccination means the post-bite treatment is greatly simplified. If an animal bites you, gently wash the wound with soap and water, and apply iodine-based antiseptic. If you have not been vaccinated you will need to receive rabies immunoglobulin as soon as possible.

Typhoid This serious bacterial infection is spread via food and water. Symptoms include high and slowly progressive fever, headache, a dry cough and stomach pain. Vaccination,

DON'T LET THE BEDBUGS BITE

Bedbugs live in the cracks of furniture and walls and migrate to the bed at night to feed on you. They are more likely to strike in high-turnover accommodation, especially hostels, though they can be found anywhere. An appearance of cleanliness is no guarantee there are no bedbugs. Protect yourself with the following strategies:

➡ Ask the hotel or hostel what it does to avoid bedbugs. It's a common problem and reputable establishments should have a pest-control procedure in place.

➡ Keep your luggage elevated off the floor to avoid having the critters latch on – this is one of the common ways bedbugs are spread from place to place.

➡ Check the room carefully for signs of bugs – you may find their translucent light-brown skins or poppyseed-like excrement.

If you do get bitten, try the following:

➡ Treat the itch with antihistamine.

➡ Thoroughly clean your luggage and launder all your clothes, sealing them afterwards in plastic bags to further protect them.

➡ Be sure to tell the management – if staff seem unconcerned or refuse to do anything about it, complain to the local tourist office.

recommended for all travellers spending more than a week in Malaysia, is not 100% effective, so you must still be careful with what you eat and drink.

INSECT BITES & STINGS

Lice Most commonly inhabit your head and pubic area. Transmission is via close contact with an infected person. Treat with numerous applications of an anti-lice shampoo containing permethrin.

Ticks Contracted after walking in rural areas. If you are bitten and experience symptoms such as a rash at the site of the bite or elsewhere, fever, or muscle aches, see a doctor. Doxycycline prevents tick-borne diseases.

Leeches Found in humid rainforest areas. They don't transmit disease, but their bites can be itchy for weeks afterwards and can easily become infected. Apply an iodine-based antiseptic to any leech bite to prevent infection.

Bees or wasps If allergic to their stings, carry an injection of adrenaline (eg an Epipen) for emergency treatment.

SKIN PROBLEMS

Fungal rashes can occur in moist areas that get less air, such as the groin, the armpits and between the toes. Treatment involves keeping the skin dry, avoiding chafing and using an antifungal cream such as Clotrimazole or Lamisil. The fungus *tinea versicolor* causes small, light-coloured patches, most commonly on the back, chest and shoulders. Consult a doctor.

Immediately wash all wounds in clean water and apply antiseptic. If you develop signs of infection (increasing pain and redness), see a doctor. Divers should be particularly careful with coral cuts as they become easily infected.

SUNBURN

Always use a strong sunscreen (at least SPF 30), and wear a wide-brimmed hat and sunglasses outdoors. If you become sunburnt, 1% hydrocortisone cream applied twice daily to the burn is helpful.

TRAVELLERS DIARRHOEA

By far the most common problem affecting travellers, travellers diarrhoea is usually caused by bacteria. Treatment consists of staying well hydrated; use a solution such as Gastrolyte. Antibiotics such as Norfloxacin, Ciprofloxacin or Azithromycin will kill the bacteria quickly.

Loperamide is just a 'stopper', but it can be helpful in certain situations, such as if you have to go on a long bus ride. Seek medical attention quickly if you do not respond to an appropriate antibiotic.

Giardiasis is relatively common. Symptoms include nausea, bloating, excess gas, fatigue and intermittent diarrhoea. The treatment of choice is Tinidazole, with Metronidazole being a second option.

WOMEN'S HEALTH

Sanitary products are readily available in Malaysia. Birth-control options may be limited, so bring adequate supplies of your own form of contraception.

Heat, humidity and antibiotics can contribute to thrush. Treat with antifungal creams and pessaries such as Clotrimazole. A practical alternative is a tablet of fluconazole (Diflucan).

Internet Access

Malaysia is blanketed with hot spots for wi-fi connections (usually free). Internet cafes are less common these days, but they do still exist if you're not travelling with a wi-fi enabled device.

In reviews, the wi-fi symbol indicates that free wi-fi is available.

Legal Matters

In any dealings with the local police forces it will pay to be deferential. You're most likely to come into contact with them either through reporting a crime (KL has a tourist-police booth at the **Malaysia Tourism Centre** (MaTiC; Map p250; ☎03-9235 4900; www.matic.gov.my/en; 109 Jln Ampang; ⏰8am-10pm; Bukit Nanas) for this purpose) or while driving. Minor misdemeanours may be overlooked, but don't count on it.

Drug trafficking carries a mandatory death penalty. A number of foreigners have been executed in Malaysia, some for possession of very small quantities of heroin. Even possession of small amounts of marijuana can bring a lengthy jail sentence and a beating with the *rotan* (cane).

Medical Services

KL is an increasingly popular destination for health tourism, for everything from cosmetic surgery to dental veneers. Medical centres and dentists are found in all the big malls and a private consultation will cost around RM50. Pharmacies are all over town; the most common is Watsons, in most malls.

Hospital Kuala Lumpur (☎03-2615 5555; www.hkl.gov.my; Jln Pahang; MTitiwangsa, Titiwangsa) City's main hospital, north of the centre.

Twin Towers Medical Centre KLCC (☎03-2382 3500; http://ttmcklcc.com.my; level 4, Suria KLCC, Jln Ampang; ⏰8.30am-5pm Mon-Fri, to 1pm Sat; MKLCC) Handily located in the mall attached to the Petronas Towers, with a second clinic near KL Sentral.

Kien Fatt Medical Store (☎03-2078 3229; 59 Jln Petaling; ⏰8.30am-5.30pm

Mon-Sat; Ⓜ Pasar Seni) In business since 1943, this traditional pharmacy sells both Chinese and Western medicines. A qualified English-speaking doctor is available for consultations.

Tung Shin Hospital (☎03-2037 2288; www.tungshin.com.my; 102 Jln Pudu; Ⓜ Plaza Rakyat) A general hospital with a Chinese traditional medicine clinic.

Klinik Medicare (☎03-2938 3333; 2nd fl, Mid Valley Megamall; ⏰10am-10pm; Ⓡ Mid Valley) For check-ups and emergency treatments. Based in Mid Valley Megamall.

Money

Most banks and shopping malls provide international ATMs (typically on the ground floor or basement level). Moneychangers offer better rates than banks for changing cash and (at times) travellers cheques; they're usually open later and at weekends and are found in shopping malls.

ATMs & Credit Cards

Mastercard and Visa are the most widely accepted brands of credit card. You can make ATM withdrawals with your PIN, or banks such as Maybank (Malaysia's biggest bank), HSBC and Standard Chartered will accept credit cards for over-the-counter cash advances. Many banks are also linked to international banking networks such as Cirrus (the most common), Maestro and Plus, allowing withdrawals from overseas savings or chequing accounts.

Contact details for credit-card companies in Malaysia:

American Express (www.americanexpress.com/malaysia)

Diners Card (www.diners.com.my)

MasterCard (www.mastercard.com/sea)

Visa (www.visa-asia.com)

Currency

The ringgit (RM) is made up of 100 sen. Coins in use are one sen, five sen, 10 sen, 20 sen and 50 sen; notes are RM1, RM5, RM10, RM50 and RM100.

Taxes & Refunds

Since 2015 a goods and sales tax (GST) of 6% has been levied on most goods and services in Malaysia. There are some exemptions (mainly for fresh and essential foods), but generally you'll now find this tax added to most things you buy, including restaurant meals and souvenirs.

Travellers Cheques & Cash

Malaysian banks are efficient and there are plenty of moneychangers. Banks usually charge a commission for cash and cheques (around RM10 per transaction, with a possible extra fee for each cheque), whereas moneychangers have no charges but more variable rates.

All major brands of travellers cheques are accepted. Cash in major currencies is also readily exchanged, though the US dollar has a slight edge.

Opening Hours

Banks 10am to 3pm Monday to Friday, 9.30am to 11.30am Saturday

Restaurants noon to 2.30pm and 6pm to 10.30pm

Shops 9.30am to 7pm Monday to Saturday, malls 10am to 10pm daily

Post

Pos Malaysia Berhad runs a fast and efficient postal system. Post offices are generally open from 8am to 5pm Monday to Saturday but closed on the first Saturday of the month and on public holidays.

Aerograms and postcards cost 50 sen to send to any destination. Letters weighing 20g or less cost RM1.20 to Asia, RM1.40 to Australia or New Zealand, and RM2 to all other countries. Parcel rates range from around RM20 to RM60 for a 1kg parcel, depending on the destination. Main post offices sell packaging materials and stationery.

For international postal services, go to the **main post office** (Map p248; ☎03-2267 2267; www.pos.com.my; Jln Tun Tan Cheng Lock; ⏰8.30am-6pm Mon-Fri, to 1pm Sat; Ⓜ Pasar Seni), across the river from Central Market. Branch post offices are found all over KL, including:

Pos Malaysia Suria KLCC (Map p250; www.pos.com.my; Lot C21, Suria KLCC; ⏰10am-6pm; Ⓜ KLCC)

Pos Malaysia Sungai Wang Plaza (Map p252; www.pos.com.my; lot T54-56, Sungai Wang Plaza, Jln Sultan Ismail; ⏰10am-8pm Mon-Fri, to 6pm Sat & Sun; AiraAsia-Bukit Bintang)

Pos Malaysia Masjid India (Map p256; www.pos.com.my; 303 Jln TAR; ⏰8.30am-5.30pm Mon-Fri, to 1pm Sat; Medan Tuanku)

Pos Malaysia Brickfields (Map p260; ☎03-2274 1535; www.pos.com.my; 75 Jln Thambipillai; ⏰8.30am-5.30pm Mon-Fri, to 1pm Sat; KL Sentral)

Pos Malaysia Bangsar (Map p262; www.pos.com.my; 48 Jln Telawi; ⏰8.30am-10pm Mon-Fri, to 1pm Sat; Ⓜ Bank Rakyat-Bangsar)

DHL Bangsar (www.dhl.com.my; 60 Jln Telawi; ⏰9am-9pm Mon-Fri, 10am-6pm Sat, 11am-5pm Sun; Ⓜ Bank Rakyat-Bangsar)

DHL Chinatown (Map p249; www.dhl.com.my; ground fl, Central Market, Jln Hang Kasturi; ⌚10am-9.30pm)

Public Holidays

As well as fixed secular holidays, various religious festivals (which change dates annually) are national holidays. These include Chinese New Year (in January/February), the Hindu festival of Deepavali (in October/November), the Buddhist festival of Wesak (April/May) and the Muslim festivals of Hari Raya Haji, Hari Raya Puasa, Mawlid al-Nabi and Awal Muharram (Muslim New Year).

Fixed annual holidays include the following.

New Year's Day 1 January

Federal Territory Day 1 February (Kuala Lumpur and Putrajaya only)

Sultan of Selangor's Birthday Second Saturday in March (Selangor only)

Labour Day 1 May

Yang di-Pertuan Agong's (King's) Birthday First Saturday in June

National Day (Hari Kebangsaan) 31 August

Christmas Day 25 December

Safe Travel

KL is generally very safe, but watch for pickpockets on crowded public transport. One ongoing irritation is the state of the pavements. The covers thrown over drains can give way suddenly, so walk around them. Flooding can also be a problem – carry an umbrella against the rain and be prepared to roll up your trousers to wade through giant puddles.

Animal Hazards

Rabies occurs in Malaysia, so any bite from an animal should be treated very seriously. Be cautious around monkeys, dogs and cats. On jungle treks look out for centipedes, scorpions, spiders and snakes. Mosquitoes are likely to be the biggest menace. The risk of malaria is low and antimalarial tablets are rarely recommended, but dengue fever is a growing problem, so take precautions to avoid mosquito bites by covering up exposed skin or wearing a strong repellent containing DEET.

Scams

The most common scams involve seemingly friendly locals who invite you to join rigged card games, or shops that trick travellers into buying large amounts of gold jewellery or gems at elevated prices.

Theft & Violence

Theft and violence are not particularly common in Malaysia. However, muggings and bag snatches do happen and physical attacks have been known to occur, particularly after hours and in rundown areas of KL. Thieves on motorbikes target women for grab raids on their handbags; where possible walk against the direction of traffic and carry your bag over the arm that's furthest from the road.

Be wary of demonstrations, particularly over religious or ethnic issues, as these can turn violent.

Use credit cards only at established businesses and guard your credit-card numbers closely.

Carry a small, sturdy padlock you can use for cheap hotel-room doors and hostel lockers, and to keep prying fingers out of your bags in left-luggage rooms.

Telephone

Landline services are provided by the national monopoly Telekom Malaysia (www.tm.com.my).

International Calls

The easiest and cheapest way to make international calls is to buy a local SIM card for your mobile phone. Only certain payphones permit international calls. You can make operator-assisted international calls from local Telekom offices. To save money on landline calls, buy a prepaid international calling card (available from convenience stores).

Local Calls

Local calls cost eight sen for the first two minutes. Payphones take coins or prepaid cards, which are available from TM offices and convenience stores. Some also take international credit cards. You'll also find a range of discount calling cards at convenience stores and mobile-phone counters.

Mobile Phones

If you have arranged global roaming with your home provider, your GSM digital phone will automatically tune in to one of the region's digital networks. If not, buy a prepaid SIM card for one of the local networks on arrival. The rate for a local call is around 40 sen per minute. There are three mobile-phone companies, all with similar call rates and prepaid packages:

Celcom (www.celcom.com.my)

DiGi (www.digi.com.my)

Maxis (www.maxis.com.my)

AREA & TELEPHONE CODES

Country code for Malaysia ☎60

Kuala Lumpur ☎03

Melaka ☎06

Penang ☎04

Singapore ☎02

Time

Malaysia is eight hours ahead of GMT/UTC. Noon in KL:

- 8pm in Los Angeles
- 11pm in New York
- 4am in London
- 2pm in Sydney and Melbourne

Toilets

Western-style sit-down loos are now the norm, but there are still a few places with Asian squat toilets. Toilet paper is often not provided; instead, you will find a hose or a spout on the toilet seat, which you are supposed to use as a bidet, or a bucket of water and a tap. If you're not comfortable with the 'hand-and-water' technique, carry packets of tissues or toilet paper wherever you go.

Tourist Information

Tourism Malaysia (www.tourismmalaysia.gov.my) has a network of domestic offices that are good for brochures and free maps but rather weak on hard factual information. Its overseas offices are useful for pre-departure planning. There are regional offices in Kuala Lumpur.

Visit KL (Kuala Lumpur Tourism Bureau; Map p260; ☎03-2698 0332; www.visitkl.gov.my; 11 Jln Tangsi; ⏲8.30am-5.30pm Mon-Fri; 📶; Ⓜ Masjid Jamek)

Malaysia Tourism Centre (MaTiC; Map p250; ☎03-9235 4900; www.matic.gov.my/en; 109 Jln Ampang; ⏲8am-10pm; Bukit Nanas)

Travellers with Disabilities

For the mobility impaired, Kuala Lumpur can be a nightmare. There are often no footpaths, kerbs can be very high, construction sites are everywhere, and crossings are few and far between. On the upside, taxis are cheap and both Malaysia Airlines and KTM (the national rail service) offer 50% discounts for travellers with disabilities.

Before setting off, get in touch with your national support organisation (preferably with the travel officer, if there is one). Also try the following:

Accessible Journeys (www.disabilitytravel.com) In the US.

Mobility International USA (www.miusa.org) In the US.

Nican (www.nican.com.au) In Australia.

Tourism for All (www.tourismforall.org.uk) In the UK.

Download Lonely Planet's free Accessible Travel guide from http://lptravel.to/AccessibleTravel.

Visas

Visitors must have a passport valid for at least six months beyond the date of entry. You may also be asked to provide proof of a ticket for onward travel and sufficient funds to cover your stay.

Only under special circumstances can Israeli citizens enter Malaysia. Nationals of most other countries are given a 30-, 60- or 90-day visa on arrival. Full details of visa requirements are available at www.kln.gov.my.

Immigration Office (☎03-6205 7400; 69 Jln Sri Hartamas 1, off Jln Duta; ⏲7.30am-1pm & 2-5.30pm Mon-Fri) Handles visa extensions; offices are opposite Publika mall.

Visa Extensions

Depending on your nationality, it may be possible to extend your visa at an immigration office in KL for an additional one or two months. Extensions tend to be granted only for genuine emergencies. It's normally easier to hop across the border to Thailand, Singapore or Indonesia and re-enter the country – this counts as a new visit, even if you re-enter the same day.

Women Travellers

Dressing modestly and being respectful, especially in areas of stronger Muslim religious sensibilities, will ensure you travel with minimum hassle. When visiting mosques, cover your head and limbs with a headscarf and sarong (many mosques lend these out at the entrance).

Be proactive about your own safety. Treat overly friendly strangers, both male and female, with a good deal of caution. After dark, take taxis and avoid walking alone in quiet or seedy parts of town.

Language

The official language of Kuala Lumpur, Melaka and Penang is Malay, or Bahasa Malaysia, as it's called by its speakers. It belongs to the Western Austronesian language family and is very similar to Indonesian.

There are several Indian and Chinese languages spoken in the region as well, such as Hokkien, Cantonese, Tamil and Malayalam. English is also widely understood.

Malay pronunciation is easy to master. Each letter always represents the same sound and most letters are pronounced the same as their English counterparts, with *c* pronounced as the 'ch' in 'chat' and *sy* as the 'sh' in 'ship'. Note also that *kh* is a guttural sound (like the 'ch' in the Scottish *loch*), and that *gh* is a throaty 'g' sound.

Syllables generally carry equal emphasis – the main exception is the unstressed *e* in words such as *besar* (big) – but the rule of thumb is to stress the second-last syllable.

BASICS

In Malaysia, *kamu* is an egalitarian second-person pronoun, equivalent to 'you' in English. The polite pronoun for the equivalent of English 'I/we' is *kami*. In polite speech, you wouldn't normally use first-person pronouns, but would refer to yourself by name or form of address, eg *Makcik nak pergi ke pasar* (Auntie wants to go to the market).

When addressing a man or a woman old enough to be your parent, use *pakcik* (uncle) or *makcik* (aunt). For someone only slightly older than yourself, use *abang* or *bang* (older brother) and *kakak* or *kak* (older sister). For people old enough to be your grandparents, *datuk* and *nenek* (grandfather and grandmother) are used. For a man or woman you meet on the street you can also use *encik* or *cik* respectively.

WANT MORE?

For in-depth language information and handy phrases, check out Lonely Planet's *Malay Phrasebook*. You'll find it at **shop.lonelyplanet.com**, or you can buy Lonely Planet's iPhone phrasebooks at the Apple App Store.

Hello. — *Helo.*

Goodbye.
(by person leaving) — *Selamat tinggal.*
(by person staying) — *Selamat jalan.*

Yes. — *Ya.*

No. — *Tidak.*

Please.
(to ask for something) — *Tolong.*
(to offer something) — *Silakan.*

Thank you. — *Terima kasih.*

You're welcome. — *Sama-sama.*

Excuse me. — *Maaf.*

Sorry. — *Minta maaf.*

How are you? — *Apa khabar?*

Fine, thanks. — *Khabar baik.*

What's your name? — *Siapa nama kamu?*

My name is ... — *Nama saya ...*

Do you speak English? — *Bolehkah anda berbicara Bahasa Inggeris?*

I don't understand. — *Saya tidak faham.*

ACCOMMODATION

Do you have any rooms available? — *Ada bilik kosong?*

How much is it per night/person? — *Berapa harga satu malam/orang?*

Is breakfast included? — *Makan pagi termasukkah?*

air-con	*pendingin udara*
bathroom	*bilik air*
campsite	*kawasan perkhemahan*
double room	*bilik untuk dua orang*
guesthouse	*rumah tetamu*
hotel	*hotel*
mosquito coil	*ubat nyamuk*
single room	*bilik untuk seorang*
window	*tingkap*
youth hostel	*asrama belia*

DIRECTIONS

Where is ...?	*Di mana ...?*
What's the address?	*Apakah alamatnya?*
Can you write the address, please?	*Tolong tuliskan alamat itu?*
Can you show me (on the map)?	*Tolong tunjukkan (di peta)?*
Go straight ahead.	*Jalan terus.*
Turn left.	*Belok kiri.*
Turn right.	*Belok kanan.*

at the corner	*di simpang*
at the traffic lights	*di tempat lampu isyarat*
behind	*di belakang*
in front of	*di hadapan*
near	*dekat*
next to	*di samping/di sebelah*
opposite	*berhadapan dengan*

EATING & DRINKING

We'd like a table for (five), please.	*Tolong bagi meja untuk (lima) orang.*
Can I see the menu?	*Minta senarai makanan?*
What's in this dish?	*Ini termasuk apa?*
I'd like ...	*Saya mahu...*
I'm a vegetarian.	*Saya makan sayur-sayuran sahaja.*
Not too spicy, please.	*Kurang pedas.*
Please add extra chilli.	*Tolong letak cili lebih.*
Thank you, that was delicious.	*Sedap sekali, terima kasih.*
Please bring the bill.	*Tolong bawa bil.*

Key Words

bottle	*botol*
breakfast	*makan pagi*
children's menu	*menu kanak-kanak*
cold	*sejuk*
cup	*cawan*
dinner	*makan malam*
drink	*minuman*
food	*makanan*
food stall	*gerai*
fork	*garfu*
glass	*gelas*
grocery store	*kedai makanan*
highchair	*kerusi tinggi*
hot (warm)	*panas*
knife	*pisau*
lunch	*makan tengahari*
market	*pasar*
menu	*menu*
plate	*pinggan*
restaurant	*restoran*
spicy	*pedas*
spoon	*sudu*
vegetarian (food)	*sayuran saja*
with	*dengan*
without	*tanpa*

Meat & Fish

(dried) anchovies	*ikan bilis*
beef	*daging lembu*
brains	*otak*
catfish	*ikan keli*
chicken	*ayam*
cockles	*kerang*
crab	*ketam*
duck	*itik*
fish	*ikan*
freshwater fish	*ikan air tawar*
goat	*kambing*
lamb	*anak biri-biri*
liver	*hati*
lobster	*udang karang*
mussels	*kepah*
mutton	*biri-biri*
oysters	*tiram*
pig	*babi*
rabbit	*arnab*
salted dried fish	*ikan kering*
saltwater fish	*ikan air masin*
shrimp	*udang*
squid	*sotong*
tripe	*perut*

Fruit & Vegetables

apple	*epal*
banana	*pisang*
beans	*kacang*
cabbage	*kubis*
carrot	*lobak*
cauliflower	*kubis bunga*
coconut	*kelapa*
corn	*jagung*
cucumber	*timun*
eggplant	*terung*
guava	*jambu*
jackfruit	*nangka*
mango	*mangga*
mangosteen	*manggis*
mushrooms	*kulat*
onion	*bawang*
orange	*oren*
papaya	*betik*
peanuts	*kacang*
pineapple	*nenas*
potato	*kentang*
pumpkin	*labu*
soursop	*durian belanda*
starfruit	*belimbing*
watermelon	*tembikai*

Other

bread	*roti*
cake	*kueh*
chilli sauce	*sambal*
noodles	*mee*
oil	*minyak*
(black) pepper	*lada hitam*
rice (cooked)	*nasi*
rice (uncooked)	*beras*
salt	*garam*
soy sauce	*kicap*
sugar	*gula*
sweets	*manisan*
tofu	*tahu*
vinegar	*cuka*

Drinks

beer	*bir*
boiled water	*air masak*
citrus juice	*air limau*
coconut milk	*air kelapa muda*
coffee	*kopi*
cordial	*pekatan*
frothed tea	*teh tarik*
milk	*susu*
palm tree spirits	*todi*
rice wine	*tuak*
tea	*teh*
water	*air*
(grape) wine	*wain*

EMERGENCIES

Help!	*Tolong!*
Go away!	*Pergi!*
I'm lost.	*Saya sesat.*
There's been an accident.	*Ada kemalangan.*
Call a doctor!	*Panggil doktor!*
Call the police!	*Panggil polis!*
I'm ill.	*Saya sakit.*
It hurts here.	*Sini sakit.*
I'm allergic to (antibiotics).	*Saya alergik kepada (antibiotik).*

SHOPPING & SERVICES

I'd like to buy ...	*Saya nak beli ...*
I'm just looking.	*Saya nak tengok saja.*
Can I look at it?	*Boleh saya lihat barang itu?*
I don't like it.	*Saya tak suka ini.*
How much is it?	*Berapa harganya?*
It's too expensive.	*Mahalnya.*
Can you lower the price?	*Boleh kurang sedikit?*
There's a mistake in the bill.	*Bil ini salah.*

Signs

Masuk	Entrance
Keluar	Exit
Buka	Open
Tutup	Closed
Pertanyaan	Information
Dilarang	Prohibited
Tandas	Toilets
Lelaki	Men
Perempuan	Women

credit card	*kad kredit*
mobile phone	*telefon bimbit*
phonecard	*kad telefon*
post office	*pejabat pos*
signature	*tanda tangan*
tourist office	*pejabat pelancong*

TIME & DATES

What time is it?	*Pukul berapa?*
It's (seven) o'clock.	*Pukul (tujuh).*
Half past (one).	*Pukul (satu) setengah.*

in the morning	*pagi*
in the afternoon	*tengahari*
in the evening	*petang*

yesterday	*semalam*
today	*hari ini*
tomorrow	*esok*

Monday	*hari Isnin*
Tuesday	*hari Selasa*
Wednesday	*hari Rabu*
Thursday	*hari Khamis*
Friday	*hari Jumaat*
Saturday	*hari Sabtu*
Sunday	*hari Minggu*

January	*Januari*
February	*Februari*
March	*Mac*
April	*April*
May	*Mei*
June	*Jun*
July	*Julai*
August	*Ogos*
September	*September*
October	*Oktober*
November	*November*
December	*Disember*

Question Words

What?	*Apa?*
When?	*Bila?*
Where?	*Di mana?*
Which?	*Yang mana?*
Who?	*Siapa?*
Why?	*Kenapa?*

TRANSPORT

Public Transport

bicycle-rickshaw	*beca*
boat	*bot*
bus	*bas*
plane	*kapal terbang*
ship	*kapal*
taxi	*teksi*
train	*keretapi*

I want to go to ...	*Saya nak ke ...*
What time does the (bus) leave?	*(Bas) bertolak pukul berapa?*
What time does the (train) arrive?	*(Keretapi) tiba pukul berapa?*
Does the bus stop at the (restaurant)?	*Bas ini berhenti di (restoran)?*
Can you tell me when we get to ...?	*Tolong beritahu saya bila kita sudah sampai di ...?*
I want to get off at ...	*Saya nak turun di ...*
The (bus) has been delayed.	*(Bas) itu telah terlambat.*
The (train) has been cancelled.	*(Keretapi) itu telah dibatalkan.*

first class	*kelas pertama*
one-way ticket	*tiket sehala*
return ticket	*tiket pergi-balik*
second class	*kelas kedua/ bisnis*

first	*pertama*
last	*terakhir*
next	*berikutnya*

airport	*lapangan terbang*
bus stop	*perhentian bas*
ticket office	*pejabat tiket*
timetable	*jadual*
train station	*stesen keretapi*

Driving & Cycling

I'd like to hire a ...	*Saya nak menyewa ...*
bicycle	*basikal*
car	*kereta*
jeep	*jip*
motorcycle	*motosikal*

child seat	*tempat duduk bayi*
diesel	*disel*
helmet	*topi keledar*
mechanic	*mekanik*
petrol/gas	*minyak*
pump	*pam*
service station	*stesen minyak*
unleaded petrol	*petrol tanpa plumbum*

Is this the road to ...?	*Inikah jalan ke ...?*
How many kilometres?	*Berapa kilometer?*
Can I park here?	*Boleh saya letak kereta di sini?*
How long can I park here?	*Beberapa lama boleh saya letak kereta di sini?*
The (car) has broken down at ...	*(Kereta) saya telah rosak di ...*
The (motorbike) won't start.	*(Motosikal) saya tidak dapat dihidupkan.*
I have a flat tyre.	*Tayarnya kempis.*
I've run out of petrol.	*Minyak sudah habis.*
I've had an accident.	*Saya terlibat dalam kemalangan.*

Numbers

1	*satu*
2	*dua*
3	*tiga*
4	*empat*
5	*lima*
6	*enam*
7	*tujuh*
8	*lapan*
9	*sembilan*
10	*sepuluh*
20	*dua puluh*
30	*tiga puluh*
40	*empat puluh*
50	*lima puluh*
60	*enam puluh*
70	*tujuh puluh*
80	*lapan puluh*
90	*sembilan puluh*
100	*seratus*
1000	*seribu*

GLOSSARY

adat – Malay customary law

alor – groove; furrow; main channel of a river

ampang – dam

Baba-Nonya – descendants of Chinese immigrants to Melaka and Penang who intermarried with Malays and adopted many Malay customs; also known as Peranakan, or Straits Chinese; sometimes spelt Nyonya

Bahasa Malaysia – Malay language; also known as Bahasa Melayu

bandar – seaport; town

baru – new; common in placenames

batik – technique of imprinting cloth with dye to produce multi-coloured patterns

batu – stone; rock; milepost

bendahara – chief minister

bomoh – spiritual healer

bukit – hill

bumiputra – literally, sons of the soil; indigenous Malays

bunga raya – hibiscus flower (national flower of Malaysia)

genting – mountain pass

gopuram – Hindu temple tower

istana – palace

jalan – road

kampung – village; also spelt kampong

kedai kopi – coffee shop

kongsi – Chinese clan organisations, also known as ritual brotherhoods, heavenman-earth societies, triads or secret societies; meeting house for Chinese of the same clan

kopitiam – traditional coffee shop

kota – fort; city

kris – traditional Malay wavy-bladed dagger

KTM – Keretapi Tanah Melayu; Malaysian Railways System

kuala – river mouth; place where a tributary joins a larger river

laut – sea

lebuh – street

lorong – narrow street; alley

LRT – Light Rail Transit (Kuala Lumpur)

mamak – Indian Muslim

masjid – mosque

merdeka – independence

muezzin – mosque official who calls the faithful to prayer

negara – country

negeri – state

nonya – see Baba-Nonya

Orang Asli – literally, Original People; Malaysian aborigines

padang – grassy area; field; also the city square

pantai – beach

pasar – market

pasar malam – night market
pelabuhan – port
penghulu – chief or village head
pengkalan – quay
perahu – sampan; small boat
Peranakan – refers to the Baba-Nonya or Straits Chinese
pulau – island

raja – prince; ruler
raja muda – crown prince; heir apparent
rakyat – common people
rattan – stems from climbing palms used for wickerwork and canes

sarong – all-purpose cloth, often sewn into a tube, and worn by women, men and children
silat – martial-arts dance form
Straits Chinese – see Baba-Nonya
sultan – ruler of one of Malaysia's nine states
sungai – river
syariah – Islamic system of law

tanjung – headland
tasik – lake
teluk – bay; sometimes spelt telok
temenggong – Malay administrator
tunku – prince

wayang – Chinese opera
wayang kulit – shadow-puppet theatre
wisma – office block or shopping centre

yang di-pertuan agong – Malaysia's head of state, or 'king'

FOOD GLOSSARY

achar – vegetable and/or fruit pickle
ais kacang – dessert of ice shavings topped with syrups, coconut milk, red beans, seeds and jelly
aloo gobi – Indian potato-and-cauliflower dish
ayam – chicken
ayam goreng – fried chicken

bak chang – rice dumpling filled with savoury or sweet meat and wrapped in leaves
bak kut teh – pork ribs and parts stewed with garlic and Chinese medicinal herbs
belacan – fermented prawn paste
belacan kangkong – water convolvulus stir-fried in prawn paste
bhindi – okra (lady's fingers)
biryani – steamed basmati rice oven-baked with spices and meat, seafood or vegetables
brinjal – aubergine (eggplant)

carrot cake – firm radish cake cubed and stir-fried with egg, garlic, chilli, soy sauce, and bean sprouts; also known as *chye tow kway*
cendol – dessert of shaved ice and mung-bean-flour 'pasta' doused with coconut milk and liquid palm sugar
chapati – griddle-fried whole-wheat bread
char kway teow – wide rice noodles stir-fried with cockles, prawns, Chinese sausage, eggs, bean sprouts, and soy and chilli sauces
char siew – sweet and sticky barbecued pork fillet
char yoke – crispy-skinned roasted pork fillet
chicken-rice – steamed chicken, served with rice boiled or steamed in chicken stock, slices of cucumber and a chilli-ginger sauce
chilli padi – extremely hot small chilli
choi sum – popular Chinese green vegetable, served steamed with oyster sauce
claypot rice – rice cooked in a clay pot with chicken, mushroom, Chinese sausage and soy sauce
congee – Chinese porridge

daun kunyit – turmeric leaf
daun pisang – banana leaf, often used as a plate in Malaysia
daun salam – leaves used much like bay leaves in cooking
dhal – dish of puréed lentils
dim sum – sweet and savoury minidishes served at breakfast and lunch; also known as *dian xin* or *yum cha*
dosa – large, light, crispy pancake

fish sauce – liquid made from fermented anchovies and salt
fish-head curry – head and 'shoulders' of large fish such as red snapper in curry sauce; also known as *kepala ikan*

gado gado – cold dish of bean sprouts, potatoes, long beans, bean curd, rice cakes and prawn crackers, topped with a spicy peanut sauce
galangal – ginger-like root used to flavour various dishes
garam masala – sweet, mild mixture of freshly ground spices
garoupa – white fish popular in Southeast Asia
ghee – clarified butter
gula jawa – brown palm-sugar sold in thin blocks

halal – food prepared according to Muslim dietary laws
hoisin sauce – thick sweet-spicy sauce made from soya beans, red beans, sugar, flour, vinegar, salt, garlic, sesame, chillies and spices
Hokkien mee – yellow noodles fried with sliced meat, boiled squid, prawns and strips of fried egg; in Penang, hot and spicy prawn and pork noodle soup

idli – steamed rice cake
ikan asam – fried fish in sour tamarind curry

ikan bilis – small, deep-fried anchovies

kangkong – water convolvulus; thick-stemmed type of spinach

kari ayam – curried chicken

kecap – soy sauce

keema – spicy minced meat

kepala ikan – fish head, usually in curry or grilled

kofta – minced-meat or vegetable ball

kopi-o – black coffee

korma – mild Indian curry with yoghurt sauce

kueh melayu – sweet pancakes with peanuts, raisins and sugar

kueh mueh – Malay cakes

kway teow – broad rice-noodles

laksa – noodles in a spicy coconut soup with bean sprouts, quail eggs, prawns, shredded chicken and dried bean curd; also called Nonya laksa to differentiate it from Penang laksa (or asam laksa), a version that has a prawn paste and tamarind-flavoured gravy

lassi – yoghurt-based drink

lombok – type of hot chilli

lontong – rice cakes in spicy coconut-milk gravy topped with grated coconut and, sometimes, bean curd and egg

lor mee – noodles with slices of meat, eggs and a dash of vinegar in a dark brown sauce

masala dosa – thin pancake rolled around spicy vegetables with rasam on the side

mee – noodles

mee goreng – fried noodles

mee pok – flat noodles made with egg and wheat

mee rebus – yellow noodles served in a thick sweetish sauce made from sweet potatoes and garnished with sliced hard-boiled eggs and green chillies

mee siam – white thin noodles in a sweet and sour gravy made with tamarind

mee soto – noodle soup with shredded chicken

murtabak – roti canai filled with pieces of mutton, chicken or vegetables

naan – tear-shaped leavened bread baked in a clay oven

nasi – rice

nasi biryani – saffron rice flavoured with spices and garnished with cashew nuts, almonds and raisins

nasi campur – buffet of curried meats, fish and vegetables, served with rice

nasi goreng – fried rice

nasi lemak – rice boiled in coconut milk, served with ikan bilis, peanuts and a curry dish

nasi padang – Malay rice and accompanying meat and vegetable dishes

pakora – vegetable fritter

pan mee – wide, thick wheat noodles tossed with dark soy and topped with ground pork, *ikan bilis* and shredded cloud ear mushrooms

pappadam – Indian cracker

phrik – chillies

pilau – rice fried in ghee and mixed with nuts, then cooked in stock

pisang goreng – banana fritter

popiah – similar to a spring roll, but not fried

pudina – mint sauce

raita – side dish of cucumber, yoghurt and mint

rasam – spicy soup

rendang – spicy coconut curry with beef or chicken

rijsttafel – literally 'rice table'; a buffet of Indonesian dishes

rogan josh – stewed mutton in a rich sauce

rojak – salad doused in a peanut-sauce dressing that may contain shrimp paste

roti – bread

roti canai – unleavened flaky bread cooked with ghee on a hotplate; eaten dipped in dhal or curry; also known as *paratha* or *roti prata*

saag – spicy chopped-spinach dish

sambal – sauce of chilli, onions and prawn paste that has been fried

sambal udang – hot curried prawns

sambar – fiery mixture of vegetables, lentils and split peas

samosa – pastry filled with vegetables or meat

santan – coconut milk

satay – pieces of chicken, beef or mutton that are skewered and grilled

Sichuan – region in south central China famous for its spicy cuisine

soto ayam – spicy chicken soup with vegetables and potatoes

steamboat – meat, seafood and vegetables cooked at the table by being dipped into a pot of boiling clear stock

tamarind – large bean from the tamarind tree with a brittle shell and a dark brown, sticky pulp; used for its sweet-sour taste

tandoori – Indian style of cooking in which marinated meat is baked in a clay oven

taro – vegetable with leaves like spinach, stalks like asparagus and a starchy root similar in size and taste to the potato

tauhu goreng – fried bean curd and bean sprouts in peanut sauce

teh tarik – tea made with evaporated milk, which is literally pulled or stretched (tarik) from one glass to another

teh-o – tea without milk

tikka – small pieces of meat or fish served off the bone and marinated in yoghurt before baking

tom yam – tomato-red hot-and-sour spicy seafood soup

umai – raw fish marinated and served with onions

won ton – mee soup dish with shredded chicken or braised beef

yong tau fu – bean curd stuffed with minced meat

yu tiao – deep-fried pastry eaten for breakfast or as a dessert

yu yuan mian – fish-ball soup

Behind the Scenes

SEND US YOUR FEEDBACK

We love to hear from travellers – your comments keep us on our toes and help make our books better. Our well-travelled team reads every word on what you loved or loathed about this book. Although we cannot reply individually to your submissions, we always guarantee that your feedback goes straight to the appropriate authors, in time for the next edition. Each person who sends us information is thanked in the next edition – the most useful submissions are rewarded with a selection of digital PDF chapters.

Visit **lonelyplanet.com/contact** to submit your updates and suggestions or to ask for help. Our award-winning website also features inspirational travel stories, news and discussions.

Note: We may edit, reproduce and incorporate your comments in Lonely Planet products such as guidebooks, websites and digital products, so let us know if you don't want your comments reproduced or your name acknowledged. For a copy of our privacy policy visit lonelyplanet.com/privacy.

OUR READERS

Many thanks to the travellers who used the last edition and wrote to us with helpful hints, useful advice and interesting anecdotes: Ane Richardsen, Anne Myles, Felicity Turner, Gene Demagalski, Helen Wood, Samuel Tan, Toni Linke.

WRITER THANKS

Simon Richmond

As always a big thank you to Penang friends Narelle, Howard, Chris, Daphne, Alison and Allen Tan. In Melaka thanks to Bob Teng.

Isabel Albiston

Huge thanks to Simon Richmond for his help and advice and to Alex Yong for his cheerful assistance with so much of my research. *Terima kasih*, also, to Noraza Yusof, Jane Rai, Scott Dunn and Ana Abdullah. For their company on the road and research tips, thanks to Kevin Chong, Siddiq Sulaiman Zainal Azhar, Fazal Mahbob, Farrah Aqlima, Matt Hobbins and Helen Armstrong.

ACKNOWLEDGEMENTS

Cover photograph: Man painting lantern in Georgetown, Malaysia; Richard l'Anson/Getty ©

THIS BOOK

This 4th edition of Lonely Planet's *Kuala Lumpur, Melaka and Penang* guidebook was researched and written by Simon Richmond and Isabel Albiston. The previous edition was also researched and written by Simon Richmond. This guidebook was produced by the following:

Destination Editors Lauren Keith, Sarah Reid
Product Editors Jessica Ryan
Senior Cartographer Julie Sheridan
Book Designer Gwen Cotter
Assisting Editors Sarah Bailey, Carolyn Bain, Judith Bamber, Imogen Bannister, Melanie Dankel, Victoria Harrison and Sam Trafford.
Cover Researcher Naomi Parker
Thanks to Louise Bastock, Jennifer Carey, David Carroll, Daniel Corbett, Evan Godt, Jane Grisman, Andi Jones, Sandie Kestell, Indra Kilfoyle, Kate Mathews, Claire Naylor, Karyn Noble, Genna Patterson, Alison Ridgway, Dianne Schallmeiner, Ellie Simpson, Angela Tinson, and Dora Whitaker.

See also separate subindexes for:

EATING P240

DRINKING & NIGHTLIFE P241

ENTERTAINMENT P242

SHOPPING P242

SPORTS & ACTIVITIES P243

SLEEPING P243

Index

8 Heeren Street (Melaka) 142

A

accommodation 15, 124-32, *see also* Sleeping *subindex*
activities, *see individual activities*, Sports & Activities *subindex*
adat 200
Air Itam 182-3
air pollution 223
air travel 218-19
ambulance 222
Ampang 53
amusement parks 22, 66, 117, 119, 121, 175, 179
animals 19, 227
animism 204
anti-Semitism 206
Aquaria KLCC 48
architecture 18-19, 209-11, **50-1**
area codes 227
Art & Garden by Fuan Wong (Penang) 179
arts 207-9, *see also individual arts*
Asianel Reflexology Spa 66
ATMs 226
Ayer Keroh 153

B

Baba & Nyonya Heritage Museum 139, 141
Badan Warisan Malaysia 48, 52
Baba-Nonya people 202
Badawi, Abdullah 195-6
Bahasa Malaysia 229-35
Balik Pulau 184
Ban Po Thar (Penang) 182
Bangsar, *see* Lake Gardens, Brickfields & Bangsar
Bank Negara Malaysia Museum & Art Gallery 85
basketry 37-8
bathrooms 228
batik 37, 53
bats 212-13
Batu Caves 9, 113-14, **3**, **9**
Batu Ferringhi 178-82
Bazaar Baru Chow Kit 85
bedbugs 224
bees 225
Berjaya Times Square Theme Park 66
bicycle travel 219-20
Bird Interpretive Centre (Bukit Fraser) 116
birdwatching 117
Blue Mansion (Penang) 159-60
boat travel 219
bomoh 205
books
- architecture 209
- environment 212, 214
- history 191, 193, 194
- Islam 203
- literature 186, 193, 207

Botanical Gardens (Penang) 183
Brickfields, *see* Lake Gardens, Brickfields & Bangsar
Buddhism 204
Buddhist Maha Vihara 101
Bukit Bintang & KLCC 43, 44-66, **44**, **250-1**, **252-3**
- accommodation 126, 127-31
- drinking & nightlife 45, 57-62
- entertainment 62-3
- food 45, 52-7
- highlights 44, 46-7
- shopping 45, 63-5
- sights 46-52
- sports & activities 65-6
- transport 45

Bukit China (Melaka) 146-7, 154
Bukit Fraser 116-18
Bukit Nanas, *see* Chinatown, Merdeka Square & Bukit Nanas
bumiputra 195
bus travel 219, 220
business hours 26, 32, 37, 226
Butterworth (Penang) 156

C

Canopy Walkway 115
car travel 220
carbon emissions 215
cell phones 14, 227
Central Market 74
Chan She Shu Yuen Clan Association Temple 74
Cheah Kongsi (Penang) 168
Cheng Ho Cultural Museum (Melaka) 142
Cheng Hoon Teng Temple (Melaka) 141-2
Chetti Museum (Melaka) 143
Chew Jetty (Penang) 161
children, travel with 22-3, 175, **22**
China-Malaysia Friendship Garden (Putrajaya) 123
Chinatown (Melaka) 139-42, 144-6, 151-2, **140**
Chinatown, Merdeka Square & Bukit Nanas 9, 43, 67-82, **8**, **67**, **73**, **248-9**
- accommodation 126, 129-31
- drinking & nightlife 68, 78-80
- entertainment 80
- food 68, 75-8
- highlights 67, 69-72, 75
- shopping 80-1
- sights 69-75
- sports & activities 81-2
- transport 68
- walks 73, **73**

Chinatown Wet Market 74
Chinese New Year 20
Chinese population 201
Chinese religions 204
Chow Kit 85, 88, 89
City of Digital Lights at i-City (Shah Alam) 119
clanhouses 168
climate 15
Cockerel Mural 76
Confucianism 204
costs 26, 125, 226
credit cards 226
culture 200-6
currency 14, 226
customs regulations 222
cycling 219-20

D

dance 63, 207-8
dangers 227
Dark Cave 113-14
deforestation 214-15
dengue fever 224
Dewan Filharmonik Petronas 47
Dharma Realm Guan Yin Sagely Monastery 48
disabilities, travellers with 228
Donna Spa 66
drama 208
drinking & nightlife 24, 31-3, **31**, *see also individual neighbourhoods*, Drinking & Nightlife *subindex*
drinks 31-2
Dutch Square 139

E

economy 186-7, 194
electricity 222

Sights 000
Map Pages **000**
Photo Pages **000**

emergencies 222
entertainment 34-5, *see also individual neighbourhoods*, Entertainment *subindex*
Entopia by Penang Butterfly Farm (Penang) 179
environmental issues 214-15
Escape (Penang) 179-80
events, *see* festivals & events

F

ferry travel 219
festivals & events 20-1, 24, 37, 203-4, **24**
film 186, 209
fire services 222
First World Indoor Theme Park (Genting Highlands) 117
flea markets 121
food 24, 25-30, **25**, **61**, *see also individual neighbourhoods*, Eating *subindex*
costs 26
etiquette 28
language 230-1, 234-5
opening hours 26
Forest Research Institute Malaysia (FRIM) 12, 115, **12**
Fraser's Hill 116-18

G

Galeri Diraja Sultan Abdul Aziz (Klang) 119
Galeri Petronas 47, 48
galleries 19, *see also individual galleries*
gardens 19, *see also individual gardens*
gay travellers 32, 222-3
Genting Highlands 117
Genting Skyway (Genting Highlands) 117
George Town (Penang) 159-78, **162-3**
accommodation 174-8
drinking & nightlife 170-2
food 164-5, 167-70
history 167
shopping 172-3
sights 159-64
sports & activities 173-4
transport 156
walks 166, **166**
Goldsmith Mural 76
government 186-7, 196
Guan Yin Temple 74
Guandi Temple 72, **51**

H

handicrafts 37, *see also individual handicrafts*
hawker food 25, 171, **61**
health 223-5
heat exhaustion & stroke 223-4
hepatitis 224
Hibiscus Garden 96
Hin Bus Depot Art Centre (Penang) 162-3
Hinduism 204
history
George Town (Penang) 167
Kampung Baru 85
Kuala Lumpur 188-96
Melaka 135
Penang 157-8, 167
HIV 224
holidays 227
Holy Name of Jesus Catholic Church (Penang) 184
Hubback, Arthur Benison 211

I

Ilham 48
immigration 197
immunisations 223
Indian population 201
internet access 225
internet resources, *see* websites
Islam 202-4
Islamic Arts Museum 9, 94, **8**, **94**
Istana Alam Shah (Klang) 119-20
Istana Kehakiman (Putrajaya) 123
itineraries 16-17

J

Jalan Alor 55
Jalan Merdeka (Melaka) 146, 152
Jeriau Waterfall (Bukit Fraser) 117
JoJoBa Spa 66

K

Kampung Baru, *see* Masjid India, Kampung Baru & Northern KL
Kampung Chetti (Melaka) 143
Kampung Pulau Betong 184
Kek Lok Si Temple (Penang) 182-3
Kek Lok Si Temple Funicular (Penang) 183
Khoo Kongsi (Penang) 168
Kids on a Bicycle (Penang) 169
kites 38
Klang 119-20
Klang Fire Station (Klang) 119
Klang Valley 118-22
Klang Valley Mass Rapid Transit 220
KL Bird Park 95
KL Butterfly Park 96
KL City Gallery 71
KL Forest Eco Park 74
KL Railway Administration and Railway Station 99, **55**
KLCC, *see* Bukit Bintang & KLCC
KLCC Park 47, 48
Komik Asia (Penang) 164
Kompleks Perdadanan Putrajaya (Putrajaya) 123
Kuan Yin Teng (Penang) 161
Kuen Stephanie Sculptures 76
Kwong Tong Cemetery 102

L

Lake Gardens, Brickfields & Bangsar 43, 92-111, **260-1**, **262**
accommodation 126, 131-2
drinking & nightlife 93, 106-7
entertainment 107
food 93, 100, 102-6
highlights 92, 94-8
shopping 93, 107-11
sights 94-102
sports & activities 111
transport 93
walks 100, **100**
Laman Seni 7 (Shah Alam) 119
languages 14, 198, 229-35
Lat Cartoon Sculptures 76
Lee, TY 210
leeches 225
legal matters 225
lesbian travellers 32, 222-3
Light Rail Transit 221
literature, *see* books
Little India (Melaka) 146-7, 154
Little India Fountain 102
local life 24
Loke Mansion 85
Lorong Kurau 106
Lostgens' 79
Lucky Gardens 105

M

Mah Meri Cultural Village 121
malaria 224
Malay language 229-35
Malay population 200-1
malls 23, 36, *see also* Shopping *index*
Maritime Museum & Naval Museum 138
markets 23, 25-6, 36-7, 174, **60-1**, *see also* Shopping *subindex*
Masjid Asy-Syakirin 48, **54**
Masjid Di Raja Sultan Suleiman (Klang) 119
Masjid India 85
Masjid India, Kampung Baru & Northern KL 43, 83-91, **17**, **83**, **256**, **258-9**
accommodation 126, 131
drinking & nightlife 84, 90
entertainment 90
food 84, 87-8, 90
highlights 83
history 85
shopping 84, 91
sights 85-7
sports & activities 91
transport 84
walks 86, 89, **86**, **89**
Masjid Jamek 75
Masjid Kampung Hulu (Melaka) 142
Masjid Kampung Kling (Melaka) 142
Masjid Negara 99
Masjid Selat Melaka (Melaka) 143
Masjid Sultan Salahuddin Abdul Aziz Shah (Shah

Sights 000
Map Pages **000**
Photo Pages **000**

Alam) 119
measures 222
Medan Pasar 74
Medan Portugis (Melaka) 143-4
medical services 225-6
Melaka 133-54, **133**, **136-7**
accommodation 151-2, 154
drinking & nightlife 147-8
food 144-7
history 135
shopping 148-9
sights 135-44
sports & activities 150
travel to/from 134
travel within 134
Melaka Bird Park (Ayer Keroh) 153
Melaka Botanical Garden (Ayer Keroh) 153
Melaka Butterfly & Reptile Sanctuary (Ayer Keroh) 153
Melaka Malay Sultanate Water Wheel 139
Melaka Zoo (Ayer Keroh) 153
Memorial Tun Abdul Razak 99
Menara KL 69, **69**
Menara Taming Sari 139
Merdeka Square 11, 70-1, **3**, **11**, **70**, *see also* Chinatown, Merdeka Square & Bukit Nanas
metalwork 38
Mid Valley 108
mobile phones 14, 227
Mohamad, Mahathir 194-6
money 14, 26, 125, 226
monkeys 114, 212
monorail 221
motorcycle travel 220
multiculturalism 192, 200-2
Museum of Ethnic Arts 74
Museum of Malay World Ethnology 98
museums 19, *see also individual museums*
music 34, 63, 208-9
Music Museum 71
Muslim Cemetery 87
Muzium Kraf 48
Muzium Orang Asli 114

N

National Monument 96
National Museum 98, **98**
national parks 214
National Planetarium 99
National Textiles Museum 71
National Visual Arts Gallery 87
New Economic Policy 194, 195
newspapers 222
nightlife, *see* drinking & nightlife
Norman, Arthur Charles 211
Northern KL, *see* Masjid India, Kampung Baru & Northern KL

O

Occupy Beach Street (Legally) (Penang) 174
oil palms 213-14
Old KL Train Station 99, **18**
opening hours 26, 32, 37, 226
Orang Asli Craft Museum 98
Orang Asli people 201-2
Orchid Garden 96

P

P Ramlee Memorial 87
pangolins 212
Pantai Pasir Panjang (Penang) 184
parks 19, *see also individual parks*
Penang 155-84, **155**, **158-9**
accommodation 174-8, 181-2, 184
drinking & nightlife 170-2, 180
food 164-5, 167-70, 180, 183-4
history 157-8, 167
shopping 173
sights 159-64, 178-80, 182-3, 184
sports & activities 174, 180
travel to/from 156
travel within 156-7
walks 166, **166**
Penang Hill 182-3
Penang Hill Funicular (Penang) 182
Penang Museum (Penang) 161
Penang National Park (Penang) 178
Penang War Museum (Penang) 183
Peranakan people 202
Perdana Botanical Garden 96
Petronas Towers 6, 46-7, **7**, **46**, **51**
Petrosains 48
Pinang Peranakan Mansion & Straits Chinese Jewelry Museum (Penang) 160-1
planning
budgeting 14, 26
children, travel with 22-3
festivals & events 20-1
itineraries 16-17
Kuala Lumpur basics 14-15
local life 24
repeat visitors 13
travel seasons 15
websites 14, 15
plants 213-14
Poh San Teng Temple 143
police 222
politics 186-7
population 187, 197-9
Porta de Santiago 139
postal services 226-7
prickly heat 224
Prison Museum (Melaka) 144
Protestant Cemetery (Penang) 161
public holidays 227
Publika 110
Pudu 49
Pudu Market 49
Pulau Ketam 121
puppets 38
Putra Bridge (Putrajaya) 123
Putra Mosque (Putrajaya) 123
Putrajaya 122-3
Putrajaya Convention Centre (Putrajaya) 123

R

rabies 224
radio 222
Ramayana Cave 114
Ramlee, P 87, 209
Razak, Najib 186, 196
reflexology 66
religion 187, 202-6
religious sites 19
Resort World Genting (Genting Highlands) 117
River of Life project 187, 211, 215
Royal Malaysia Police Museum 96
Royal Museum 99, 101, **3**
Royal Selangor Club 71
Royal Selangor Pewtersmithing Workshops 91
Royal Selangor Visitor Centre 91
Ruang Pemula 53
Rumah Penghulu Abu Seman 48

S

safety 227
Sam Kow Tong Temple 101
Sam Poh Footprint Temple (Penang) 183
scams 227
Sekeping Tenggiri 101
Sentul 87, 88
Sentul West 87
Seri Wawasan Bridge (Putrajaya) 123
Shah Alam (Klang Valley) 119, 120
shopping 10, 24, 36-9, **11**, **36**, *see also individual neighbourhoods*, Shopping *subindex*
Sin Sze Si Ya Temple 72
skin problems 225
Spa Village 66
spas 66
Sree Veera Hanuman Temple 102
Sri Kandaswamy Temple 101
Sri Mahamariamman Temple 72
Sri Mariamman Temple (Penang) 161
Sri Poyatha Venayagar Moorthi Temple (Melaka) 142
Sri Sakthi Vinayagar Temple 102
Sri Subramaniam Thuropathai Amman Alayam (Melaka) 143
Stadium Merdeka 72, 74
Stadium Negara 74
Stadthuys 135, 138
Starhill Gallery 66
St Mary's Anglican Cathedral 71
St Paul's Church 138
St Peter's Church (Melaka) 143
street art 76, 139, 169
street food 6, 60-1, 100, **6**, **60-1**
Suffolk House (Penang) 170
Sultan Abdul Samad

Building 70, **51**
Sultan Sulaiman Club 85
Sultanate Palace 139
Sungai Melaka (Melaka) 139
Sungai Penchala 101

T
Tabung Haji 52
Taman Botani (Putrajaya) 123
Taman Mini Malaysia (Ayer Keroh) 153
Taman Wetland (Putrajaya) 123
Taoism 204
Tatt Khalsa Diwan Gurdwara 85
taxes 226
taxis 220-1
Tech Dome Penang (Penang) 175
Telekom Museum 75
telephone services 14, 227
Teluk Bahang 178-82
Temple Cave 113
Teochew Puppet & Opera House (Penang) 175
Thaipusam 20, 205
The Habitat (Penang) 182
The Top at KOMTAR (Penang) 163-4, 175
Thean Hou Temple 12, 97, **12**, **97**
theft 227
theme parks 22, 66, 119, 121, 175, 179
ticks 225
time 14, 228
tipping 26, 125
Titiwangsa 87, 88
Titiwangsa Lake Gardens 87
toilets 228
tourist information 14, 228
tourist police 222
tours 221
train travel 221
travel to Kuala Lumpur 15, 218-19
travel within Kuala Lumpur 15, 219-21
travellers cheques 226
travellers diarrhoea 225
trishaws 135
Tropical Spice Garden (Penang) 179
Tuanku Mizan Zainal Abidin Mosque (Putrajaya) 123
Tun Abdul Razak Heritage Park 10, 95-6, **10**, **95**
TV 222
typhoid 224-5

U
Unesco 167
Urbanscapes 20

V
vaccinations 223
vegetarian & vegan travellers 26, 30
Victorian Fountain 71
Villa Sentosa (Melaka) 142
visas 14, 228
Vivekananda Ashram 102

W
walks
- Brickfields 100, **100**
- Chow Kit & Kampung Baru 89, **89**
- Chinatown 73, **73**
- George Town (Penang) 166, **166**
- Masjid India 86, **86**

Wat Chayamangkalaram (Penang) 164
water, drinking 223
wayang 208
weather 15
websites
- accommodation 125
- arts & culture 209
- children, travel with 23
- drinking & nightlife 32
- environment 214, 215
- expat resources 197
- food 26
- planning 14

weights 222
wildlife 212-13
women in Malaysia 206
women travellers 225, 228
woodcarving 38

Y
Yap Ah Loy 190

Z
Zacharevic, Ernest 169
Zheng He Duo Yun Zuan (Melaka) 141
Zoo Negara 114

EATING

13 Hibiscus Vintage Art Cafe (Melaka) 146

A
Acme Bar & Coffee 57
Ah Fook Chee Cheong Fun 49
Alamanda (Putrajaya) 123
Al-Amar Lebanese Cuisine 54
Alexis Bistro 105
Annalakshmi Vegetarian Restaurant 103
Antara Restaurant 78
ARCH Cafe 71
Ashley's By Living Food 104
Atmosphere 360 30, 78
Awesome Canteen (Penang) 169

B
Baboon House (Melaka) 145
Bali Hai Seafood Market (Penang) 170
Bangsar Fish Head Corner 105
Bangsar Sunday Market 104
Bee 110
Ben's 54
Bijan 55
Blue Boy Vegetarian Food Centre 52
Boey Chong Kee (Penang) 168
BTB (Penang) 170
Bulldog (Melaka) 146
Bungalow (Penang) 180
Bunn Choon 76

C
Cafe Kasah 115
Cafe Ko Cha Bi Balik Pulau (Penang) 184
Cafe Old Market Square 75-6
Cantaloupe 57
Canteen By Chef Adu 78
Capital Café 88
Capitol Satay (Melaka) 146
Cha Bou Kitchen 78
Chawan 104
Chee Cheong Fun Stall 76
Chelo's Appam Stall 105
China House (Penang) 170
Chung Wah (Melaka) 145
Cilantro 57
Colonial Cafe 103
Cozy in the Rocket (Penang) 169

D
Da Shu Xia Seafood House (Penang) 168-9
David Brown's (Penang) 183
Delicious 106
Dewakan (Shah Alam) 120
Dharma Realm Guan Yin Sagely Monastery Canteen 56
D'Istana Jalamas Café 88

E
El Cerdo 56
Enak 55

F
Fei Por 49
Ferringhi Garden (Penang) 180
Fierce Curry House 105
Food Republic 52
French Feast 55-6
Fu Er Dai (Penang) 167
Fukuya 56

G
G3 Kitchen & Bar 105
Ganga Cafe 106
Gem Restaurant 103
Glutton Street 49
Goh Thew Chik (Penang) 167
Green House Vegetarian Restaurant (Melaka) 145
Green Tomato Cafe 53
Gurney Drive Hawker Stalls (Penang) 171

H
Hai Boey Seafood (Penang) 183-4
Hameediyah (Penang) 165, 167
Hill View (Bukit Fraser) 117
Hoe Kee Chicken Rice Ball (Melaka) 145
Hon Kee 76
Hong Kee Bamboo Noodle (Penang) 167
Hornbill Restaurant 102-3
House+Co Kitchen 105

Sights 000
Map Pages **000**
Photo Pages **000**

I

ICC Pudu 49
Ikan Bakar Berempah 88
Ikan Bakar Jalan Bellamy 103
Ikan Panggang 77

J

Jalan Imbi Hawker Stalls 52
Jaslyn Cakes 104
Jassal Tandoori Restaurant 103
Jawi House (Penang) 168
Jia Siang Cafe (Penang) 184
Jonker 88 (Melaka) 144
Joo Hooi Cafe (Penang) 171
Journal by Plan b 110

K

Kafe Heng Huat (Penang) 171
Kak Som 88
Kebaya (Penang) 169-70
Kedai Makanan Dan Minuman TKS 55
Kek Lok Si Temple Restaurant (Penang) 183
Khukri 77
Khunthai (Penang) 183
Kim Lian Kee 77
Kin Kin 87-8
Kirishima (Penang) 169
Kocik Kitchen (Melaka) 145
Kompleks Makan Tanglin 102

L

Lai Foong 76
Lawanya Food Corner 103
Lebuh Presgrave Hawker Stalls (Penang) 171
Levain 54
Lg Baru (New Lane) Hawker Stalls (Penang) 171
Lima Blas 52
Limapulo 88
Limau-Limau Cafe (Melaka) 145
Little Penang Kafé 56-7
LOKL Coffee Co 77
Lot 10 Hutong 52
Low Yong Moh (Melaka) 144

M

Madras Lane Hawkers 75
Malaya Hainan 78
Mama San 56
Marco Polo 56
Masjid India Pasar Malam 88, **61**
Mei Keng Fatt Seafood Restaurant 53
Melur & Thyme 56
Merchant's Lane 77
Ming Xiang Tai Pastry Delights (Penang) 167
Moghul Mahal 78
Moody Cow (Penang) 169
Mungo Jerry 88
My Nonya Favourites (Penang) 168

N

Nam Chuan Coffee Shop 105
Nancy's Kitchen (Melaka) 144
Nasi Kandar Pelita (Bangsar) 104
Nasi Kandar Pelita (KLCC) 56
Nathalie's Gourmet Studio 110
Neroteca 54
Nerovivo 55
Nutmeg 105

O

Ocean Green (Penang) 170
Old China Café 77-8

P

Pak Putra Restaurant (Melaka) 144
Pinchos Tapas Bar 54
Poh Piah Lwee (Melaka) 144
Poomy's 105
Precious Old China 77
Prego 56
Pulau Tikus Hawker Centre (Penang) 171
Purple Cane Tea Restaurant (Melaka) 147

Q

Quay Café (Penang) 167

R

Rebung 102
Restaurant Mahbub 104
Restaurant Muar 54-5
Restoran Arzed (Bukit Fraser) 117
Restoran Beh Brothers 55
Restoran de Lisbon (Melaka) 146
Restoran K-Haleel (Penang) 180
Restoran Nyonya Suan (Melaka) 146
Restoran Rani (Batu Caves) 114
Restoran Santa 75
Restoran Win Heng Seng 52
Restoran Yarl 103
Restoran Yusoof dan Zakhir 77
Robson Heights Seafood Restaurant 104
Rococo 52

S

Sage 108
Sahara Tent 55
Salud Tapas (Melaka) 145
Sambal Hijau 101
Samira 88
Sangeetha 76
Santouka 54
Sao Nam 54
Saravana Bhavan 88
Scott's Pub & Restaurant (Bukit Fraser) 117
Sea Pearl Lagoon Cafe (Penang) 171
Seeds Garden (Melaka) 145
Sek Yuen 49
Selera Putra (Putrajaya) 123
Selvam (Melaka) 146
Seng Huat Bak Kut Teh (Klang) 120
Shucked 108
Shui Xian Vegetarian (Melaka) 144
Sisters Noodle 55
Siu Siu 104
Southern Rock Seafood 104
Sri Ananda Bahwan (Penang) 165
Sri Barathan Matha Vilas (Klang) 120
Sri Nirwana Maju 104
Strato 57
Street Kitchen (Melaka) 146
Subak 101
Suffolk House (Penang) 170
Sushi Hinata 55

T

Tamarind Springs 53
Tang City 77
Tarbush (Penang) 180
Teksen (Penang) 168
Tho Yuen Restaurant (Penang) 165
Tommy Le Baker 90
Tong Shin Hokkien Mee 52
Top View Restaurant & Lounge (Penang) 172
Tree Monkey (Penang) 180
Twenty One Kitchen & Bar 54

V

Veloo Villas (Penang) 167
Via Pre (Penang) 169
Vishal 103

W

Wai Kei (Penang) 165
WINS Boulangerie 78
Wondermama 56, 105
Wong Ah Wah 55
Wong Kee 49

Y

Yap Kee (Klang) 120
Yeast Bistronomy 105
Yut Kee 88
Yuzu 108

Z

Zaini Satay 53

DRINKING & NIGHTLIFE

Ah Weng Koh Hainan Tea 49
Aku Cafe & Gallery 79
Apartment Downtown 62
Backlane Coffee (Melaka) 147
Barlai 79
Beach Blanket Babylon (Penang) 170-1
Bilique Bangsar 107
Bistro Richard 90
Blueboy Discotheque 59
Bora Bora (Penang) 180
Butter & Beans 90
Café 55 (Penang) 176
Calanthe Art Cafe (Melaka) 147
Ceylon Bar 59
Chocha Foodstore 79

C&J Alabama Shake (Penang) 171
Claret 57
Coffea Coffee 107
Coffee Stain by Joseph 110
Coley 106
Coliseum Cafe 90
COMO 58
Constant Gardener (Penang) 170
Coppersmith 57
Daily Fix (Melaka) 147
Discovery Cafe & Guest House (Melaka) 147
DivineBliss 62
Feeka Coffee Roasters 58
Fuego 57
Geographér Cafe (Melaka) 147
Gravity (Penang) 172
Heli Lounge Bar 57
Idlers Corner (Melaka) 147-8
Inch (Penang) 172
J Co Donuts & Coffee 59
Jing-Si Books & Cafe (Penang) 172
Kaya Kaya Cafe (Melaka) 148
Kia Klemenz 106
Koong Woh Tong 79
Kopi C (Penang) 170
Library 108
Luk Yu Tea House 59
Luna 131
Mai Bar 106
Mantra Bar KL 106
Marini's on 57 62
Marketplace 62
Me & Mrs Jones (Melaka) 148
Métisser (Penang) 172
Micke's Place (Penang) 172
Mish Mash (Penang) 170
Mixx (Melaka) 148
Moontree House 79-80
Mugshot Cafe (Penang) 171-2
Nagaba 58
Neo Tamarind 59
Newens 59
Odeon Trick Art Cafe & Restaurant (Penang) 172

Sights 000
Map Pages **000**
Photo Pages **000**

Omakase + Appreciate 79
Pampas Sky Bar (Melaka) 147
Pisco Bar 57
Plan b 107
PS150 79
Pulp by Papa Palheta 106
Rabbit Hole 57
Reggae Bar 80
RGB At The Bean Hive 62
Ril's Bar 106
Seraph Awaken (Klang) 120
Seventy7 (Penang) 159
Sid's Pub @ Jonkers (Melaka) 148
Sino The Bar Upstairs 107
Sky Bar 62
Snowflake 59
Social 107
Supperclub 58
Taps Beer Bar 58
Tate 62
Three Sixty Revolving Restaurant & Sky Bar (Penang) 172
TWG Tea 58
VCR 79
Village Bar 59
Vine & Single (Penang) 170
Whisky Bar Kuala Lumpur 59
Wings 59
Woods (Melaka) 148
Zion Club 57
Zouk 58

ENTERTAINMENT

Canteen (Penang) 170
Coliseum Theatre 90
Dewan Filharmonik Petronas 62
Findars 80
Forbidden City 63
GSC Berjaya Times Square 63
GSC Mid Valley 108
GSC Pavilion KL 63
Hard Rock Café (Bukit Bintang) 63
Hard Rock Cafe (Penang) 182
Istana Budaya 90
KL Live 63
Kuala Lumpur Convention Centre 63
Kuala Lumpur Performing Arts Centre 90
Live House 58
MABA Stadium 80
Malaysian Tourism Centre 63
MAP 110
Merdekarya (Klang Valley) 118
Mud 80
No Black Tie 62
Saloma 63
Sutra Dance Theatre 90
Temple of Fine Arts 107
TGV Cineplex 63
TREC 58

SHOPPING

1 Utama (Petaling Jaya) 120-1

A

Ajuntha Textile (Klang) 121
Alexis Ampang 53
Amcorp Mall (Petaling Jaya) 121
Arcadia 110
Artis Kids Store 110
Aseana 65
Asli Craft 80
Avenue K 65

B

Bangsar Shopping Centre 111
Basket Shop 81
Batek-Lah (Penang) 173
Ben's Independent Grocer 110
Berjaya Times Square 64
Bon Ton (Penang) 173
Bonia 37
British India (Bukit Bintang) 64
British India (Publika) 37, 110

C

Cap City 108
Central Market 80
Chop Kongsi (Penang) 173
Chop Sang Kee 81
Clay House (Melaka) 149
Cocoa Boutique 64
Comoddity 109
Curve (Petaling Jaya) 120

D

Dataran Pahlawan (Melaka) 149
d.d.collective 109, 110
DR.Inc 109

E

Eu Yan Sang 49

F

Fabspy 108
Fahrenheit88 64
Fuan Wong (Penang) 173

G

Gahara Galleria 80
Gardens Mall 108
Gerak Budaya (Penang) 173
Giant B (Ayer Keroh) 153
Great Eastern Mall 53
Gurney Plaza (Penang) 173

H

House of Rinpo 81
House of Suzie Wong 64
Hueman Studio (Melaka) 149

I

I Love Snackfood 109
Isetan 65-6

J

Jadi Batek Centre 64
Jaya One (Petaling Jaya) 120
Jln Kuala Kangsar (Penang) 174
Joe's Design (Melaka) 149
Jonker Walk Night Market (Melaka) 148
Junk Bookstore 81-2
Just B 110

K

Khoon Hooi 64
Kinokuniya 65
Kompleks Kraf Kuala Lumpur 65
KWC Fashion Mall 49
Kwong Yik Seng 81

L

Lavanya Arts 107
League of Captains 91
Lebuh Campbell (Penang) 174
Lebuh Cecil (Penang) 174

Little Penang Street Market (Penang) 174
Lonely Dream 109
Lot 10 65

M

Macallum Street Night Market (Penang) 174
Malaqa House (Melaka) 149
Melium Outlet 37
Mid Valley Megamall 108
Mimpikita 109
Moon Shop (Penang) 173
Museum of Ethnic Arts 80

N

Never Follow Suit 109
Nu Sentral 107
Nurita Harith 111

O

Orangutan House (Melaka) 148
ottokedai (Penang) 173

P

Padini 37
Pavilion KL 63-4
Pedlars 53
Petaling Street Market 81, **61**
Peter Hoe at the Row 90-1
Plaza Low Yat 64
Pop-Up Market (Penang) 174
Prototype Gallery 65
Pucuk Rebung 109
Puri Padi (Melaka) 149
Purple Cane Tea Arts 81
Purple Cane Tea Square 49

R

Rattan Art Enterprises 91
Red Handicrafts (Melaka) 148
Rhino 80
Royal Selangor 63
Run Amok (Penang) 163

S

Sam's Batik House (Penang) 173
Semua House 91
Shoes Shoes Shoes 109
Shop Howard (Penang) 172-3
Shore Shopping Gallery (Melaka) 149
Silverfish Books 111
Sonali 107
Songket Sutera Asli 80
Starhill Gallery 64
Sungei Wang Plaza 64
Sunway Pyramid (Petaling Jaya) 120
Suria KLCC 65

T

Taman Connaught Night Market 64
Tanamera 80
Tham Siew Inn Artist Gallery (Melaka) 148
Thisappear 109
Thomas Chan 53
Trash & Treasure (Melaka) 148
TriBeCa 109
Tropical Spice Garden In Town (Penang) 173

U

Umyang Batik (Melaka) 149
Unique Penang (Penang) 173

W

Wah Aik Shoemaker (Melaka) 149
Wau Tradisi 80
Wei-Ling Gallery 107
White Elephant 110
World of Feng Shui 108

SPORTS & ACTIVITIES

Ampang Superbowl 66
Aziz Ma'as 82
Berjaya Times Square Theme Park 66
Biossentials Puri Spa (Melaka) 150
Camp5 (Petaling Jaya) 121-2
Celebrity Fitness 66
Chi the Spa at Shangri-la (Penang) 180
Chin Woo Stadium 81
Cruise Tasik Putrajaya (Putrajaya) 123
Dive Station Explorer 108
Eco Bike Tour (Melaka) 150
Food Tour Malaysia 82
Fraser's Hill Golf Club (Bukit Fraser) 118
FRIM Guided Forest Walk 115
George Town World Heritage Incorporated (Penang) 174
Going Places Tours 221
Hammam Spa 111
Happy Yen (Kuala Kubu Bharu) 118
Hemmant Trail (Bukit Fraser) 117
Huolong Foot Reflexology & Massage (Melaka) 150
Kampung Baru Walking Tour 91
Kampung Morten Walking Tour (Melaka) 150
Kizsports & Gym 111
KL Hop-On Hop-Off 221
KL Sky Tour 91
Kompleks Sukan Bangsar 111
Kuala Lumpur Heritage Trail 81
Kuala Lumpur Night Walk 81
Kuala Lumpur Urban Sketchers 76
LaZat 101
Majestic Spa 111
Malacca Night Cycling (Melaka) 150
Melaka River Cruise (Melaka) 150
Melaka Wonderland (Ayer Keroh) 153
Mr Durai (Bukit Fraser) 117
My Batik Visitor Centre 53
Nancy's Kitchen (Melaka) 150
Nazlina Spice Station (Penang) 174
Nonya Culinary Journey (Melaka) 150
Old KL & Nature Walk 111
Old Melaka Heritage Tour (Melaka) 150
Paddock (Bukit Fraser) 118
Penang Heritage Trust (Penang) 174
Peranakan Culinary Journey (Melaka) 150
Pierose Swiftwater (Kuala Kubu Bharu) 118
Pine Tree Trail (Bukit Fraser) 117
Putrajaya Sightseeing (Putrajaya) 123
Royal Klang Heritage Walk (Klang) 122
Royal Selangor Golf Course 66
Sarang Cookery 81
Simply Enak 82
Skytrex Melaka (Ayer Keroh) 153
Starhill Culinary Studio 65
Sunway Lagoon (Petaling Jaya) 121
Tour 51 Malaysia 221
Travel Han 221
Tropical Spice Garden Cooking Courses (Penang) 180
Tubester 91
Tugu Drum Circle 111
Visit KL Guided Walks 81
YMCA 111

SLEEPING

5 Elements Hotel 130
23 Love Lane (Penang) 176
45 Lekiu (Melaka) 152
1825 Gallery Hotel (Melaka) 154

A

Aloft Kuala Lumpur Sentral 131
AnCasa Hotel & Spa Kuala Lumpur 130
Anggun Boutique Hotel 128
Apa Kaba Home & Stay (Melaka) 152
Audi Guesthouse (Penang) 184

B

Baba Guest House (Penang) 181
BackHome 129
Bagasta Boutique Guesthouse 131
Blue Mansion (Penang) 177
Bridge Loft (Melaka) 154

C

Cafe 1511 Guesthouse (Melaka) 151
Calanthe Artisan Loft (Melaka) 152
Campbell House (Penang) 175-6
Capsule by Container Hotel (airport) 132
Casa Del Rio (Melaka) 152
Ceria Hotel 127
Chaos Hotel 127
Classic Inn 128
Clove Hall (Penang) 178

Coffee Atelier (Penang) 176
Container Hotel (Bukit Bintang) 127
Container Hotel (Penang) 175
Courtyard@Heeren (Melaka) 151

D

D'Majestic Place 127
Dorms KL 127

E

E&O Residences Kuala Lumpur 128
Eastern & Oriental Hotel (Penang) 177
Explorers Guesthouse 130

F

Fraser Place Kuala Lumpur 129

G

G Hotel Kelawai (Penang) 178
G Tower Hotel 128
Gardens Hotel & Residences 132
Gingerflower (Melaka) 151
GLOW (Penang) 177-8
Grand Hyatt Kuala Lumpur 129

H

Hangout@Jonker (Melaka) 151
Hard Rock Hotel (Penang) 182
Heeren House (Melaka) 151
Hilton Kuala Lumpur 132
Homestay Teluk Bahang (Penang) 181
Hotel 1000 Miles 130
Hotel Equatorial (Melaka) 152
Hotel Puri (Melaka) 151-2
Hotel Sportfishing (Penang) 181

I

Invito 128-9

J

Jawi Peranakan Mansion (Penang) 178

K

Kuala Lumpur Journal 127

L

Lang Hoose (Penang) 176
Lantern Hotel 129-30
Le Dream (Penang) 176
Lone Pine Hotel (Penang) 181
LZB (Penang) 181

M

Majestic Hotel 132
Majestic Malacca (Melaka) 154
Malihom (Penang) 184
Mandarin Oriental 129
Melange Boutique Hotel 127
Mesui Hotel 127
MiCasa All Suite Hotel 129
Muntri Grove (Penang) 177
Muntri Mews (Penang) 177
Museum Hotel (Penang) 177
My Chew Jetty (Penang) 161

N

Nomaps (Melaka) 151
Noordin Mews (Penang) 177

O

Opposite Place (Melaka) 152

P

Pacific Regency Hotel Suites 130-1
Paloma Inn 130
Paper Plane Hostel 130
Parkroyal Serviced Suites 129
Penaga Hotel (Penang) 178
PODs 131
Pullman Putrajaya Lakeside (Putrajaya) 122
Puncak Inn (Bukit Fraser) 116
Putrajaya Shangri-la (Putrajaya) 122

Q

Quayside Hotel (Melaka) 152

R

Rainforest Bed & Breakfast 128
Rasa Sayang Resort (Penang) 181
Reeds 131
Reggae Mansion 129
Ren i Tang (Penang) 176
Ringo's Foyer (Melaka) 151
Ritz Carlton 129
Rooftop Guesthouse (Melaka) 151
Roomies (Penang) 181
Roomies Suites (Penang) 181
Rucksack Caratel (Melaka) 152
Ryokan Muntri (Penang) 175

S

Sahabat Guest House 128
Sama-Sama Express KLIA (airport) 132
Sarang Vacation Homes 130
Sea Princess Hotel (Penang) 181
Segara Ninda (Penang) 176
Sekeping Serendah (Kuala Kubu Bharu) 118
Sekeping Sin Chew Kee 130
Sekeping Tenggiri 131
Seven Terraces (Penang) 177
Shahzan Inn Fraser's Hill (Bukit Fraser) 116
Shangri-La Golden Sands Resort (Penang) 181
Sinkeh (Penang) 176
Siok Hostel (Penang) 175
Spices Hotel (Penang) 176
St Regis Kuala Lumpur 132
Stables (Melaka) 152
Swiss-Garden Hotel & Residences (Melaka) 154

T

The Edison (Penang) 177
Tido Penang Hostel (Penang) 174-5
Time Capsule Hotel (Penang) 175
Tipsy Tiger Party Hostel (Penang) 175
Traders Hotel Kuala Lumpur 129
Tune Hotel Downtown 131
Tune Hotel KLIA2 (airport) 132

V

Villa Samadh 128
Vistana 131

W

Wolo Bukit Bintang 127

Y

Ye Olde Smokehouse Fraser's Hill (Bukit Fraser) 116
YMCA 131
You Le Yuen (Penang) 176
YY38 Hotel 128

Kuala Lumpur, Melaka & Penang Maps

Sights

- Beach
- Bird Sanctuary
- Buddhist
- Castle/Palace
- Christian
- Confucian
- Hindu
- Islamic
- Jain
- Jewish
- Monument
- Museum/Gallery/Historic Building
- Ruin
- Shinto
- Sikh
- Taoist
- Winery/Vineyard
- Zoo/Wildlife Sanctuary
- Other Sight

Activities, Courses & Tours

- Bodysurfing
- Diving
- Canoeing/Kayaking
- Course/Tour
- Sento Hot Baths/Onsen
- Skiing
- Snorkelling
- Surfing
- Swimming/Pool
- Walking
- Windsurfing
- Other Activity

Sleeping

- Sleeping
- Camping

Eating

- Eating

Drinking & Nightlife

- Drinking & Nightlife
- Cafe

Entertainment

- Entertainment

Shopping

- Shopping

Information

- Bank
- Embassy/Consulate
- Hospital/Medical
- Internet
- Police
- Post Office
- Telephone
- Toilet
- Tourist Information
- Other Information

Geographic

- Beach
- Gate
- Hut/Shelter
- Lighthouse
- Lookout
- Mountain/Volcano
- Oasis
- Park
- Pass
- Picnic Area
- Waterfall

Population

- Capital (National)
- Capital (State/Province)
- City/Large Town
- Town/Village

Transport

- Airport
- Border crossing
- Bus
- Cable car/Funicular
- Cycling
- Ferry
- LRT
- Metro/MTR/MRT station
- Monorail
- Parking
- Petrol station
- Skytrain/Subway station
- Taxi
- Train station/KTM
- Underground station
- Other Transport

Note: Not all symbols displayed above appear on the maps in this book

Routes

- Tollway
- Freeway
- Primary
- Secondary
- Tertiary
- Lane
- Unsealed road
- Road under construction
- Plaza/Mall
- Steps
- Tunnel
- Pedestrian overpass
- Walking Tour
- Walking Tour detour
- Path/Walking Trail

Boundaries

- International
- State/Province
- Disputed
- Regional/Suburb
- Marine Park
- Cliff
- Wall

Hydrography

- River, Creek
- Intermittent River
- Canal
- Water
- Dry/Salt/Intermittent Lake
- Reef

Areas

- Airport/Runway
- Beach/Desert
- Cemetery (Christian)
- Cemetery (Other)
- Glacier
- Mudflat
- Park/Forest
- Sight (Building)
- Sportsground
- Swamp/Mangrove

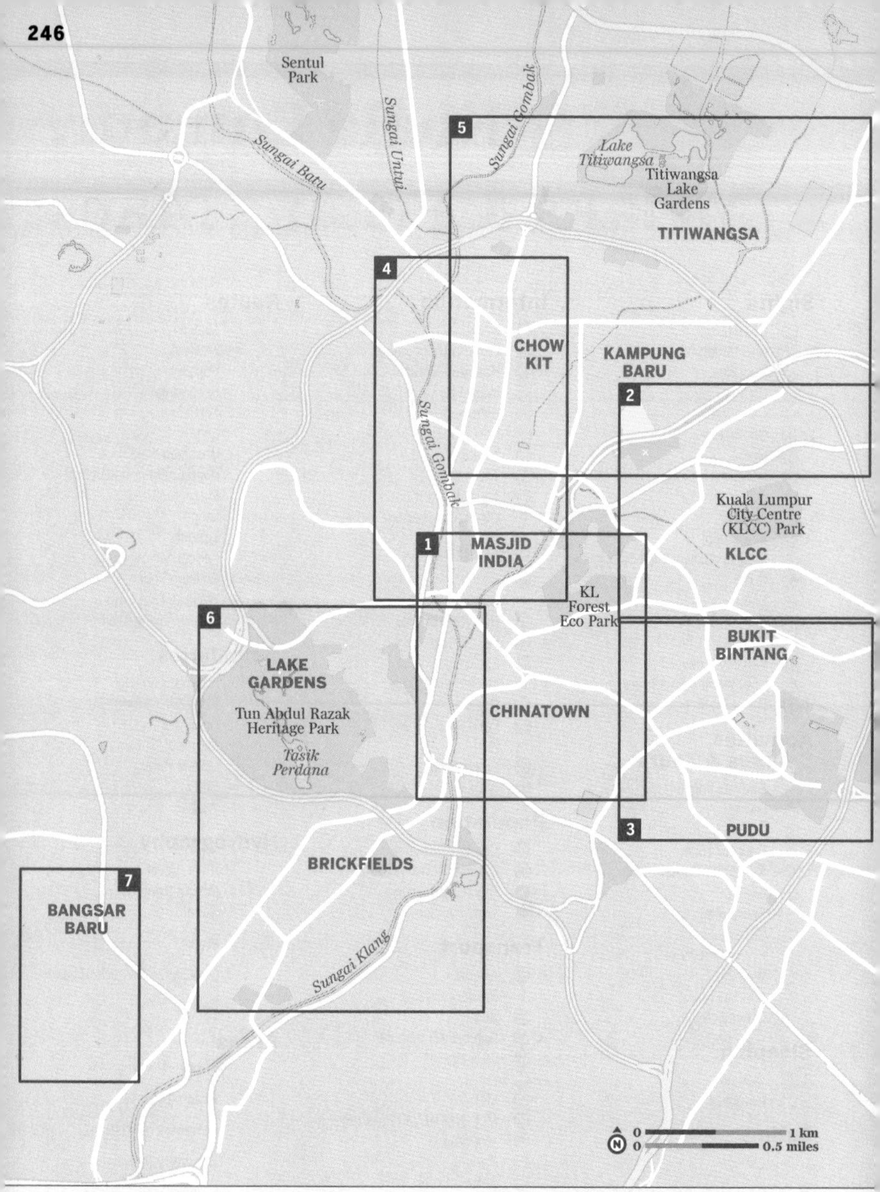

Sentul Park

Sungai Batu

Sungai Untui

Sungai Gombak

5

Lake Titiwangsa

Titiwangsa Lake Gardens

TITIWANGSA

4

CHOW KIT

KAMPUNG BARU

2

Sungai Gombak

Kuala Lumpur City Centre (KLCC) Park

KLCC

1

MASJID INDIA

KL Forest Eco Park

6

LAKE GARDENS

Tun Abdul Razak Heritage Park

Tasik Perdana

BUKIT BINTANG

CHINATOWN

3

PUDU

BRICKFIELDS

7

BANGSAR BARU

Sungai Klang

0 1 km
0 0.5 miles

MAP INDEX

1 Chinatown & Merdeka Square (p248)

2 KLCC (p250)

3 Bukit Bintang (p252)

4 Masijd India & Chow Kit (p256)

5 Kampung Baru & Titiwangsa (p258)

6 Lake Gardens & Brickfields (p260)

7 Bangsar Baru & Mid Valley (p262)

CHINATOWN & MERDEKA SQUARE *Map on p248*

Top Sights **(p69)**
1 Menara Kuala Lumpur F2
2 Merdeka Square A4
3 Sri Mahamariamman Temple B6

Sights **(p72)**
4 #tanahairku mural D4
5 Central Market B5
6 Chan She Shu Yuen Clan Association Temple C8
7 Chettiar House C3
8 Chinatown Wet Market C6
9 Cockerel Mural C5
10 Ernest Zacharevic Mural C3
11 Goldsmith Mural C7
12 Guan Yin Temple C8
13 Guandi Temple C6
14 KL City Gallery A4
15 KL Forest Eco Park G2
16 Kuen Stephanie Sculptures C5
17 Lat Cartoon Sculptures C3
18 Lee Rubber Building B6
19 Lostgens' C7
20 Masjid Jamek B4
21 Medan Pasar B4
22 Muzium Musik A4
23 National Textiles Museum A4
24 OCBC Building B5
25 Royal Selangor Club A3
26 Sin Sze Si Ya Temple B5
27 St Mary's Anglican Cathedral A3
28 Stadium Merdeka D8
29 Stadium Negara E7
30 Sultan Abdul Samad Building A4
31 Telekom Museum D3
32 Victorian Fountain A4

Eating **(p75)**
33 Antara Restaurant F3
ARCH Cafe ....(see 14)
34 Atmosphere 360 ....F2
35 Bunn Choon C7
36 Cafe Old Market Square B4
Canteen By Chef Adu ....(see 23)
37 Cha Bou Kitchen C8
38 Chee Cheong Fun Stall C6
39 Hon Kee C6
40 Ikan Panggang C6
41 Khukri C5
42 Kim Lian Kee C6
43 Lai Foong C5
LOKL Coffee Co ....(see 82)
44 Madras Lane Hawkers C6
45 Malaya Hainan C7
46 Merchant's Lane C7
47 Moghul Mahal F2
48 Old China Café C7
49 Precious Old China B5
Restoran Santa ....(see 53)
50 Restoran Yusoof dan Zakhir B5
51 Sangeetha C3
52 Tang City C6
53 WINS Boulangerie C3

Drinking & Nightlife **(p78)**
Aku Cafe & Gallery ....(see 60)
Barlai ....(see 91)
54 Chocha Foodstore C7
55 Koong Woh Tong C6
56 Luna Bar G2
Moontree House ....(see 19)
57 Omakase + Appreciate C3
PS150 ....(see 46)
58 Reggae Bar C6
59 VCR G6

Entertainment **(p80)**
60 Findars C7
61 MABA Stadium D6
62 Mud B3
63 Panggung Bandaraya B3

Shopping **(p80)**
64 Asli Craft B5
65 Basket Shop C7
66 Chop Sang Kee C4
Gahara Galleria ....(see 23)
67 House of Rinpo A4
68 Junk Bookstore C4
69 Kwong Yik Seng C5
70 Museum of Ethnic Arts B5
Petaling Street Market ....(see 85)
71 Purple Cane Tea Arts C7
72 Rhino B5
Songket Sutera Asli ....(see 5)
Tanamera ....(see 72)
73 Wau Tradisi B5

Sports & Activities **(p81)**
74 Chin Woo Stadium D7
75 Going Places Tours C6
76 KL By Cycle A4
77 Kuala Lumpur Heritage Trail A4
78 Kuala Lumpur Night Walk B5
Sarang Cookery ....(see 90)
79 Travel Han B6

Sleeping **(p129)**
80 5 Elements Hotel C6
81 AnCasa Hotel & Spa Kuala Lumpur D5
82 BackHome C3
83 Explorers Guesthouse C5
84 Hotel 1000 Miles C3
85 Lantern Hotel C6
86 Pacific Regency Hotel Suites G2
87 Paloma Inn F6
88 Paper Plane Hostel F6
89 Reggae Mansion C4
90 Sarang Vacation Homes G6
91 Sekeping Sin Chew Kee G6

CHINATOWN & MERDEKA SQUARE

Key on p247

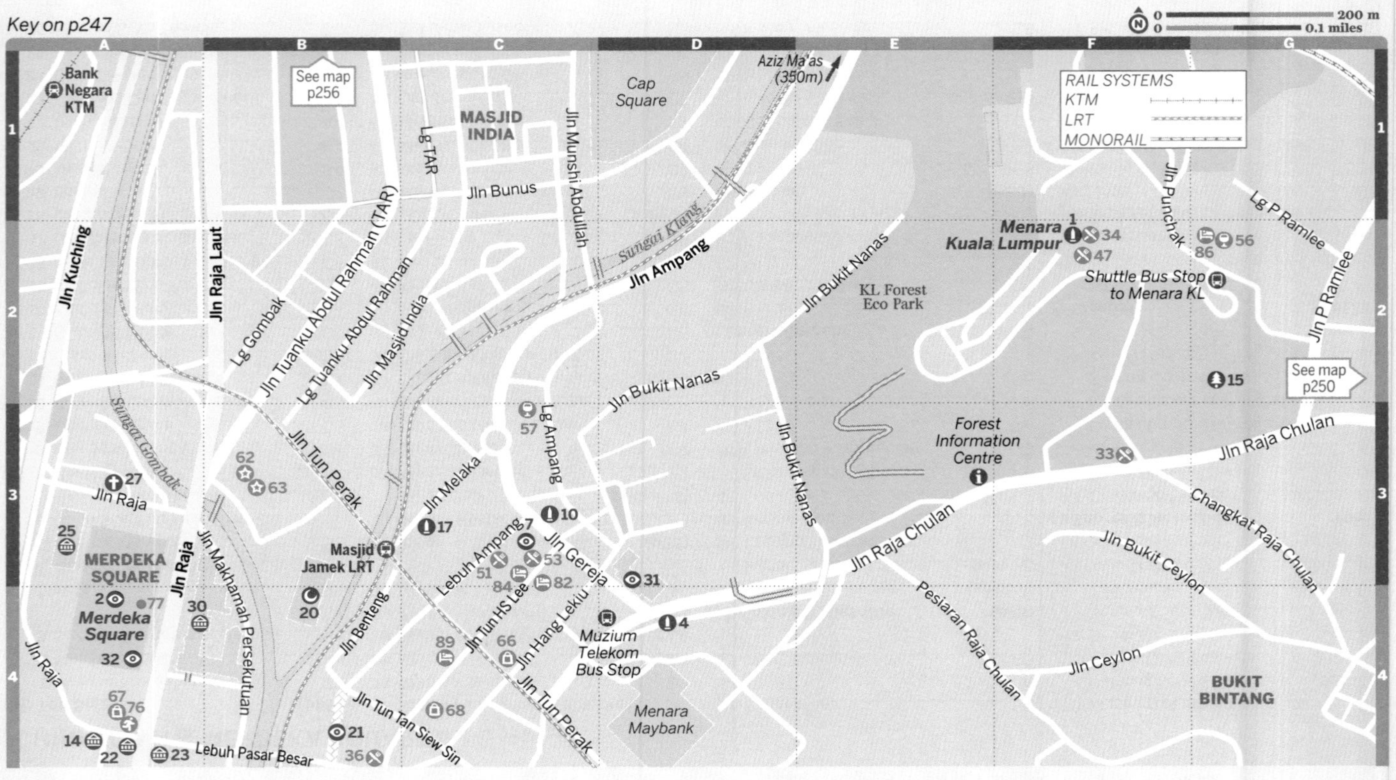

CHINATOWN & MERDEKA SQUARE

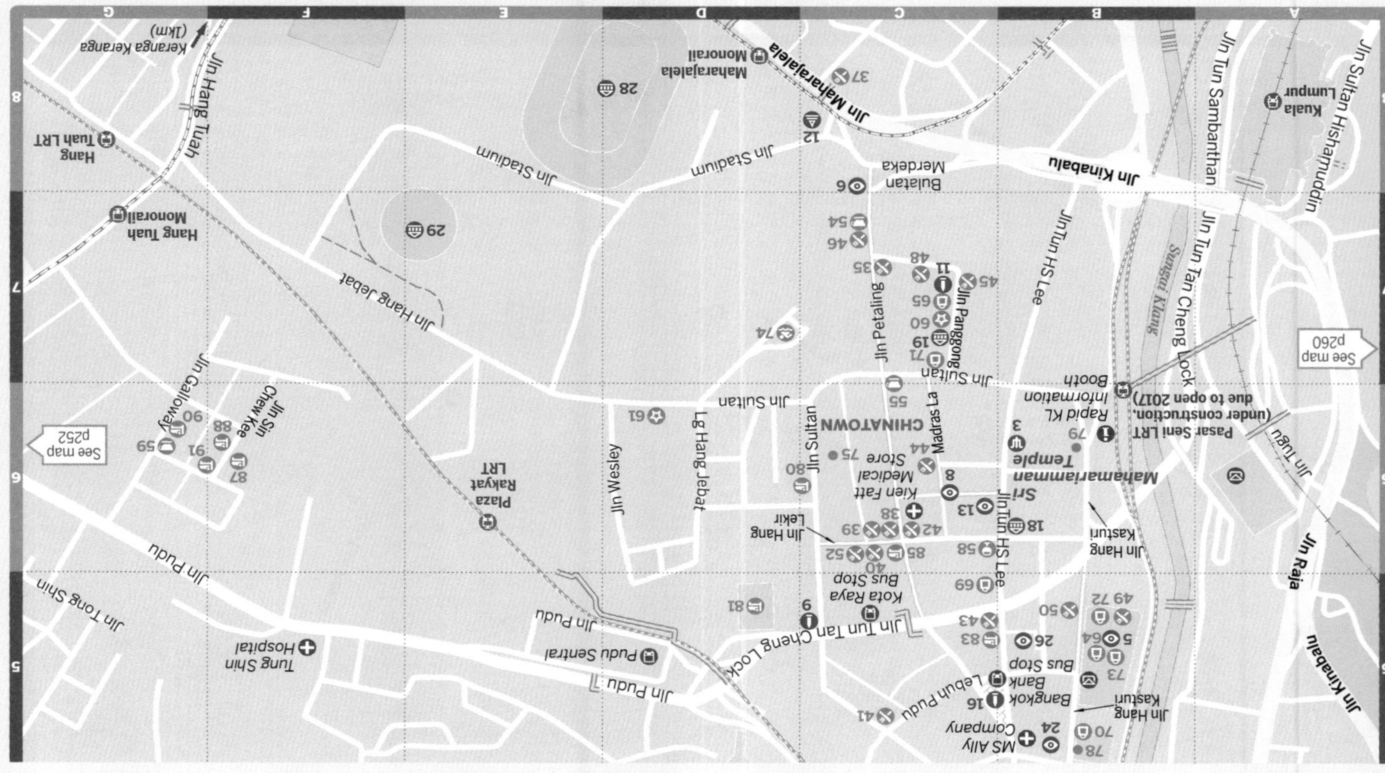

KLCC

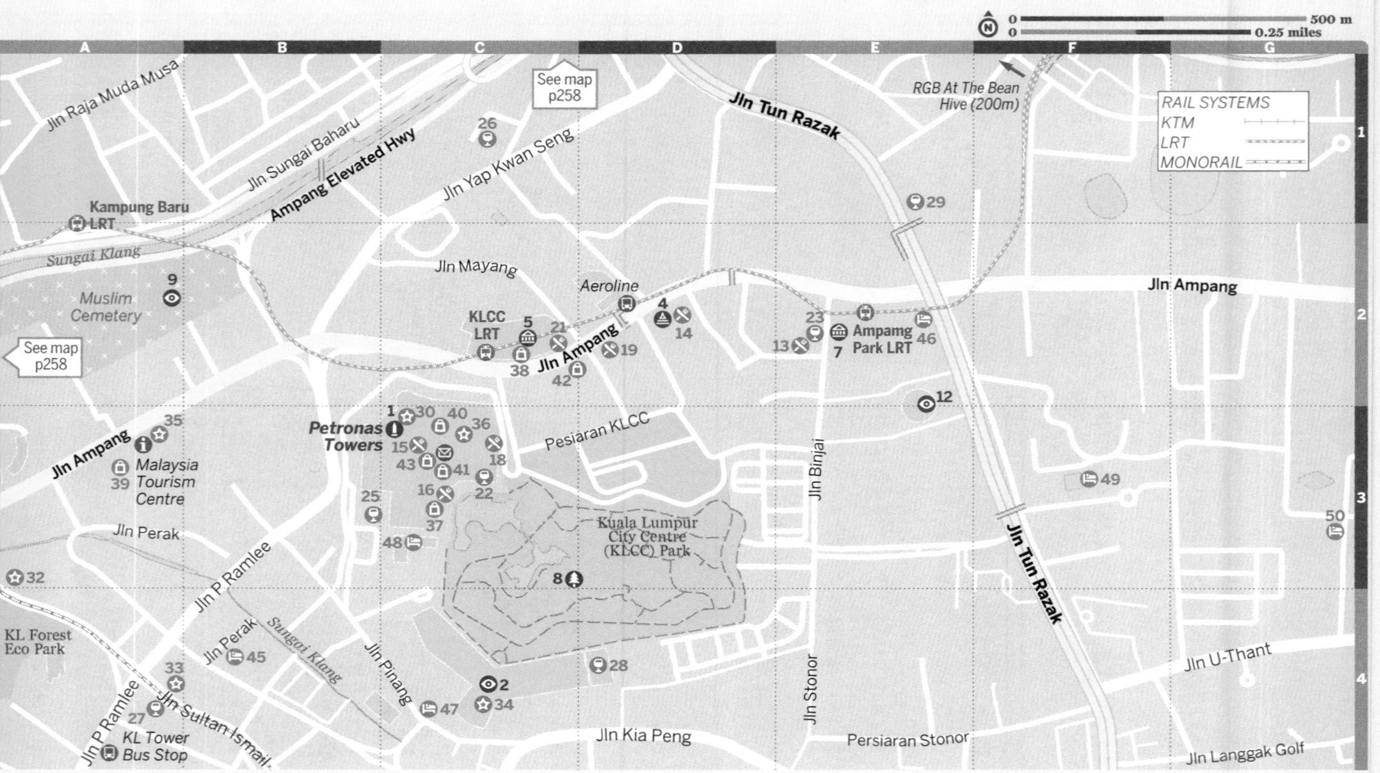
0 500 m
0 0.25 miles
RAIL SYSTEMS
KTM
LRT
MONORAIL
Jln Raja Muda Musa
Jln Sungai Baharu
Ampang Elevated Hwy
Jln Yap Kwan Seng
See map p258
Jln Tun Razak
RGB At The Bean Hive (200m)
Kampung Baru LRT
Sungai Klang
Muslim Cemetery
9
See map p258
Jln Mayang
Aeroline
KLCC LRT
Jln Ampang
Ampamg Park LRT
Petronas Towers
Pesiaran KLCC
Jln Binjai
Malaysia Tourism Centre
Jln Perak
Kuala Lumpur City Centre (KLCC) Park
Jln P Ramlee
KL Forest Eco Park
Jln Pinang
Jln Stonor
Jln U-Thant
Jln Sultan Ismail
KL Tower Bus Stop
Jln Kia Peng
Persiaran Stonor
Jln Langgak Golf

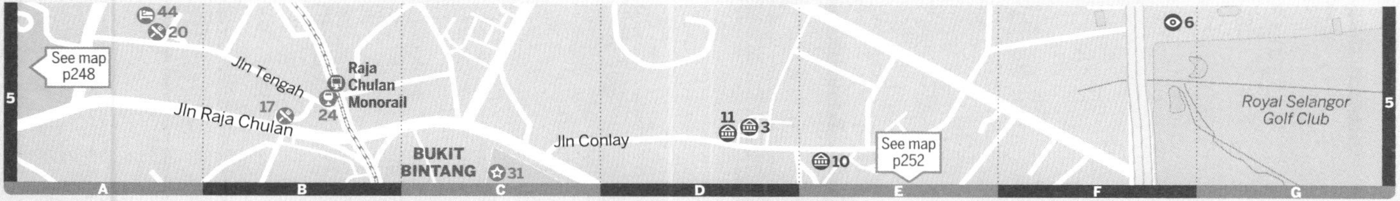

Top Sights (p46)
1 Petronas Towers ... C3

Sights (p48)
2 Aquaria KLCC ... C4
3 Badan Warisan Malaysia ... D5
4 Dharma Realm Guan Yin Sagely Monastery ... D2
5 Discoveria ... C2
Galeri Petronas ... (see 43)
6 Goethe Institut ... F5
7 ILHAM ... E2
8 KLCC Park ... C3
9 Muslim Cemetery ... A2
10 Muzium Kraf ... E5
Petrosains ... (see 43)
11 Rumah Penghulu Abu Seman ... D5
12 Tabung Haji ... E2

Eating (p56)
13 Acme Bar & Coffee ... E2
Cantaloupe ... (see 23)
Cilantro ... (see 49)
14 Dharma Realm Guan Yin Sagely Monastery Canteen ... D2
15 Little Penang Kafé ... C3
16 Mama San ... C3
17 Marco Polo ... B5
18 Melur & Thyme ... C3
19 Nasi Kandar Pelita ... D2
Strato ... (see 23)
20 Sushi Hinata ... A5
21 Wondermama ... C2

Drinking & Nightlife (p62)
22 Apartment Downtown ... C3
DivineBliss ... (see 46)
23 Fuego ... E2
24 Heli Lounge Bar ... B5
25 Marini's on 57 ... B3
26 Marketplace ... C1
27 Neo Tamarind ... A4
28 Sky Bar ... D4
29 Tate ... E1

Entertainment (p62)
30 Dewan Filharmonik Petronas ... C3
31 GSC Pavilion KL ... C5
32 Hard Rock Café ... A3
33 KL Live ... A4
34 Kuala Lumpur Convention Centre ... C4
35 Saloma ... A3
36 TGV Cineplex ... C3

Shopping (p65)
37 Aseana ... C3
38 Avenue K ... C2
39 Cocoa Boutique ... A3
40 Isetan ... C3
41 Kinokuniya ... C3
Kompleks Kraf Kuala Lumpur ... (see 10)
42 Prototype Gallery ... C2
43 Suria KLCC ... C3

Sports & Activities (p65)
Tour 51 Malaysia ... (see 42)

Sleeping (p127)
44 E&O Residences Kuala Lumpur ... A5
45 Fraser Place Kuala Lumpur ... B4
46 G Tower Hotel ... E2
47 Grand Hyatt Kuala Lumpur ... C4
48 Mandarin Oriental ... C3
49 MiCasa All Suite Hotel ... F3
Traders Hotel Kuala Lumpur ... (see 28)
50 Villa Samadhi ... G3

Key on p254

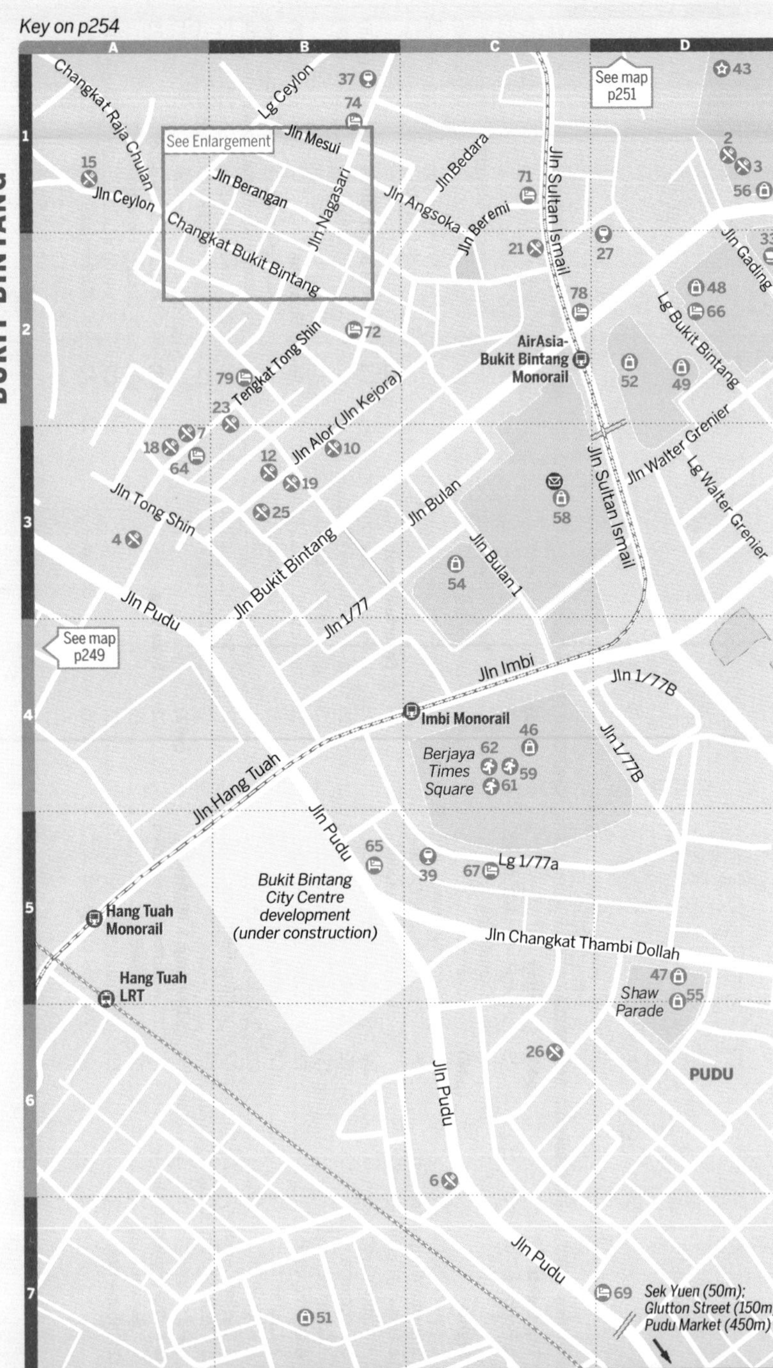

A
B
C
D
1
2
3
4
5
6
7
Changkat Raja Chulan
Lg Ceylon
Jln Mesui
See Enlargement
Jln Berangan
Jln Nagasari
Changkat Bukit Bintang
Jln Ceylon
JlnBedara
Jln Angsoka
Jln Beremi
Jln Sultan Ismail
See map p251
Jln Gading
Lg Bukit Bintang
AirAsia-Bukit Bintang Monorail
Tengkat Tong Shin
Jln Alor (Jln Kejora)
Jln Walter Grenier
Lg Walter Grenier
Jln Tong Shin
Jln Bulan
Jln Bulan 1
Jln Bukit Bintang
Jln Pudu
Jln 1/77
See map p249
Jln Imbi
Jln 1/77B
Imbi Monorail
Berjaya Times Square
Jln Hang Tuah
Lg 1/77a
Bukit Bintang City Centre development (under construction)
Hang Tuah Monorail
Jln Changkat Thambi Dollah
Hang Tuah LRT
Shaw Parade
PUDU
Sek Yuen (50m); Glutton Street (150m); Pudu Market (450m)

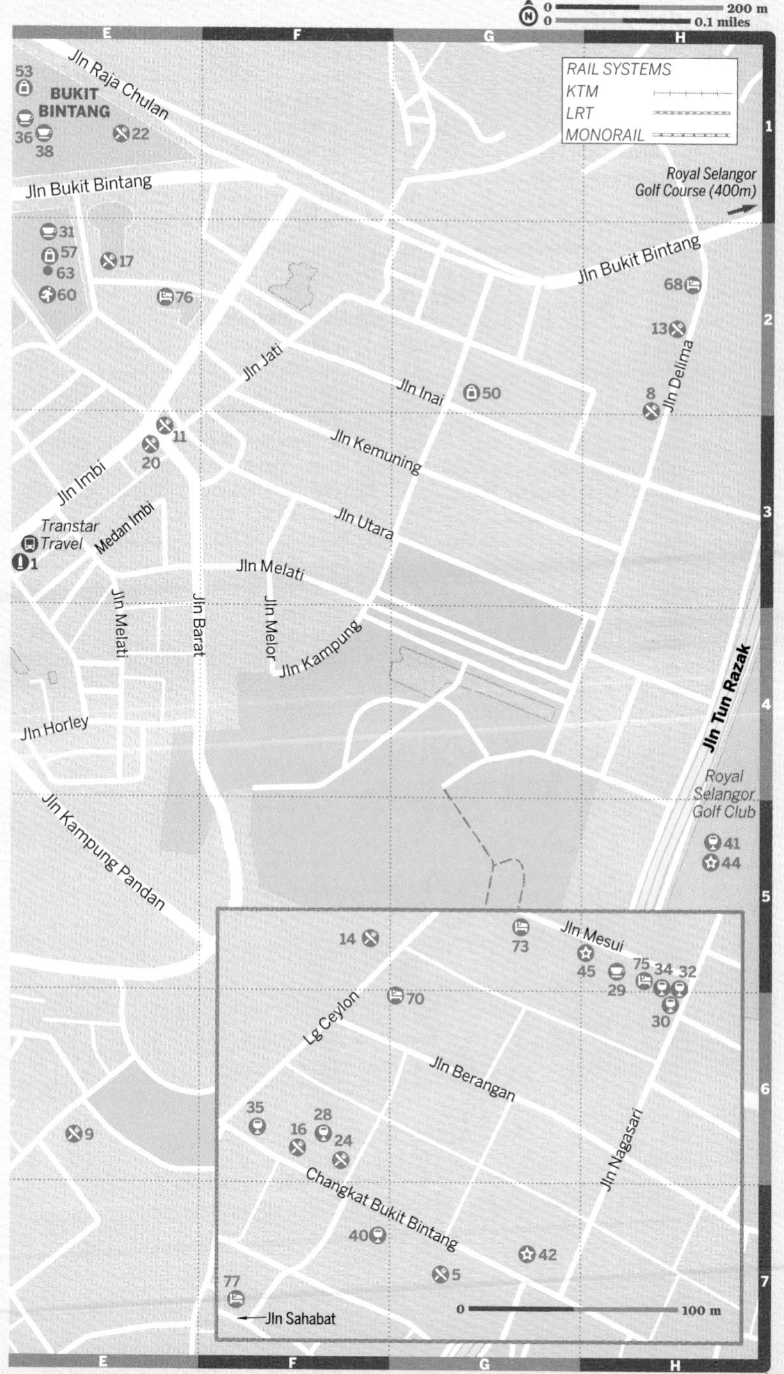
BUKIT BINTANG
RAIL SYSTEMS
KTM
LRT
MONORAIL
0 200 m
0 0.1 miles
E
F
G
H
1
2
3
4
5
6
7
BUKIT BINTANG
Jln Raja Chulan
Jln Bukit Bintang
Royal Selangor Golf Course (400m)
Jln Jati
Jln Inai
Jln Delima
Jln Kemuning
Jln Imbi
Jln Utara
Transtar Travel
Medan Imbi
Jln Melati
Jln Barat
Jln Melor
Jln Kampung
Jln Horley
Jln Tun Razak
Royal Selangor Golf Club
Jln Kampung Pandan
Jln Mesui
Lg Ceylon
Jln Berangan
Jln Nagasari
Changkat Bukit Bintang
Jln Sahabat
0 100 m
53
36
38
22
31
57
63
60
17
76
68
13
50
8
11
20
1
41
44
14
73
45
75
34
32
29
30
70
35
28
16
24
9
40
42
5
77

BUKIT BINTANG *Map on p252*

Sights **(p46)**

1 #districtcreative #artforlife mural E3

Eating **(p52)**

Ah Weng Koh Hainan Tea .... (see 9)
2 Al-Amar Lebanese Cuisine D1
3 Ben's D1
Bijan .... (see 15)
4 Blue Boy Vegetarian Food Centre A3
5 El Cerdo G7
Enak .... (see 57)
6 Fei Por C6
Food Republic .... (see 53)
7 French Feast A3
8 Fukuya H2
9 Imbi Market at ICC Pudu E6
10 Jalan Alor B3
11 Jalan Imbi Hawker Stalls E3
12 Kedai Makanan Dan Minuman TKS B3
13 Levain H2
Lima Blas .... (see 45)
Lot 10 Hutong .... (see 52)
14 Neroteca F5
15 Nerovivo A1
16 Pinchos Tapas Bar F6
17 Prego E2
18 Restaurant Muar A3
19 Restoran Beh Brothers B3
20 Restoran Win Heng Seng E3
Rococo .... (see 72)
21 Sahara Tent C2
22 Santouka E1
23 Sao Nam B2
Sisters Noodle .... (see 19)
Tong Shin Hokkien Mee .... (see 64)
24 Twenty One Kitchen & Bar F6
25 Wong Ah Wah B3
26 Wong Kee C6

Drinking & Nightlife **(p57)**

27 Blueboy Discotheque D2
28 Ceylon Bar F6
COMO .... (see 44)
29 Feeka Coffee Roasters H5
J Co Donuts & Coffee .... (see 53)
30 Kuala Lumpur Pub Crawl H6
31 Luk Yu Tea House E2
32 Nagaba H5
33 Newens D2
34 Pisco Bar H5
35 Rabbit Hole F6
36 Snowflake E1
Supperclub .... (see 44)
37 Taps Beer Bar B1
38 TWG Tea E1
Village Bar .... (see 57)

Whisky Bar Kuala Lumpur ....(see 42)
39 Wings C5
40 Zion Club F7
41 Zouk H5

Entertainment (p62)

42 Forbidden City G7
43 GSC Pavilion KL D1
GSC Berjaya Times Square ....(see 46)
44 Live House H5
45 No Black Tie H5

Shopping (p63)

46 Berjaya Times Square C4
British India ....(see 53)
47 Eu Yan Sang D5
48 Fahrenheit88 ....D2
49 House of Suzie Wong D2
50 Jadi Batek Centre G2
Khoon Hooi ....(see 57)
51 KWC Fashion Mall B7
52 Lot 10 ....D2
53 Pavilion KL E1
54 Plaza Low Yat C3
55 Purple Cane Tea Square D5
56 Royal Selangor D1
57 Starhill Gallery E2
58 Sungei Wang Plaza C3

Sports & Activities (p65)

59 Ampang Superbowl C4
60 Asianel Reflexology Spa E2
61 Berjaya Times Square Theme Park C4
Celebrity Fitness ....(see 52)
Donna Spa ....(see 57)
62 JoJoBa Spa C4
Spa Village ....(see 76)
63 Starhill Culinary Studio E2

Sleeping (p127)

64 Anggun Boutique Hotel A3
65 Ceria Hotel B5
66 Chaos Hotel D2
67 Classic Inn C5
68 Container Hotel H2
69 D'Majestic Place D7
Dorms KL ....(see 64)
70 Invito G6
71 Kuala Lumpur Journal C1
72 Melange Boutique Hotel B2
73 Mesui Hotel G5
74 Parkroyal Serviced Suites B1
75 Rainforest Bed & Breakfast H5
76 Ritz Carlton E2
77 Sahabat Guest House F7
78 Wolo Bukit Bintang C2
79 YY38 Hotel B2

MASJID INDIA & CHOW KIT

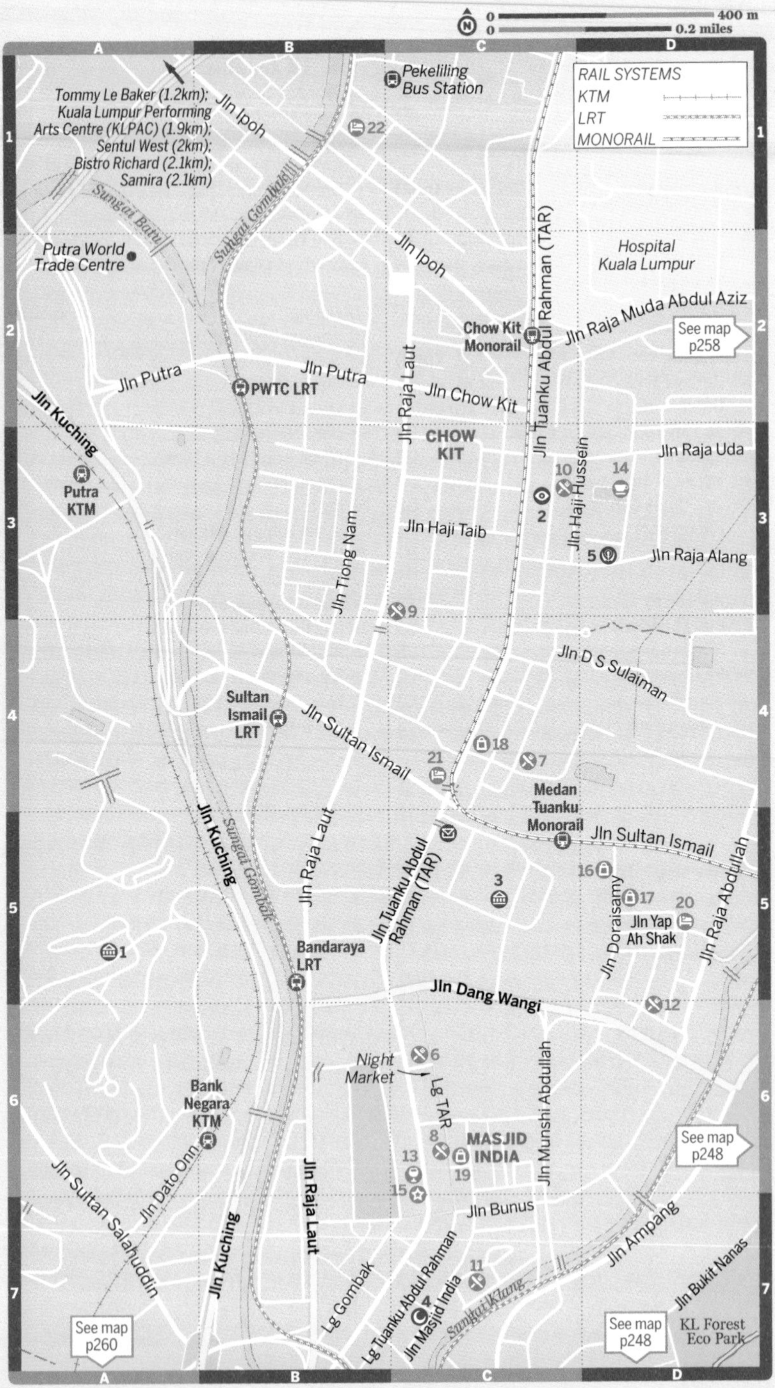

0 — 400 m
0 — 0.2 miles

RAIL SYSTEMS
KTM
LRT
MONORAIL

Tommy Le Baker (1.2km);
Kuala Lumpur Performing
Arts Centre (KLPAC) (1.9km);
Sentul West (2km);
Bistro Richard (2.1km);
Samira (2.1km)

Jln Ipoh
Pekeliling
Bus Station
22
Sungai Batu
Sungai Gombak
Putra World
Trade Centre
Jln Ipoh
Jln Tuanku Abdul Rahman (TAR)
Hospital
Kuala Lumpur
Jln Raja Muda Abdul Aziz
Chow Kit
Monorail

See map p258

Jln Putra
PWTC LRT
Jln Putra
Jln Raja Laut
Jln Chow Kit
Jln Kuching
CHOW
KIT
Jln Raja Uda
10
14
Putra
KTM
2
Jln Haji Hussein
Jln Haji Taib
Jln Tiong Nam
5
Jln Raja Alang
9
Jln D S Sulaiman
Sultan
Ismail
LRT
Jln Sultan Ismail
18
21
7
Medan
Tuanku
Monorail
Jln Kuching
Sungai Gombak
Jln Raja Laut
Jln Tuanku Abdul
Rahman (TAR)
Jln Sultan Ismail
16
3
17
20
Jln Doraisamy
Jln Yap
Ah Shak
Jln Raja Abdullah
1
Bandaraya
LRT
Jln Dang Wangi
12
6
Night
Market
Lg TAR
Jln Munshi Abdullah
Bank
Negara
KTM
8
MASJID
INDIA
13
19

See map p248

15
Jln Bunus
Jln Dato Onn
Jln Sultan Salahuddin
Jln Kuching
Jln Raja Laut
Jln Ampang
Lg Gombak
Lg Tuanku Abdul Rahman
11
4
Jln Masjid India
Sungai Klang
Jln Bukit Nanas
KL Forest
Eco Park

See map p260

See map p248

MASJID INDIA & CHOW KIT

Sights (p85)

1 Bank Negara Malaysia Museum & Art Gallery ... A5
2 Bazaar Baru Chow Kit ... C3
3 Loke Mansion ... C5
4 Masjid India ... C7
5 Tatt Khalsa Diwan Gurdwara ... D3

Eating (p87)

6 Capital Café ... C6
7 Kin Kin ... C4
Limapulo ... (see 16)
8 Masjid India Pasar Malam ... C6
9 Mungo Jerry ... C3
Murtabak Ana ... (see 10)
10 Pak Ngah Bihun Sup ... C3
11 Saravana Bhavan ... C7
12 Yut Kee ... D6

Drinking & Nightlife (p90)

Butter & Beans ... (see 16)
13 Coliseum Cafe ... C6
14 Nam Kee ... D3

Entertainment (p90)

15 Coliseum Theatre ... C6

Shopping (p91)

16 League of Captains ... D5
17 Peter Hoe at the Row ... D5
18 Rattan Art Enterprises ... C4
19 Semua House ... C6

Sleeping (p131)

20 Reeds ... D5
21 Tune Hotel Downtown ... C4
22 Vistana ... B1

KAMPUNG BARU & TITIWANGSA

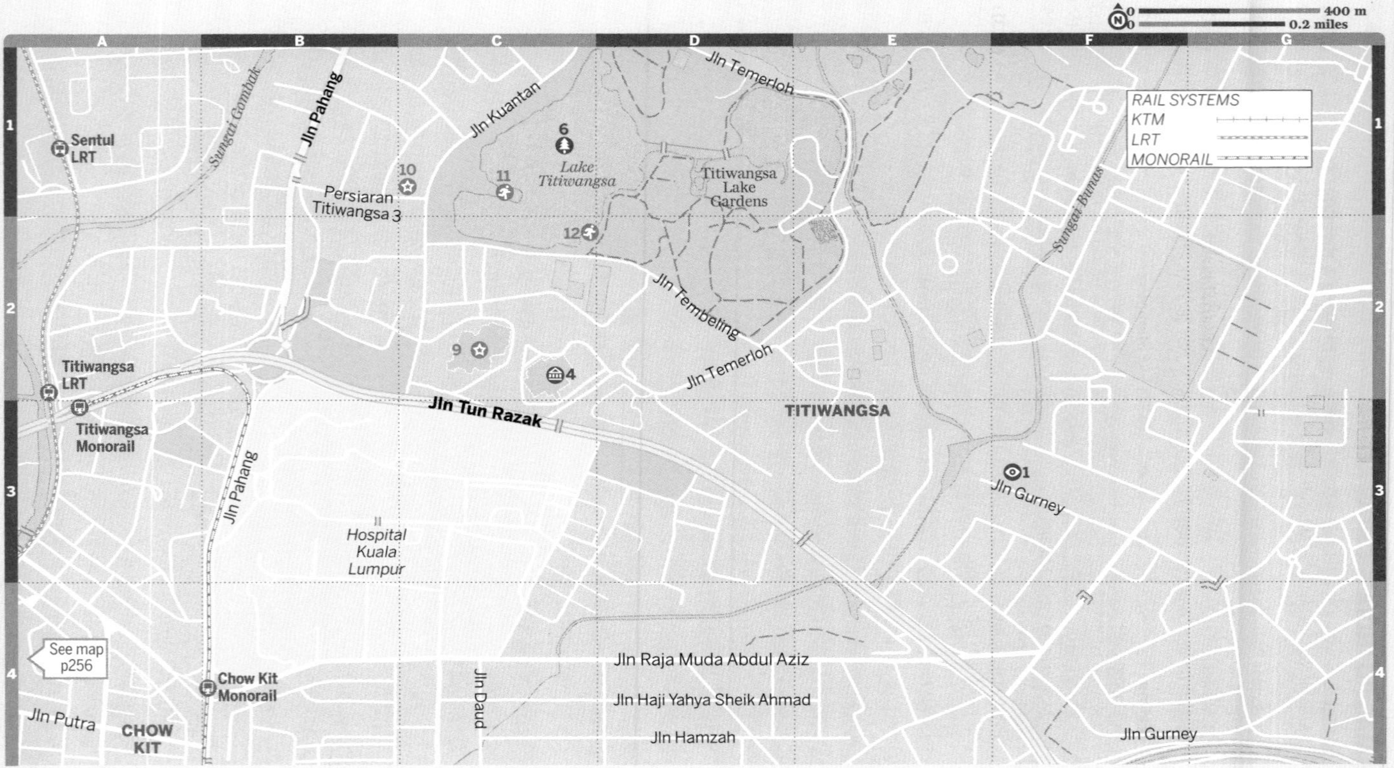

KAMPUNG BARU & TITIWANGSA

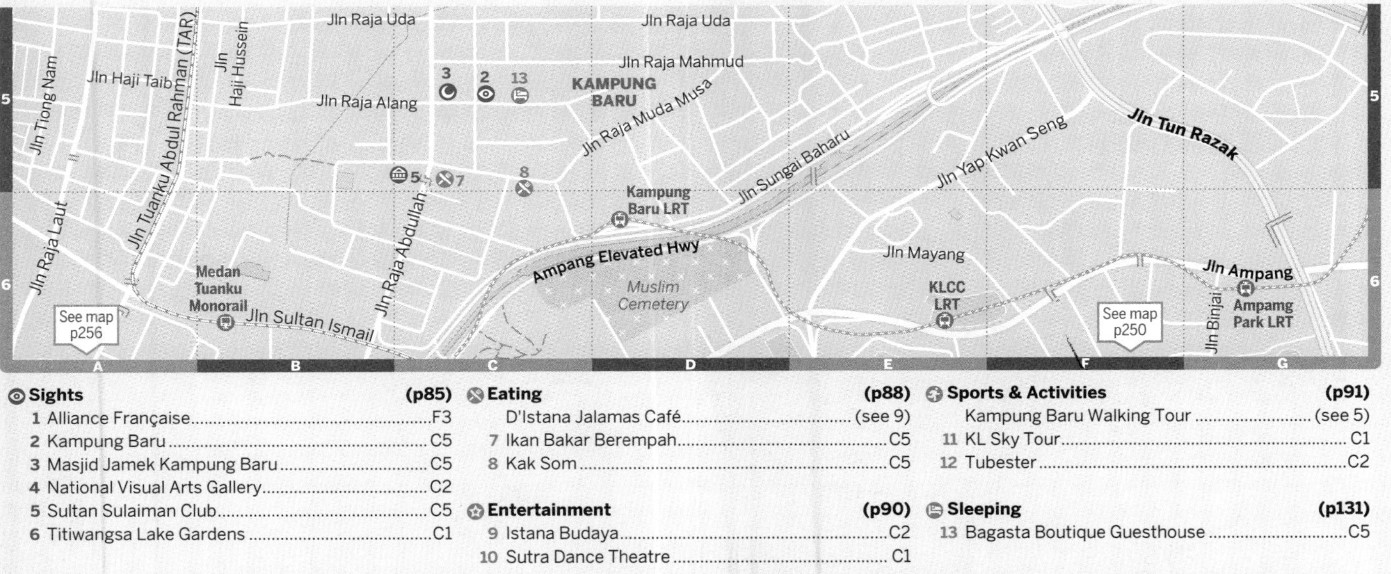

Sights (p85)

1 Alliance Française ... F3
2 Kampung Baru ... C5
3 Masjid Jamek Kampung Baru ... C5
4 National Visual Arts Gallery ... C2
5 Sultan Sulaiman Club ... C5
6 Titiwangsa Lake Gardens ... C1

Eating (p88)

D'Istana Jalamas Café ... (see 9)
7 Ikan Bakar Berempah ... C5
8 Kak Som ... C5

Entertainment (p90)

9 Istana Budaya ... C2
10 Sutra Dance Theatre ... C1

Sports & Activities (p91)

Kampung Baru Walking Tour ... (see 5)
11 KL Sky Tour ... C1
12 Tubester ... C2

Sleeping (p131)

13 Bagasta Boutique Guesthouse ... C5

LAKE GARDENS & BRICKFIELDS

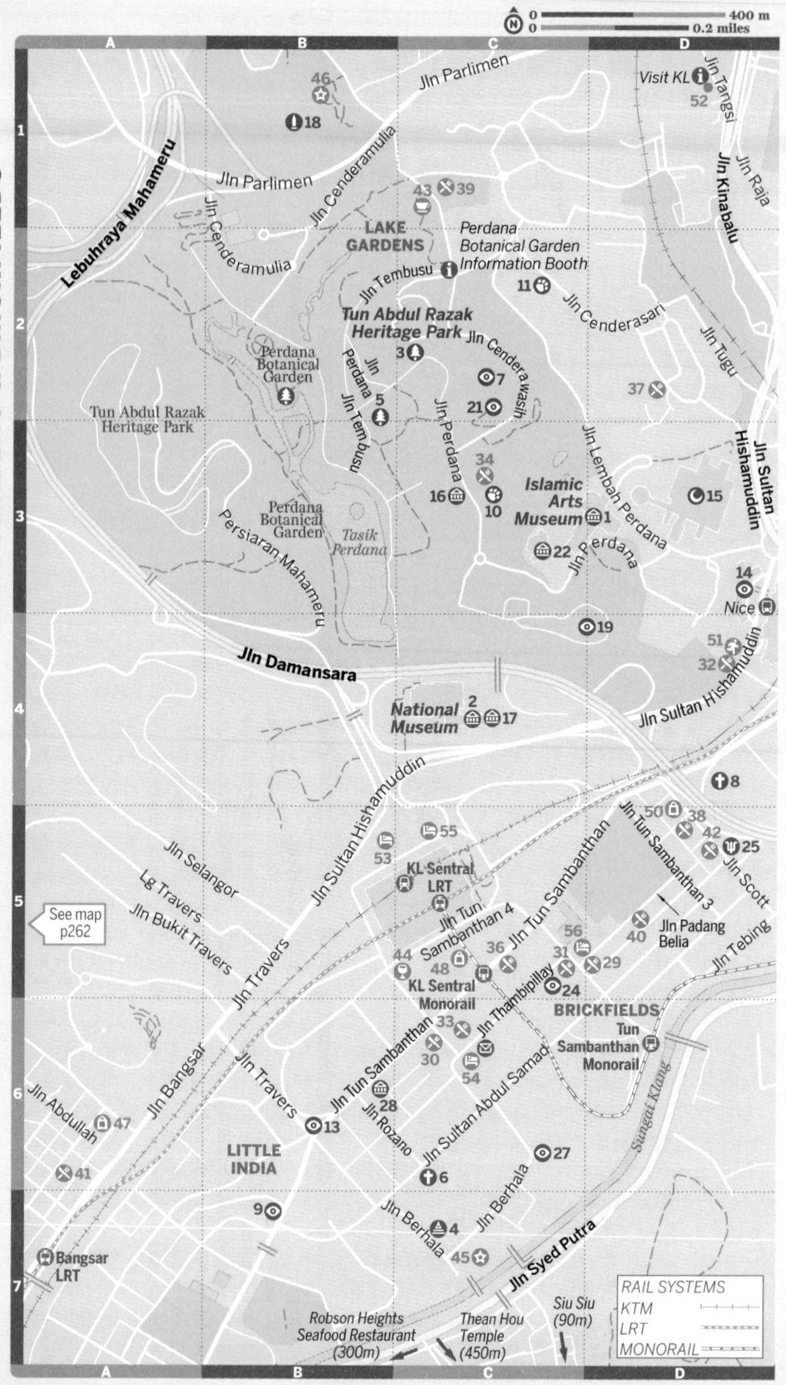

Top Sights (p94)

1 Islamic Arts Museum D3
2 National Museum................ C4
3 Tun Abdul Razak Heritage Park.................................. C2

Sights (p99)

4 Buddhist Maha Vihara..........C7
5 Deer Park B2
6 Evangelical Zion Lutheran Church.............................. C6
7 Hibiscus Garden.................. C2
8 Holy Rosary Church D4
9 Jln Tun Sambanthan Garland Sellers...................B7
10 KL Bird Park......................... C3
11 KL Butterfly Park C2
12 Kwong Tong Cemetery E7
13 Little India Fountain............ B6
14 Malayan Railway Administration Building D3
15 Masjid Negara D3
16 Memorial Tun Abdul Razak C3
17 Museum of Malay World Ethnology.......................... C4
18 National Monument............. B1
19 National Planetarium D4
20 Old KL Train Station E3
Orang Asli Craft Museum ....(see 17)
21 Orchid Garden...................... C2
22 Royal Malaysian Police Museum C3
23 Royal Museum E5
24 Sam Kow Tong Temple........C5
25 Sree Veera Hanuman Temple D5
26 Sri Kandaswamy Temple..... E5
27 Sri Sakthi Vinayagar Temple C6
28 Vivekananda Ashram B6

Eating (p102)

29 ABC Stall D5
30 Ammars C6
Annalakshmi Vegetarian Restaurant................(see 45)
31 Brickfields Pisang Goreng...C5
32 Colonial Cafe.........................D4
Fierce Curry House .... (see 47)
33 Gem Restaurant C6
34 Hornbill Restaurant.............C3
35 Ikan Bakar Jalan Bellamy E6
Islamic Arts Museum Restaurant..................(see 1)
36 Jassal Tandoori Restaurant.........................C5
37 Kompleks Makan Tanglin....D2
38 Lawanya Food Corner..........D5
39 Rebung................................. C1
40 Restoran Yarl D5
41 Southern Rock Seafood A6
42 Vishal....................................D5

Drinking & Nightlife (p106)

Coley .... (see 47)
43 Kia Klemenz C1
44 Mai Bar C5

Entertainment (p107)

45 Temple of Fine Arts C7
46 Tugu Drum Circle B1

Shopping (p107)

47 DR.Inc....................................A6
Lavanya Arts .... (see 45)
48 Nu Sentral.............................C5
49 Sonali E5
50 Wei-Ling Gallery....................D5

Sports & Activities (p111)

51 Majestic Spa.........................D4
52 Old KL & Nature Walk D1
YMCA .... (see 56)

Sleeping (p131)

Aloft Kuala Lumpur Sentral...................... (see 44)
53 Hilton Kuala Lumpur B5
Majestic Hotel .... (see 32)
54 PODs C6
55 St Regis Kuala Lumpur C5
56 YMCA C5

BANGSAR BARU & MID VALLEY

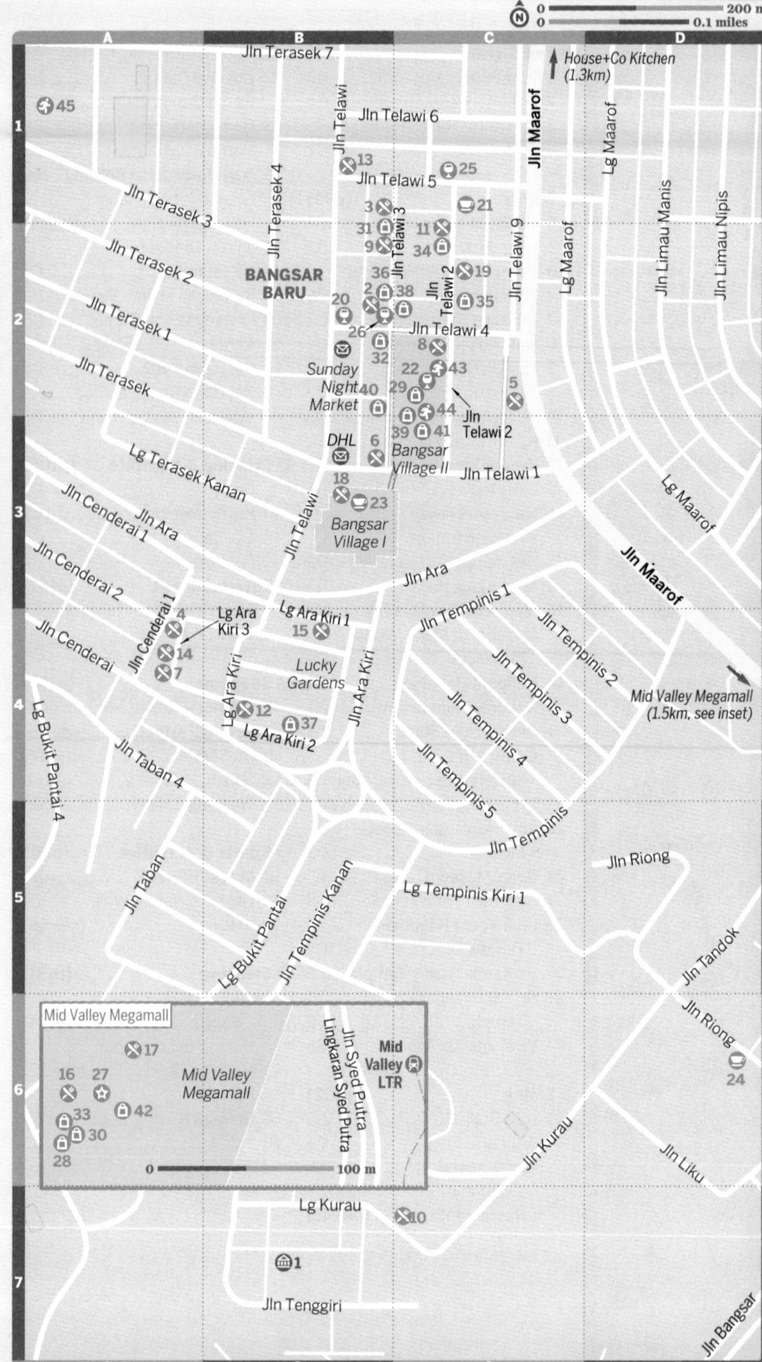

BANGSAR BARU & MID VALLEY

Sights (p101)

1 Sekeping Tenggiri....B7

Eating (p104)

2 Alexis Bistro....B2
3 Ashley's By Living Food....B1
4 Bangsar Fish Head Corner....A4
5 Bangsar Sunday Market....C2
6 Chawan....B3
7 Chelo's Appam Stall....A4
8 Delicious....C2
9 G3 Kitchen & Bar....B2
10 Ganga Cafe....C7
11 Jaslyn Cakes....C2
12 Nam Chuan Coffee Shop....B4
13 Nasi Kandar Pelita....B1
Nutmeg....(see 29)
14 Poomy's....A4
15 Restaurant Mahbub....B4
16 Sage....A6
17 Shucked....A6
Sri Nirwana Maju....(see 32)
18 Wondermama....B3
19 Yeast Bistronomy....C2
Yuzu....(see 33)

Drinking & Nightlife (p106)

20 Bilique Bangsar....B2
21 Coffea Coffee....C1
Library....(see 16)
22 Mantra Bar KL....C2
23 Plan b....B3
24 Pulp by Papa Palheta....D6
25 Ril's Bar....C1
26 Sino The Bar Upstairs....B2
Social....(see 40)

Entertainment (p107)

27 GSC Mid Valley....A6

Shopping (p109)

28 Cap City....A6
29 Comoddity....C2
d.d.collective....(see 41)
30 Fabspy....A6
Gardens Mall....(see 33)
31 I Love Snackfood....B2
32 Lonely Dream....B2
33 Mid Valley Megamall....A6
34 Mimpikita....C2
35 Never Follow Suit....C2
36 Nurita Harith....B2
37 Pucuk Rebung....B4
38 Shoes Shoes Shoes....C2
39 Silverfish Books....C3
40 Thisappear....B2
41 TriBeCa....C3
42 World of Feng Shui....A6

Sports & Activities (p111)

Dive Station Explorer....(see 33)
43 Hammam Spa....C2
44 Kizsports & Gym....C2
45 Kompleks Sukan Bangsar....A1

Sleeping (p131)

Gardens Hotel & Residences....(see 33)
Sekeping Tenggiri....(see 1)

Our Story

A beat-up old car, a few dollars in the pocket and a sense of adventure. In 1972 that's all Tony and Maureen Wheeler needed for the trip of a lifetime – across Europe and Asia overland to Australia. It took several months, and at the end – broke but inspired – they sat at their kitchen table writing and stapling together their first travel guide, *Across Asia on the Cheap*. Within a week they'd sold 1500 copies. Lonely Planet was born.

Today, Lonely Planet has offices in Franklin, London, Melbourne, Oakland, Dublin, Beijing and Delhi, with more than 600 staff and writers. We share Tony's belief that 'a great guidebook should do three things: inform, educate and amuse'.

Our Writers

Simon Richmond

Curator, Melaka and Penang Journalist and photographer Simon Richmond has specialised as a travel writer since the early 1990s and first worked for Lonely Planet in 1999 on their *Central Asia* guide. He's long since stopped counting the number of guidebooks he's researched and written for the company, but countries covered include Australia, China, India, Iran, Japan, Korea, Malaysia, Mongolia, Myanmar (Burma), Russia, Singapore, South Africa and Turkey. His travel features have been published in newspapers and magazines around the world, including in the UK's *Independent*, *Guardian*, *Times*, *Daily Telegraph* and *Royal Geographical Society Magazine*; and Australia's *Sydney Morning Herald* and *Australian* newspapers and Australian *Financial Review Magazine*.

Read more about Simon at:
https://auth.lonelyplanet.com/profiles/simonrichmond

Isabel Albiston

Chinatown, Merdeka Square & Bukit Nanas, Masjid India, Kampung Baru & Northern Kuala Lumpur and Lake Gardens, Brickfields & Bangsar After 6 years working for the *Daily Telegraph* in London, squeezing in as many trips as annual leave would allow, Isabel left to spend more time on the road. A job as writer for a magazine in Sydney, Australia was followed by four years living and working in Buenos Aires, Argentina. Isabel started writing for Lonely Planet in 2014, having been back in the UK just long enough to pack a bag for a research trip to Malaysia, and has contributed to five Lonely Planet guides.

Read more about Isabel at:
https://auth.lonelyplanet.com/profiles/IsabelAlbiston

Published by Lonely Planet Global Limited
CRN 554153
4th edition – Jun 2017
ISBN 978 1 78657 530 2

10 9 8 7 6 5 4 3 2 1
Printed in China